Planning Practice

Planning Practice: Critical Perspectives from the UK provides the only comprehensive overview of contemporary planning practice in the UK. Drawing on contributions from leading researchers in the field, it examines the tools, contexts and outcomes of planning practice. Part I examines planning processes and tools, and the extent to which theory and practice diverge, covering plan-making, Development Management, planning gain, public engagement and place-making. Part II examines the changing contexts within which planning practice takes place, including privatisation and deregulation, devolution and multi-level governance, increased ethnic and social diversity, growing environmental concerns and the changing nature of commercial real estate. Part III focuses on how planning practice produces outcomes for the built environment in relation to housing, infrastructure, economic progress, public transport and regeneration. The book considers what it means to be a reflective practitioner in the modern planning system, the constraints and opportunities that planners face in their daily work, and the ethical and political challenges they must confront.

Jessica Ferm is Lecturer in Planning and Urban Management and coordinator of the Bartlett School of Planning's "Planning Practice" module. She is a practice-focused academic with research interests in the intersections between spatial planning and the economy. She is actively involved in planning in London. Prior to academia, she worked for 10 years in planning practice.

John Tomaney is Professor of Urban and Regional Planning in the Bartlett School of Planning, University College London. His work focuses on the governance of local and regional development and spatial planning and the political, social and cultural foundations of regions. Prior to this post at UCL, he was Director of the Centre for Urban and Regional Development Studies at Newcastle University.

Planning Practice

Critical Perspectives from the UK

Edited by Jessica Ferm and John Tomaney

NEW YORK AND LONDON

First published 2018
by Routledge
711 Third Avenue, New York, NY 10017

and by Routledge
2 Park Square, Milton Park, Abingdon, Oxon, OX14 4RN

Routledge is an imprint of the Taylor & Francis Group, an informa business

Library of Congress Cataloging-in-Publication Data
Names: Ferm, Jessica, editor. | Tomaney, John, 1963- editor.
Title: Planning practice : critical perspectives from the UK / edited by Jessica Ferm and John Tomaney.
Description: New York : Routledge, 2018. | Includes bibliographical references.
Identifiers: LCCN 2018000816 | ISBN 9780815384830 (hardback) | ISBN 9780815384847 (pbk.)
Subjects: LCSH: City planning—Great Britain.
Classification: LCC HT169.G7 P514 2018 | DDC 307.1/2160941—dc23
LC record available at https://lccn.loc.gov/2018000816

ISBN: 978-0-8153-8483-0 (hbk)
ISBN: 978-0-8153-8484-7 (pbk)
ISBN: 978-1-351-20331-9 (ebk)

Typeset in Sabon
by Swales & Willis Ltd, Exeter, Devon, UK

Printed and bound in Great Britain by
TJ International Ltd, Padstow, Cornwall

Contents

List of Figures vii
List of Tables ix
List of Boxes x
Biographies xi
Preface xx
Acknowledgements xxi
List of Abbreviations xxiii

1 Introduction: Contexts and Frameworks for Contemporary Planning Practice 1
JOHN TOMANEY AND JESSICA FERM

2 Devolution and Planning 20
JOHN TOMANEY AND CLAIRE COLOMB

PART I
Practices of Planning 37

3 Plan-making: Changing Contexts, Challenges and Drivers 39
JESSICA FERM

4 Contemporary Challenges in Development Management 55
BEN CLIFFORD

5 Challenges and Emerging Practices in Development Value Capture 70
PATRICIA CANELAS

6 Public Participation and the Declining Significance of Planning 85
YASMINAH BEEBEEJAUN

7 The Design Dimension of Planning: Making Planning Proactive Again 101
MATTHEW CARMONA

PART II
Changing Contexts for Planning Practice 121

8 Private Consultants, Planning Reform and the Marketisation of Local Government Finance 123
MIKE RACO

9 Localism and Neighbourhood Planning 138
ELENA BESUSSI

10 The Evolving Intersection of Planning and the Commercial Real Estate Market 158
TOMMASO GABRIELI AND NICOLA LIVINGSTONE

11 Planning for Diversity in an Era of Social Change 174
CLAIRE COLOMB AND MIKE RACO

12 Sustainable Development and Planning 189
CATALINA TURCU

PART III
Planning in Practice 203

13 Planning for Housing: The Global Challenges Confronting Local Practice 205
NICK GALLENT

14 Planning for Infrastructure 220
JOHN TOMANEY, PETER O'BRIEN AND ANDY PIKE

15 Planning for Economic Progress 235
JESSICA FERM, MICHAEL EDWARDS AND EDWARD JONES

16 Planning for Public Transport: Applying European Good Practice to UK Regions? 250
IQBAL HAMIDUDDIN AND ROBIN HICKMAN

17 Planning for the Regeneration of Towns and Cities 266
CLAUDIO DE MAGALHÃES AND NIKOS KARADIMITRIOU

18 Conclusion: Beyond Reflective, Deliberative Practice 281
JESSICA FERM AND JOHN TOMANEY

Index 301

Figures

2.1	Pendulum swings in economic development governance in England	26
4.1	Total number of planning applications received compared to central government's formula grant for local authorities in England, 2009–2017	60
7.1	The 'Pink Book'	102
7.2	Birmingham: the team working on the centre of the city from the late 1980s onwards transformed it from a vehicle- to people-dominated space	105
7.3	The design governance toolbox	107
7.4	This recent infill housing development was listed on the council's website under the title 'The future of housing design'	111
7.5	Extract from the Liverpool Knowledge Quarter, the Climax Plan	113
7.6	Extract from the South Quay Masterplan	114
7.7	Extract from the Fairfield Park Design Code	115
7.8	Newhall, Harlow, a high-quality contemporary urban extension, coded by Studio REAL	117
7.9	Hammarby Sjöstad, created through a skilled urban design process and now delivering long-term economic, social, health and environmental benefits to its city	118
9.1	Distribution of all London's wards (white) and neighbourhood areas (black) across selected variables	148
9.2	Changes in Neighbourhood Planning Area for the Elephant and Walworth Neighbourhood Plan	150
9.3	Map and location of Camley Street Neighbourhood Planning Area	152

11.1 Ethnic groups other than White in England and Wales, 1991–2001–2011 census data 176
16.1 Valenciennes – the region and location in France 254
16.2 Valenciennes, tram double-tracking at stations, and single track beyond 255
16.3 Kassel – the region and location in Germany 258
16.4 Kassel Königsplatz – the tram and tram–trains interchange in the city centre 259
17.1 The Olympic Village in London, regeneration through property development. The built environment outcomes are clear, but how can it produce the desired social outcomes? 271
17.2 The Heygate Estate in London: landownership could have given the local authority a powerful tool to shape the outcomes of the redevelopment towards the aspirations of the existing community, but many argue this has been wasted 275

Tables

2.1	Devolution deals in England in 2016	29
5.1	Mechanisms for development value capture	75
8.1	The 10 largest UK-based planning consultancies	130
12.1	Ten OPL principles guiding the delivery of Elmsbrook	197
14.1	The 'four sublimes that drive megaproject development'	225
14.2	Transitions in approaches to governing and planning infrastructure funding and financing at the city/city-region scale	227

Boxes

3.1 Stages in production of the Welborne Plan 46
12.1 The NPPF's view on the economic, social and environmental role of planning 193
13.1 Identification of sites for development 210
14.1 Defining infrastructure 221
14.2 Structural characteristics that affect infrastructure 223

Biographies

The Editors

Jessica Ferm is Lecturer in Planning and Urban Management and coordinator of the masters module on "Planning Practice" at the Bartlett School of Planning. She is a Royal Town Planning Institute (RTPI)-accredited town planner and practice-focused academic with research interests in spatial planning, economic development and social sustainability. Her current research activities explore the relationship between planning, development and the ability of diverse economic activities to thrive. She has recently completed and published research on the pressures facing industrial accommodation in London, and is part of a team (with Ben Clifford, Nicola Livingstone and Patricia Canelas) assessing the impacts of office-to-residential conversions through permitted development (funded by the Royal Institute of Chartered Surveyors [RICS]). She is actively involved in planning in London – as a member of Just Space Economy and Planning, the London Planning and Development Forum, and the London Industry and Logistics Sounding Board, convened by London First and the Greater London Authority. Prior to academia, she worked for 10 years in planning practice in both the public and private sectors – at the planning and regeneration consultancy Urban Practitioners and the London Borough of Enfield.

John Tomaney is Professor of Urban and Regional Planning in the Bartlett School of Planning, University College London (UCL). Prior to his post at UCL, he was Henry Daysh Professor of Regional Development Studies and Director of the Centre for Urban and Regional Development Studies at Newcastle University, and Professor of Regional Studies and Monash University. He is a Fellow of the Academy of Social Sciences (UK), a Fellow of the Regional Australia Institute, and holds visiting positions at the University of New South Wales, University College Dublin and Newcastle University (UK). He is the co-author of *Local and Regional Development* (2017, with Andy Pike and Andrés Rodríguez-Pose) and co-editor of the

Handbook of Local and Regional Development (2011) and *Local and Regional Development – Major Works* (2015, with Andy Pike and Andrés Rodríguez-Pose). He has undertaken work for international organisations and national, regional and local governments in several countries. His work focuses on the governance of local and regional development and spatial panning, and the political, social and cultural foundations of regions.

The Contributors

Yasminah Beebeejaun is Senior Lecturer in Urban Politics and Planning at the Bartlett School of Planning, with particular expertise in participation, race and gender. She completed her BA (Hons) in Town and Regional Planning and her PhD at the University of Sheffield. She has been an international visiting scholar at the University of Illinois at Urbana–Champaign, University of Illinois, Chicago, the University of Michigan and the American Philosophical Society. Her research focuses on social justice within planning, and her particular interests are diversity in planning and community engagement. Her work has been published in a range of journals, including *Environment and Planning C*, *Journal of Urban Affairs*, *Planning Theory and Practice* and *Urban Studies*. She is editor of *The Participatory City* (2016). Her research has been funded by the Arts and Humanities Research Council (UK), the American Philosophical Society and the British Academy.

Elena Besussi is Teaching Fellow in Plan Making and a PhD candidate in Planning Studies at the Bartlett School of Planning. She has 10 years' experience in academic research, teaching and professional consultancy in the UK. Between 2002 and 2005, she has been a research fellow at the Centre for Advanced Spatial Analysis at UCL, and since 2006 she has been a planning advisor supporting local residents' participation in spatial planning and urban regeneration, at Willowbrook Centre in Southwark until 2007, and now independently. She has produced academic and professional research for national organisations (Brunel University Research Archive, RICS) and international institutions, including the European Commission. Elena's PhD research considers local government practices in the management of public property assets under conditions of fiscal austerity, and discusses their consequences, on a theoretical level, for current interpretations of urban politics, and on a practical level, for questions of distributional justice expressed in terms of levels and spatial distribution of public service provision.

Patricia Canelas is a Research Associate, and recently completed her PhD at the Bartlett School of Planning, where she focused on the nexus between planning and property markets in the context of urban regeneration. She is an architect and urban designer, with degrees from the Universidade Lusiada and Universidade Catolica in Lisbon, and an MA in Architecture from the University of California, Berkeley, where she was a Pinto-Fialon Fellowship recipient. Between 2001 and 2010, she worked in architecture practice, including setting up her own practice where she completed several projects, including office and retail spaces, and single and multi-family homes. She has held a fixed-term lectureship position in Real Estate and Planning at the University of Reading, and she has been a tutor at the Bartlett School of Planning since 2012. Patricia has been involved in international research projects in China, the USA, Portugal and the UK, and has contributed to the RICS-funded research on office-to-residential permitted development led by Ben Clifford.

Matthew Carmona is Professor of Planning and Urban Design at the Bartlett School of Planning. His research has focused on the policy context for delivering better-quality built and natural environments, having worked on a range of research projects examining design policies and guidance, design coding, residential design and development processes, measuring quality in planning, managing external public space, and the governance of design. Matthew is the founder and Chair of the Place Alliance, is on the editorial board of *Urban Design Quarterly*, is European Associate Editor for the *Journal of Urban Design*, and edits the *Design in the Built Environment* book series for Ashgate. He is a regular advisor to government and government agencies both in the UK and overseas, and writes a column for *Town and Country Planning*, the journal of the Town and Country Planning Association. He has previously lectured at the University of Nottingham, and before that worked as a researcher at Strathclyde and Reading Universities and as an architect in practice. He is a Design Council Commission for Architecture and the Built Environment (CABE) Built Environment Expert. Between 2003 and 2011, Matthew served as Head of the Bartlett School of Planning.

Ben Clifford is Senior Lecturer in Spatial Planning and Government, Programme Director for the MSc in Spatial Planning and MSc Tutor at the Bartlett School of Planning. He is a political geographer, with research interests centred on the implications of the modernisation of the state for the practice of planning in the UK. He is the lead author (with Mark Tewdwr-Jones) of *The Collaborating Planner?* (2013), based on his PhD (from King's College London). Prior to academia, Ben was seconded to the Department for Communities and Local Government to assist with the major consultation on planning reform and the redrafting of the Planning Policy Statement on local spatial planning. He then acted as a policy advisor on the Killian Pretty

Review, a national review of the planning application process. His recent research has focused on devolution and policy mobility around spatial planning between the UK and Ireland, the effectiveness of planning for nationally significant infrastructure, and the implications of deregulation in Development Management.

Claire Colomb is Reader in Planning and Urban Sociology at the Bartlett School of Planning, and has been an academic at UCL since 2005. She holds a first degree in Politics and Sociology (Institut d'Études Politiques de Paris) and a PhD in Planning (UCL). Her research interests cover urban and regional governance, the politics of planning and urban regeneration in European cities, urban social movements and grassroot mobilisations around planning issues (including Neighbourhood Planning), European spatial planning and territorial cooperation, and comparative planning systems and cultures. She is co-author of *European Spatial Planning and Territorial Cooperation* (2010, with S. Dühr and V. Nadin) and author of *Staging the New Berlin: Place Marketing and the Politics of Urban Reinvention* (2011). She was involved with Mike Raco in a large EU-funded project on the governance of urban diversity (2013–2017).

Michael Edwards joined the UCL staff in 1969. He has had a long career researching the relationship between property markets and planning, mainly in the UK and Europe. He is active in London planning, campaigned for over two decades on the King's Cross development, and is now a lead member of Just Space, supporting community groups since 2009 in challenging the various iterations of the London Plan. Mike has degrees in Philosophy, Politics and Economics from Oxford (1961–1964) and Town Planning from UCL (1964–1966). In the 1960s, he was employed at Nathaniel Lichfield and Associates, and in that capacity worked on the Milton Keynes Master Plan, other new settlements, retail schemes and cost benefit analysis. He is a founder member of the International Network for Urban Research and Action and of the Planners Network UK. He held a Leverhulme Emeritus Fellowship focusing on the land and housing crisis in the UK, working with Bob Colenutt (University of Northampton), which led to a commission to contribute the housing paper to the Government Office for Science Foresight Programme 2015. In 2014, he was the recipient of a UCL Career Achievement Award in Public Engagement for his work bringing planning students and London community groups together to work on London planning. A full publications list and blog is available at http://michaeledwards.org.uk.

Tommaso Gabrieli is a Lecturer in Real Estate at the Bartlett School of Planning, and a theoretical economist by training. Inspired by the Ambrosian tradition of social welfare, Tommaso has a long-lasting interest in the socio-economic dynamics of cities, especially the extent of social mobility, the existence of poverty traps and the relative policy implications. His current research focuses on the links between spatial segregation and poverty traps, the application of game theory and real options to real estate valuation and policy, as well as work on behavioural economic theory and asset pricing. He holds a PhD in Economics from the University of Warwick and an MSc in Economics from the London School of Economics (LSE). Before joining UCL, Tommaso held academic positions at the University of Reading, City University London, University of Warwick and the Catholic University of Milan.

Nick Gallent is Professor of Housing and Planning and Head of the Bartlett School of Planning. Nick is a housing specialist whose research focuses on UK planning policy as it pertains to housing delivery and as it affects rural communities. He has conducted research for a wide range of funding bodies. His research has been disseminated in 13 published books, mainly dealing with housing, planning, rural communities and the countryside, and in a number of peer-reviewed articles and book contributions. His most recent book, *Politics, Planning and Housing Supply in Australia, England and Hong Kong* (with Nicole Gurran and Rebecca Chiu), was published in 2016. Nick is a Chartered Town Planner and a Fellow of the Royal Institution of Chartered Surveyors. He became a Fellow of the Academy of Social Sciences in 2015. He maintains a range of professional interests, and is currently Chair of the RTPI's Partnership and Accreditation Panel.

Iqbal Hamiduddin is Lecturer in Transport Planning and Housing at the Bartlett School of Planning. He is particularly interested in the social impacts of different housing and transport regimes, and the policy implications for well-being and social sustainability. Drawing the fields of transport and housing policy together, his recently completed doctoral research examined the social impacts of residential car reduction strategies. In the transport field, he was a member of the EU SINTROPHER project, coordinated from the Bartlett by Professor Sir Peter Hall, and was a lead member of the recently completed SYNAPTIC project (2011–2013) with Peter Hall and Robin Hickman (Bartlett School of Planning) and Peter Jones (UCL Engineering). In housing, he is currently leading a project supported by the UCL Grand Challenges scheme, with Nick Gallent (Bartlett School of Planning) and John Kelsey (Bartlett School of Construction & Project Management), to explore the viability of the German *Baugruppen* or group-build style of approach to housing development in England (2013–).

Robin Hickman is Reader in Transport Planning and the City and Director of the MSc in Transport and City Planning at the Bartlett School of Planning. He has been a Visiting Research Associate and

Research Fellow at the Transport Studies Unit, University of Oxford, and a Visiting Lecturer at the University of Malta. He worked previously in consultancy as an Associate Director at Halcrow, leading on transport research, on masterplanning and transport research at Llewelyn Davies, and local transport planning at Surrey County Council. He has research interests in transport and climate change, urban structure and travel, integrated transport and urban planning strategies, the affective dimensions of travel, discourses in travel, multi-criteria appraisal, and sustainable transport strategies in the UK, Europe and Asia. He has authored and co-authored a range of books and best practice guides, including the *Handbook on Transport and Development* (2015) and *Transport, Climate Change and the City* (2014). He gained his PhD at the Bartlett in 2007.

Edward Jones completed his PhD in 2017 at the Bartlett School of Planning on the operation and governance of Tech City in East London (funded by the Economic and Social Research Council [ESRC]). During his time at the School of Planning, he worked as a Research Assistant on a number of projects: London's Industrial Land (with Jessica Ferm), resulting in publications in *Urban Studies* and *European Planning Studies*, Revealing Local Economies in Suburban London (with Michael Edwards and Jessica Ferm) and the online cataloguing of the late Sir Peter Hall's photographic archive. He has taught on two masters courses at UCL – "Spatial Planning: Concepts and Contexts" and "Design and Real Estate Development". Ed has an undergraduate degree in international history from the LSE and a masters degree from the University of Reading. He practised as a local authority town planner in London (Boroughs of Enfield and Camden) for seven years before starting his PHD research, and is an RTPI-accredited town planner. Since October 2017, Ed has been working in the economic research team of the City of London Corporation.

Nikos Karadimitriou is Senior Lecturer in Planning and Property Development at the Bartlett School of Planning. Before joining the Bartlett in 2006, he worked as a Research Officer at the University of Reading, Department of Real Estate and Planning – Centre for Planning Studies (2003–2006). His first degree was in Planning and Regional Development in Greece, where he also worked as a planning consultant on the Urban Audit Pilot Project of DG Regio and the Unification of the Archaeological Sites of Athens, and as a planner on the Organising Committee for the Olympic Games in Athens (2004). His PhD from UCL explored housebuilders and the use of previously developed land. His research and publications span several different areas of regeneration, from social segregation and community consultation to property development and housebuilding. He has worked on research projects funded by the European Commission, the ESRC, the

National Housebuilders Council, the House Builders Federation, the Foundation for Urban and Regional Studies, the Greek Ministry of Industry & Technology and the British Council.

Nicola Livingstone is Lecturer in Real Estate at the Bartlett School of Planning. Before coming to UCL in 2014, she worked at Heriot-Watt University, Edinburgh, where she also completed both her undergraduate degree and PhD. Nicola's research falls into two distinct but complementary dimensions: the first is critical social theory, and the second is real estate. Nicola's PhD, awarded in 2011, examined the growth of charity retailing in the UK from a Marxist perspective. Her current real estate research is focused on international liquidity, the restructuring of property markets and how sustainable real estate is evolving. She has recently completed a project on liquidity for the Investment Property Forum. In addition to real estate research, Nicola's research interests include the third sector, the political economy of charity, and food insecurity. She has completed commissioned work on food aid for the Scottish Government, and is currently working on a project for the British Academy/Leverhulme on the 'lived experiences' of emergency food providers. Her current research is focused on how the retail market is changing through online and multi-channel interfaces, food insecurity in the UK, and the role of 'charity' in the 21st century.

Claudio de Magalhães is Professor in Urban Regeneration and Management and Director of the MSc in Urban Regeneration at the Bartlett School of Planning, with a background in architecture and urban planning. In the early stages of his career, he worked for 12 years as a planner in local and regional government in Brazil, acquiring considerable experience in urban governance and in the management of urban investment programmes for urban and regional development. He has worked as an academic in the UK since the mid-1990s, first at Newcastle University, and since 1999 at UCL. His interests have been in planning and the governance of the built environment, the provision and governance of public space, property development processes and urban regeneration policy. Claudio has conducted research for British research councils, professional bodies such as RICS and CABE, UK Government departments and local authorities, and has published widely on property markets and globalisation, capacity-building for urban governance, the relationship between urban governance, the built environment and property markets, and the management of public spaces. His most recent research looks at the practical and theoretical issues confronting Business Improvement Districts in England as urban governance tools.

Peter O'Brien is a Research Associate in the Centre for Urban and Regional Development Studies at Newcastle University. Previously, he was the Director of the Tyne and Wear City Region Partnership, where he was responsible for the development and delivery of the Tyne and Wear City Region Economic Review and the Tyne and Wear City Region Multi Area Agreement and preparing the submission to government to establish the North East Local Enterprise Partnership. Other roles Peter has held include Assistant Chief Executive at the North East Assembly and Regional Policy Officer at the Trades Union Congress. Peter's research focuses on the funding, finance and governance of urban infrastructure.

Andy Pike is Henry Daysh Professor of Regional Development Studies and Director of the Centre for Urban and Regional Development Studies at Newcastle University. He is a Fellow of the Academy of Social Sciences. His research concerns the geographical political economy of local and regional development. His work has a strong policy orientation and builds upon close policy engagement, and has informed local and regional development policy for the European Commission, United Nations International Labour Organization, the Organisation for Economic Cooperation and Development, UK Government departments and local and regional governments.

Mike Raco is Professor of Urban Governance and Development and Director of Research at the Bartlett School of Planning. He has a BA in Geography and a PhD from the Royal Holloway University of London. His thesis was on the topic of "Business Associations and the Politics of Local Economic Development in the UK", under the supervision of Professor Rob Imrie. He has held lectureships at the Universities of Glasgow (1997–2000), Reading (2000–2005) and King's College London (2005–2011). His research focuses on the themes of urban governance, sustainable cities and the changing nature of welfare states. Mike is currently leading an EU-funded project entitled Divercities that is examining the relationships between urban policy and diversity in European cities. His other recent work has examined: changing governance arrangements in the EU, UK and East Asia; the planning system and community engagement in London; the new localism and Big Society in England; the role of contracts and privatisation on local democracy and welfare reform; understandings of culture-led urban development and resilience planning in London and Hong Kong; and the governance and management of the London Olympics 2012.

Catalina Turcu is Senior Lecturer in Sustainable Development and Planning, and Director of the MSc in Sustainable Urbanism at the Bartlett School of Planning. She has a background in public policy and sustainability (PhD, LSE 2010), international housing and social change (MSc Dist, LSE 2001), urbanism studies (MA Dist, University of Architecture and Urbanism 'Ion Mincu' [UAUIM] 1999) and architecture (BArch DipARch, UAUIM 1998). Prior to joining academia in the UK, Catalina worked as an architect and urban designer (Farells Architects, Llewelyn Davies Yeang, Levitt Bernstein Associates) and environmental development officer (Affinity Housing Group) in London. Before that, Catalina was a Lecturer at UAUIM in Bucharest, where she established her own architectural practice (Zona Architects). Catalina has 15 years of joint academic and professional experience, is registered with the Architects Registration Board (UK) and Order of Romanian Architects, and is a member of the Royal Institute of British Architects. Catalina's research interests are broadly located within the area of urban sustainability studies, at the interface between spatial, environmental, social and institutional aspects of urban development. More specifically, she is interested in social sustainability, energy efficiency in buildings, urban retrofit, multi-occupancy housing, sustainability indicators and certification schemes, institutions, and pro-environmental behaviour.

Preface

This book has its origins in our teaching in the Bartlett School of Planning at University College London. Over several years, we have taught a course aiming to introduce our students to the world of planning practice. The course is designed around contributions from leading practitioners in different fields of planning from the public, private and non-governmental sectors, including officers, politicians, developers and citizen activists. As well as hearing from and debating with practitioners, students are introduced to the academic debates that surround each area of practice. One challenge we faced in running this course was the absence of a suitable text. While there is a large academic literature that examines the role of planners, the planning system and planning outcomes, we were struck by the absence of a single book that addresses and analyses the dilemmas, constraints and opportunities that face planners in their daily practice. This book seeks to fill that gap.

In developing our course, and in designing this book, we have drawn on the repository of academic expertise in the Bartlett School of Planning, the UK's largest planning school, which accommodates over 600 students in our undergraduate, postgraduate and doctoral programmes. Being part of such a large planning school provides an environment in which there are a diverse range of academic interests, perspectives and methods, but what unites us is a strong orientation to addressing practical planning issues. This book, then, seeks both to give expression to this distinctive aspect of the Bartlett School of Planning's research and teaching, and to contribute to debates about the problems of planning practice in the UK, which are of wide relevance.

Jessica Ferm and John Tomaney
London, November 2017

Acknowledgements

This book is necessarily a collective effort. Our sincere thanks go to:

Krystal LaDuc, Kathryn Schell and staff at Routledge for endorsing our proposal for the book and seeing it through to publication;

the three anonymous reviewers;

the many practitioners and speakers who have contributed so willingly to the "Planning Practice" module which provided the inspiration for the book: Michael Ball (Waterloo Development Group), Simon Bevan (London Borough of Southwark), Natalie Broughton (now London Borough of Hackney, previously London Borough of Enfield), Bethany Cullan (London Borough of Camden), Jenny Frew (Department for Communities and Local Government), Mike Geddes (HS2 Action Alliance), Brian Ham (Home Group), John Lett, Jennifer Peters and Jörn Peters (in the London Plan team at the Greater London Authority), Sue Vincent (LB Camden and Urban Design London), Dan Taylor (London Borough of Southwark) and Ivan Tennant (AECOM, previously Plan Projects);

Ben Clifford and Peter Rees for their annual contributions to the module;

our masters students on the "Planning Practice" module at the Bartlett School of Planning, who have over the years shared with us their questions, and in many cases insights, from their own professional practice;

our contributing authors for responding admirably to the brief we gave them and for their timely delivery;

Nick Gallent (Head of the Bartlett School of Planning) and Mike Raco (Director of Research at the Bartlett School of Planning) for supporting and encouraging us in this endeavour, and Michael Edwards for his comments on an earlier draft of the introduction;

our Bartlett School of Planning colleagues for helpful comments made during our departmental research exchange seminars, which helped us to develop our approach to the book;

the organisers and our academic colleagues attending the *Planning Research Conference* held at Queen's University Belfast in September 2017, where we presented our thoughts on the conclusions of the book.

The usual disclaimers apply.

Abbreviations

AAP	Area Action Plan
BME	Black and Minority Ethnic
CABE	Commission for Architecture and the Built Environment
CAZ	Central Activities Zone
CBA	Cost Benefit Analysis
CIL	Community Infrastructure Levy
CIP	Community Investment Programme
CLT	Community Land Trust
CRE	Commission for Racial Equality
DC	Development Control
DCLG	Department for Communities and Local Government
DCO	Development Consent Order
DEFRA	Department for Environment, Food and Rural Affairs
DfT	Department for Transport
DM	Development Management
DoE	Department of Environment
EAN	Elephant Amenity Network
EEB	Economics Evidence Base
EIA	Environmental Impact Assessment
ESRC	Economic and Social Research Council
ETS	Emissions Trading System (EU)
EWNF	Elephant and Walworth Neighbourhood Forum
EZ	Enterprise Zone
GDP	Gross Domestic Product
GFC	Global Financial Crisis
GLA	Greater London Authority
HM	Her Majesty's
HS2	High Speed 2
IEM	Internal Energy Market (EU)
IFC	International Financial Centre
IPC	Infrastructure Planning Commission
JSEP	Just Space Economy and Planning
LEP	Local Enterprise Partnership

LFC	London Finance Commission
LIP	London Infrastructure Plan 2050
LPA	Local Planning Authority
LRT	Light Rapid Transit
LSOA	Local Super Output Area
MBW	Metropolitan Board of Works
MCA	Multi-Criteria Analysis
MHCLG	Ministry of Housing, Communities and Local Government
NAO	National Audit Office
NDF	National Development Framework (Wales)
NDP	Neighbourhood Development Plan
NEF	New Economics Foundation
NF	Neighbourhood Forum
NHB	New Homes Bonus
NI	Northern Ireland
NLE	Northern Line Extension
NP	Neighbourhood Plan
NPF	National Planning Framework (Scotland)
NPPF	National Planning Policy Framework (England)
NSIP	Nationally Significant Infrastructure Project
NWB	North West Bicester
ODPM	Office of the Deputy Prime Minister (former UK Government department responsible for planning)
OFWAT	Office of Water Services (UK government)
OPL	One Planet Living
PD	Permitted Development
PPA	Planning Performance Agreement
PPG	Planning Policy Guidance
PPP	Public–Private Partnership
PPS	Planning Policy Statement
PRC	Public Realm Credit
RDA	Regional Development Agency
RIBA	Royal Institute of British Architects
RICS	Royal Institute of Chartered Surveyors
RRA	Race Relations Act
RTPI	Royal Town Planning Institute
SD	Sustainable Development
SHLAA	Strategic Housing Land Availability Assessment
SNP	Scottish National Party
SPD	Supplementary Planning Document
TCPA	Town and Country Planning Association
UCL	University College London

1 Introduction

Contexts and Frameworks for Contemporary Planning Practice

John Tomaney and Jessica Ferm

Introduction

Historically, planning practice occurred on behalf of the state within relatively closed national borders and in a context where technocratic modernism gave planners and planning authorities a high degree of power to shape private enterprise in order to achieve their objectives. In many democratic societies in the Global North, they were criticised for the way they exercised their power. Faga (2010: 235) suggests:

> From the 1930s to the 1950s, master builders, such as New York's Robert Moses, envisioned great plans and built them with little debate or discussion. Many of these plans were highly disruptive, displacing people and neighborhoods for the sake of highways, infrastructure, and new development. The community did not have a voice in these planning decisions, and those who tried to speak up were quickly and effectively silenced.
>
> (see also Caro, 1974; Jacobs, 1961)

In the UK, similar criticisms were levelled at planners by sociologists who saw large scale post-war planning programmes concerned with 'slum clearance' and 'comprehensive redevelopment' as overriding the interest of local communities in the cause of modernisation (Dennis, 1970, 1972; Davies, 1972). The experience of planning practice in the comprehensive redevelopment of cities gives weight to the criticism that planning has not always operated with a strong sense of the wider public interest (Caro, 1974; Jacobs, 1961).

The untrammelled power of planning has long gone. Today, local (and central) government planners operate in systems of governance "in which boundaries between and within the public and private sectors have become blurred" (Stoker, 1998: 17). At the urban and regional scale, government is institutionally, economically and politically constrained, and increasingly, local and regional governments are compelled to act with other players to deliver development within multi-level governance systems.

Across the Global North, the local state is enrolled in urban growth machines or local growth coalitions (Logan and Molotch, 2007; Stone, 1989) which are concerned with "blending public and private resources" in ways that enhance corporate power (Peters and Pierre, 2012: 74) and raise important questions about accountability and democratic control.

The aim of this book is to chart the terrain of contemporary planning practice and the complexities planners face in the regulation and management of land use and the production of the built environment. The contemporary practice of planning involves multiple actors. These include professional planners, in the public and private sectors, but also developers, citizens, corporations, non-governmental organisations, politicians, the media and others. It occurs in specific historical, legal and cultural contexts. It is shaped by – and contributes to – the transformation of social and economic structures. At the same time, planning practice is affected by shifts in academic understandings, which are themselves embedded in the broader societal contexts within which they are produced and consumed. Planning practice is embedded within and interacts with forms of private enterprise that reflect particular varieties of capitalism. It is a political activity that mobilises, mediates and regulates interests in the use of land and property. Planning practice occurs in a context in which transformation of the built environment is accelerating and the very purposes of planning are subject to ideological challenge both from the neo-liberal right, where it is often seen as a damaging constraint on private interests, and from the left, where it is viewed as an instrument of corporate interests. The practice of planning occurs in a political climate where its value is openly challenged. Processes of decentralisation and devolution mean that planning occurs increasingly within structures of multi-level governance.

The planner is critically concerned with identifying, animating and mediating between different interests in the development process, giving rise to the need for multiple skills. In the late 1980s, Thomas and Healey (1991) identified five role models for planners as social reformer, public bureaucrat, intermediator, policy analyst and urban development manager. A critique of planners, particularly their technocratic approach, led to a substantial body of research around communicative planning and notions of public participation (Forester, 1999; Healey, 1997). As Ted Kitchen (2007: 241) writes in his book *Skills for Planning Practice*:

> I have seen during my professional lifetime a substantial shift in thinking away from the idea that planners know best by virtue of the fact that they are the planners and it is their job to know the best, and towards the idea that planning is about adding value to the ways people experience places by working with them to improve those places.

This conception of the planner as a 'deliberative practitioner' (Forester, 1999), communicator and collaborator (Healey, 1997) contrasts with other depictions of the planner that have emerged in literature on the relationship between planning and property. Early critique suggested that planners are willing collaborators in the capitalist project in order to enhance land values and increase the competitiveness of their localities (Smith, 1986, 2002), thereby supporting the urban growth-machine (Logan and Molotch, 2007). A more nuanced view of planners has emerged since, however, portraying planners as "parties to a structural dilemma" who can use their regulatory power to "decommodify space and extract broad based benefits" (Wolf-Powers, 2005: 381). The crafting of land use plans by local authority planners in order to increase the scope for planning gain when departures from the plan are subsequently allowed was documented by Edwards (1990). However, the dependence of planners on private development to secure social and community benefits has increased substantially as public funding for infrastructure and public services has decreased, so that we are now, Rydin (2013) argues, in an era of 'growth-dependent planning'. Whereas planners may previously have acted primarily to enforce controls that shield lower-yielding activities from market forces, they are now left with little option but to support the principle of the highest and best use, with the aim of securing as much public benefit as possible from the property-led development that takes place. Despite this, public sector planners still have a strong sense of public service and working for the 'greater good' (Clifford and Tewdwr-Jones, 2013). One of the aims of this book is therefore to work towards a theory (or theories) of planning practice which navigates these different conceptions of planners and planning practice, in the context of the global processes of economic, political and environmental change, the austerity state and a hostile ideological framework in the UK within which planners work.

Planning developed as a profession during the 20th century with distinctive forms of education and accreditation, associations, hierarchies and, latterly, ethical statements. However, since planning as a practice is a political activity and occurs within a framework of legislation that is constantly changing, planning education necessarily shies away from arming its students with knowledge that is likely to be out of date once they graduate. Students who study planning are often only exposed to the very real challenges and dilemmas of planning practice when they start working in the field. In addition, many of those working in or impacted by planning have had no formal planning education at all. Even those graduates with accredited planning degrees will find that there are contrasts between the theory of planning and planning practice itself, between how people think planning is done and how it actually is done.

The aim of this book is to explore some of these contrasts, and to reflect upon the challenges and dilemmas that confront contemporary planning practice and its practitioners. In doing so, we reflect on the adequacies and limitations of existing theories of planning practice, and point to future directions for theoretical inquiry. In this chapter, we consider the contemporary social, economic, political and ideological contexts within which planning occurs. First, we look in general terms at the contemporary global contexts and challenges to planning practice, identifying some ideological and structural conditions that frame the space for planning. Second, we pay particular attention to the frameworks within which British planning occurs. Third, we set out the contemporary case for planning and what this means for the profession and practitioners. One emerging theme is that the case for planning is by no means widely agreed. Finally, we outline the remainder of the book, which comprises a series of chapters that address the different dimensions of contemporary planning practice.

Frameworks of Planning Practice

The practice of planning occurs in an intellectual and political atmosphere where its very value is called into question. The notion that planning is a hindrance in the promotion of economic development is suggested by both academics and policy-makers. Edward Glaeser argues in *The Triumph of the City* (2012) that planning restrictions, such as the protection of historic landmarks, zoning regulations, building height limits and Green Belts, have impeded the development of cities, which are the prime sources of potential productivity improvements in the economy. Local land use policies are blamed by some economists for raising the cost of land purchases and the prices of residential and commercial property and impeding urban growth in places as diverse as Boston and New York, the Randstad and the UK, while cities such as Houston which have abandoned zoning are offered as success stories of urban development (Cheshire and Hilber, 2008; Cheshire and Shepperd, 2002; Glaeser, 2012; Glaeser and Ward, 2009; Robert-Nicoud and Hilber, 2013; Vermeulen and van Ommeren, 2009). Some political scientists view planning not as a rational means of mediating conflicting interests in the use of land, but as a vehicle for professional, bureaucratic and vested interests (Pennington, 2002, 2005). Another version of this argument suggests that society and economy are now too complex to plan, and that the planning profession is founded on 'hubris' (Cheshire, 2006; Webster and Lai, 2003).

Alongside the ideological challenge to planning, accelerating processes of economic and social change are transforming the context within which it occurs. Increasing global movements of people, firms, commodities, capital, culture and ideas are transforming cities and regions. Powerful global cities, which contain the command and control functions of the world economy, can coexist with shrinking post-industrial cities within the same national boundaries. The sources of capital in cities and regions in the Global North are increasingly diverse, originating in China, the Gulf, South East Asia and elsewhere. The privatisation of state assets, including land and infrastructure, is a powerful attractor for such investment, and the funding, financing and planning of urban development becomes increasingly complex.

The free flow of people and resources is made possible by the growing integration and deregulation of international markets, which are said to be characteristic of a neo-liberal age, founded on "the belief that open, competitive and unregulated markets liberated from all forms of state interference represent the optimal mechanism for economic development" (Brenner and Theodore, 2002: 350). Growing international integration, deregulated markets and financialisation of urban development were the proximate causes of the global financial crisis and the ensuing Great Recession. In the Global North, the costs of stabilising the banking sector, together with declining state revenues, have increased the fiscal stresses on governments and engendered large-scale retrenchment. Schäfer and Streeck (2013: 9–10) argue: "governments, at the prodding of 'financial markets', jointly try to turn the tax and debt state that existed before 2008 into an austerity or consolidation state defined by balanced budgets and a (gradual) decline in public indebtedness". Austerity now provides an enduring framework within which planning is practised. This means diminished public resources and capacity to shape the development of cities and regions, forcing the adoption of new approaches to funding and financing urban growth in which planners are embroiled. Faltering growth is the background to the early signs that the long movement towards globalisation may be slowing, or even reversing, in response to rising populism.

Longer-term planning pressures arise from population changes. Migration, both internal and across borders, is transforming cities and regions, and poses new challenges for planning practice. Population growth places new stresses on the built environment, and planners now engage with increasingly diverse communities. Elsewhere, cities and regions may contain an ageing population, which has implications for the future fiscal health of governments, and for the design of public services and the planning of settlements. Endemic forms of ill-health such as obesity are distributed unevenly within and between cities and regions, and place new strains on them. Environmental and resource pressures also pose challenges for planning practice. Most obviously, climate change requires new approaches to the production and management of the built environment. This is closely tied to concerns about the way we produce and consume finite resources. The future of cities depends on the production and management of energy, minerals, water, waste and food, all of which are subject to conflict on a global and local scale. The practice of planning occurs within a testing and rapidly changing context. The complexities of the development process, the proliferation of actors involved in it and the multiplying social, economic and environmental pressures at play in cities and regions, together with the ideological assault on planners and their practice, mean that the case for planning cannot be assumed.

Frameworks of Planning Practice in the UK

The main focus of this book is planning practice in the UK, where the global processes described in the previous section take on a particular character. The UK is a multi-national state – comprising England, Wales, Scotland and Northern Ireland – which recently has been transformed through processes of devolution and no longer appears to be a very united kingdom. Planning itself occurs within frameworks of Parliamentary democracy, a body of common law, judicial action, and the evolving relationships between central and local government. The Town and Country Planning Act 1947 and associated legislation established the state's right to regulate land use, and the permission of a local planning authority is required before any development can occur. Decisions are made case-by-case, primarily on the basis of whether or not the proposed development is in accordance with the local 'development plan'. The development plan is not legally binding, so although it might indicate areas where specific land uses and densities are preferred, developers are permitted to make a case for departure from the plan in their planning application. Hence, planning in the UK is often referred to as 'discretionary'. This differs from the system of zoning in the US and Japan, for instance, where zoning ordinances are legally binding. It also differs from the systems prevalent in much of Continental Europe and Scandinavia, where local authorities are responsible for preparing detailed plans for sites which are legally binding, but where more strategic plans have less weight. In the UK, despite various reforms, this essential framework of land use regulation remains intact, although the public ownership of development rights has been eroded in many ways.

Planning in the UK occurs within a distinctive political economy in which there has been a growing role for markets in the allocation of resources since the late 1970s and the deregulation of the financial sector in the 'Big Bang' of 1986 initiated by the Thatcher government. Urban and regional inequalities have grown rapidly, and are among the widest in the Organisation for Economic Cooperation and Development. The economy of London and adjacent southern regions of England has grown at rates well above the national average, while the remaining regions (with the exception of Scotland) have grown at much lower rates (McCann, 2016). These developments occur within the context of highly concentrated and opaque patterns of landownership and where homeownership has been promoted as the primary mode of personal wealth accumulation (Hetherington, 2015). However, in Scotland there is a lively debate on proposals to improve the transparency of landownership through a public register of controlling interests in land, following the Land and Reform Act 2016 (Milne, 2016).

Despite the trend towards a more deregulated or lightly regulated planning system, planners and their practices remain subject to criticism. The former UK Prime Minister, David Cameron, in 2012, identified planners as being among the bureaucrats who were stifling private enterprise and the aspirations of citizens:

> We're determined to cut through the bureaucracy that holds us back. That starts with getting the planners off our backs, getting behind the businesses that have the ambitions to expand and meeting the aspirations of families that want to buy or improve a home.
>
> (David Cameron, quoted in BBC News, 2012)

In 2011, the then Chancellor of the Exchequer, George Osborne, and his ministerial colleague, Eric Pickles, claimed that:

> our planning system is a deterrent to international investment, and a barrier to the expansion of home-grown enterprise. When planning acts as a break on growth, and on the much needed new jobs and new businesses, reform is imperative . . . planning has come to be seen as a tool to say "no" to growth; as a means to block and delay.
>
> (Osborne and Pickles, 2011)

A sense that planning inhibits growth has survived several changes of government. Academic research by economists in the UK has emphasised the 'costs of planning' which contribute to increased house prices and market volatility, increased office rents and lower retail productivity, and the misallocation of investment away from (lower-cost) greenfield sites – through policies such as the Green Belt – towards (higher-cost) brownfield sites (Cheshire, 2013). Drawing on such analysis, Her Majesty's Treasury (2015) has maintained that planning impedes the growth of productivity, increases the cost and uncertainty of investment, hinders competition by raising barriers to entry, adaptation and expansion, constrains the agglomeration of firms and labour mobility, and encourages speculation in land. Powerful voices in society identify planning as a source of inefficiency in the development process and assert the value of markets as the best means of allocating resources, including the use of land and the production and management of the built environment. In this analysis, planning failures lie at the heart of the UK's low productivity and the underperformance of its urban and regional economies.

The UK planning system has been subject to successive rounds of deregulation over the past 30 years, expanding the range of development and change of use that can take place without the need for planning permission (permitted development), and through innovations such as Enterprise Zones. In 2010, regional planning strategies were abolished and the National Planning Policy Framework (Department for Communities and Local Government, 2012) was introduced. It consolidated and reduced the quantity of national planning guidance and introduced a presumption in favour of (sustainable) development, with a bias towards economic growth. There has been a raft of new legislation, in particular the Deregulation Act 2015 and Housing and Planning Act 2016. The latter allows, for instance, 'permission in principle' on sites allocated for development and further extensions of permitted development rights, most notably the conversion of offices to residential use without the need for full planning permission.

The creation of devolved administrations in Scotland, Wales and Northern Ireland, together with the creation of the London Mayor and Assembly, has created a series of new political spaces and the possibility of divergent planning practices in different parts of the UK. In England, the Coalition government (2010–2014) abolished the mechanisms of regional spatial planning established by the previous Labour administration and switched the policy focus towards the urban scale which is viewed as the engine of economic growth. City Deals and Devolution Deals, which in some cases include new statutory planning powers, have been offered to selected local authorities, typically on condition that a directly elected Metro Mayor becomes part of the governance arrangements. Another strand of reforms under the move towards decentralisation has been the introduction of Neighbourhood Planning, facilitated by the Localism Act 2011, which gives communities the power to create a Neighbourhood Forum and prepare a Neighbourhood Plan. These plans must be in conformity with the Local Plan and National Planning Policy Framework, but if approved and adopted, have statutory status. Whether or not this represents a genuine shift towards grassroots involvement and decision-making in planning matters is a subject of current debate (Parker and Street, 2015).

Contemporary reforms have occurred within the context of a UK 'austerity state'. Local government has borne the brunt of local expenditure cuts, and planning departments have been hit especially severely. There have been significant reductions in local authority budgets and staff: between 2010 and 2015, a third fewer staff overall, with an average decrease of 37% in planning policy staff and 27% decrease in Development Management staff. At the same time, planning services became an increasingly significant source of income for local authorities (e.g. through pre-application advice, application fees and the New Home Bonus), but this was not often reflected in the funding provided to planning departments (Royal Town Planning Institute/ARUP, 2015).

Such financing mechanisms generally favour localities with higher levels of development.

In the mid-2000s, in the context of a development boom, the UK Government identified a shortfall in the number of planners and the skills of existing planners, particularly as a new 'spatial planning' approach was developed which sought to place planning at the centre of the strategic coordination of the spatial impacts of sector policies and decisions. The introduction of 'spatial planning' by the New Labour government led to reforms, including: the replacement of a single development plan by a 'suite' of documents within a Local Development Framework, which could be updated separately so as to speed up the plan-making process; a collaborative front-loaded process of identifying issues and evaluating options, to promote a more inclusive and consensual process; the introduction of 'tests of soundness' emphasising an evidence-based approach; and a focus on implementation and annual monitoring to encourage the delivery of wider outcomes (Nadin, 2007). The Egan Review saw the planning of sustainable communities as involving a concern with governance, transport and connectivity, the provision of public, private and community services, and encompassing environmental, economic, housing and social and cultural dimensions (see also Barker, 2006; House of Commons, 2008). Egan (2004: 4, 10) sought to identify the range of skills required by the planner:

> Delivering better communities requires not only the professional skills of planning, architecture and surveying, but also a broad range of generic skills, behaviour and knowledge – such as governance of communities, economic planning for prosperity, communication (especially listening to and selling to communities), risk taking, and above all leadership and partnership working . . . it is the generic skills, behaviour and knowledge that will make the difference between successful delivery and failure. Skills such as the ability to create a vision, leadership to achieve buy-in to the vision, communication, teamworking, project management, process re-engineering, understanding sustainable development, effective financial management, understanding the economics of development and the processes of local democracy.

Despite austerity and state retrenchment, these objectives for planning practice remain relevant, but the conditions for implementing them have become much more difficult. Planners are called upon to be astute strategic actors with a detailed grasp of the dynamic social, political and economic context within which they operate, but to achieve this with fewer resources and powers.

The setting within which planning is practised in the UK is complex and challenging. The global processes that are transforming cities and regions are refracted through the distinctive relationships between state and market that shape the UK. The UK has a longstanding planning system, but this has been transformed recently by its place in the deregulated austerity state and the evolving system of multi-level governance. Planning and planners are subject to ideological attack for their supposed role in hindering economic development.

The Case for Planning

In a context where the value of planning is in question, it is necessary to consider why it remains important. In the UK, many of the claims that attend the apparent failures of planning can be firmly challenged. Land supply restrictions seem a poor explanation of the exceptional scale of regional inequalities in the UK. While acknowledging that planning restrictions can distort land and housing prices, a more credible explanation of regional inequalities would emphasise changes in the sectoral structure of the economy linked to the effects of globalisation as the cause. While building new homes on the Green Belt may help to solve London's housing crisis, planning restrictions in themselves clearly have not stopped the city from growing rapidly in recent decades. Moreover, problems of urban development in slower-growing northern cities appear to owe more to broader regional structural conditions than the operation of the planning system (McCann, 2016). Much of current orthodoxy on UK planning confuses causes and outcomes. It seems likely, for instance, that any efforts to develop housing on the Green Belt will require more, not less, planning. Planning plays a critical role in shaping, regulating and stimulating markets and enhancing the capacity of city and regional governance systems to manage these tasks.

The 'costs of planning' literature typically overlooks the benefits of planning. In the UK, the Town and Country Planning Association has been at the forefront of reviving an interest in the utopian tradition of planning, founded on principles of social justice and human well-being. Ellis and Henderson (2014, 2016) argue that bold thinking about alternative imaginary futures is required if we are to address the major issues of our time, such as inequality and climate change, but that recent 'reforms' and deregulation, driven by neo-liberal ideology, undermine our ability to do so. Town planning has lost its purpose, it is "no longer an active movement for visionary and holistic place-making, which was its core inspiration and primary function" (Ellis and Henderson, 2016: 14). Klosterman (1985) argues that there are strong economic arguments for planning that arise from the need to: secure public goods (including the infrastructure required to underpin economic growth and activity); address the negative externalities (such as congestion, pollution and climate change) arising from development, but which can act as an encumbrance on the economy; solve the prisoner's dilemma, where individuals pursue self-interest at odds with the interests of society as a whole; and address distributional consequences which may result from development that advantages some social groups or places over others.

Moreover, the critique of planning rests on a narrow measure of the value of planning determined by its contribution to economic growth, typically measured by Gross Domestic Product (GDP). But there has been a surge of interest in the limits to understanding human progress in terms of economic growth, and measuring it in terms of GDP, which fails to capture all aspects of the development process or the contribution to human well-being (Michaelson, 2015). This has led to the search for new approaches to understanding and measuring urban and regional development which go beyond simple measures of economic output (Tomaney, 2015). In an important sense, the planning system adjudicates between the competing values that are at play in our contested understandings of development and growth. Campbell (1996) identifies a triangle of conflicting goals for planning and three associated conflicts. The conflicting goals of planning comprise equity and social justice, economic development and environmental protection – the trilemma of sustainable development. Interposed between these goals are conflicts based around the ownership and use of property, the costs and benefits of development, and deployment of finite resources. There is considerable scope for dispute about how we measure each of Campbell's goals, depending on the values we deploy in their definitions.

An additional argument for planning arises from the new 'place-based' approaches to the promotion of economic development. These approaches promote local institutional transformation to allow regions to reach their development potential. They are based on recognition that countries are internally diverse and heterogeneous, that national policies typically favour capital cities and national elites, and that what is required is bottom-up, multi-level governance arrangements that build on local social capital to identify and develop embedded local economic assets. Such approaches require widely agreed plans rather than solutions provided by national technocratic elites and 'market forces'. Strategic planning engages with complex problems in an integrated way, allowing for the creation of strategic visions of shared futures at a larger than project-level scale (Albrechts, 2004). In this perspective, planning concerns coordination and integration and "thinking of all the different needs of, and opportunities for, an area in order to guide where new infrastructure investment should go. It is about taking as comprehensive a view as possible by engaging with relevant stakeholders" (Rydin, 2011: 31). The planner is not just a regulator of the use of land and property, but "a proactive and strategic coordinator of all policy and actions that influence spatial development; as to do this in the interests of more sustainable development" (Nadin, 2007: 43).

The (theoretical) economic rationale for planning would imply that policy must to seek to constrain market externalities and promote sustainable growth, even if that restricts particular development opportunities (at least in the short term). However, it should also support the business economy by ensuring that crucial local and national infrastructure, which would not otherwise be brought forward by the market, is both delivered and maintained. The value of planning in economic terms is thus about much more than resolving externalities. It is also concerned with a broader set of economic outcomes than growth alone, and with stretching economic horizons beyond the short term, to ensure their achievement. Successful planning thus provides an important platform for long-term sustainable economic development. Despite the ideological hostility to planning, it has proved impossible to dispense with it completely because society in general values the stability and certainty it provides, especially in a period of rapid social and economic change.

Outline of the Book

Chapter 2 provides further important context for the remainder of the book. John Tomaney and Claire Colomb consider how planning is practised in the context of a devolved UK that has experienced ad hoc, piecemeal decentralisation, with uneven implications for planning. Devolution to Scotland, Wales and Northern Ireland is creating space for forms of spatial planning practice that diverge from those in England. In England, London still has its own powers over strategic planning, exercised by the Mayor and Greater London Assembly. Other cities, notably Manchester, are progressing strategic spatial planning frameworks. In other parts of England, a strategic vacuum exists. The complexities of spatial planning provide a lens through which we can investigate the wider relevance and impact of the theory and practice of multi-level governance.

Following the chapter on devolution, and in order to develop our understanding of contemporary planning practice, the remainder of the book is structured in three parts, under the themes of 'tools', 'contexts' and 'outcomes'. In each part, our contributors – whose first authors are all academics in the Bartlett School of Planning – reflect on the opportunities and challenges for contemporary planning practice in their areas of expertise.

Part I is concerned with exploring the range of tools and processes that come under the banner of planning practice, and broadly correspond to areas of specialist work for planning practitioners. It is particularly concerned with how theory informs practice, how practice diverges from theory, and the challenges facing professional planning practitioners as they go about their everyday practice. Chapter 3 by Jessica Ferm looks at plan-making, which covers the area of planning work that is variously called forward planning, strategic planning, strategy-making or planning policy. This is at the core of what planning is, and refers to attempts to make plans for, and reduce risk in, an uncertain future. The chapter starts by revealing how patchy (up-to-date) Local Plan coverage is, particularly in England. It then examines the practice and drivers of plan-making, and how these have changed in the last two decades. It argues that the political focus on the housing crisis and emphasis on viability in policy has rendered the practice of plan-making less creative and visionary, and the delivery of housing (and growth) have overtaken place-making and social transformation as the main drivers. The other major area of work that planning practitioners in the UK engage in is Development Management. Drawing on empirical work with planners in England and Scotland, Chapter 4 by Ben Clifford explores the dilemmas and challenges that planners face in the process of managing and guiding development from planning application decision-making to delivery. Long neglected by planning scholars, Development Management is facing growing pressures within a sphere increasingly shaped by austerity, outsourcing and deregulation, and the challenges for everyday practice are manifold, with impacts on development quality, democratic accountability, community engagement and the delivery of social and environmental objectives. An important part of the work of planning officers in local authorities is capturing the development value for public benefit or infrastructure financing, which is becoming increasingly challenging – and important – in an age of austerity. In Chapter 5, Patricia Canelas goes into further depth on the challenges and emerging practices involved in capturing development value, drawing on interviews with planners, developers, valuers and community representatives involved in, or affected by, contemporary urban developments. Chapter 6 further explores the practice of public engagement or participation in planning. Drawing on her research on participative processes in planning, Yasminah Beebeejaun argues that while there is a strong desire for participation in theory, the reality is that communities seldom behave in ways that have been welcomed by either practitioners or theorists. The reasons for this are complex, relating to the increasingly constrained position of participation in planning, the ways in which community opposition is understood, and the overwhelming emphasis on consensus. Chapter 7 by Matthew Carmona – the final chapter in this first part of the book – looks more specifically at role of design and place-making in planning. He argues that despite top-down approaches to masterplanning being discredited decades ago, there is a need to remember some of the early vision, to make planning more proactive again and reintroduce a stronger design dimension to planning, which requires that planners do more than simply allocate sites, write policies and regulate development. Carmona investigates potential approaches to doing so, discussing some of the conundrums and the best tools to improve practice – and design outcomes – in the future.

Part II of the book examines the changing contexts for planning practice. It elaborates on some of the themes outlined in this introduction, and explores the impacts of these changing contexts on planning practice and the dilemmas or challenges faced by planning practitioners in the face of them. In Chapter 8, Mike Raco considers the profound impact of growing privatisation and the relentless expansion of the role of the private sector in influencing the design, financing and governance of the planning system. He examines the impact of austerity cuts and the growing power and influence of the global consultancy industry as new markets for expert advice and 'successful' policy models have opened up in the wake of globalisation and territorial competition. These changing contexts mean that the private sector now, arguably, has a bigger role to play in shaping the form and character of places and spaces in England than at any time since 1945, and yet public sector-led models of the planning system still permeate everyday thinking. Chapter 9, by Elena Besussi, explores the ambivalent concept and practice of Neighbourhood Planning in England under the Localism Act as both a bottom-up, community-led practice and as a top-down policy. Academics and practitioners have raised questions about the neo-liberal and exclusionary nature of Neighbourhood Planning given its requirement to comply with broader government agendas for growth. Besussi explores these contradictions in two case studies of Neighbourhood Planning in London, where tensions raised by neo-liberal urban politics are particularly tangible, and where communities' attempts to challenge top-down agendas through Neighbourhood Planning and more radical means are examined. Chapter 10 turns to the evolving relationship between planning and real estate. Tommaso Gabrieli and Nicola Livingstone consider the intersection between planning and commercial real estate in the UK, and how it has evolved, adapted and responded to globalisation and consequent regulatory and industry changes after the global financial crisis. Drawing on interviews with professionals in commercial real estate and planning, they reveal how the rapidly changing investment and development context in London over the last decade has wide-ranging implications for planning practice, which seeks to balance sustainable social and economic real estate impacts, and successfully 'add value'. Next, our attention is turned to the changing human contexts affecting planning. In Chapter 11, Claire Colomb and Mike Raco discuss how the UK planning system and local planning practice have responded to the ethnic, cultural, religious and demographic diversification of British society generated by 20th- and 21st-century waves of migration. Diversity has gradually become an object of concern and attention for planners due to the perceived challenges (but also opportunities) that a more culturally and ethnically diverse society poses. Colomb and Raco contrast the normative calls for 'planning for diversity' with the ambiguities, contradictory outcomes, dilemmas and challenges of doing so in practice. Finally, we consider the changing environmental context which planning is framed by and seeks to impact. Chapter 12, by Catalina Turcu, examines planning for sustainable urban development in policy and practice, with a particular emphasis on the environmental dimension of sustainability, low-carbon and energy-efficient urban development. Through a review of the policy, legislative and fiscal contexts and an examination of North West Bicester – the first eco-town in England – she reveals challenges for the delivery of sustainable development in practice. These include the lack of a strong framework for the delivery of sustainable development at the national policy level in the four UK nations, the challenges posed by Neighbourhood Planning in England and community-led planning elsewhere, and the impact of austerity measures which have hindered the ability of local planning to deliver sustainable development in practice.

The third part of the book examines the various outcomes of planning practice, looking at what we plan 'for' – housing, infrastructure, economic progress, transport connections and regeneration. Nick Gallent introduces the thorny issue of planning for housing in Chapter 13. The production and consumption of housing is now highly financialised, and most housing today is built speculatively, either for owner occupation or rental, but mostly for investment and as mechanisms for wealth accumulation. The implications of this context for planning for housing are explored, looking at the different strategic and development planning approaches and tools that have emerged, reflecting on planning's apparent inability to shape housing outcomes – in terms of type and mix of housing provided and its 'affordability' – in the strongest markets, where outcomes seem largely to be driven by investment pressure. In Chapter 14, John Tomaney, Peter O'Brien and Andy Pike examine the challenge confronting planners in providing large-scale strategic physical infrastructure developments in the context of global financial crisis, faltering economic recovery and austerity, where national and local state actors are being compelled into the increasingly speculative activities of entrepreneurial urbanism. They examine the complexity and contradictions of such infrastructure at the UK scale and in Scotland, London and northern England. Central to understanding the planning of strategic infrastructure is its contemporary transformation from public good to private asset class. The challenge for planners, they argue, is to locate and anchor new sources of private capital, develop new and 'innovative' instruments and models of infrastructure provision, and new or reformed institutional and governance arrangements. In Chapter 15, Jessica Ferm, Michael Edwards and Edward Jones reflect on the tensions of planning for economic progress in the UK, where the dominant framing of the economy overemphasises the role of specialisation and agglomeration as growth strategies, underplaying the role of economic diversity and the costs of agglomeration. They argue that the way 'evidence' on the economy is prepared and used by planners results in a narrow framing of the economy, and thus approach to planning, drawing on their involvement in the preparation of the Economics Evidence Base for London which informs the London Plan. In Chapter 16, Iqbal Hamiduddin and Robin Hickman examine the problem of planning for high-quality public transport infrastructure beyond the main cities of the UK, particularly in the smaller urban areas and their hinterlands, where residents are significantly more car-dependent. The challenges in practice of transferring innovative transport solutions from mainland Europe to the UK are examined through an examination of the implementation of two innovative rail-based tramway models in mainland Europe. Chapter 17, by Claudio de Magalhães and Nikos Karadimitriou, looks at the changing contexts for urban regeneration and how planning practitioners are responding. The focus is on the increasing use of private-led land redevelopment projects in public/private partnerships as a key tool in the delivery of public policy, from housing to transport, employment and economic development, and the complex relationship between the public sector and property markets the use of that tool engenders. As the chapter will show, to engage in it effectively, planning practitioners need skills and knowledge – in property valuation, risk management and stakeholder management – which have not traditionally been part of their education.

In the final chapter of the book, we bring together the theoretical, practical and political messages of the collective chapters, examining the limitations of *reflective* and *deliberative* practice through a re-examination of debates concerning communicative planning and collaborative practice. It also traces the shift from rational-scientific models of planning to evidence-based approaches and, latterly, to viability-based planning. The final chapter draws attention to the structural constraints within which planning occurs and the limits they place on planning practice. It also discusses the implications of the changing nature of the state, in particular evolving multi-level governance, considering the opportunities this provides for divergent practices, but also the limits it places on planning practice. A further theme explored in the chapter is the increasing role of the private sector in shaping the performance of the planning system, with profound ethical and political implications. Finally, it considers the likely future directions of planning practice and the shifting purposes of planning in a context of rising inequality, austerity and a splintering state.

References

All listed URLs were last accessed on 1 March 2018.

Albrechts, L. (2004) Strategic (spatial) planning reexamined, *Environment and Planning B: Planning and Design*, 31, pp.743–758.

Barker, K. (2006) *Barker Review of land use planning. Final report – recommendations.* Available at: https://www.gov.uk/government/uploads/system/uploads/attachment_data/file/228605/0118404857.pdf.

BBC News (2012) Planning rules on extensions to be relaxed "to boost economy", 6 September. Available at: www.bbc.co.uk/news/uk-politics-19496204.

Brenner, N. and Theodore, N. (2002) Cities and the geographies of "actually existing neoliberalism", *Antipode*, 34(3), pp.349–379.

Campbell, S. (1996) Green cities, growing cities, just cities? Urban planning and the contradictions of sustainable development, *Journal of the American Planning Association*, 62(3), pp.296–312.

Caro, R. (1974) *The power broker: Robert Moses and the fall of New York*. New York: Knopf.

Cheshire, P. (2006) Resurgent cities, urban myths and policy hubris: what we need to know, *Urban Studies*, 43(8), pp.1231–1246.

Cheshire, P. (2013) Land market regulation: market versus policy failures, *Journal of Property Research*, 30(3), 170–188.

Cheshire, P. and Hilber, C. (2008) Office space supply restrictions in Britain: the political economy of market revenge, *Economic Journal*, 118(529), pp.F185–F221.

Cheshire, P. and Sheppard, S. (2002) The welfare economics of land use planning, *Journal of Urban Economics*, 52, pp.242–269.

Clifford, B. and Tewdwr-Jones, M. (2013) *The collaborating planner? Practitioners in the neoliberal age*. Bristol: Policy Press.

Davies, J. (1972) *The evangelistic bureaucrat: a study of a planning exercise in Newcastle upon Tyne*. London: Tavistock Publications.

Dennis, N. (1970) *People and planning: the sociology of housing in Sunderland*. London: Faber.

Dennis, N. (1972) *Public participation and planner's blight*. London: Faber.

Department for Communities and Local Government (2012) *National Planning Policy Framework*, 27 March. London: The Stationery Office.

Edwards, M. (1990) What is needed from public policy? In P. Healey and R. Nabarro (eds) *Land and property development in a changing context*. Aldershot: Gower, pp.175–185.

Egan, J. (2004) *The Egan Review: skills for sustainable development*. Available at: http://webarchive.nationalarchives.gov.uk/20070402223805/http://communities.gov.uk/index.asp?id=1502251.

Ellis, H. and Henderson, K. (2014) *Rebuilding Britain: planning for a better future*. Bristol: Policy Press.

Ellis, H. and Henderson, K. (2016) *English planning in crisis: 10 steps to a sustainable future*. Bristol: Policy Press.

Faga, B. (2010) Focus on civic engagement. In G. Hack et al. (eds) *Local planning: contemporary principles and practice*. Washington, DC: ICMA Press, pp.234–242.

Forester, J. (1999) *The deliberative practitioner: encouraging participatory planning processes*. Cambridge, MA: MIT Press.

Glaeser, E. (2012) *The triumph of the city*. London: Pan.

Glaeser, E. and Ward, B. (2009) The causes and consequences of land use regulation: evidence from Greater Boston, *Journal of Urban Economics*, 65, pp.265–278.

Healey, P. (1997) *Collaborative planning: shaping places in fragmented societies*. Basingstoke: Macmillan.

Her Majesty's Treasury (2015) *Fixing the foundations: creating a more prosperous nation*. Cm 9098. Presented to Parliament by the Chancellor of the Exchequer by command of Her Majesty. Available at: https://www.gov.uk/government/uploads/system/uploads/attachment_data/file/443898/Productivity_Plan_web.pdf.

Hetherington, P. (2015) *Whose land is our land? The use and abuse of Britain's forgotten acres*. Bristol: Policy Press.

House of Commons (2008) Communities and Local Government Committee. *Planning matters – labour shortages and skills gaps. Eleventh report of session 2007–08. Volume 1. Report with formal minutes*. HC 517-I. London: The Stationery Office.

Jacobs, J. (1961) *The death and life of great American cities*. New York: Random House.

Kitchen, T. (2007) *Skills for planning practice*. Basingstoke: Palgrave Macmillan.

Klosterman, R. (1985) Arguments for and against planning, *Town Planning Review*, 56(1), p.5.

Logan, J and Molotch, H. (2007) *Urban fortunes: the political economy of place*. 2nd Ed. Berkeley, CA: University of California Press.

McCann, P. (2016) *The UK regional-national economic problem: geography, globalisation and governance*. London: Routledge.

Michaelson, J. (2015) GDP: what aren't we measuring? 21 October, *Commonwealth Foundation People's Forum*. Available at: http://cpf.commonwealthfoundation.com/measuring-gdp-alternatives/.

Milne, R. (2016) Scotland's land register consultation starts, *The Planner*, 15 September. Available at: www.theplanner.co.uk/news/scotland%E2%80%99s-land-register-consultation-starts.

Nadin, V. (2007) The emergence of the spatial planning approach in England, *Planning Practice and Research*, 22(1), pp.43–62.

Osborne, G. and Pickles, E. (2011) Planning reforms boost local power and growth, *Financial Times*, 4 September.

Parker, G. and Street, E. (2015) Planning at the neighbourhood scale: localism, dialogic politics, and the modulation of community action, *Environment and Planning C*, 33(4), pp.794–810.

Pennington, M. (2002) *Liberating the land: the case for private land-use planning*. London: IEA.

Pennington, M. (2005) The dynamics of interventionism: a case study of British land use regulation. In P. Kurrild-Klitgaard (ed.) *The dynamics of intervention: regulation and redistribution in the mixed economy. Advances in Austrian economics*, vol. 8. Bingley: Emerald Group Publishing, pp.335–356.

Peters, B.G. and Pierre, J. (2012) Urban governance. In K. Mossberger, S. Clarke and P. John (eds) *The Oxford handbook of urban politics*. Oxford: Oxford University Press, pp.71–86.

Robert-Nicoud, F. and Hilber, C. (2013) On the causes and consequences of land use regulations. Available at: www.voxeu.org/article/causes-and-consequences-land-use-regulations.

Royal Town Planning Institute/ARUP (2015) *Investing in delivery: how we can respond to the pressures on local authority planning*. RTPI Research Report no.10, October. Available at: www.rtpi.org.uk/media/1496890/RTPI%20Arup%20Research%20Report%20Investing%20in%20Delivery%2010%20October%202015.pdf.

Rydin, Y (2011) *The purpose of planning*. Bristol: Policy Press.

Rydin, Y. (2013) *The future of planning*. Bristol: Policy Press.

Schäfer, A. and Streeck, W. (2013) Introduction: politics in the age of austerity. In A. Schäfer and W. Streeck (eds) *Politics in the age of austerity*. Cambridge: Polity Press, pp.1–25.

Smith, N. (1986) Gentrification, the frontier and the restructuring of urban space. In N. Smith and P. Williams (eds) *Gentrification of the city*. Boston, MA: Allen & Unwin, pp.15–34.

Smith, N. (2002) New globalism, new urbanism: gentrification as global urban strategy. In N. Brenner and N. Theodore (eds) *Spaces of neoliberalism: urban restructuring in North America and Western Europe*. Malden, MA: Blackwell, pp.80–103.

Stoker, G. (1998) Governance as theory: five propositions, *International Social Science Journal*, 155, pp.17–28.

Stone, C. (1989) *Regime politics: governing Atlanta, 1946–1988*. Lawrence, KS: University Press of Kansas.

Thomas, H. and Healey, P. (1991) *Dilemmas of planning practice*. Aldershot: Avebury Technical.

Tomaney, J. (2015) Region and place III: well-being, *Progress in Human Geography*, 41(1), pp.99–107.

Vermeulen, W. and van Ommeren, J. (2009) Does land use planning shape regional economies? A simultaneous analysis of housing supply, internal migration and local employment growth in the Netherlands, *Journal of Housing Economics*, 18(4), pp.294–310.

Webster, C. and Lai, L. (2003) *Property rights, planning and markets: managing spontaneous cities*. Cheltenham: Edward Elgar.

Wolf-Powers, L. (2005) Upzoning New York City's mixed-use neighbourhoods: property-led economic development and the anatomy of a planning dilemma, *Journal of Planning Education and Research*, 24, pp.279–393.

2 Devolution and Planning

John Tomaney and Claire Colomb

Introduction: Planning in a Devolved UK

The constitution of the United Kingdom has been transformed since 1997 by devolution. The establishment of devolved administrations in Scotland, Wales and Northern Ireland and a directly elected Mayor and Assembly in London created new centres of political power and new legislative frameworks through which planning is enacted. A more uncertain and partial process of decentralisation has been initiated in England, notably since 2010. The UK is characterised by asymmetrical devolution in which different territories are accorded different powers, but in each case land use planning has been an important devolved power. Devolution in the UK is often described as a process, not an event. That is, the devolution legislation enacted by the New Labour government in 1997–2001 did not so much establish an enduring constitutional settlement, but rather created the conditions for instability and enduring contention.

Planning as a state activity (understood here in a broad sense) and as a form of public policy is closely bound with debates on constitutional arrangements and evolving multi-level governance structures in changing states. The interplay of devolution and planning can be viewed through the prism of 'territorial politics':

> that arena of political activity concerned with the relations between the central political institutions in the capital city and those interests, communities, political organisations and governmental bodies outside the central institutional complex, but within the accepted boundaries of the state, which possess, or are commonly perceived to possess, a significant geographical or local/regional character.
>
> (Bulpitt, 2008: 59)

It is also closely bound with longstanding debates on the transformation of the role of the central and local state in territorial management in a post-Fordist or post-Keynesian era and the objective of 'rebalancing' the 'national' economy – that is, among other things, encouraging growth outside London and the South East of England (Pike and Tomaney, 2009; Pike et al., 2015). In principle, devolution allows public policies to be better matched to citizens' local preferences and conditions.

This chapter examines the contemporary context for planning practice in a devolved UK, which gained increasing salience in the aftermath of the 2014 referendum in which voters rejected the proposal for Scotland to become an independent country, but which compelled the UK Government to initiate a new wave of constitutional reform. It examines debates on devolution in the rest of UK which were stoked in the wake of the referendum, looking at the planning implications of further devolution in Northern Ireland and Wales, and at recent developments in England. In the conclusion, we reflect on the significance of the developments analysed for planning practice, and on the implications of the outcome of the referendum on the UK's membership of the EU as of June 2016.[1]

Planning in Scotland

Since the Scotland Act of 1998, which initiated devolution, the Scottish Parliament has had full responsibility for spatial planning and related fields such as transport and local government. The reforms introduced by the first two Scottish Governments (a coalition between Labour and Liberal Democrats) until 2010, mainly through the Planning etc. (Scotland) Act 2006, echoed many of the planning reforms passed in England at the same time by the then New Labour government (Nadin, 2007; Lloyd and Peel, 2009). From 2010 onwards, the newly elected UK Coalition government (Conservative–Liberal Democrat) set out to reform the English planning system through the 2011 Localism Act, which dismantled many of New Labour's spatial planning initiatives (see below and Rozee, 2014). Following the electoral victory of the Scottish National Party (SNP) in the Scottish Parliamentary election in 2011, a divergence between the planning policy agendas of the Scottish and UK Governments became more apparent (Tomaney and Colomb, 2013).

Spatial planning in Scotland acquired a relatively high profile on the political agenda of the SNP government post-2011. While similarities remained in the respective planning discourses of the UK and Scottish Governments in the post-recession era – for example, the emphasis on 'sustainable economic growth' and calls for more efficiency in Development Management (the system and processes of planning control and permission) – the Scottish Government was keen to state the value of planning as a positive means of steering spatial development. The strategic and visionary element of planning supported the SNP's image of an independent, prosperous, low-carbon Scotland. In recent years, however, there has been some debate about the extent of this divergence and distinctiveness (Keating, 2005; Allmendinger, 2006; Clifford and

Morphet, 2015; Morphet and Clifford, 2014), but evidence suggests that the devolution arrangements of the late 1990s in the UK have allowed greater experimentation to occur in planning strategies and delivery styles – that is, they have generated a diversity of 'spatial plannings' between and within the nations of the UK, highlighting "distinctiveness in territorial management in the broader sense" (Haughton et al., 2009).

The 3rd National Planning Framework (NPF3) for Scotland, which was published just before the referendum in the summer of 2014, following an extensive consultation process, included a positive vision for the territory of Scotland (Scottish Government, 2014). It was presented as the spatial expression of the SNP government's Economic Strategy (Scottish Government, 2010), setting out a 20–30-year vision for development and investment in support of 'sustainable economic growth' and the transition to a low-carbon economy, emphasising the need to balance economic growth with the conservation of natural assets, the stewardship of natural resources and the development of renewable energy. Additionally, themes of social, regional and inter-generational equity figured prominently as policy objectives in NPF3 and in the Scottish Government's Economic Strategy in ways that were absent in the UK Coalition government's National Planning Policy Framework for England (DCLG, 2012; Tomaney and Colomb, 2013).

Scottish Planning Policy and NPF3 are instruments to guide planning decisions in a range of sectors such as economic development, regeneration, energy, environment, climate change, transport and digital infrastructure. Their potential is linked to their capacity to influence the investment decisions of the Scottish Government, public agencies, local planning authorities and private investors, as well as to the financing capacity of the Scottish Government. The Scottish Government's room for manoeuvre has been limited by its inability to borrow directly on capital markets to fund infrastructure projects. Additionally, the UK Parliament at Westminster retains competence in some key policy areas, such as taxation, energy and airports, which are fundamental levers in shaping the territorial and spatial development of any jurisdiction. Energy policy and the control of the National Grid are not devolved matters, and this is a source of contention between the Scottish and UK Governments because of the SNP's rejection of nuclear power and support for the development of renewable energy.

Following the 2014 referendum, the key areas of planning-related activities of the Scottish Government included energy policy (including a ban on fracking for shale gas), the Community Empowerment Act (passed in June 2015; see Scottish Parliament, 2015), and land reform – a sensitive and contentious issue (for a discussion, see Wightman, 2015a, 2015b) – which was put on hold prior to the referendum. The Land Reform (Scotland) Act was passed in March 2016 (Scottish Parliament, 2016). Some of its provisions were strongly opposed by the Conservatives and large landowners, such as powers to force the sale of private land to community groups, and improvements in both the common good land regime and 'right to roam' arrangements – while campaigners for land reform argued the Act did not go far enough (Brooks, 2016).

The Scottish Parliament elections of 2016 resulted in the SNP retaining control of the Scottish Government. It set out proposals for further reforms of the planning system (Scottish Government, 2017), including making community planning a statutory aspect of development plan-making, abolishing strategic (city-region) development plans, giving Scotland's National Planning Framework and Scottish Planning Policy stronger statutory status with greater clarity on regional priorities, improving the Local Development Plan process, designating more land for housing, and removing the need to apply for planning permission for more types of development.

Planning in Northern Ireland

The post-conflict conditions of Northern Ireland (NI), where the signing of the Good Friday Agreement in 1998 brought an end to several decades of violence, led to the creation of the Northern Ireland Assembly, founded on a consociational model of government, designed to create a power-sharing Executive involving the local political parties. In the aftermath of the Scottish referendum, attention was on the protracted negotiation of a 'Stormont Agreement' between the various parties in the NI and UK Governments (Boland, 2014; Her Majesty's [HM] Government, 2014). This agreement, following months of deadlock which threatened the power-sharing arrangements born out of the peace process, partly focused on the implementation of the UK Government's desired welfare and financial cuts (Birrell, 2015), but included other significant aspects such as the devolution of responsibility for the raising of corporation tax – a power which even Scotland lacks – ostensibly allowing NI to compete (or cooperate) with the Republic of Ireland for mobile investment. This agreement proved fragile, and in 2017 the Northern Ireland devolution arrangements were suspended following the failure to establish a new Executive in the aftermath of elections to the Northern Ireland Assembly.

In 2012, the NI Government published a Regional Development Strategy (NI Department of Infrastructure, 2012), which set out the spatial aspects of its programme, in particular spatial planning, transport, sustainable development and housing priorities. This was followed by efforts to create a new planning system. A contentious reform of the NI local government and planning system took effect on 1 April 2015, and involved the reduction in the number of local authorities and the devolution of powers from the NI Executive to 11 new district councils. This includes planning (including local development plan-making and Development Management), area-based urban regeneration and community development. The NI Executive retains responsibility for 'regionally significant' planning applications. The context for these changes was a system in which local authorities were stripped of a wide range of powers in the late 1960s (including planning) and only had a consultative role. According to the Planning (Northern Ireland) Order 1991, Local Plan preparation, development control and enforcement were in the hands of the NI Department of the Environment. But the effort to reform the system has been slow and fraught. The devolution of planning powers to NI local authorities is a challenging process, which requires capacity-building and a 'culture change'. Additionally, a proposed Northern Ireland Planning Bill was withdrawn in late 2013, although some of the aborted bill's provisions were implemented through administrative action. A *Strategic Planning Policy Statement for Northern Ireland* was agreed upon in 2015 (NI Department of Infrastructure, 2015), which sets out the planning policy objectives for securing the development of land in NI under the reformed two-tier planning system, and constitutes the strategic framework for the preparation of Local Development Plans.

Planning in Wales

The Government of Wales Act 1998 established the National Assembly of Wales, but in contrast to the primary law-making powers given to the Scottish Parliament, the Act limited the National Assembly to enacting secondary legislation only when authorised by the UK Parliament. The Government of Wales Act 2006 enhanced the Welsh Assembly's powers, and the Commission on Devolution in Wales (2014) advocated a 'reserved powers' model for Wales, which would offer more clarity, consistency and equity across the devolved nations of the UK. It also supported the devolution of certain tax and borrowing powers and specific planning powers to allow the Welsh Assembly to manage Welsh natural resources more effectively. It recommended that all energy planning consents (non-renewable and renewable) below 350MW should be devolved, and that the UK Government should have a statutory duty to take account of Welsh planning policies when exercising its retained responsibilities for larger projects. Other proposals relate to the devolution of regulatory powers over transport including ports, rail, buses and taxis, possible elements of social protection (e.g. housing) and control over the Crown Estate – all of them relevant for planning policy, and some of which were taken on board in the plans proposed by the UK Government (Wales Office and The Rt Hon Stephen Crabb MP, 2015). The new Conservative government's priorities included plans to grant new powers to the Welsh Assembly in the fields of energy, transport and the running of elections, which were enacted in the Wales Act 2017.

A significant part of planning competences was devolved to the Welsh Assembly government under the Government of Wales Act 2006, which stipulated a duty to promote sustainable development. A Wales Spatial Plan was approved in 2004, and updated in 2008. The Welsh Government introduced the Planning (Wales) Bill to the National Assembly in October 2014 to propose a reform of the planning system. The Planning (Wales) Act was approved in May 2015 (Welsh Assembly, 2015), and has been described as the foundation for a "renaissance of strategic planning" in Wales (Morris, 2015). The Act foresees the preparation of a National Development Framework (NDF) by 2018 (which will replace the Wales Spatial Plan and set out a 20-year land use framework for Wales) and the introduction of Strategic Development Plans for some parts of the country to tackle larger-than-local cross-boundary issues (e.g. in Cardiff and Swansea), in addition to existing Local Development Plans. In combination with two other pieces of legislation – the Environment (Wales) Bill and the Well-being of Future Generations (Wales) Act 2015, the Welsh planning system is being geared towards supporting the sustainable use, management and development of Welsh resources, as the country is likely to be strongly affected by the impacts of climate change. A reform of local government has also been under discussion, with proposals spelled out in early 2017 in a *Local Government Reform White Paper*. Corresponding to the proposed NDF's commitment to strategic, larger-than-local planning, in 2017 the UK Government, the Welsh Assembly government and the Cardiff Capital Region (the city of Cardiff and nine neighbouring local authorities) agreed a City Deal which creates a framework for strategic planning – including housing, transport planning and land use – in South East Wales.

Towards Regional Planning in England

England is the largest country in the UK, but has not experienced devolution of the type seen in other countries. There has been a long post-war search for a stable and effective regional planning system, with the regional and local scales being the focus for action in different periods. Under New Labour, a strong emphasis was placed on the regional scale through the creation of Regional Development Agencies (RDAs) and the proposal to create elected regional assemblies. The incoming Coalition in 2010 swiftly abandoned this approach, abolishing RDAs and their associated Regional Spatial Strategies.

'Localism' and the 'Big Society' were buzzwords in the early days of the UK Coalition government (Swain and Baden, 2012; Wills, 2016). Both terms were vaguely defined, but rhetorically signalled a reduced role for the state in the management of urban and regional change, and a shift of power from the central state beyond local authorities to 'local communities' (DCLG, 2010). In planning terms, the apparatus of spatial planning established by the previous Labour government in the form of Regional Development Agencies and Regional Spatial Strategies was abolished by

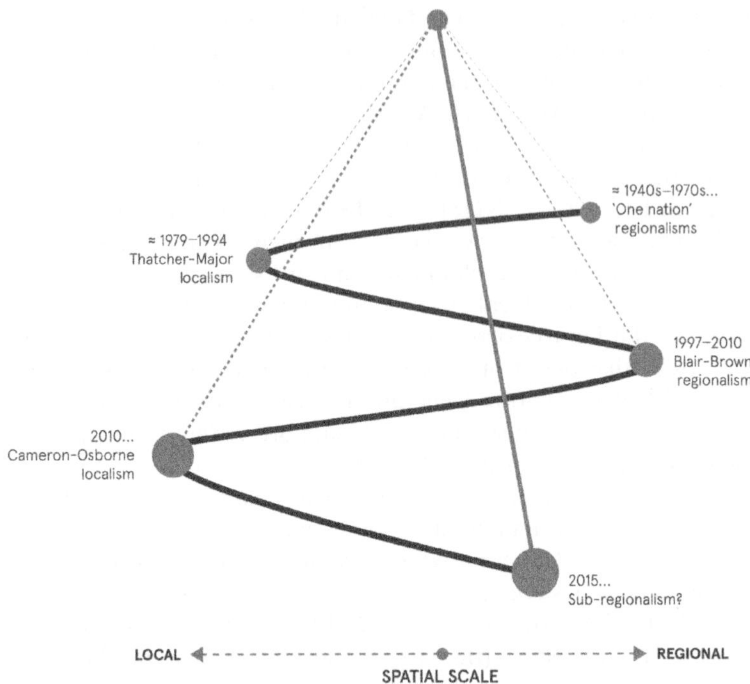

Figure 2.1 Pendulum swings in economic development governance in England
Source: Pike et al. (2016).

the incoming government (Rozee, 2014). Newly instituted non-statutory Local Enterprise Partnerships (LEPs) in theory brought together public and private actors at a local scale to promote local economic growth (Pike et al., 2015). This 'downscaling' of planning was accompanied by concerns over the system's ability to achieve broader and longer-term spatial objectives (Gallent et al., 2013; Baker and Wong, 2013; Boddy and Hickman, 2013). In the 2011 Localism Act, the Coalition government stipulated a formal 'Duty to Cooperate' for local authorities to work with their neighbours in the preparation of their development plans. In parallel, a new tier of 'Neighbourhood Planning' was introduced to give the right to residents to prepare a plan for a designed area subject to a referendum (Brownill and Bradley, 2017; Davoudi and Madanipour, 2015; DCLG, 2014; Locality, 2015; Wills, 2016). Underlying these approaches was the assumption that a proliferation of Local and Neighbourhood Plans and their attendant spillovers can be resolved through cooperative and voluntaristic means, although there is scant evidence of this practice (Boddy and Hickman, 2013). In 2015, tensions had become apparent within the Conservative government's agenda between, on the one hand, the promise to take the decentralisation and Localism Agenda further (by giving more power to local authorities and local communities over the control of development), and on the other, the imposition of top-down pressures for local authorities to accept new developments at all costs and release land for housing (HM Treasury, 2015).

While spatial planning arrangements in England were quickly abolished by the Coalition government in 2010, London remained an exception. The creation of a directly elected Mayor and Assembly in 1999 (the Greater London Authority) included the power to create a statutory spatial strategy ('The London Plan'). Strategic spatial planning in London is the shared responsibility of the Mayor of London, London Boroughs and the City of London. The London Plan is the Mayor's overarching strategic planning policy, with which the individual spatial plans of the London Boroughs and City of London must conform. The Mayor has a duty to keep The London Plan under review, and it is expected to provide an integrated economic, environmental, transport and social framework for the spatial development of London over a 25-year period, for instance designating 'Opportunity Areas' for new housing and commercial development and 'Intensification Areas', which vary in physical size and growth potential, but collectively are earmarked to provide land for hundreds of thousands of new jobs and homes. The Mayor has overall responsibility for designating the Opportunity Areas, while the Boroughs lead on development activity within the Opportunity Areas.

The London Plan is not covered by the Duty to Cooperate, but the Mayor does have to consult with the Boroughs and with local authority areas that border the administrative boundaries of London within the broader city-region. The perceived success of mega-events such as the London Olympics in 2012 and mega-infrastructure such as Crossrail ('The Elizabeth Line') have bolstered claims that London's governance arrangements have delivered effective spatial planning. However, episodes such as the aborted London Garden Bridge, proposed by Mayor Boris Johnson, with its "extremely murky procurement process, hazy costs, and utter lack of practical benefits" (O'Sullivan, 2017) also suggest some of the dangers in so much power resting in the office of the Mayor. At the same time, the steering capacity of the Mayor – and more widely of London Boroughs – in the planning and urban development fields has been constrained by the increasing influence of private developers and weight given to 'viability' considerations in the development and planning obligation negotiation process (Wainwright, 2014, 2015). Successive London Mayors, backed by key economic actors, have recurrently pleaded for more devolution for London, especially in fiscal terms. With the prospect of Brexit, the London Finance Commission (LFC), convened by the Mayor, called for more tax and spending powers for London to support its continuous demographic and economic growth (LFC, 2017). The challenge arising from such demands when considered at a larger scale is:

> how to operate a system which provides London with greater incentives and control (and therefore responsibilities), while at the same time not being seen to diminish the significant contribution that the capital makes to the national finances and therefore to public services in other parts of the country.
>
> (McGough, 2016)

There is no formal strategic planning framework for the wider functional urban region which extends beyond the Mayor's jurisdiction – i.e. the city-region or South East as a whole. As there are noticeable differences in the institutional capacity, statutory responsibilities and resources between the Greater London Authority, London Boroughs and local authorities and LEPs in South East England, this makes governance, long-term planning for housebuilding, and assembling public and private (particularly international) infrastructure difficult (O'Brien et al., forthcoming). London's particular and distinct geography, and complex questions of governability, has resulted in a "number of ad-hoc solutions to the city's governance problems" (Travers, 2015: 26), while there have also long been arguments for planning and coordinating infrastructure and development within and beyond London's administrative boundaries as "urban geographers and planners have generally seen London as an area of economic and social activity that extends far beyond the continuous built-up area of the city" (Travers, 2015: 337).

Alongside the broad shift to localism – and partly responding to its weaknesses as well as the powers granted to London – there has been a growing focus on city-regions as the scale to which political powers should be decentralised in England. This has found expression in the form of 'Devolution Deals' with Combined Authorities – statutorily defined groups of local authorities – which have typically included increased planning powers. The most significant development in this context was the signing of the 'Greater Manchester Agreement' between the Chancellor of the Exchequer, George Osborne, and the leaders of 10 local councils in Greater Manchester on 3 November 2014 (Jenkins, 2015; Tomaney and McCarthy, 2015). The establishment of a directly elected Mayor for Greater Manchester, with the power, among other things, to create a statutory spatial development plan including provisions for employment land, housing and infrastructure to 2033 (HM Treasury and Greater Manchester Combined Authority, 2014). A draft Greater Manchester Spatial Framework was published in late 2016, including proposals to build on the Green Belt that caused local controversy (Williams, 2016). Following the Scottish independence referendum, the UK Government agreed additional Devolution Deals with ad hoc groups of local authorities, largely replicating the Manchester Agreement, and typically involving some statutory strategic planning powers (Table 2.1). In each case, new Combined Authorities agreed to be governed by directly elected Mayors,

Table 2.1 Devolution deals in England in 2016

	Cambridge and Peterborough	*Greater Manchester*	*Liverpool City Region*	*Tees Valley*	*West Midlands*	*West of England*
30-year investment fund	£600m	£900m	£900m	£450m	£1.1bn	£900m
Education and skills	Apprenticeship Grant for Employers, Adult Skills Budget Post-16 further education system	Apprenticeship Grant for Employers, Adult Skills Budget Post-16 further education system	Apprenticeship Grant for Employers, Adult Skills Budget Post-16 further education system	Adult Skills Budget	Adult Skills Budget	Apprenticeship Grant for Employers, Adult Skills Budget Post-16 further education system
Housing and planning	£170m Affordable Housing Grant Strategic planning Mayoral Development Corporations	£30m per year Housing Investment Fund Strategic Planning Land Commission Compulsory purchase powers Mayoral Development Corporations	Strategic planning Compulsory purchase powers Mayoral Development Corporations Control of Key Route Network	Mayoral development Corporations	Compulsory purchase powers	Strategic planning Compulsory purchase powers Mayoral Development Corporations
Transport	Consolidated transport budget. Local roads network. Bus franchising. Smart ticketing	Consolidated transport budget Local roads network Bus franchising Smart ticketing	Consolidated transport budget Local roads network Bus franchising Smart ticketing	Consolidated transport budget	Consolidated transport budget Local roads network Bus franchising. Smart ticketing	Consolidated transport budget Local roads network Bus franchising Smart ticketing
Health and social care	Planning for health and social care integration	Control of £6bn integrated health and social care budget	Planning for health and social care integration			

Source: Centre for Cities (2016).

and elections were held in May 2017. In other places, mooted Devolution Deals – such as in the North East, Sheffield, West Yorkshire and Greater Lincolnshire – did not materialise, or collapsed because of an inability to agree local priorities or governance structures.

Conclusion

Devolution provides an important context within which planning occurs in the UK. The creation of devolved administrations in Scotland, Wales and Northern Ireland made space for divergences in planning priorities and practices with England. In London, the Mayor's London Spatial Plan offers the only example of a strategic framework for land use development. Despite the existence of a Local Plan-based system in the rest of England, and a putative 'localism' after 2010, the space for sub-national discretion there has been more limited. The creation of a small number of Combined Authorities led by directly elected Mayors raises the prospect of the return of more strategic forms of spatial planning in England following their abolition in 2010, but it will take some time before judgements about the effectiveness of these arrangements can be made.

The developments described above raise the prospect of planning better matched to the diversity of conditions and preferences in the UK, but as Pike et al. (2012: 25) note, there is "limited evidence that any economic dividend of devolution has emerged yet". This remains difficult to discern because the likely effects are overridden by the role of national economic growth in decisively shaping the pattern of spatial disparities, and in determining the scope and effects of spatial economic policy and decentralisation. Additionally, asymmetrical devolution raises the question, in England for instance, whether decentralisation to selected city-regions empowered by directly elected Mayors, without the development of broader mechanisms for inter-regional redistribution and territorial equalisation or regional economic development strategies, will create an archipelago of dynamic metropolitan areas surrounded by hinterlands of small towns and rural areas struggling with issues of demographic and economic decline (Tomaney, 2016). The most pressing planning issues in England – a North–South divide that is neither sustainable for the residents of the 'North' nor for the residents of the overheated South East; a chronic shortage of affordable, adequate housing for significant parts of the English population; the threat of climate change, resource depletion and natural disasters such as flooding; the needed improvements in transport infrastructure – all demand strategic planning at a scale that may be higher than the city or city-region. Some degree of higher-level adjudication is important to reconcile conflicting territorial interests to secure key infrastructure, amenities or housing developments across the territory. As with any rescaling of government and governance, "there is the potential for a radical reworking of the distribution of winners and losers in both societal and spatial terms, which may be progressive or it may be regressive" (Haughton et al., 2009: 10).

The Brexit referendum of 2016 created intense political and economic uncertainty. The referendum was held as a UK-wide franchise, with no separate requirements for majorities in each of the four constituent nations of the UK. The results revealed a highly divided UK: Scotland, Northern Ireland and London voted in favour of remaining; large parts of England and Wales voted to leave. Those results might have a strong impact on the relationships between the four nations of the UK, with Scotland's First Minister airing the possibility of convening a second referendum on Scottish independence. The possibility of an independent Scotland negotiating to remain within the EU while the rest of the UK is out of it would mean the creation of a 'hard' border. Such a prospect would have an impact on the North of England and generate new challenges for the Anglo-Scottish border (Shaw, 2016; Colomb, 2017). In Northern Ireland, there are fears that the recreation of a hard border between the Republic of Ireland and NI, and the loss of significant amounts of EU structural funds which have supported economic and social development in the region, could jeopardise the peace process. In the long term, an effective Brexit might increase scope for policy differentiation between the UK nations once their governments have been freed from the constraints of EU harmonisation (Hazell and Renwick, 2016).

In this chapter, we have charted the impact of devolution on planning practice. Devolution holds the promise of achieving spatial planning better matched to local conditions. But we began by noting that devolution occurs within the context of territorial politics in which power over the allocation of land use is critical. Therefore, it is important to recognise that effective planning practice rests not just on the deployment of technical skills, but on knowledge of the political economy of (local and regional) growth and development. Planners in the public, private and non-governmental sectors are necessarily implicated both in debates about how to promote sustainable development in diverse economic conditions and those that concern territorial politics in a devolving state.

Note

1 Parts of this chapter are based on an earlier paper: Colomb and Tomaney (2016).

References

All listed URLs were last accessed on 1 March 2018.

Allmendinger, P. (2006) Escaping policy gravity: the scope for distinctiveness in Scottish spatial planning. In M. Tewdwr-Jones and P. Allmendinger (eds) *Territory, identity and spatial planning*. London: Routledge, pp.153–166.

Baker, M. and Wong, C. (2013) The delusion of strategic spatial planning: what's left after the Labour Government's English regional experiment? *Planning Practice and Research*, 28(1), pp.83–103.

Birrell, D. (2015) Lessons from the Stormont House Agreement, *Centre on Constitutional Change Blog*, 17 February. Available at: https://www.centreonconstitutionalchange.ac.uk/blog/lessons-stormont-house-agreement.

Boddy, M. and Hickman, H. (2013) The demise of strategic planning? The impact of the abolition of Regional Spatial Strategy in a growth region, *Town Planning Review*, 84(6), pp.743–768.

Boland, V. (2014) Northern Ireland's parties reach broad deal but obstacles remain, *Financial Times*, 23 December. Available at: www.ft.com/cms/s/0/03732d42-8abd-11e4-8e24-00144feabdc0.html.

Brooks, L. (2016) A new dawn for land reform in Scotland? *The Guardian*, 17 March. Available at: https://www.theguardian.com/uk-news/scotland-blog/2016/mar/17/a-new-dawn-for-land-reform-in-scotland.

Brownill, S. and Bradley, Q. (eds) (2017) *Localism and neighbourhood planning: power to the people?* Bristol: Policy Press.

Bulpitt, J. (2008) *Territory and power in the United Kingdom: an interpretation*. Colchester: ECPR.

Centre for Cities (2016) Everything you need to know about metro-mayors: an FAQ. Available at: www.centreforcities.org/publication/everything-need-know-metro-mayors/#whois.

Clifford, B. and Morphet, J. (2015) A policy on the move? Spatial planning and state actors in the post-devolutionary UK and Ireland, *Geographical Journal*, 181(1), pp.16–25.

Colomb, C. (2017) A European perspective on Anglo-Scottish cross-border cooperation: lessons from EU-funded territorial cooperation programmes, *Journal of Borderland Studies*. Online preview, 24 April. Available at: www.tandfonline.com/eprint/Bxy63DXhsGiz5r5ukvMJ/full.

Colomb, C. and Tomaney, J. (2016) Territorial politics, devolution and spatial planning in the UK: results, prospects, lessons, *Planning Practice & Research*, 31(1), pp.1–22.

Commission on Devolution in Wales (2014) *Empowerment and responsibility – legislative powers to strengthen Wales*. Available at: https://www.gov.uk/government/publications/empowerment-and-responsibility-legislative-powers-to-strengthen-wales.

Davoudi, S. and Madanipour, A. (eds) (2015) *Reconsidering localism*. London: Routledge.

DCLG (2010) *Decentralisation and the Localism Bill: an essential guide*. Available at: https://www.gov.uk/government/publications/decentralisation-and-the-localism-bill-an-essential-guide--2.

DCLG (2012) *National Planning Policy Framework*. London: DCLG. Available at: https://www.gov.uk/government/uploads/system/uploads/attachment_data/file/6077/2116950.pdf.

DCLG (2014) *Giving communities more power in planning local development. Appendix 2: neighbourhood planning*. Available at: https://www.gov.uk/government/policies/giving-communities-more-power-in-planning-local-development/supporting-pages/neighbourhood-planning.

Gallent, N., Hammiduddin, I. and Maddedu, M. (2013) Localism, down-scaling and the strategic dilemmas confronting planning in England, *Town Planning Review*, 84(5), pp.563–582.

Haughton, G., Allmendinger, P., Counsell, D. and Vigar, G. (2009) *The new spatial planning: territorial management with soft spaces and fuzzy boundaries*. London: Routledge.

Hazell, R. and Renwick, A. (2016) *Brexit: its consequences for devolution and the union*. UCL Constitution Unit Briefing Paper. Available at: https://www.ucl.ac.uk/constitution-unit/research/europe/briefing-papers/briefing-paper-3.

HM Government (2014) *Stormont House Agreement*. Available at: https://www.gov.uk/government/uploads/system/uploads/attachment_data/file/390672/Stormont_House_Agreement.pdf.

HM Treasury (2015) *Fixing the foundations: creating a more prosperous nation*. Available at: https://www.gov.uk/government/uploads/system/uploads/attachment_data/file/443898/Productivity_Plan_web.pdf.

HM Treasury and Greater Manchester Combined Authority (2014) *Devolution to the Greater Manchester Combined Authority and transition to a directly elected mayor*. Available at: https://www.gov.uk/government/publications/devolution-to-the-greater-manchester-combined-authority-and-transition-to-a-directly-elected-mayor.

Jenkins, S. (2015) The secret negotiations to restore Manchester to greatness, *The Guardian*, 12 February. Available at: www.theguardian.com/uk-news/2015/feb/12/secret-negotiations-restore-manchester-greatness.

Keating, M. (2005) Policy divergence and convergence in Scotland under devolution, *Regional Studies*, 39(4), pp.453–463.

LFC (2017) *Devolution: a capital idea*. Available at: https://www.london.gov.uk/sites/default/files/devolution_-_a_capital_idea_lfc_2017.pdf.

Lloyd, G. and Peel, D. (2009) New Labour and the planning system in Scotland: an overview of a decade, *Planning Practice and Research*, 24(1), pp.103–118.

Locality (2015) Neighbourhood planning. Available at: http://mycommunityrights.org.uk/neighbourhood-planning/.

McGough, L. (2016) Three questions the new London Finance Commission needs to answer, *Centre for Cities Blog*, 28 July. Available at: www.centreforcities.org/blog/three-questions-new-london-finance-commission-needs-answer/.

Morphet, J. and Clifford, B. (2014) Policy convergence, divergence and communities: the case of spatial planning in post-devolution Britain and Ireland, *Planning Practice and Research*, 29(5), pp.508–524.

Morris, H. (2015) A new vision for Wales, *The Planner*, July 10. Available at: www.theplanner.co.uk/features/a-new-vision-for-wales.

Nadin, V. (2007) The emergence of the spatial planning approach in England, *Planning Practice and Research*, 22(1), pp.43–62.

NI DoE (2015) *Strategic Planning Policy Statement for Northern Ireland*. Available at: https://www.planningni.gov.uk/index/policy/spps.htm.

NI Department of Infrastructure (2012) Regional Development Strategy 2035. Available at: https://www.infrastructure-ni.gov.uk/publications/regional-development-strategy-2035.

O'Brien, P., Pike, A. and Tomaney, J. (forthcoming) Governing the ungovernable? Financialisation and the governance of transport infrastructure in the London global city-region, *Progress in Planning*.

O'Sullivan, F. (2017) The death of London's Garden Bridge, and the end of an era, *Citylab*. Available at: https://www.citylab.com/design/2017/05/the-death-of-londons-garden-bridge-marks-the-end-of-an-era/524886.

Pike, A. and Tomaney, J. (2009) The state and uneven development: the governance of economic development in England in the post-devolution UK, *Cambridge Journal of Regions, Economy and Society*, 2(1), pp.13–34.

Pike, A., Kempton, L., Marlow, D., O'Brien, P. and Tomaney, J. (2016) *Decentralisation: issues, principles and practice*. Available at: https://research.ncl.ac.uk/ibuild/outputs/reports/Pike%20et%20al.%202016%20Decentralisation%20-%20Issues%20Principles%20and%20Practice%20-%20Final%20Draft-1.pdf.

Pike, A., Marlow, D., McCarthy, A., O'Brien, P. and Tomaney, J. (2015) Local institutions and local economic development: the Local Enterprise Partnerships in England, 2010–, *Cambridge Journal of Regions Economy and Society*, 8(2), 185–204.

Pike, A., Rodríguez-Pose, A., Tomaney, J., Torrisi, G. and Tselios, V. (2012) In search of the "economic dividend" of devolution: spatial disparities, spatial economic policy, and decentralisation in the UK, *Environment and Planning C: Government and Policy*, 30(1), pp.10–28.

Rozee, L. (2014) A new vision for planning – there must be a better way? *Planning Theory and Practice*, 15(1), pp.124–138.

Scottish Government (2010) *A low carbon economic strategy for Scotland: Scotland – a low carbon society*. Available at: www.scotland.gov.uk/Publications/2010/11/15085756/12.

Scottish Government (2014) *Ambition, opportunity, place. Scotland's Third National Planning Framework*. Edinburgh: Scottish Government.

Scottish Government (2017) *A consultation on the future of the Scottish planning system*. Available at: https://consult.scotland.gov.uk/planning-architecture/a-consultation-on-the-future-of-planning/.

Scottish Parliament (2015) *Community Empowerment (Scotland) Act 2015*. Available at: www.legislation.gov.uk/asp/2015/6/contents/enacted.

Scottish Parliament (2016) *Land Reform (Scotland) Act 2016*. Available at: www.legislation.gov.uk/asp/2016/18/contents/enacted.

Shaw, K. (2016) What will happen to the England–Scotland border following Brexit? *ESRC Blog*, 27 July. Available at: https://blog.esrc.ac.uk/2016/07/27/what-will-happen-to-the-england-scotland-border-following-brexit/.

Swain, C. and Baden, T. (2012) Where next for strategic planning? *Town and Country Planning*, 81(9), pp.363–368.

Tomaney, J. (2016) Limits of devolution: localism, economics and post-democracy, *Political Quarterly*, 87(4): 546–552.

Tomaney, J. and Colomb, C. (2013) Planning for independence? The evolution of spatial planning in Scotland and growing policy differences with England, *Town and Country Planning*, 82(9), pp.371–373.

Tomaney, J. and McCarthy, A. (2015) The Manchester model, *Town and Country Planning*, May, pp.233–236.

Travers, T. (2015) *London's Boroughs at 50*. London: Biteback.

Wainwright, O. (2014) The truth about property developers: how they are exploiting planning authorities and ruining our cities, *The Guardian*, 17 September. Available at: https://www.theguardian.com/cities/2014/sep/17/truth-property-developers-builders-exploit-planning-cities.

Wainwright, O. (2015) Revealed: how developers exploit flawed planning system to minimise affordable housing, *The Guardian*, 25 June. Available at: https://www.theguardian.com/cities/2015/jun/25/london-developers-viability-planning-affordable-social-housing-regeneration-oliver-wainwright.

Wales Office and The Rt Hon Stephen Crabb MP (2015) *Powers for a purpose: towards a lasting devolution settlement for Wales*. Available at: https://www.gov.uk/government/publications/powers-for-a-purpose-towards-a-lasting-devolution-settlement-for-wales.

Welsh Assembly (2015) *Planning (Wales) Act 2015*. Available at www.legislation.gov.uk/anaw/2015/4/contents/enacted.

Wightman, A. (2015a) *Land Matters Blog*. Available at: www.andywightman.com/.

Wightman, A. (2015b) Scottish land reform is on the agenda. And the rest of the UK should take note, *The Guardian*, 25 June. Available at: www.theguardian.com/commentisfree/2015/jun/25/scottish-land-reform-bill.

Williams, J. (2016) We can finally reveal which parts of Greater Manchester's green belt could be built upon, *Manchester Evening News*, 20 October. Available at: www.manchestereveningnews.co.uk/news/greater-manchester-green-belt-gmsf-12053737.

Wills, J. (2016) *Locating localism*. Bristol: Policy Press.

Part I

Practices of Planning

3 Plan-making

Changing Contexts, Challenges and Drivers

Jessica Ferm

Introduction

Despite an abundance of anti-planning rhetoric in government and media communications, support for spatial strategy or plan-making[1] still persists, and extends across the public and private sectors. Even during the Thatcher years of so-called 'roll-back' planning, when "neoliberal ideas about deregulation were at their height" (Healey, 2007: 140), many plans continued to be prepared, whereas experiments that promoted a project-led approach to urban development, in the absence of strategic plans, created uncertainty and increased risk for developers and investors and a range of adverse consequences for the market (see Allmendinger and Haughton, 2013: 11). As Leonora Rozee, former Deputy Chief Executive of the Planning Inspectorate, insists (2014: 124):

> We cannot create a stable and creative economy, a fair and healthy society and a culturally and ecologically diverse and attractive environment without long-term visionary planning which operates within a flexible hierarchical framework that can accommodate change and the unexpected whilst providing sufficient certainty to investors at all levels.

However, the approach to strategic planning has changed substantially over the years. Since the turn of the last century, when it was a highly ideological activity, "embedded in the reformist ideas of a number of visionary individuals" (Davoudi, 2006: 17), there was a shift in the role of the planner from 'expert' to 'facilitator' in line with a 'communicative turn' in planning (Healey, 1992), and a shift in the type of evidence and knowledge that has informed planning, "away from simple descriptive physical surveys represented in detailed maps and blueprints" towards more analytical evidence that includes social-economic dimensions, supporting the systems view of cities (Davoudi, 2006: 17). As the contexts within which plan-making takes place change, so there continue to be significant changes.

This chapter has been guided by the following questions: (1) How are plans made? (2) What are the contemporary drivers? (3) What challenges are planners facing in their practice? The discussion reflects on how these processes, drivers and challenges have changed over time and how they are framed by the broader contemporary contexts discussed in Chapter 1 by John Tomaney and Jessica Ferm – in particular, austerity, deregulation and decentralisation. In writing this chapter, I have drawn on interview material with planning practitioners in the public and private sectors, insights gained during my teaching, which involves guest speakers from practice, as well as my own professional experience in a local authority planning policy team and working as a planning consultant.

Plan-making can take place at many scales: "the nation, a wider region, an urban node, a neighbourhood, a new development, or a redevelopment area where a new 'piece of city' is proposed" (Healey, 2007: 198). This chapter focuses mostly on the statutory development plan – which includes the local (development) plan,[2] and in some places also the regional plan[3] and the Neighbourhood Plan – but acknowledging that non-statutory plans prepared for smaller areas or sites are hugely influential in the preparation of the 'higher-tier' plans. The chapter will argue that plan-making has become a more rigorous and collaborative activity, with more of an emphasis on what can realistically be delivered, which has had implications for how we view 'creativity' in the process of planning. Even though the 'communicative turn' in planning remains strong, the failure of so many local authorities to produce up-to-date Local Plans means that in these places the potential for public participation in the plan-making process has been lost entirely. Although statutory plans are led by the public sector, much of the work that goes into plan-making is done by the private sector, with the work of public sector planners (in policy) dominated by the management of consultants' contracts and their members' expectations. The broader implications of this are not discussed here, but analysed in more detail by Mike Raco in Chapter 8.

The chapter is divided into three sections. The first provides an overview of plan-making in the UK. Drawing on publicly available data from the Department of Communities and Local Government (DCLG) and published reports, it reveals the geographical differences in coverage of Local Plans and exposes the challenges for government. The second section considers what plan-making involves in theory and how it plays out in practice, focusing mostly on the question of 'how' we make plans, examining the interplay between knowledge, creativity and politics. The third section examines the changing drivers of plan-making, revealing how the delivery of housing and growth have overtaken place-making and social transformation as drivers. The final section draws conclusions and reflects on these contemporary challenges for plan-making in practice.

The Struggle to Get a Plan in Place

The UK is said to have a 'plan-led' planning system. Decisions on planning applications are made primarily on the basis of policies set out in the development plan, which in turn is required to conform to national-level guidance or frameworks[4] (for an explanation of the similarities and differences between the four nations, see Cave et al., 2013). The weight of the development plan in decision-making has always been a subject of debate, however. In a background paper prepared to inform the Raynsford Review of Planning (Town and Country Planning Association, 2017: 4), it is argued that there was always ambiguity in the presumption in favour of the plan, introduced through the Planning and Compensation Act in 1991, but that it was further undermined by the presumption in favour of (sustainable) development in the 2012 National Planning Policy Framework (NPPF), which "made the status of the plan even harder to understand" and "had the effect of reducing the weight of the plan in decisions on housing". Certainly, if the plan is to have any weight, it needs to be 'up-to-date', otherwise developers can defer to national-level guidance or frameworks. As the Conservative Party (2010) explained:

> We will legislate that if new local plans have not been completed within a prescribed period, then the presumption in favour of sustainable development will automatically apply. In other words, if a local planning authority does not get its local plan finalised in reasonable time, it will be deemed to have an entirely permissive planning approach, so all planning applications will be accepted automatically if they conform with national planning guidance.

Geographical coverage of up-to-date plans varies across the UK. It is almost absent in Northern Ireland due to the fact that responsibility for making Local Plans only transferred to local councils in 2015. In Wales, there is good coverage: all 25 local planning authorities (LPAs) have an adopted a Local Plan, although 11 of those pre-date 2012, and are therefore more than five years old at the time of writing. There appears to be no publicly available data for Scotland. The coverage in England is very patchy. Of the 386 LPAs in England, 56% are without an up-to-date Local Plan found to be sound against the NPPF.[5] The geography of this coverage reveals that "plan-making is lagging in some particular areas including authorities surrounding Manchester, Birmingham and London where difficult choices about Green Belt appears to be halting progress" (Lichfields, 2017: 2).

A recent report to the UK Government prepared by the Local Plans Expert Group (2016) sought to understand the causes behind slow or incomplete Local Plan preparation in England and found that local authorities were struggling to agree housing needs with adjoining authorities under the Duty to Cooperate[6] and suffering from a lack of an agreed methodology on Strategic Housing Market Assessments, among other problems. This, according to the Housing White Paper (DCLG, 2017: 13), is undermining our ability to address the housing crisis: "the uncertainty this creates about when and where new homes will be built is both unpopular and affects the entire house building process, slowing it right down".

The city of York's draft Local Plan was not approved for consultation in 2014 due to members' nervousness that it would fail the NPPF's 'test of soundness'. The only relevant document which is a material consideration for planning decisions is a draft Local Plan document from 2005.[7] As City of York Council states on its website: "If we don't adopt an up to date Local Plan, development will still happen, but decisions will be taken in regard to the NPPF without local people having a say on setting local policies" (City of York Council, 2017). This goes against the government's ambitions for the planning system, as stated by the Minister of State for Housing and Planning in July 2015 (DCLG, 2015): "We are committed to a planning system that provides communities with certainty on where new homes are to be built. Local plans produced in consultation with the community are therefore the cornerstone of our planning reforms."

The discussion here raises the concern that, despite good intentions, the patchy coverage of plans across the UK and the fact that the weight of the plan itself is now under question, undermines the impact of consultation in Local Plan-making (see Chapter 6 by Yasminah Beebeejaun for further discussion). The next section takes a closer look at the processes and practical challenges of plan-making, integrating reflections from theory and practice.

The Process of Plan-making

In an attempt to summarise the complex nature of contemporary plan-making, Patsy Healey (2008: 865) suggests that it involves: "draw[ing] on diverse sources and forms of knowledge and imagination to generate one or more strategic ideas, which give a sense of direction and focus to those involved in place-management and place-development processes". Although the bringing together of knowledge and imagination was a feature of the Geddesian 'survey–analysis–plan' approach in the early 20th century, the knowledge was limited to physical survey data, and the role of the planner "was seen as being imaginative and visionary, not only in setting the goals, but also in taking a creative leap from the analysis of the survey to the making of the plan" (Davoudi, 2006: 17). As planning moved away from a simple concern with the physical arrangement of land, buildings and the spaces between them towards broader questions of the interplay between physical, economic and social aspects (the systems view of planning), this required a more analytical approach to evidence-gathering, and the role of knowledge in the process of planning acquired greater weight.

The question of what constitutes knowledge in planning has, however, shifted over the years. Whereas rational, scientific approaches dominated in the first half of the 20th century, in the latter half the question of what constitutes knowledge was opened up to debate. Rydin (2007) suggests that the communicative turn was effectively an argument for a broader view of knowledge in planning, bringing local (or lay) knowledge to bear on planning processes, as well as scientific and technical knowledge, to create 'multiple knowledges'. In practice, Alexander (2005) argues that the balance between these knowledges changes depending on the scale of the plan. At the neighbourhood or community scale, local knowledge is highly valued in the planning process, but higher up the governance scale, the issues become more complex and require bringing together domains of specialised knowledge, and ultimately "appreciative knowledge loses some of its value" (Alexander, 2005: 100).

The upsurge of interest in evidence-based policy under New Labour in the late 1990s was driven by a renewed enthusiasm for evidence, rooted in the instrumental view of the policy–research interface, whereby "the relationship between evidence and policy is unproblematic, linear and direct" (Davoudi, 2006:15). But this is a simplification (Young et al., 2002), and the role of power and politics in all this is key: "power procures the knowledge which supports its purposes, while it ignores or suppresses that knowledge which does not serve it" (Flyvbjerg, 1998: 226). Hence, Davoudi (2006: 21) argues: "It takes more than knowledge and ideas to make policy" and "Policy process is as much about power relations and competition over agenda setting as it is about finding the truth and solving problems."

One public sector planner with more than 20 years' professional experience reflected on the impact of the New Labour reforms. Prior to the Planning and Compulsory Purchase Act 2004, policies had to be 'justified', but there were no tests of soundness, so planners would "fudge everything and go with what their politicians wanted". The focus in the independent examinations was on 'objections' to the plan. Now, "you've probably got to do more work because you need to make sure everything is sound, rather than just the bits that people are going to object to". On the other hand, budget cuts have meant that LPAs don't always have adequate up-to-date evidence. For example, in this planner's LPA, their: "strategic flood risk assessment is way out of date – from 2006 or 2007 – we should really be updating that now. We're taking risks really with going with what we've got. That's a resourcing issue."

At the same time, even though "the evidence stage is really critical, because that's what you get tested on . . . there's a massive amount of choice in terms of where [housing] sites actually go, and a lot of politics comes into it". So, for example, the requirement in the NPPF for planners to consider viability in both plan-making and planning decisions, an absence of an explicit 'brownfield first' policy and the requirement for local authorities to demonstrate a five-year housing supply has, in practice, meant more latitude to consider greenfield sites for housing delivery. However, politicians have historically strongly opposed any building on greenfield sites, and this opposition is still apparent since "there are lots of residents out there in groups and parish councils and the like who don't want to see development on greenfield sites . . . and that filters through to what the politicians want". Local authority officers are therefore increasingly seeking to engage members early in the policy- and plan-making process, in order to encourage cross-party engagement and support for the plan as it progresses. In cities with elected Mayors, the politically driven nature of plan-making is even more apparent. In London, the election of a new Mayor prompts the preparation of a new London Plan, the direction of which is in accordance with the Mayor's election manifesto. This provides the opportunity for a much more direct relationship between the plan and the Mayor's political priorities than in a typical local authority context. In Greater Manchester, where a strategic spatial framework – developed jointly with 10 councils – had controversially proposed building housing on the Green Belt, the Mayor for the Combined Authority of Greater Manchester, who was elected in May 2017, pledged a radical re-write of the spatial framework in his election manifesto (Williams, 2017). Thus, although planning is inherently a political process, in the case of cities (or regions) with elected Mayors, the influence of politics seems to be even more explicit.

In terms of the role of appreciative knowledge, there is a perception among local authority planners that consultation is taken more seriously by officers than it ever was. As one planner said:

> Back in the day, [my boss] wasn't keen on us going to area forums or ward forums, he was very "anti" them. We just avoided community engagement at all costs on the basis of concerns that these forums lacked diversity and representation of the whole community . . . officers knew best and we had our evidence.

The greater enthusiasm for consultation today has no doubt been encouraged by the Localism Agenda. "The fact that neighbourhood planning exists also affects the content and the way you produce a local plan", leading to a more place-based approach that will help communities see the benefit of engaging in the Local Plan and ultimately encouraging officers to be more proactive in consulting with their communities.

If evidence were the primary input into the process of plan-making, then lower-tier plans (for smaller sites or areas) would have to conform with and follow (in temporal terms) higher-tier plans. However, it is far from a linear, hierarchical process. In reality, landowners and developers come forward with proposals for sites in an ad-hoc manner, and the higher-level plans might have to work to accommodate these proposals. This means that there may be a compromise in terms of the strategic vision and that developers and landowners have more influence in the plan-making process than might be apparent from reports on consultation. The increasing pressure on local authorities to speed up the preparation of their Local Plans has exacerbated these pressures and means there is even less clear progression from evidence-gathering through to plan-making. Evidence does not always precede the plan. From the perspective of local residents and businesses trying to engage with the plan, this is confusing and can be seen as lacking transparency. Box 3.1 lists the evidence-based documents and stages involved in the preparation of a Local Plan (for Welborne), as well as the variety of consultants engaged in its preparation (for a fuller discussion of the role of consultants in planning, see Chapter 8 by Mike Raco).

Commissioned evidence that does not fit the council's agenda does not always see the light of day. In Camden, a Freedom of Information request revealed that a consultants' report on the suitability of various employment sites for redevelopment (for housing) was never made public, presumably since it did not support the council's intention to release particular sites for housing redevelopment (for a discussion, see Ferm and Jones, 2016). Similarly, a private sector planning consultant who is regularly commissioned to undertake evidence-based studies for Neighbourhood Forums suggested that evidence is quite often "just ditched if it doesn't suit them".

So if evidence is not as central to plan-making as we might have assumed, what else comes into play? Other studies have emphasised how planners are much more pragmatic in their search for solutions to problems, relying on experience, what they learned in their planning education, rules of thumb and best practices applied by others (Krizek et al., 2009; Hack, 1984). Far from carefully assessing the multiple knowledges before them, "too often a suggested policy action is justified with reference to a single source of evidence that fits the practitioner's or author's preconception . . . they ignore evidence that does not agree with their position" (Krizek et al., 2009: 469). Weiss (2001) elaborates on this,

Box 3.1 Stages in production of the Welborne Plan

Date	*Document*	*Prepared or led by*
March and June 2009	Stakeholder Visioning Workshops for the North of Fareham Strategic Development Area	Urban Design and Mediation
July 2009	Fareham SDA Capacity Analysis Study	David Lock Associates
August 2011	Fareham Borough Local Plan Part 1: Core Strategy (Adopted)	Fareham Borough Council
July 2012	Options consultation	Fareham Borough Council
August 2012	Concept masterplan options study	LDA Design
April 2012	Preferred concept masterplan option report	LDA Design
Nov 2013	Welborne Employment Strategy	Wessex Economics
Dec 2013	Welborne SRTM Modelling Analysis	MVA/TfSH
Jan 2014	Concept masterplan	LDA Design
	Welborne Plan Parking Strategy	FBC
Apr 2014	Welborne Wastewater Infrastructure: Initial Infrastructure Assessment	Albion Water
	Welborne M27 Junction 10 – Preferred Option Note	HCC/FBC/HA
May 2014	Welborne Planning Obligations and Affordable Housing Supplementary Planning Document	Fareham Borough Council
June 2014	Welborne Design Guidance SPD	FBC/LDA Design
	Welborne Concept Masterplan phasing plan	FBC
July 2014	Welborne Infrastructure Funding Strategy	GVA
June 2015	Local Plan Part 3: The Welborne Plan	FBC

Source: Adapted from *The Welborne Plan*, Appendix A (Fareham Borough Council, 2015).

arguing that research or evidence is only one contender for influence among many competitors, including: (1) ideology (people's basic values), (2) interests (both people's and organisations' self-interest), (3) institutional norms and practices, and (4) prior information (new information has to fit in with current understandings).

The role of the imagination or creativity in the plan-making process receives little attention in the literature. Most commentators agree that it forms a key part. For example, Albrechts (2017: 195) suggests:

> The construction of different futures, which lies at the very heart of transformative practices, requires creativity and original synthesis. To construct visions for the future, we need both the solidity of the analysis that seeks to discover a place that is and that might exist, and the creativity of the designing of a place that would otherwise not be.

On the other hand, there is an acknowledgement that (broadly) there has been a transition from a mode of planning led by creativity to one led by knowledge. This has not, however, been a linear transition. In Davoudi's account of the role of evidence in plan- and policy-making processes, she shows how planning in the 1980s and 1990s in the UK was criticised for its lack of imagination and creativity (2006: 21) at a time when planning was almost reduced to a regulatory function and Local Plans were notoriously dry and wordy. This led to a renewed emphasis on the 'spatial', and design, in planning under New Labour, alongside the revival of evidence-based planning (Nadin, 2007).

For my graduating students, the private sector is seen to offer more scope to use their creative skills in planning and urban design, whereas public sector jobs are often perceived to be dominated by bureaucracy. Finn Williams, who is spearheading Public Practice, an initiative to encourage talented young planners (and architects) to work in the public sector, claims that the appeal of planning weakened over the years as the "agency that used to be afforded to the Town Planner is now fragmented between officers specializing in Development Management, Planning Policy, Placemaking, Conservation, Regeneration, Housing, Sustainability, Building Control and Enforcement". This, he argues, "inevitably result[s] in each specialist taking a more blinkered approach, which makes thinking holistically and planning proactively an extraordinarily complex task of coordination" (Williams, 2016: 55). Ten years ago, the work of plan-making was outsourced to the private sector almost entirely, taking much creative work away from public sector planners and reducing their role to project management. However, there is a perception in the public sector that there has been a 'shift back'. Part of that is due to perceived poor quality of consultants' work, since with budget cuts, you get what you pay for: "With staff cut backs it's much easier politically to justify cutting consultants' budgets than making redundancies." So planners in the public sector are again doing more of the creative work by necessity. However, as Mike Raco shows in Chapter 8, planning consultancies' incomes have continued to rise, suggesting a shift in the nature of their work as changing legislation and policy means councils are better off spending their limited budgets on technical studies and viability assessments than on recruiting consultants to prepare an Area Action Plan. Even where private sector planners are preparing site plans on behalf of landowner or developer clients, the potentially creative side of plan-making is suppressed by technical calculations and viability exercises. One planning consultant commented: "I never thought master-planning would be all about spreadsheets."

Changing Drivers of Plan-making

In the introduction to this chapter, the quote from Leonora Rozee (2014: 124) suggested that the purpose of long-term visionary planning is broad, namely to "create a stable and creative economy, a fair and healthy society and a culturally and ecologically diverse and attractive environment". These aspirations are familiar to me from my days working in planning practice, where our briefs tended to be focused on improving and transforming places, turning around their economic fortunes, and dealing with their complex socio-economic issues. However, with political priorities focused on addressing 'the housing crisis' and requirements for local planning authorities to meet objectively assessed needs for housing, increasingly the primary driver of strategic spatial planning has become the delivery of housing. Difficulties in assessing housing needs has, according to the report of the Local Plans Expert Group (2016: 15), been "a key barrier to plan progression".

In assessing housing needs, there is little or no scope for public participation in the process of agreeing on an area's capacity, which remains a technical process. Once communities tend to get involved in planning (at neighbourhood scales), housing capacity for that area has normally already been agreed in the development plan. The scale of change is already a 'given', therefore matters for consultation (or local determination, in the case of Neighbourhood Plans) are limited to the detail of how it might be delivered, and exactly where, in what configuration etc. Allmendinger and Haughton (2010: 809) claim:

> where spatial planning could have provided a forum for meaningful debate over radically different alternative visions of development futures, instead it has provided a forum for legitimating a government-led

> agenda dominated by economic growth and meeting housebuilding targets, allied to some hard-to-enforce commitments to improving quality of place. Any search for radical alternatives is in effect displaced to outside the spatial planning arena.

The greater emphasis on viability and deliverability of plans since the recession following 2008 has also significantly driven the nature of plan-making. During the recession, development activity across the UK slowed significantly, and in some places stalled altogether. The response has been to bring a greater focus to 'viability' and 'deliverability' of development proposals and plans in all parts of the UK. This has brought a greater need for flexibility in plans, meaning that councils have moved away from a 'blueprint' approach to plan-making. In some places, the need for flexibility has meant that councils have avoided preparing a plan with any formal planning status, and have chosen instead to prepare more abstract documents, which become 'material planning considerations', but allow for change and flexibility. So, for example, the London Borough of Redbridge prepared the *Ilford Regeneration Delivery Prospectus* for the development of one of its main town centres,[8] but it is not clear what weight this will have in the planning decision process.

The emphasis on viability has also affected the content of plans. One local authority planner claimed it had "forced us to think more innovatively than we ever have done before in terms of how we really maximise the use of land". So, for example, there is now even more emphasis on the vertical mix of uses such as high-density residential development incorporating schools and other social infrastructure, which reflects a shift in thinking. Viability considerations have also forced planners to be more spatially nuanced in their demands on development, for example, identifying employment-led areas where affordable workspace might be secured instead of affordable housing. Borough-wide plans are now considered to be more 'spatial' and fine-grained than in the past, when they tended to just set out borough-wide policies, without taking different approaches in different areas. On the other hand, the emphasis on viability can mean that planners or urban designers have to make compromises that jar with their professional opinions. So, for example, one consultant explained how a design for a scheme that had included mixed use and 'active' ground floor uses was ultimately turned into a purely residential scheme due to viability concerns. So consultants might well compromise design principles and the vision, as they can't be seen to be 'putting off' investment or development.

This emphasis on viability and deliverability, coupled with the context of austerity, has put the property industry in a more powerful position with respect to plan-making, and has meant that there are benefits for the public sector in working jointly or cooperatively with the private sector. This happens in a number of ways. First, as part of the assessment of availability of strategic housing land, local authorities rely on landowners to come forward as part of the process of identifying sites. Second, landowners, developers and housebuilders are increasingly more involved in the preparation of site masterplans and supplementary planning documents. This can vary from drawing up a supplementary planning document (SPD) on behalf of a local authority to funding an SPD for a local authority in an area where a landowner or developer has vested interests, working closely with LPAs on the preparation of site masterplans or planning applications which then inform the higher-tier plan – the SPD or Area Action Plan (AAP). So, although the higher-tier Local Plans tend to be prepared by the public sector, they are invariably informed by lower-tier site plans that are developer/landowner-led. One consultant explained how they worked up a strategic masterplan for a site, in partnership with a local council, where all the up-front work was done by consultants on behalf of their landowner client. After a few years of this work, the council decided to 'break away' and continued working on the masterplan, which eventually became an Area Action Plan, formally adopted by the council. But, the consultant observed, the strategic diagram in the AAP was "almost the mirror image" of their planning application, so "lots of the things we did directly informed their thinking". This chimes with my experience working in local authority planning policy on the preparation of Area Action Plans, where negotiations with landowners pre-dated any consultation on the AAP. So it can be the case that land deals, key ideas and important decisions are made in discussion with, say, the regeneration team of the council before the work even comes into the domain of the planning policy team. This inevitably fuels consultation apathy, where the local community understandably sense that they have little influence over many of the important decisions that will affect them.

Conclusions

This chapter has focused on plan-making – the area of planning practice that has the longest history and is seen as the most creative and visionary, with the potential to transform places. We know that in the latter half of the 20th century there was a 'communicative turn' in planning, and over the turn of the millennium, a revival in so-called evidence-based planning. However, little has been written on the practice of plan-making since New Labour's reforms in the early 2000s. The main aim of the chapter has been to investigate the changes that have taken place – in the practice and drivers of plan-making.

Decentralisation in the UK has had a significant impact. It has provided an opportunity for Scotland, Wales and Northern Ireland to do things differently. In England, national-level guidance has been streamlined and neighbourhoods given powers to develop their own statutory plans. This has nurtured locally driven (and thus more creative) solutions, and encouraged a more proactive approach towards community engagement in all areas of planning. However, the actions of the UK Government have not been coherent, with austerity and deregulation at the same time undermining local control and resources. The national political focus on the housing crisis has dominated plan-making, with increasing pressures on local planning authorities to quickly produce Local Plans that conform with national-level policy, demonstrate a five-year housing supply and are based on solid evidence, such that the majority of local planning authorities in England – which do not have the support of the higher-level regional tier of planning – are struggling to produce up-to-date Local Plans that are found to be sound. At a site level, the creative and collaborative processes involved in plan-making have been quashed by housing delivery calculations and viability spreadsheets.

Political agendas have long been acknowledged as a strong influence in plan-making. The increasing weight placed on evidence-gathering in legislation has tempered this to some extent at the local level, although politicians are still swayed by voters' opinions on key emotive issues such as the Green Belt. At the regional and local levels, where there is an elected Mayor the political agenda is a more explicit driver of the plan-making process. With the expansion of City Deals and elected Metro Mayors across England (see Chapter 2 by John Tomaney and Claire Colomb), this is likely to become accentuated further. Although strong, politically engaged local members can help to bring the concerns of their local constituents and residents to the fore, where the political agenda is influenced more remotely – say at the regional level – this only accentuates communities' perceptions that important decisions are made elsewhere before plans are even consulted on.

The process of plan-making is significantly more complicated than it was in the past. Plans used to be the output of a creative process driven mostly by one individual – 'the town planner' – or small team (based in the public sector). However, the more onerous requirements for collaboration and evidence-gathering, coupled with declining public sector resourcing for planning, has meant a much bigger role for the private sector in plan-making (both in preparing evidence and in making area-based proposals). For the policy planner, much creative work goes on to inform consultants' briefs and to pull together all the work into a coherent whole for their district or region. But this work needs to be done alongside the management of consultants and their contracts, as well as the statutory consultation and political processes to get plans adopted. All in all, the task of plan-making is one of coordination, and more onerous than it ever was. In the context of budget cuts to planning departments, the use of consultants in plan-making has been seen as an obvious place to make savings. The upside of this has been more engagement of public sector planners in the creative work of plan-making. Finn Williams (2016) points to some encouraging signs of a revival of interest in public service, and a new generation of architects, urban designers and planners who are choosing to go into the public sector, as well as innovations in London Boroughs such as Croydon, which has created the first in-house architecture department in decades. Whether or not this will lead to a more widespread return to the ethos of public sector plan-making remains to be seen.

Acknowledgements

I would like to thank the practitioners – in both private and public practice – who agreed to be interviewed for this chapter, and the guest speakers who have contributed to the session on plan-making in my "Planning Practice" module over the years. I am also grateful to ex-colleagues at Urban Practitioners and the London Borough of Enfield who both inspired and supported me during my years working in planning practice. All opinions are my own.

Notes

1 I have deliberated at length over what terminology to use to refer to the processes that are the focus of discussion in this chapter. 'Spatial strategy-making' feels most accurate, and yet is rather a mouthful for repetitive use. Therefore, I have chosen to use the term 'plan-making'. However, the process involves more than devising a 'blueprint' two-dimensional plan, rather it is a spatial expression of multi-faceted policies, which I would ask that the reader keep in mind.

2 The terminology across the countries of the UK differs. In England, since 2010, the government refers to 'local plans'. In Scotland, Wales and Northern Ireland, these same plans are referred to as 'local development plans'. They are, essentially, the same. For brevity, this chapter will mostly use the term 'Local Plan'.

3 Regional planning was abolished in most of England with the incoming Coalition government in 2010, but in London it remains, and in Scotland, strategic development plans exist in four of the largest cities.

4 Either the National Planning Framework for Scotland, the Wales Spatial Plan, the Regional Development Strategy for Northern Ireland, or National Planning Policy Framework for England.

5 Calculated from figures compiled by the Department for Communities and Local Government (30 June 2017).

6 The NPPF states that local authorities have a 'Duty to Cooperate' with neighbouring authorities in the preparation of their Local Plans, in order to meet objectively assessed housing needs across Housing Market Areas. These tend not to coincide with local authority boundaries.

7 From the Meeting of the Council, Thursday 9 October 2014 (Item 45). Available at: http://democracy.york.gov.uk/mgAi.aspx?ID=36260.

8 https://www.redbridge.gov.uk/business-and-regeneration/regeneration/ilford-regeneration-delivery-prospectus/.

References

All listed URLs were last accessed on 1 March 2018.

Albrechts, L. (2017). Strategic planning as a catalyst for transformative practices. In B. Haselsberger (ed.) *Encounters in planning thought: 16 autobiographical essays form key thinkers in spatial planning*. New York: Routledge, pp.184–201.

Alexander, E. (2005) What do planners need to know? Identifying needed competencies, methods, and skills, *Journal of Architectural and Planning Research*, 22(2), pp.91–106.

Allmendinger, P. and Haughton, G. (2010) Spatial planning, devolution, and new planning spaces, *Environment and Planning C: Government and Policy*, 28, pp.803–818.

Allmendinger, P. and Haughton, G. (2013) The evolution and trajectories of English spatial governance: neoliberal episodes in planning, *Planning Practice & Research*, 28(1), pp.6–26.

Cave, S., Rehfisch, A., Smith, L. and Winter, G. (2013) Comparison of the planning systems in the four UK countries. Research Paper 082-13, 19 June. Available at: www.niassembly.gov.uk/globalassets/documents/raise/publications/2013/environment/8213.pdf.

City of York Council (2017) New Local Plan. Available at: https://www.york.gov.uk/info/20051/planning_policy/710/new_local_plan.

Conservative Party (2010) *Open source planning: the Conservative planning Green Paper*. London: Conservative Party.

Davoudi, S. (2006) Evidence-based planning: rhetoric and reality, *disP*, 165(2), pp.14–24.

DCLG (2012) *National Planning Policy Framework*. London: DCLG. Available at: https://www.gov.uk/government/uploads/system/uploads/attachment_data/file/6077/2116950.pdf.

DCLG (2015) Local Plans. House of Commons Written Statement made by Minister of State for Housing and Planning (Brandon Lewis). Available at: www.parliament.uk/documents/commons-vote-office/July%202015/21%20July/8-Communities-and-Local-Government-Local-Plans.pdf.

DCLG (2017) *Fixing our broken housing market*. London: DCLG.

Fareham Borough Council (2015) *Local Plan Part 3: the Welborne Plan*, June 2015.

Ferm, J., and Jones, E. (2016) Mixed use "regeneration" of employment land in the post-industrial city: challenges and realities in London, *European Planning Studies*, 24(10), pp.1913–1936.

Flyvbjerg, B. (1998) *Rationality and power: democracy in practice*. Chicago, IL: University of Chicago Press.

Hack, G. (1984) Research for urban design. In J. Snyder (ed.) *Architectural research*. New York: Van Nostrand Reinhold, pp.125–145.

Healey, P. (1992). Planning through debate: the communicative turn in planning theory. *Town Planning Review*, 63(2), p.143.

Healey, P. (2007) *Urban complexity and spatial strategies*. London: Routledge.

Healey, P. (2008). Knowledge flows, spatial strategy making, and the roles of academics. *Environment and Planning C: Government and Policy*, 26(5), pp.861–881.

Krizek, K., Forsyth, A. and Schively Slotterback, C. (2009) Is there a role for evidence-based practice in urban planning and policy? *Planning Theory and Practice*, 10(4), pp.459–478.

Lichfields (2017) *Planned and deliver. Local Plan-making under the NPPF: a five-year progress report*. April 2017. Available at: http://lichfields.uk/media/3000/cl15281-local-plans-review-insight_mar-2017_screen.pdf.

Local Plans Expert Group (2016) *Local Plans: report to the Communities Secretary and the Minister for Housing and Planning*. Available at: https://www.gov.uk/government/uploads/system/uploads/attachment_data/file/508345/Local-plans-report-to-government.pdf.

Nadin, V. (2007) The emergence of the spatial planning approach in England, *Planning Practice and Research*, 22(1), pp.43–62.

Rozee, L. (2014) A new vision for planning – there must be a better way? *Planning Theory and Practice*, 15(1), pp.124–138.

Rydin, Y. (2007) Re-examining the role of knowledge within planning theory, *Planning Theory*, 6(1), pp.52–68.

Town and Country Planning Association (2017) *The Raynsford Review of Planning. Provocation Paper 1: do we have a plan-led system?* July 2017. Available at: https://www.tcpa.org.uk/Handlers/Download.ashx?IDMF=7de55c0f-5be8-4c5c-8f41-1fcd08d4c1e5.

Weiss, C. (2001). What kind of evidence in evidence-based policy? Keynote paper presented at the *Third International, Interdisciplinary Evidence-Based Policies and Indicator Systems Conference*, July, University of Durham, UK.

Williams, F. (2016) Finding the beauty in bureaucracy: public service and planning. In R. Brown, K. Hannah and R. Holdsworth (eds) *Making good – shaping places for people*. London: Centre for London, pp.52–63.

Williams, J. (2017) New mayor Andy Burnham to re-write controversial green belt masterplan, *Manchester Evening News*, 11 May.

Young, K., Ashby, D., Boaz, A. and Grayson, L. (2002) Social science and the evidence-based policy movement, *Social Policy and Society*, 1(3), pp.215–224.

4 Contemporary Challenges in Development Management

Ben Clifford

Introduction: The Executive Arm of Planning

Development Management matters. The "executive arm of the planning process", it "gives effect to the planning objectives of the development plan" and is critically important for "the quality of the outcome" (Audit Commission, 1992, in Tewdwr-Jones, 1995: 166). In the UK system, Development Management (DM) – formerly referred to as Development Control (DC) – describes the part of the planning system responsible for the processing of planning applications and enforcement of planning regulations, and in a mixed-market economy where most development is brought forward by the private sector, is the point at which policies can actually be implemented so that the development plan is realised in shaping the physical environment.

Haar described the permitting system as "the heart of British planning", and the system of DC made possible through the nationalisation of development rights in 1947 as "one of the glories of the British system" (Haar, 1984, in Booth, 2003: 1). Many other commentators have, however, been rather less kind. Writing in 1973, McLoughlin noted that "Development control . . . seems to have become stigmatized as a bureaucratic chore and . . . its practitioners the 'Cinderellas' of the profession" (in Booth, 2003: 107), with concerns about its apparently reactive and time-wasting nature and overwhelming concern with trivia compared to the higher-status and more visionary process of plan-making. It has also been called "the Child that grew up in the cold" on account of the way the granting and refusing of planning permissions was apparently an add-on in 1947 to an older system of preparing plans dating back to 1909, with which it was given equal status (in Booth, 1999: 278).

This longstanding negative perception is undoubtedly because DM involves a great deal of direct contact with the public and elected politicians, and difficult exercises in professional planning judgement on a day-to-day basis which can often involve dealing with conflict (Harrison, 1972; Clifford, 2006). DM has, however, been remarkably flexible and responsive to change over the last 70 years and remains vitally important in effective planning (Booth, 1999, 2003). The system has always faced challenges, but recent and on-going planning reforms implemented by central and devolved government across the UK – many linked to an obsession with deregulation in the pursuit of economic growth – combined with a challenging era for local government (particularly due to the politics of austerity) have meant the dilemmas for planning practice in DM are manifold.

In this chapter, having first briefly considered some existing academic literature on DM, I outline some of the key challenges in contemporary DM practice through the eyes of frontline local authority planners. These accounts come from interviews with four planners in Greater London authorities, two planners in the North East of England, and two in Scotland conducted specifically for this book. All interviewees are referred to by an appropriate pseudonym to preserve anonymity. A wider understanding of the issues comes from my on-going engagement with planning reform (see, e.g., Clifford and Tewdwr-Jones, 2013). In doing so, I concentrate on the dilemmas of practice against an understanding of the value of planning as a process that should serve the public interest, maximising public benefit and furthering sustainability.

Understanding the British Approach to Managing Development

The essentials to the approach to DM taken across the UK are that prior permission from the state (usually the local authority) is required before development (given a wide-ranging definition in legislation) can commence, and that in determining whether to grant such permission, planners will consider not just the development plan, but also other circumstances known as 'material considerations'. Each case is thus decided on its own merits, and the development plan is more indicative than blue-print. This weighing-up process involves considerable discretion, which distinguishes the British system from most others internationally, and makes the determining of planning permission an exercise involving professional judgement rather than simply an administrative process. Commenting about this discretionary approach, Booth (2003: 182) argues that "it is at once the system's inherent weakness and its greatest strength".

Since 1947, while the core tenants of prior permission linked to universal control and discretion linked to indicative plans have remained, the practice of DC has evolved, with particular concern in the 1980s on the need for speed and efficiency to support "wealth-creating enterprise" (Booth, 2003). This deregulatory impulse has remained a constant theme up to the present day. The 2000s saw the emergence of the idea of 'Development Management' rather than 'Development Control', nomenclature which quickly spread throughout the UK (Morphet and

Clifford, 2014). The shift was supposedly about more than just name change, but also about culture change, to try to take a more proactive role in facilitating development and proactive working to deliver – being a "seeker and shaper of development opportunities" (Planning Advisory Service [PAS], 2008: 7) rather than just reactive control.

Whatever this positive image of proactive engagement involves, DM inevitably still involves the working through of considerable tensions. Some of these go back to the very origins of the system, and the diversity of both explicit and implicit reasons as to why we want to control development, ranging from notions of amenity and public order to fear of fire, concerns about public health, issues around movement within settlements, desire for open space, the limiting of externalities such as pollution, and ensuring compatible mixes of uses, preventing sprawl and protecting agricultural land, to issues over the appearance of buildings. It also involves trying to serve both tactical and strategic elements at the boundary between the public and the private, and doing this all in an explicitly political environment (Punter, 1993).

Underlying this is a notion of serving the 'public interest' (and indeed, the idea that local authorities are the appropriate trustees of that interest). This links to ideals of planning furthering the delivery of a 'the good life', yet this is often poorly articulated, with DM an accumulation of value-laden ideas and practice at the intersection of public interest, private property and public participation (Booth, 2003). Planners have long been critiqued for their ability to really have a higher knowledge of the public good, for their indifference to difference. Nevertheless, to lose sight of the public interest is to lose sight of the very purpose of planning.

This purpose does appear to have been lost in recent government reforms, which seem to have focused on planning – and particularly DM – as a bureaucratic barrier preventing economic growth and development, and have heavily involved deregulatory impulses such as extending permitted development. They have also continued the now well-established trend for central government to primarily view the DM system through a managerialist lens, with much talk of the efficiency of the system. This perspective has been developing for some time, even though, as Glasson and Booth (1992: 64) comment: "to represent developers as being at the mercy of a lumbering bureaucracy is clearly far from the truth".

Although many planners now work in the private sector, including consultants who prepare planning applications and assist clients through the DM process and a smaller number who work directly for public clients doing contracted-out work, the system remains the responsibility of local government, and so a 'public' system. It is therefore heavily impacted not just by direct reform of planning, but also by reforms of local government more generally. The overarching theme of these reforms has been an increasingly neo-liberalised local government, with New

Public Management providing the model of reform. This has involved an emphasis on performance and efficiency and the ideal of providing a service for 'customers' (Clifford, 2012).

Some of the key challenges for contemporary DM in the UK clearly have well-established antecedents. The literature on DC and DM is, however, surprisingly sparse, particularly in recent years. This is not to say there is not a wealth of valuable scholarship on particular relevant topics, like sustainability or land value capture, but the amount written directly about DC and DM and considering this as a system in general is not as voluminous as might be expected given the real-world impacts on our environment. Perhaps this is linked to an enduring idea that DM somehow has a lesser status than policy, or perhaps in an internationalised academy there is less interest in a peculiarly British system compared to more readily comparable plan-making. This is compounded by the fact so few planners write about their experience in practice. I therefore addressed the question of contemporary dilemmas in DM practice by asking serving local government planners what the key issues for them are. I now turn to consider the key challenges identified by these planners.

Delivering Planning in an Age of Austerity

The shift in nomenclature from 'Development Control' to 'Development Management' was supposed to also involve a shift in culture to a more proactive approach by planners. In the interviews conducted for this chapter, there was some evidence that this had indeed happened. Several interviewees explained how they take a proactive approach to trying to deliver development and the Local Plan: for example, Molly described participating in a quarterly Development Forum with developers and the business community in her city.

Planning remains, however, distinctly political and impacted by institutional constraints which can vary greatly between over 400 local planning authorities (LPAs) across the UK. There was discussion in the interviews about some examples where it was difficult to get local politicians to proactively set out a vision for the future of their city, and how the appetite for growth could vary greatly between different authorities. Dave commented: "If you're in a local authority that still can't get a Local Plan through since 2004 because members won't have a brick laying on a bit of green grass, or whatever it might be, how can you manage development?" As discussed by Jessica Ferm in Chapter 3, a significant number of LPAs still lack up-to-date plans. The degree to which DM truly meets the vision set out by the Planning Advisory Service (2008) a decade ago is thus highly variable.

Beyond local politics, however, a key challenge to successful Development Management relates directly to the on-going programme of centrally driven austerity. These austerity politics have resulted in large cuts to the funding of local government in all parts of the UK, where it is traditionally more dependent on central grants rather than locally raised finance, making it susceptible to cuts in this grant. These have amounted to over a 30% reduction for English local authorities since 2010 (Gardner, 2017). These cuts have fallen particularly heavily on planning services, which are often viewed as something where staff cuts will have less immediate consequence than other service areas such as social services (NAO, 2014, in Harris, 2015).

In interview, Jane felt that austerity and these associated staffing implications were the biggest contemporary challenge for DM planners: "As a local authority planner, the biggest challenge for us is probably lack of resources to actually do the job that we need to do because local government continues to have its budgets cut again and again." Giving a flavour of the level of these cuts, Doreen explained that her team of 74 staff in 2005 now stood at 34, while Terri explained that 25 planners 10 years ago had now been reduced to 11, but with a volume of work that was not reduced.

The implications of this were both personal (Jane explained how there had been constant restructuring and she had needed to reapply for her own job many times, with the resultant stress and distraction), but also impacted the ability to deliver the same level of service to all stakeholders with far fewer staff. Natalie explained that she had team members "running a case load of 90 planning applications" and that officers with just four or five years' experience were given large applications to manage. As a result, Martin was concerned officers did not have time to "actually reflect on things". In some senses, then, austerity threatens the ability of local authority planners to take a more proactive, engaging 'Development Management' approach and threatens to strip them back to a more regulatory 'Development Control' style.

Despite the continuation of austerity politics, across the country planning application numbers have increased in recent years, so for some authorities the only option to cope with this has been the use of short-term consultants to help process applications, but there were concerns that such consultants could lack local knowledge. It has not just been planning departments in local authorities that have faced cuts, and staff reductions in other departments have also had an impact, reducing their ability to respond to queries from planners. Again this appears to threaten a positive, proactive planning agenda. Figure 4.1 shows the total number of planning applications compared to the total 'formula grant' from central government received by local authorities in England from 2009 to 2017.

Although there were many negative consequences resulting from austerity-driven cuts to DM teams in local authorities, the degree and results of cuts have varied between authorities. Doreen was aware of another local authority which had privatised its planning department, but was grateful for the political decision not to do that where she worked, explaining: "If you want your city to regenerate and to develop how you want it, you need your planning team at the heart of that and I think that

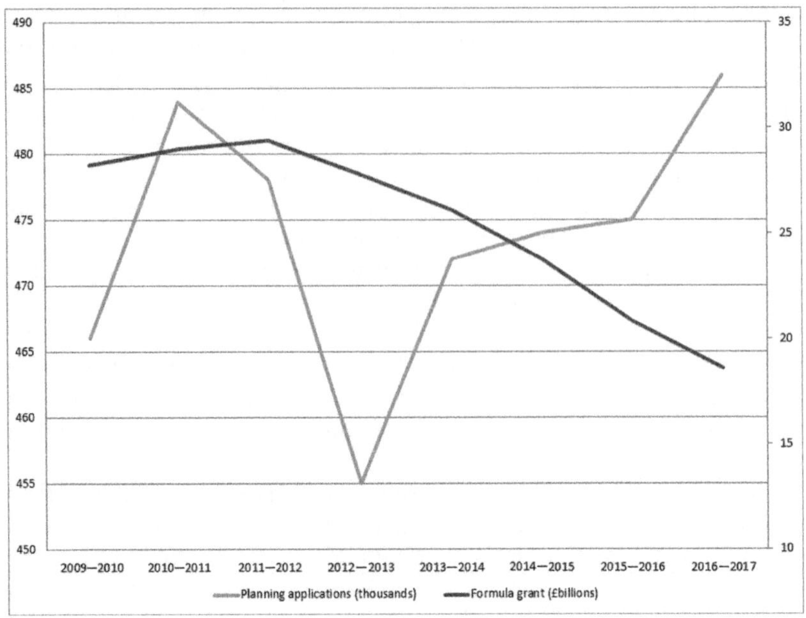

Figure 4.1 Total number of planning applications received compared to central government's formula grant for local authorities in England, 2009–2017

Source: Publicly available data held by MHCLG on (1) on Local Government Finance Settlement: England, and (2) planning applications statistics, available at: https://www.gov.uk/government/statistical-data-sets/live-tables-on-planning-application-statistics.

we're lucky that that's actually been recognised at the senior management level." Dave explained that although his department had suffered cuts, these had not been as large as in some other local authorities he was aware of, because the council's leadership saw planning as able to deliver growth, and thus income, in the future:

> Authorities have got to wake up to it, there will be no government grant in 2020 . . . the planning division creates income and that income is not only by pre-apps, that income is not only through planning application fees, but that is income, indirectly created by CIL [Community Infrastructure Levy] receipts, Section 106 receipts, business rates receipts and new home bonus receipts and council tax receipts.

This narrative of planning as able to deliver for local authorities is indicative of the idea that in public sector reforms what Vivien Lowndes (2005) terms 'institutional entrepreneurs' can sometimes exploit reforms and find opportunity in them. The implications of austerity have thus been somewhat variegated, but clearly have presented a huge challenge for

DM practice in the UK in terms of the ability to provide a reasonable level of service, to simply keep up with the workload, and to work in the proactive, engaging and reflective way which years of government policy has apparently worked to see.

The Mantra of 'Viability' and the Funding of Infrastructure

Governmental austerity has also impacted the ability of the public sector to fund the physical, social and green infrastructure which supports quality of life. For many years, some of the shortfall in the public funding of local infrastructure has been made up through the capturing of development value through so-called 'planning gain', such as that gathered through Section 106 of the Town and Country Planning Act 1990 in England and Wales or Section 75 of the Town and Country Planning (Scotland) Act 1997. Securing this planning gain is a key task of DM planners, through their negotiations with developers as part of the process of the granting of planning permission, and is seen as one of the best ways they can deliver public benefit and mitigate impacts of new development.

Changes in central government policy – particularly the wording of the National Planning Policy Framework (NPPF) (Department for Communities and Local Government [DCLG], 2012) – have, however, restricted the ability of planners in this vital area of practice under the mantra of not adversely impacting the 'viability' and hence delivery of development (see McAllister et al., 2013). Assessing this also involves expensive consultant assessment reports, due to a lack of relevant expertise within local authorities sufficient to argue against the assessments produced by the consultants used by developers.

Natalie put the current approach to 'viability' at the top of all contemporary challenges in DM, and these concerns were shared among all those planners interviewed. Jane felt she could no longer secure all the benefit she would like to see from schemes due to the mantra of viability even in areas with high pressure for development:

> So, for example, we've been approached by developers to talk about large mixed-use schemes, we really want to focus on providing more jobs and more homes, more affordable homes, those are our priorities and normally, what we're told is "You can't have everything." At the moment, our policies require 40% affordable housing, and if you're lucky, you achieve about 20/25%.

There was some feeling that the fixed-tariff Community Infrastructure Levy in England had made things harder as it was less immediately obvious where the money was being spent and therefore where the public benefit was, and this had come alongside a general shift in planning over the last decade to favour the developer more. It was widely argued that the government's approach to viability was a constraint on trying to secure public benefit through planning.

Concern was also expressed in Scotland. Although the wording of the Scottish Planning Policy (Scottish Government, 2014) is different from the NPPF in England and local authorities have been less restricted, the direction of travel appears similar, and Molly commented that in future: "planners are going to be spending quite a lot of their time trying to assess viability assessments, so the developers can get out of these huge developer contributions, and that's where it's going to become very tricky". The result of this was concerns about the ability to deliver what Molly called "the actual amount of infrastructure that is needed for a growing city". These issues are discussed further in Chapter 5 by Patricia Canelas, but it is important to note the discussion of this topic by DM practitioners. The emphasis placed on viability and restrictions on negotiating planning gain have been promoted by central government as a way of getting development delivered, but to planners in practice represent a real challenge in their ability to offset some of the consequences of development (which can undermine public support for it) and secure public benefit like affordable housing.

The Ability to Actually Manage Development

The statutory purpose of planning has been defined across the UK as contributing to the achievement of sustainable development (DCLG, 2012; Department of the Environment Northern Ireland, 2015; Welsh Government, 2016). While this captures well the traditional planning concerns with balancing social equity, environmental protection and economic growth within an overall frame of maximising the public benefit, the term is highly open to redefinition (Campbell, 2016). We have seen this in recent years in the UK, where the statutory purpose of planning has not changed, but the way sustainable development is defined has shifted. Thus, in the NPPF, although all three elements (social, economic, environment) are present, the economic role of planning is listed first, alongside comments such as "it is clear that development which is sustainable can be approved without delay" (DCLG, 2012: 4). In Scotland, while the Scottish Planning Policy does mention protecting and enhancing natural and cultural resources, these are not mentioned in the list of 'core values of the planning service', and the first key paragraph gives the purpose of the planning system as "increasing sustainable economic growth" rather than delivering sustainable development (Scottish Government, 2014: 4).

This increasingly pro-growth approach to government policy was perceived by interviewees to have shifted the balance within planning. For example, interviewees in England felt that since the adoption of the NPPF there had been a general shift to make planning more pro-development, and Doreen felt this had been to the detriment of the ability to plan for sustainable communities:

> Pre-NPPF, the responsibility was on the developer to demonstrate to us, as a local planning authority, that something was acceptable and how it would work. NPPF came in and suddenly that emphasis, that shift was local planning authorities were now the body who had to demonstrate why something would have a significant adverse impact.

In Scotland, despite less anti-planning rhetoric from central government ministers than has been seen under the recent Coalition and current Conservative government in England, there seems to have been a similar shift in policy, with Nancy worrying that the 2014 version of the Scottish Planning Policy clearly placed a much greater emphasis on planning supporting economic growth than the social or environmental elements of sustainable development, and Patrick commenting that the change was unnecessary: "It's this concept which is just based on nothing. We've never said we weren't open for business, but it has to be the right business in the right locations and respecting what you've actually got." The concern seemed to be that these shifts in central government policy over-privileged economic growth and weakened the hand of DM planners when trying to consider environmental and social aspects in their decision-making processes.

The same sentiment from central government has also seen a further deregulation of planning through extending 'permitted development' (PD), in an interesting echo of ideas from the 1980s that to stimulate development and the associated economic growth, things should be removed from the scope of DM. There have been some changes to PD across the UK in recent years, including increases to how much householders can extend their properties without planning permission and, most notably, in England, allowing office buildings to be changed to residential use without needing planning permission (as was always the case before 2013) as part of a 'prior approval' process which further complicates the system (Muldoon-Smith and Greenhalgh, 2016).

These policy changes were not popular with the frontline DM planners interviewed, particularly office-to-residential PD. Martin felt permitted development reduced the ability of DM planners to be effective placemakers: "it puts a jeopardy on everything that you're trying to achieve through design negotiation and it's setting a precedent which is not place-based". Dave did acknowledge that office-to-residential PD had delivered housing and helped the authority with its five-year supply (as did Jane), but felt that this benefit was outweighed by the disadvantages, and he argued that this PD "completely undermines the plan-led system".

In many cases, there were examples of negative consequences from the lack of control DM planners now had. Jane's serious concerns about office-to-residential PD were around the loss of "huge amounts of employment floorspace", office tenants in some cases being evicted to make way for housing "because residential prices are so much better than offices", and a lack of ability to have mixed rather than purely residential neighbourhoods: "It just doesn't really fit with the idea of sustainable development." Doreen was concerned that they could no longer negotiate improvements around amenity on office-to-residential schemes, but also could not get any Section 106 monies to help fund local infrastructure or services impacted by the new housing units.

Terri had found it difficult to explain to local councillors "that for £80 you can convert an office block, and we can't look at the amenity, the space standards, all the things that normally we would do with an application". Martin had examples of PD rights being used as a 'bargaining chip' to get the authority to approve something through planning permission which it might not otherwise have allowed, as the alternative was a PD scheme which was 'abhorrent', so 'lowering the barrier of acceptability'. Dave gave an example of a PD office-to-residential scheme where the units were $14m^2$ each, as self-contained studio units, and was concerned about people's quality of life in such accommodation.

Views on the new PD rights for householders were slightly more mixed. Jane accepted the householder rights as a reasonable thing for central government to have introduced, particularly given that the housing market conditions in London have made it harder for people to move house when they need more space, but Natalie was concerned about the increases to householder PD, and noted that "this causes huge amounts of complaints to us from neighbours [even though] there's nothing we can do about it as long as it complies with the legislation". She added: "It's also resulting in absolutely appalling relationships between adjoining properties." Doreen noted concerns from residents about householder permitted development. The changes had also apparently led to confusion and a consequent increase in enforcement workload, which was commented on by both the English and Scottish planners.

Through the increases in PD, we see a weakening of the ability of DM planners to exert control in their management of the built environment. Combined with changes to central government policy that prioritise economic development over all else, the balance between social equity, environmental protection and economic growth is disrupted and there is less chance to secure public benefit through the DM process.

Performance Pressure and Engagement

In 2008, the biggest single issue impacting the professional lives of planners (interviewed at the time) was meeting performance targets which were centred around the time taken to process planning applications (see Clifford and Tewdwr-Jones, 2013). Since that time, we have seen some move away from such a focus on central government-set targets for local government in general, but no let-up in the concern about the efficiency of DM. In the specific interviews for this chapter, it was certainly still seen as an issue impacting practice, albeit now alongside a host of other challenges.

Doreen felt the need to balance speed of decisions against quality of design within quite tight timeframes often presented dilemmas about where to make trade-offs. She further explained that meeting performance targets was now more challenging than 10 years ago, "because you're trying to meet the same standards and targets with probably only a third of the staff and cuts to the other departments you are trying to consult". Patrick described the challenges of meeting performance targets with reduced resources as "like firefighting without a hose".

A lot of the pressure on meeting DM targets was because of the consequences of not meeting them: in England, central government has the power to put the local authority into 'special measures', which was seen as undesirable by the senior leadership and politicians of many local authorities. In Scotland, ministers can actually reduce the planning fees that an under-performing planning authority can charge, so as a result, "our bosses are very much focused on speed" (Molly).

This emphasis on speed has long been perceived by planners to have a range of detrimental consequences (see Clifford, 2016), and some of the usual concerns were repeated by the interviewees for this chapter, including that the focus was "too much on efficiency (how quick you do things) rather than looking at quality", and that this could "become defeating in terms of morale in the organisation" (Patrick).

The most commonly cited concern in these interviews was about the reduced scope to negotiate improvements to a scheme. Terri observed:

> You look at a major application and you think, "Do we dare refuse this one, or do we just try and work on it, or do we just say that on balance, it's probably alright?", and we'll just let it go, and that's really not allowing you to do your job to your full ability, it's not allowing you to express what you really want to see because you're constrained by these threats that government has over you.

This is clearly linked to where planners think they can add most value in DM: on the case-by-case negotiation of proposals, bringing to bear their professional expertise to try to secure improvements perceived to be in the public interest.

That said, the threat of refusing poor schemes, and a desire on all sides to avoid this, had apparently led to an increased emphasis on pre-application discussions to try to sort out issues before an application is submitted rather than on negotiation during the processing period. This might be viewed as a positive thing, although, according to Natalie, it often only worked with the very big developers and there were more challenges around medium- and smaller-scale developments, where developers are often less willing to work collaboratively with the local authority at the pre-application stage.

Given the resource constraints in local government and pressure on performance targets, there was no great sense of a high priority being attached to public participation. That is not to say it was not viewed as an important part of DM, but rather that in the last 10 years the amount of emphasis placed on it was much less than the previous decade when the Labour administrations in the UK, Scottish and Welsh Governments had introduced innovative reforms around community engagement in DM (see Clifford, 2013). Thus, although the UK Coalition government had introduced Neighbourhood Planning on the policy side in England, Jane did not think much had happened on the DM side with regard to engagement for some years. Patrick expressed his personal view: "I think the problem with the planning service over the last decade or so has been that it's been far too much about developers, development and business and not about communities."

Although the priority might be more about delivering development, there was still a sense that participation is an important part of what DM was and should be. Terri felt the front-facing public interaction work she did was where she most added value as a planner. This could, however, be challenging. For a big developer, she felt, there was "no emotional attachment", whereas local residents and householder applications could "bring out a lot of emotions . . . we've been to some very difficult meetings where we've had people in tears and we've had to sit and explain things". Although there might not have been many recent changes to how DM engages the public, this is within a context of a system that is arguably increasingly pro-development following the NPPF, which can lead to tensions with a public who still want to be closely involved in decision-making (for further discussion about engaging the public in planning, see Chapter 6 by Yasminah Beebeejaun).

It is clear the emphasis placed by central government on the speed of planning application processing remains high, and this impacts contemporary planning practice by reducing the space for negotiation and potentially reducing the attention paid to community engagement and consultation processes. Balancing between these competing demands on time is a key challenge for the DM practitioner.

Conclusion: Challenged but Vital

The challenges for contemporary DM practice in the UK are manifold. As discussed in Chapter 1 by John Tomaney and Jessica Ferm, in recent years it has felt like planning has been under attack. Much of the focus for both negative comment and the resulting reforms has been on DM. The rhetoric has been most negative in England, but despite some differences post-devolution, similar trends are apparent to a greater or lesser degree across the UK. Planning reform remains, as it was a decade ago, a constant conveyor belt of initiatives. The dilemmas presented to DM planners in how they go about achieving what we expect of their role are manifold and continual.

The challenges identified by practising planners include both planning and local government issues. On the direct planning side, we have seen an increase in PD as part of a broader deregulatory push. This reduces the ability of planners to actually exercise control, which, even in a more proactive engaging system, is really what underpins the ability to safeguard certain standards within the environment and try to implement the vision contained in the development plan. Smaller changes can be as important incrementally as more dramatic development proposals, but the system has been weakened considerably in its ability to manage these. We have also seen an increasing emphasis on economic growth as the goal of planning, making harder the balance with social equity and environmental protection. The ability to capture public benefit from development through planning gain has also been severely constrained. This might lead to more being built, but this comes at the price of impact on local infrastructure which austerity era local government can ill afford.

Austerity politics have led to severe cuts to local government funding in the UK. Planning teams have been slashed, even though workloads have not. This reduces the ability to be proactive, reflective and actually keep up with the vast amount of reform being implemented by governments obsessed with tinkering with planning instead of confronting far bigger issues in our political economy. Potential reforms in England undermine the very nature of the approach to DM that has developed over decades of practice in the UK (see Ellis and Henderson, 2016), while potential further privatisation through alternative providers risks the very sense of place ownership that should be at the heart of local planning.

Alongside all of this, the focus on performance above almost all else has remained. This has an inherently negative view of DM: it implies it does not add value itself, and essentially that planners need to get out of the way to allow development to happen. The realities of development economics show this to be based largely on a false premise, as demonstrated by the number of unimplemented planning consents for housing. The relenting pressure on efficiency neglects all other potential goals and outcomes that we might want from DM, such as democracy, community engagement and social justice. In the words of Booth (2003: 24), the focus on delay as the sole narrative around DM for decades has left the system with "inadequate intellectual resources" to counter the sustained attack.

The future of DM depends on being able to counter this attack, however. There remains a vital role for planning in improving our lives and environments. An adequately resourced local government planning department with the power of planning policy and tools of regulation behind it is key to this. Regulation is not a dirty word, and a 'bonfire of red tape' ignores the very real harm that can occur if the state does not have adequate means to keep people safe and protect environmental quality. Furthermore, given that people understandably still care very much about their surroundings and the appearance and location of new development, there must be adequate opportunity for them to be engaged and articulate the vision of the 'good life' they want planning to deliver. DM can provide that opportunity if given the space to do so.

Allmendinger (1996: 231) questions the assumption that "all planners are benign and imbued with liberal conceptions of democracy and they all agree on what is the 'public good'". This may be the case, but in my research over several years, it has been clear that many public planners care passionately about the role and try very hard to maximise the value they deliver. Despite the structural constraints, they strive to continue to deliver public benefit. Through this, there is hope for the future of DM. After 70 years, the distinctive British approach to DM is also well embedded, so while an end to constant government reform seems unlikely, so is the fundamental deconstruction of the system. For that system to deliver the public good it really ought to, however, will take a shift in the current approach to planning and local government, which is presenting very real challenges and dilemmas for practitioners. This must be something we hope for. Development Management matters.

Acknowledgements

I am very grateful to the editors for their helpful feedback on the much longer earlier version of this chapter.

References

All listed URLs were last accessed on 1 March 2018.

Allmendinger, P. (1996) Development control and the legitimacy of planning decisions: a comment, *Town Planning Review*, 67(2), pp.229–233.

Booth, P. (1999) From regulation to discretion: the evolution of development control in the British planning system 1909–1947, *Planning Perspectives*, pp.277–289.

Booth, P. (2003) *Planning by consent: the origins and nature of British Development control*. London: Routledge.

Campbell, S. (2016) The Planner's Triangle revisited: sustainability and the evolution of a planning ideal that can't stand still, *Journal of the American Planning Association*, 82(4), pp.388–397.

Clifford, B. (2006) Only a town planner would run a toxic-waste pipeline through a recreational area: planning and planners in the British press, *Town Planning Review*, 77(4), pp.423–455.

Clifford, B. (2012) Planning in an age of customers: British local authority practitioners, identity and reactions to public sector reform, *Town Planning Review*, 83(5), pp.553–574.

Clifford, B. (2013) Rendering reform: local authority planners and perceptions of public participation in Great Britain, *Local Environment*, 18(1), pp.110–131.

Clifford, B. (2016) Clock-watching and box-ticking: British local authority planners, professionalism and performance targets, *Planning Practice and Research*, 31(4), pp.383–401.

Clifford, B. and Tewdwr-Jones, M. (2013) *The collaborating planner?* Bristol: Policy Press.

DCLG (2012) *National Planning Policy Framework*. London: DCLG. Available at: https://www.gov.uk/government/uploads/system/uploads/attachment_data/file/6077/2116950.pdf.

Department of the Environment Northern Ireland (2015) *Strategic Planning Policy Statement for Northern Ireland*. Belfast: Department of the Environment Northern Ireland.

Ellis, H. and Henderson, K. (2016) *English planning in crisis: 10 steps to a sustainable future*. Bristol: Policy Press.

Gardner, A. (2017) Big change, little change? Punctuation, increments and multi-layer institutional change for English local authorities under austerity, *Local Government Studies*, 43(2), pp.150–169.

Glasson, B. and Booth, P. (1992) Negotiation and delay in the development control process, *Town Planning Review*, 63(1), pp.63–78.

Harris, M. (2015). Four reasons why cuts to planning are a false economy, *RTPI Blog*. Available at: www.rtpi.org.uk/briefing-room/rtpi-blog/four-reasons-why-cuts-to-planning-are-a-false-economy/.

Harrison, M. (1972) Development control: the influence of political, legal and ideological factors', *Town Planning Review*, 43(3), pp.254–274.

Lowndes, V. (2005) Something old, something new, something borrowed . . .: how institutions change (and stay the same) in local governance, *Policy Studies*, 24(3/4), pp.291–309.

McAllister, P., Wyatt, P. and Coleman, C. (2013) Fit for policy? Some evidence on the application of development viability models in the United Kingdom planning system, *Town Planning Review*, 84(4), pp.517–541.

Morphet, J. and Clifford, B. (2014) Policy convergence, divergence and communities: the case of spatial planning in post-devolution Britain and Ireland, *Planning Practice & Research*, 29(5), pp.508–524.

Muldoon-Smith, K. and Greenhalgh, P. (2016) Greasing the wheels, or a spanner in the works? Permitting the adaptive re-use of redundant office buildings into residential use in England, *Planning Theory and Practice*, 17(2), pp.175–191.

Planning Advisory Service (2008) *Development management guidance and discussion document*. London: Planning Advisory Service.

Punter, J. (1993) Development interests and the attack on planning control: "planning difficulties" in Bristol 1985–1990, *Environment and Planning A*, 25, pp.521–538.

Scottish Government (2014) *Scottish Planning Policy*. Edinburgh: Scottish Government.

Tewdwr-Jones, M. (1995). Development control and the legitimacy of planning decisions, *Town Planning Review*, 66(2), pp.163–181.

Welsh Government (2016). *Planning Policy Wales*. Cardiff: Welsh Government.

5 Challenges and Emerging Practices in Development Value Capture

Patricia Canelas

Introduction

This chapter discusses current challenges and emerging practices faced by local planning authorities (LPAs) in capturing development value. It examines how the fiscal climate, changes to policy and the interests of the property industry affect the way LPAs capture this value. A specific focus of the chapter is on what is colloquially known as 'planning gain', the broader gain – financial or in-kind – that can be secured through the development process. Planning gain is associated with the uplift in land value that takes place as a result of planning permission being granted, and has its roots in the 1947 Town and Country Planning Act. It can be defined as the "policies that evolved in Britain, particularly in the last two decades, to enable (but not require) LPAs to negotiate with private developers seeking planning permission for contribution towards the physical and social infrastructure connected with proposed developments" (Crook and Monk, 2011: 997). This involves securing financial contributions and commitments from developers – through 'planning obligations' in a legal agreement – to undertake specific work towards affordable housing, highway works, schools or other public facilities. It is generally accepted that planning gain "should support the delivery of sustainable development – including affordable housing, facilities and infrastructure – that benefits the community and contributes to economic growth" (Henneberry, 2016: 116). Planning gain is implemented in England and Wales via Section 106 of the Town and Country Planning Act 1990 (and equivalent parts of legislation in the rest of the UK). In addition to planning gain, there is also consideration of the challenges and practices of other methods of capturing development value: the Community Infrastructure Levy (CIL, a more explicit 'development tax' introduced in 2010), Planning Performance Agreements (PPAs) and Public Realm Credits (PRCs) (more on these later).

The chapter draws on 19 in-depth interviews conducted between 2013 and 2015 with council planners and property industry actors operating in three Inner London LPAs – Westminster City Council, the

Royal Borough of Kensington and Chelsea, and the London Borough of Camden. Given the chapter's focus on emerging practices and the influence of the property industry, this focus on London is justified as it is in London where the property industry exerts its strongest influence, and – as the chapter will show – where the most recent innovative practices have emanated. Some of these practices have been rolled out by central government in national policy and guidance, hence this experience is of interest to planners and scholars elsewhere.[1] Challenges to development value capture have arisen from top-down imposed budget cuts and central government reforms, such as the Comprehensive Spending Review of 2010 and 2013, the Growth and Infrastructure Act of 2013, amendments to the Town and Country Planning (General Permitted Development) Order and the introduction of the Community Infrastructure Levy, all with application across England. Additional challenges emerge from the changing interests and practices of the property industry operating across the UK. These involve developers' growing interest in the so-called build-to-rent market, in inner city redevelopment and in the adaptive re-use of existing buildings.

Development value capture is facing significant challenges. LPAs are squeezed between central government fiscal interventions, policy and legislative changes, and the interests of the property industry. The chapter shows that while the property industry often publicly presents the operation of planning system as a hindrance to development and calls for deregulation (Adams, 2001; Booth, 2003), in practice, property industry players are heavily involved in shaping the way it operates. The remainder of the chapter is divided into three sections: first, there is an overview of the argument for development value capture (the 'why'), the ways development value is captured in the UK (the 'how') and a consideration of what planning gain is used for (the 'what'); second, there is a review of the challenges and novel ways of capturing development value happening on the ground; third, the chapter concludes with some implications for planning practice and theory.

Capturing Development Value: Why, How and for What?

The planning system in the UK is hierarchical and discretionary (Adams, 2001; Booth, 2003; Clifford and Tewdwr-Jones, 2013). Its hierarchical nature means that central government significantly influences local planning policy, which needs to comply with national level policy. Central government also retains control over LPAs' resources, particularly through the local government funding system (Clifford and Tewdwr-Jones, 2013). Regarding its discretionary nature, in contrast with regulatory systems, planning applications in a discretionary system are judged on their own merits rather than just against their compliance with a pre-established land use plan (Booth, 2003). These two key features of the UK planning system are relevant to understand the dynamics at play in development value capture.

The debates on development value capture in the literature focus on three key questions:

- Why should development value be taxed?
- What is the best way to capture it (e.g. explicit or implicit taxes)?
- To what ends should this value captured be put to use?

One broadly accepted principle behind development value capture is that developers should cover the costs of the infrastructure needed to make new development acceptable in planning terms. That is, certain infrastructure should be in place alongside the development, and the developer seeking planning permission should cover its costs. This might include roads, schools or other physical and social infrastructure needed to meet the needs of, and mitigate the impacts created by, a new development. Although it has a longer history, expressed through notions of 'betterment' (e.g. Penny, 1966), the widespread use of planning gain throughout English LPAs grew only in the late 1980s (Rowley and Crook, 2016).

This growth was accompanied by what some refer to as 'the entrepreneurial turn' in local government (see Chapter 8 by Mike Raco). Harvey (1989) argues that urban governance became, in the 1980s, more concerned with ways development could foster economic growth and that, in contrast with its managerial role of the previous decades, urban governance was assuming an entrepreneurial role. This is reflected in the imperative of linking the planning system to the objectives of promoting economic growth, and LPAs increasingly adopting an enabling role to private investment (see, e.g., Coiacetto, 2000; Alexander, 2001; Adams and Tiesdell, 2010, 2013). By the 1990s, a significant part of the urban development process was being led by the private sector (Henneberry, 2016). Already in this decade, public spending cuts started pushing LPAs to seek contributions from the private sector and to shape market-led property development to help support the provision and maintenance of amenities previously provided by the public sector (Healey, 1998).

Since the early 2000s, it has been argued that planners should be perceived, and perceive themselves, as market actors (Alexander, 2001; Adams and Tiesdell, 2010; Henneberry and Parris, 2013), and that contemporary urban development requires strong cooperation between planners and property industry actors (Healey, 1998; Coiacetto, 2000; Alexander, 2001; Adams and Tiesdell, 2010, 2013). Coiacetto (2000: 353) maintains that: "in order to shape urban development, planners have to influence the actions of the players who actually build cities. This requires a solid understanding of the perspective, actions and strategies of those builders". Shaping market-led development and influencing the property industry is, however, challenging because "the defence of private property is deeply entrenched in English law and culture. From this perspective planning represents a recent statutory interference in property rights" (Adams, 2001: 12–13).

After several unsuccessful attempts to introduce national development taxes, the use of the locally managed planning gain gradually extended and was eventually endorsed by central government (Department of the Environment, Transport and the Regions, 1998) as a way to secure affordable housing (Crook and Monk, 2011; Crook et al., 2016). The rationale for the use of planning gain to secure affordable housing rested on the understanding that planning consent increases the land value and that this betterment should be captured and shared by the wider community. Although the use of planning obligations for affordable housing provision has had its critics (Joseph Rowntree Foundation, 1994; Oxley, 2008), it has generally been perceived as a successful and practical way of securing affordable units (e.g. Crook et al., 2016) particularly in the context of buoyant development markets (e.g. Crook and Monk, 2011: 1013).

The literature amply discusses the advantages and disadvantages of implicit and explicit forms of development value capture. Implicit forms, such as Section 106 agreements, are subject to possible negotiation, whereas explicit forms, when set, are certain and non-negotiable. The claimed advantages of implicit value capture mechanisms include enabling planners to adapt to the different phases of the property cycle and different property sub-markets, adjusting and phasing contributions if needed (Crook et al., 2016). Through Section 106 agreements, planners have secured on-site affordable housing, contributing to the development of socio-economically mixed communities (Rowley and Crook, 2016). Claimed disadvantages of implicit forms of development value capture include their uncertainty, lack of transparency, time taken to negotiate and high transaction costs (e.g. Healey et al., 1992; Crook and Monk, 2011). A further criticism is that planning gain is highly dependent on buoyant development markets and on the negotiation skills of planners at the LPAs (Crook et al., 2016).

The Community Infrastructure Levy was introduced in 2010 as a response to some of the perceived disadvantages of securing planning gain through Section 106 agreements. CIL is an explicit tax charging a fixed rate per square metre of net increase in floor space (when new build exceeds 100m^2 gross internal area), varying according to use and location and set by each LPA. LPAs have discretionary powers to define what infrastructure can be funded by the CIL and indeed whether to charge the CIL at all. The LPAs that opt to implement the CIL are required to publish a Regulation 123 list where the items to be covered by the CIL are specified, and items on that list cannot be charged through Section 106 agreements (CIL Review Team, 2016). CIL is expected to bring greater certainty to development value contributions and therefore reduce transaction costs for both LPAs and developers. With the introduction of CIL, contributions set under Section 106 are scaled back to site-specific infrastructure and affordable housing (Burgess et al., 2013; Mulliner and Maliene, 2013; Crook, 2016).

Since the early 2010s, LPAs in the UK have experienced significant budget cuts, such that planning in an age of austerity seems to be the new paradigm (Clifford and Tewdwr-Jones, 2013; *London Evening Standard*, 2013; Local Government Association, 2014; Harris, 2015; Besussi, 2016). One of the implications of these budget cuts is that LPAs are becoming more dependent on the private sector to finance some of their day-to-day activities. A recent example is the growing use of Planning Performance Agreements as means to subsidise councils. PPAs are a voluntary project management tool where applicants and LPAs enter into an arrangement "to agree timescales, actions and resources for handling particular applications" in exchange for an additional fee (Department of Communities and Local Government [DCLG], 2015).

Figures from the DCLG suggest than half the major planning applications assessed in England in the last quarter of 2015 were being subjected to PPAs (Kochan, 2016). There is no precise format for PPAs. Planning guidance on the topic advises that: "it is for the local planning authority and the applicant to discuss and agree a suitable process, format and content which is proportionate to the scale of the project and the complexity of the issues to be addressed" (DCLG, 2015).

PPAs are not the only additional mechanism for development value capture LPAs have adopted to cope with austerity. Other coping mechanisms include the supplementary planning document *Public Realm Credits – Operating a system in Westminster* (Westminster City Council, 2011). The financial contributions from developers sought by LPAs discussed in this chapter, and their nature and possible uses, are summarised in Table 5.1.

The financial viability of development has become critical in both Section 106 agreements and the setting of CIL charges (Crosby et al., 2013; Crook, 2016; Henneberry, 2016; Sayce et al., 2016). Henneberry (2016) traces references to viability in development value capture policy back to 2005. This includes references in the National Planning Policy Framework (NPPF) (DCLG, 2012: para.173) indicating that:

> To ensure viability, the costs of any requirement likely to be applied to development, such as requirements for affordable housing, standards, infrastructure contributions or other requirements should, when taking into account of the normal cost of development and mitigation, provide competitive returns to a willing land owner and willing developer to enable the development to be deliverable.

Table 5.1 Mechanisms for development value capture

Contributions	*Nature*	*Uses*
Section 106	Negotiated (implicit tax)	Local infrastructure needs, including affordable housing (except items included in Regulation 123 if CIL is implemented)
Community Infrastructure Levy	Fixed tariff (explicit tax)	Wider and local infrastructure as determined by each LPA's Regulation 123 list, except affordable housing
Planning Performance Agreements	Negotiated fee and management tool	The salaries of council planners and planning departments running costs
Other, e.g. Public Realm Credits	Ad hoc	Public space investment

Source: Patricia Canelas.

Subsequent planning practice guidance further stresses that capturing development value should not compromise the financial viability of development (DCLG, 2014, 2016). The 2013 Growth and Infrastructure Act introduced a temporary appeal mechanism that allowed developers to challenge affordable housing obligations previously agreed and settled under Section 106 agreements at any point in time. The rationale for the new procedure was that "unrealistic Section 106 agreements negotiated in differing economic conditions can be an obstacle to house building" (DCLG, 2013: 2).

There is an on-going debate over the limitations of using viability appraisals in planning gain negotiations (e.g. Henneberry, 2016; Sayce et al., 2016; Park, 2017). It has been argued that the degree of input data uncertainty, based on a wide range of assumptions, and the different results obtained, depending on the valuation methodology used, make viability appraisals prone to challenges from both developers and planners (see, e.g., Henneberry, 2016). Also, it has been claimed that "many developers openly admit that viability appraisals can be manipulated to demonstrate most predetermined outcomes" and that "it is increasingly clear that negotiation over viability is a war of attrition that the local authority is very unlikely to win" (Park, 2017: 79). Ultimately, research suggests that the introduction of development viability appraisals in planning gain, together with other complex set of factors, undermines LPAs' capacity to secure affordable housing (Sayce et al., 2016).

Challenges and Novel Ways of Capturing Development Value

Securing Affordable Housing

The provision of affordable housing in the UK through central and local government funding has shrunk significantly in the last decades (Rydin, 2013). After the decades of public housing provision that followed the Second World War, starting in the 1980s, affordable housing provision grew critically reliant on development value capture (Rydin, 2013; Crook et al., 2016). Recent figures suggest that about 60% of all affordable housing in England is provided through Section 106 agreements (Burgess et al., 2013; Mulliner and Maliene, 2013). Provision of affordable housing through planning gain can follow one of three routes: (1) on-site, (2) off-site and (3) monetary contributions to LPAs' affordable housing funds. The London Plan establishes that off-site provision of affordable housing, or monetary contributions to LPAs' affordable housing funds, should be accepted only in exceptional cases.

However, a growing trend towards inner-city brownfield redevelopment (Karadimitriou, 2005), makes securing on-site affordable housing more challenging, as development is more expensive than on greenfield suburban sites (Calavita and Mallach, 2009; Crook et al., 2016). London First, a business funded advocacy group, also endorses off-site provision (London First and Turley, 2016). Interviews with local authority planners revealed that it is common to find inner-city developers proposing off-site affordable housing or monetary contributions as an alternative to using some of their prime land for affordable housing. They also revealed LPAs' preference for securing affordable housing on-site as a way to incentivise mixed-income neighbourhoods and thus tackle urban polarisation. Securing affordable housing on-site nevertheless brings a practical dilemma for LPAs, particularly in expensive inner-city locations, inasmuch as larger numbers of affordable housing units can be achieved through off-site or in lieu contributions than through on-site provision. As one planner claimed: "for the money they give us you would get five units in Covent Garden but you might get 15 in another part of the city, but you are just creating potentially polarised neighbourhoods". LPAs thus struggle to find the grounds to contest what seems to be a growing trend towards off-site provision.

Additionally, the expansion of the build-to-rent market (Evans, 2015) brings further challenges to securing affordable housing. The build-to-rent sector is a long-term business model based on income return. Without capital return, as there are no sales, planners at LPAs have claimed that developers often make a case that they cannot afford to provide affordable housing, based on their viability models that exclude capital gains. In light of the growth of the sector and its negative impact on LPAs' capacity to secure affordable housing, one planner stated that LPAs were trying to enter into agreements with build-to-rent developers where the developers agreed to pay affordable housing obligations in the event of selling the scheme.

Securing affordable housing through planning obligations is mostly effective in buoyant property markets. Planners in London interviewed for this research emphasised the additional challenges they faced securing affordable housing during the market downturn that followed the 2007–2008 global financial crisis. This is also very likely to be the case in less buoyant property markets in the rest of the UK. Council planners also claimed that provisions in the 2013 Growth and Infrastructure Act, which enabled developers to renegotiate planning gain previously agreed with LPAs or appeal to the Planning Inspectorate, represented a top-down challenge to LPAs' autonomy and legitimacy in managing planning gain negotiations. The renegotiation of planning obligations had always been possible, but required the voluntary agreement of both parties: the LPAs and the developers. The changes imposed by central government have interfered with the power dynamics involved in planning gain discussions, tilting the forces towards the interests of developers.

Deregulation and the Expansion of Permitted Development Rights

Developers can also bypass affordable housing contributions and other planning obligations when proposing schemes that fall under Permitted Development Rights (PD Rights). The Town and Country Planning (General Permitted Development) (England) Order determines what uses fall under PD Rights, or in other words, the development activity that does not require full planning permission. The 2013 amendment extended PD Rights to include office-to-residential conversions. Initially a temporary measure, it was made permanent in 2016. The policy rationale was that with reduced planning requirements, the market would bring forward more quickly this adaptive re-use of space. This would contribute to reducing redundant office space while speeding up housing delivery. With PD Rights, a prior notification to the relevant LPA is enough to guarantee exemption from full planning consent. This presents new challenges to development value capture. Although LPAs are able to apply CIL charges to conversions, they cannot negotiate Section 106 payments for issues that fall outside the remit of prior approval. For example, affordable housing is not an issue for consideration under prior approval, and some LPAs argue that they have lost millions of pounds in affordable housing as a result of the inclusion of offices to residential conversions into PD Rights (Fort, 2016).

Planners at the three London LPAs interviewed for this research expressed their concerns over this policy. For instance, one planner maintained:

> it's a big loss, what happens is that the market is very geared towards high-value housing, so we are losing office space and what we are gaining is housing for very affluent people, and not really very high-density housing either. We really need to make use of all the land we have available, and the PD Rights that are coming forward don't make the best use of space.

Some LPAs were granted exemptions in the initial pilot phase of the policy. This included parts of London Boroughs falling within London's Central Activities Zone (CAZ) alongside other parts of London, including the whole of Royal Borough of Kensington and Chelsea and parts of the London Borough of Camden outside the CAZ. Since these exemptions were only temporary, many LPAs are in the process of implementing Article 4 directions as a mechanism to provide exemption for key sites. However, there are financial and resourcing implications for boroughs that go down this route, which is a burden unpalatable to many in the context of austerity.

Community Infrastructure Levy

The three LPAs studied for this research were, in mid to late 2015, in the process of, or at the first stages in, implementing the CIL. More recent research for the government suggests that CIL implementation does not seem to offer what it promised – "a fairer, faster, more certain and transparent system" of securing contributions from development (CIL Review Team, 2016: 5–6). On the contrary, CIL implementation has been perceived as too complex, to the point that developers, who were first keen on seeing the gradual scale-back of Section 106 replaced by the CIL, are now showing nostalgia for Section 106 agreements (CIL Review Team: 11). The research also found that many LPAs have chosen not to implement the CIL, since they prioritise affordable housing over infrastructure. Affordable housing cannot be secured through the CIL, and CIL channels contributions from developers into other infrastructure needs, thus some LPAs have preferred not to introduce the CIL and to continue to use Section 106 agreements (CIL Review Team, 2016).

Using Section 106 agreements, instead of the CIL, LPAs seem to be able to secure greater levels of affordable housing and other planning obligations that better respond to site-specific constraints. Section 106 agreements offer greater flexibility than the CIL. With Section 106, LPAs can consider the phases of the property cycle and the characteristics of local property markets and adjust, phase or postpone the contributions from developers if necessary. The research found that the nature of the items included and the extent of Regulation 123 lists (where the items to be covered by the CIL are specified) vary significantly between the different CIL-charging LPAs, and that the latest LPAs introducing the CIL have fewer items on their list than the forerunners. This allows the later adopters a greater range of infrastructure that can still be negotiated under Section 106 agreements.

Public Realm Credits

Other public goods that can be delivered through Section 106 agreements if not covered by the CIL include public space. LPAs' budget constraints affect, among other things, their capacity to invest in public space, which means that contributions from developers for this end have become increasingly important. In May 2011, Westminster City Council adopted a supplementary planning document, *Public Realm Credits – Operating a System in Westminster*, aimed at capturing development value for public space improvements (Westminster City Council, 2011). A group of developers represented by the Westminster Property Association approached the council and the parties negotiated this new policy called Public Realm Credits. Property developers could invest in public space improvements agreed and approved by the council, and in return they would receive PRCs. These credits could be used at a later point in time to offset planning obligations for public space triggered by any planning application developers subsequently submitted to the council.

With the implementation of PRCs, developers' voluntary capital investment in the public space could be institutionalised. Developers with several schemes in the same area were particularly keen on these unsolicited public space improvements, inasmuch as these investments would have a positive impact on the value of their properties. From the point of view of the council, PRCs incentivised private investment in the public space (Westminster City Council, 2011), which the council was particularly pleased to see in the run-up to the 2012 London Olympic Games. According to the planners, this would help promote local economic growth. The disadvantage of this policy was that at the time of a new planning application, if developers chose to offset their PRCs, there would be limited remaining funds for the public space works that should go along the new development. This policy was discontinued with the introduction of the CIL, and the developers interviewed were disappointed to see the policy rescinded, as it had given them greater control over the timing and allocation of their development value contributions.

Planning Performance Agreements

Austerity has played a role in giving the property industry greater power to influence planning policies and greater control over Development Management and planning gain negotiations. According to one Westminster

City Council planner, the council approached the Westminster Property Association asking for its cooperation in dealing with budget cuts. The cuts would require the council to cut 25% of staff, which meant that the service would go 'belly-up'. The members of the Westminster Property Association agreed to pay a supplement to planning application fees to cover the costs of keeping the service intact. The council established a figure of £30,000 per application. A property developer from the Westminster Property Association maintained: "Westminster is short of funds, short of resources, the money has to come from somewhere, so they are looking at alternative methods of funding." Following negotiations, the Westminster Property Association, the Leader of Westminster City Council and the Deputy Mayor of London wrote together to the then Chancellor of the Exchequer, George Osborne, asking him to formalise the use of Planning Performance Agreements. As described in the media, they asked the Chancellor for property companies to be allowed to pay higher application fees to help to subsidise council planning departments (Allen and Pickard, 2014).

According to the chairman of the Westminster Property Association as quoted in the *London Evening Standard* (2013), "when considering a major application, it is a small price to pay, and benefits everyone". The same source claimed that developers, through the fees of PPAs, were indirectly paying the wages of 11 of the 62 planning officers at Westminster City Council. A planner interviewed whose salary was being paid with these funds maintained:

> I'm still an employee of the council, so it's not my job to make it happen for them, it's not my job to rush through their planning applications, it's not my job to put additional resources into making things happening for them. It's my job to be some sort of arbiter, I suppose, between what they want to do and what can really happen.

A property developer refuted that PPAs were being used to pay planners' salaries, and said: "it doesn't work that way, it goes into this big magical pot". The developer further claimed: "We don't actually pay for any planning officer time, because we don't think that's appropriate, because these guys have to get us planning consents and if we were paying them that would be a conflict." Whether the fees from PPAs were being used to pay for the salaries or not, this situation seemed to be rather uncomfortable for property developers.

The discomfort property developers expressed with this situation could be explained by their awareness of the conflict of interest planners on such contracts might experience. As the media have asserted, planners' salaries being paid by PPAs raises the question whether "developers are only paying for more efficient decision-making processes, and not permissions" (Allen and Pickard, 2014). But this is not all: planners are likely to end up in a weaker position negotiating planning gain when their salaries are being paid by the developers the planners have to negotiate with. Moreover, PPAs are an additional development cost that the developers are covering, which ultimately means that part of the development value available for subsidising infrastructure is being channelled into subsidising the running costs of the LPAs.

Conclusions

Emerging challenges to, and novel ways of capturing, development value spring from the dynamic interplay between fiscal and planning policy and the interests and practices of the property industry. LPAs have long been embroiled in the turn to urban entrepreneurialism, which is intensified in response to budget cuts. Central government-imposed budget cuts hinder the everyday functioning of LPAs, pushing them into innovative ways of self-financing, including capturing funds from developers' contributions. The urgency in capturing development value to fund public goods and the running costs of LPAs increases as their budget shrinks. But capturing development value is dependent on growth and development viability. If these are compromised, whether at certain phases of the property cycle or at certain geographical locations, LPAs end up with very limited opportunities to continue to shape urban development.

Additional challenges to securing planning obligations that LPAs face derive from planning deregulation and policy emphasis on economic growth, including policies around development viability. These destabilise the power dynamics between LPAs and developers, tilting the forces towards the interests of developers. Policies resulting from property industry lobbying, such as Planning Performance Agreements and Public Realm Credits, also further empower developers with greater levels of control over Development Management and the uses of development value funds captured. The introduction of these property industry lobby-led policies also shows where developers prefer to spend their development contributions. These novel uses and formats of capturing development value moreover render contributions for affordable housing more residual.

LPAs have fought back against some of the central government-imposed policies. This has included challenging policies such as PD Rights for office-to-residential conversions, choosing not to implement the CIL or reducing the number of items charged under the CIL, and continuing to make extensive use of Section 106 agreements. However, LPAs have few powers to oppose property industry interests, as their financial reliance on the industry grows, including for funding their running costs.

Acknowledgments

I would like to thank Michael Edwards, Ed Jones and Daniel Fitzpatrick for their comments, and the editorial team of this book for their support.

Note

1 As Crook et al. (2016: 6) note: "the systems in Scotland and Wales are not dissimilar to those in England . . . [however,] the advent of devolved administrations means that there are increasing differences between the nations of Britain in the way these issues are being handled". For more on planning gain in Scotland and Wales, see, for instance, Rowley and Crook (2016). Additionally, see Scottish Parliament Information Centre (2013) for more on planning gain in Northern Ireland and for a comparison of the planning systems of the four UK countries.

References

All listed URLs were last accessed on 1 March 2018.

Adams, D. (2001) *Urban planning and the development process.* London: Routledge.

Adams, D. and Tiesdell, S. (2010) Planners as market actors: rethinking state–market relations in land and property, *Planning Theory & Practice*, 11(2), pp.187–207.

Adams, D. and Tiesdell, S. (2013) *Shaping places: urban planning, design and development.* London: Routledge.

Alexander, E. (2001) Why planning vs. markets is an oxymoron: asking the right question, *Planning and Markets*, 4(1), pp.1–8.

Allen, K. and Pickard, J. (2014) Planners seek cash for fast ruling, *Financial Times*, 11 February. Available at: www.ft.com/cms/s/0/d24dd15e-9314-11e3-b07c-00144feab7de.html#axzz3qoEn2YSp.

Besussi, E. (2016) Extracting value from the public city: urban strategies and the state-market mix in the disposal of municipal assets. In B. Schönig and S. Schipper (eds) *Urban austerity: impacts of the global financial crisis in cities in Europe.* Berlin: Theater der Zeit, pp.89–102.

Booth, P. (2003) *Controlling development: certainty and discretion in Europe, the USA and Hong Kong. The Natural and Built Environment Series 9.* London: Routledge.

Burgess, G., Crook, T. and Monk, S. (2013) *The changing delivery of planning gain through Section 106 and the Community Infrastructure Levy.* Cambridge: Cambridge Centre for Housing and Planning Research.

Calavita, N. and Mallach, A. (2009) Inclusionary housing, incentives, and land value recapture, *Land Lines*, 21(1), pp.15–21.

CIL Review Team (2016) *A new approach to developer contributions: a report by the CIL Review Team.* Available at: https://www.gov.uk/government/publications/community-infrastructure-levy-review-report-to-government.

Clifford, B. and Tewdwr-Jones, M. (2013) *The collaborating planner? Practitioners in the neoliberal age.* Bristol: Policy Press.

Coiacetto, E. (2000) Places shape place shapers? Real estate developers' outlooks concerning community, planning and development differ between places, *Planning Practice and Research*, 15(4), pp.353–374.

Crook, T. (2016) Planning obligations policy in England: de facto taxation of development value. In T. Crook, J. Henneberry and C. Whitehead (2016)

Planning gain: providing infrastructure and affordable housing. Chichester: Wiley-Blackwell, pp.63–114.

Crook, T. and Monk, S. (2011) Planning gains, providing homes, *Housing Studies*, 26(7–8), pp.997–1018.

Crook, T., Henneberry, J. and Whitehead, C. (2016) *Planning gain: providing infrastructure and affordable housing*. Chichester: Wiley-Blackwell.

Crosby, N., McAllister, P. and Wyatt, P. (2013) Fit for planning? An evaluation of the application of development viability appraisal models in the UK planning system, *Environment and Planning B: Planning and Design*, 40(1), pp.3–22.

DCLG (2012) *National Planning Policy Framework*. London: DCLG. Available at: https://www.gov.uk/government/uploads/system/uploads/attachment_data/file/6077/2116950.pdf.

DCLG (2013) *Section 106 affordable housing requirements: review and appeal*. Available at: https://www.gov.uk/government/uploads/system/uploads/attachment_data/file/192641/Section_106_affordable_housing_requirements_-_Review_and_appeal.pdf.

DCLG (2014) Viability and decision taking. Available at: https://www.gov.uk/guidance/viability#viability-and-decision-taking.

DCLG (2015) Before submitting an application: planning performance agreements. Available at: http://planningguidance.communities.gov.uk/blog/guidance/before-submitting-an-application/planning-performance-agreements/.

DCLG (2016) *Planning obligations*. Available at: https://www.gov.uk/guidance/planning-obligations.

Department of the Environment, Transport and the Regions (1998) *Planning and affordable housing*. Circular 6/98. London: The Stationery Office.

Evans, J. (2015) Investors bet on build-to-let for UK's "generation rent", *FT. Com*, 5 December. Available at: https://www.ft.com/content/43956e6e-9a87-11e5-a5c1-ca5db4add713.

Fort, L. (2016) Reading loses £3.8m and 257 affordable homes after rule change, *getreading*, 30 January. Available at: www.getreading.co.uk/news/local-news/reading-loses-38m-257-affordable-10808792.

Harris, M. (2015) Four reasons why cuts to planning are a false economy, *RTPI Blog*. Available at: www.rtpi.org.uk/briefing-room/rtpi-blog/four-reasons-why-cuts-to-planning-are-a-false-economy.

Harvey, D. (1989) From managerialism to entrepreneurialism: the transformation in urban governance in late capitalism, *Geografiska Annaler. Series B, Human Geography*, 71(1), pp.3–17.

Healey, P. (1998) Regulating property development and the capacity of the development industry, *Journal of Property Research*, 15(3), pp.211–227.

Healey, P., Purdue, M. and Ennis, F. (1992) Rationales for planning gain, *Policy Studies*, 13(2), pp.18–30.

Henneberry, J. (2016) Development viability. In T. Crook, J. Henneberry and C. Whitehead (eds) *Planning gain: providing infrastructure and affordable housing*. Chichester: Wiley-Blackwell, pp.115–139.

Henneberry, J. and Parris, S. (2013) The embedded developer: using project ecologies to analyse local property development networks, *Town Planning Review*, 84(2), pp.227–250.

Joseph Rowntree Foundation (1994) *Inquiry into Planning for Housing*. York: Joseph Rowntree Foundation.

Karadimitriou, N. (2005) Changing the way UK cities are built: the shifting urban policy and the adaptation of London's housebuilders, *Journal of Housing and the Built Environment*, 20(3), pp.271–286.

Kochan, B. (2016) How performance agreements are driving change in local authority planning departments, *Planning Resource*, 18 March. Available at: www.planningresource.co.uk/article/1387869/performance-agreements-driving-change-local-authority-planning-departments.

Local Government Association (2014) *Under pressure: how councils are planning for future cuts*. Available at: https://www.local.gov.uk/sites/default/files/documents/under-pressure-how-counci-471.pdf.

London Evening Standard (2013) Property: Westminster planners' "untenable burden" – and a £26,000 load for the developers, *Evening Standard*, 21 November. Available at: www.standard.co.uk/business/business-news/property-westminster-planners-untenable-burden-and-a-26000-load-for-the-developers-8954219.html.

London First and Turley (2016) *The off-site rule: improving planning policy to deliver affordable housing in London*. Available at: http://londonfirst.co.uk/wp-content/uploads/2016/02/The-Off-Site-Rule.pdf.

Mulliner, E. and Maliene, V. (2013) Austerity and reform to affordable housing policy, *Journal of Housing and the Built Environment*, 28(2), pp.397–407.

Oxley, M. (2008) Implicit land taxation and affordable housing provision in England, *Housing Studies*, 23(4), pp.661–671.

Park, J. (2017) *One hundred years of housing space standards: what now?* Available at: www.levittbernstein.co.uk/site/assets/files/2682/one_hundred_years_of_housing_space_standards.pdf.

Penny, P. (1966) The compensation and betterment problem in town planning, *South African Journal of Economics*, 34(4), pp.257–269.

Rowley, S. and Crook, T. (2016) The incidence and value of planning obligations. In T. Crook, J. Henneberry and C. Whitehead (eds) *Planning gain: providing infrastructure and affordable housing*. Chichester: Wiley-Blackwell, pp.140–174.

Rydin, Y. (2013) *The future of planning: beyond growth dependence*. Bristol: Policy Press.

Sayce, S. et al. (2016) *Viability and the planning system: the relationship between economic viability testing, land values and affordable housing in London*. London: Boroughs of Barking and Dagenham, Brent, Camden, Croydon, Enfield, Greenwich, Islington, Lambeth, Merton, Newham, Southwark, Tower Hamlets and Waltham Forest.

Scottish Parliament Information Centre (2013) *Comparison of the planning systems in the four UK countries*. SPICe Briefing 13/35. Available at: www.parliament.scot/ResearchBriefingsAndFactsheets/S4/SB_13-35.pdf.

Westminster City Council (2011) *Public realm credits – operating a system in Westminster*. Available at: http://transact.westminster.gov.uk/docstores/publications_store/Public_Realm_Credits_SPD_Adopted_May_2011.pdf.

6 Public Participation and the Declining Significance of Planning

Yasminah Beebeejaun

Introduction

The importance of listening to, and respecting, the public's viewpoint has never seemed so important as details emerge of the fire at Grenfell Tower, one of the worst modern tragedies in peacetime England. Yet the idea of a reciprocal participatory process that respects communities and enhances collective services seems difficult to secure. Despite being a key aspiration of the planning system, participation appears to have uneven and negligible impacts upon planning and development practices. Even when planners strive hard to mobilise effective and sustained participation, the problem of power relations between professional planners and the public persists (see Aitken, 2009; Clarke and Agyeman, 2011). Whether professionals engage with tenants or residents, service users, or simply 'the public' who may have a stake in development and planning decisions, there are important concerns regarding mutual respect and progressing from being heard to being listened to across and within all sectors.[1]

Community engagement is in principle a key component of the post-war planning system (Rydin, 1999). The emphasis on community involvement has intensified in recent decades, reflecting a set of wider governance reforms (see Raco and Flint, 2001; Durose et al., 2012), and more recently, a desire to reinforce or recreate ideas about neighbourhood attachment through the Conservative government's Localism Agenda (see Chapter 9 by Elena Besussi). Successive UK Governments have sought to bring planning closer to local communities despite the highly centralised nature of the British political system. While opportunities to subvert and challenge existing power relations exist, communities have to engage with the procedures and practices of professional fields in order to gain influence (Taylor, 2007: 314).

This chapter focuses on aspects of the English experience for public participation in formal planning processes, and relates to British experiences despite some differences in approaches to community engagement. In Scotland, for example, an established system of community planning exists, yet concerns remain that this is not well integrated with the current planning system (see Scottish Government, 2017). The statutory requirements of planning systems clearly vary between countries, as well as their cultural and social understandings (Beebeejaun, 2006). However, Anglo-American planning theory heavily influences public participation debates despite the great differences with the nature of American planning and social, economic and cultural distinctions. In terms of planners' relationships with others and the treatment of knowledge, there are wider implications for theory and practice.

In this chapter, I firstly set out important aspects of the framework for understanding public participation within the English planning system. I argue that understanding public participation is conceptualised in highly constrained ways. These create particular barriers and a range of possibilities that differ from other policy areas. Secondly, I develop a set of challenges regarding how publics are characterised in planning and a set of key problems that emerge. I draw out some key themes within current conceptions of planning and their implications for theory and practice. I argue that while there has been a great deal of support for participation in wider debates, mainstream literature, including collaborative planning, has occupied a problematic position. Despite the sustained emphasis on ideal forms of participation (Innes and Booher, 2004), empirical work examining the mainstream; mundane but important statutory processes is lacking within the literature (exceptions include McClymont, 2011; Clifford 2016; McClymont and O'Hare, 2008; Mace, 2013).

The Expanding Public

Previous conceptions of the public and community have taken an approach that imagines much more homogeneity within localities and grapples with the complications of a public interest as supporting planning activity (see Campbell, 2012). While there is a great deal of diversity within seemingly traditional communities, planning's difficulties in engaging with other forms of difference along racial, ethnic, religious or gendered lines, as well as sexuality, has been noted for several decades (see Chapman and Lowdnes, 2009; Doan, 2015; Royal Town Planning Institute/Commission for Racial Equality Working Party, 1983; Sweet and Ortiz Escalante, 2015; Thomas and Krishnarayan, 1994a, 1994b; Thomas, 2004). Despite this significant field of literature, many individuals and groups continue to be marginalised within planning practice. Participation is infused with great potential and hope for many communities, but the reality is often disappointing (Beebeejaun, 2016).

There are clear spatial dimensions to planning, thus it differs from other forms of service provision in that it affects geographical communities as well as groups that share perceived attributes or interests. The spatial dimensions of planning mean it is more difficult to remove oneself or opt out from the impacts of policy in the ways education may be privately consumed, except by moving to a different area. Planning may divide, but it also brings together a range of people, often in opposition to a planning proposal.

Public participation has been given much attention within planning theory and practice. This is not surprising given the rejection of technocratic forms of planning since the late 1960s onwards, and the erosion of a singular public interest, as well as the shift of planning to the private sector, requires that planning must continuously rework its own legitimacy. The 'communicative turn', as it is known within planning theory, has dominated debates since the 1980s. Key theorists include Patsy Healey, Judy Innes and John Forester. These debates are complex, drawing on the theories of Jürgen Habermas and John Dewey, to argue for a reinvigorated public realm to empower decision-making. As well as this, the idea of the public as stakeholders, and the planner as mediator, brings together disparate groups to weave together a shared spatial future predominate.

While these theoretical insights are important, along with their substantive critique, this chapter does not substantively discuss them. Planning theorist Crystal Legacy develops an interesting perspective in the Canadian and Australian context, arguing that we can understand some long-term planning processes as integrating traditional 'rational-comprehensive' models with moments of deliberation where wider stakeholder groups are drawn in. Indeed, sustained planning processes, particularly at the regional scale, offer scope for more innovative and deliberative ways of doing planning (see Baker et al., 2010). The task for planners is to manage these 'parallel processes' (see Legacy, 2010, 2012).

However, one of the key planning reforms of the UK Coalition government (2010–2015) was to abolish the regional planning scale, centralising further some planning powers and devolving others down to the local level. This process has been problematic, with much recent work turning to the potential of Neighbourhood Planning as a mechanism to enable greater community control over planning (see Parker and Salter, 2017). Innes and Booher (2004) note that the statutory ways of doing planning "simply do not work", yet they remain the main mechanism for public involvement. Implementing deliberative forms of planning requires a form of democracy and governmental capacity that is far more extensive than the current English planning system has the capacity to deliver. However, these problems are not confined to the English context. Given the evident 'hollowing out' of the state, firstly through governance and latterly through austerity, what space can statutory forms of participation occupy in planning?

Assessing participation is a complex task. Yvonne Rydin's analysis of planning participation, considering 50 years of planning within Barry Cullingworth's book *British Planning*, provides an important overview of the English experience (Cullingworth, 1999). The influence of Thatcherism and the emergence of the pro-growth mandate of planning in contrast to previous plan-led imperatives loomed large. However, hope was seen in the form of Local Agenda 21, an initiative that tried to integrate public participation with sustainability initiatives. While Local Agenda 21 is no longer a central policy field in the UK, successive initiatives have not produced radically different forms of participation and public impact. Today, we see moves towards co-production, the 'smart city' agenda and Neighbourhood Planning, which has also been synonymous with popular understandings of planning. But what about the on-going, if ever-changing, mainstream practice of planning?

Planning Practice

The post-war planning system was part of a set of bold ideas about tackling inequality in all aspects of society (Cullingworth, 1999). The value of community involvement was acknowledged 60 years ago. Opening the Second Reading debate on the 1947 Town and Country Planning Bill, the Minister for Town and Country Planning, Lewis Silkin, stated: "The people whose surroundings are being planned must be given every chance to take an active part in the planning process, particularly when the stage of detail is reached."[2] While many of the details of the participatory system have changed during the intervening six decades, the substantive rationale for public participation has not. Public participation is generally invited as a response to planning policy or a specific development application. Over time, there have been attempts to include the public in earlier stages of planning, but this is not general practice across local authorities (see Baker et al., 2010). The shift from presumption in favour of the plan – a document with a broad vision of the area for all sectors of the community – to presumption for development has significantly altered the framework for assessing participation. Public participation in plan-making is framed around development, particularly engagement with increased housebuilding. This change reflects shifts noted in the late 1980s and 1990s.

A critical issue that arises is how participation can be seen to benefit or be welcome when representations must also follow pro-growth strategies. An ideal of public participation remains central to claims for a legitimate and fair planning system that achieves a putative public interest. However, Alan Mace (2013: 1144) points out the contradictions that these goals create for communities: "Once again we hear of local communities being empowered, of the rollback of government but still within the context of the rollout of the neoliberal; people and places are to be given a responsible voice in seeking more development." Communities' objections to development are represented as self-interested because they contradict national planning policy, without acknowledgement that planning has moved away from more holistic spatial strategies.

The origins of demands for public participation exist in tension with the current requirements of the statutory planning system. Current regulations are set out in the Town and Country Planning (Local Planning) (England) Regulations 2012. While guidance has been altered in the last few decades, the current regulations reflect a categorisation of public engagement with a set of statutory bodies and interest groups, communities of identity and the public in general. There are guidelines on a range of groups which must be consulted regarding local planning, and supplementary planning documents that include religious or faith-based groups and groups based on other collective identities such as ethnicity, race, age etc. The public can make representations within the time limits set out in the regulations. Time periods are short for each stage of consultation, although authorities are encouraged to 'front-load'. Through consultation at earlier stages, it is hoped that there will be fewer objections at later stages. Turning to planning applications for development, the public have 21 days to respond to planning applications, although this can be extended for complex or contentious applications. While the details are specific to the English system, the general principles of limited and structured public consultation are the norm of many planning systems. Examples of best practice – such as Port Alegre participatory budgeting – have become renowned, but are difficult to replicate as they are the result of extensive and embedded work in particular locations. Efforts to develop community organising have been fragmented in the UK due to their co-optation by the state, and they diverge significantly from more established forms of community empowerment (see Thomas, 2016).

While these mechanisms enshrine the principle of time, albeit limited, to engage with planning, as well as setting out how planning is publicised, this does not provide many insights into the political approach to participation. The National Planning Policy Framework (NPPF), the principal policy statement for the system, only contains one mention of participation, although not public participation, compared to nearly 50 mentions of the community. The ethos is encapsulated by the exhortation that "local planning authorities should aim to involve all sections of the community". Yet under the current Conservative government, there have been few if any signs of engagement with the difficulties for some groups to participate in planning. While they have produced several legally required documents such as equality impact assessments, these have demonstrated a parlous lack of concern with the consequences of planning policy.[3]

Contradictions of Participation

The mechanics of the planning system are based upon a notion of consultation that appeals to fairness. But within this framework, how have the public fared? People should have the right to comment on schemes that affect them. This benevolent bureaucracy often conflicts with the more radical roots of participation based on a longstanding critique of planning. The outcomes of schemes that displaced marginalised communities, particularly Black communities in US cities, led to a groundswell of critique exemplified by the work of Sherry Arnstein and Paul Davidoff. This work acted to challenge power relations within planning. While the US has similar concerns regarding the efficacy of planning, there are much stronger sectors of civil society, and racial, ethnic, LGBTQ+ and religious groupings have much greater engagement and impact on political debates (see Thomas and Ritzdorf, 1997).

However, these radical roots have become co-opted into other policy arenas, notably co-production and modes of power-sharing (Durose et al., 2012). The ideals of community engagement have been influential outside planning, and have subsequently spread to many other policy areas, particularly regeneration. Here, the underpinning rationale for such engagement is that development can only have lasting impacts when the communities affected are involved (Dargan, 2009). Within England, the New Deal for Communities embodied the most well-resourced schemes that aimed to enhance community voice as a mechanism to deliver more responsive regeneration schemes in the country's most deprived areas. A related and important field of work in political science has argued for mechanisms to democratise fields of policy, arguing that the public bring important perspectives and can create mutually beneficial partnerships within various sectors, including education and policing (see Fung, 2009).

Participation remains a highly normative concept both within and outside planning. These principles developed, in part, through the planning system have moved to homes elsewhere. Much participation around planning issues is outside the constraints of the formal system (see Sundaresan, 2016). But it also marks the troubled circumstances of planning, as there are limited recent theoretical insights that break with the dominant themes of communicative planning within the discipline. While there is a proliferation of attention to best practice within planning, there are few indicators of change everyday planning. This is an important area to address, as the first and perhaps only engagement with planning many people will have is through objecting to planning development.

Planning Not Fit for the Public or a Public Not Fit for Planning?

A history of planning participation shows that limited numbers and sections of the community engage with planning, especially in the development of policy. Despite efforts being made to engage a variety of groups, successes have been short-lived and are heavily reliant on enthusiastic individuals and the political commitment of time and resources (Booth, 1996). The Local Plan-making system, coordinated by the local authority, is the cornerstone of local policy, although much recent attention has focused on Neighbourhood Planning. Research continues to show that the public, whether making representations as part of a group or as individuals, consider their viewpoints to have little influence on policy-making, and despite initiatives to encourage further participation, significant barriers remain (see Baker et al., 2010; Bedford et al., 2002; Beebeejaun, 2004).

When initiatives have been developed such as the extensive work in the preparation of the Sheffield Unitary Development Plan to target a range of groups, including women, unemployed people, parents with young children, and people with disabilities, the outcomes were mixed and the initiative did not continue (Booth, 1996). The Leeds Unitary Development Plan made extensive efforts to involve the public, and lasted from initial consultation in 1992 to final adoption in August 2001. Around 27,000 objections were received during the different stages of progress. By some measures, it seems to be a successful example of engaging the public and generating interest in planning. However, it supported a rationale for streamlining the plan-making system, given the resource implications and length of the process. The time-length needed for good or extensive participation is not supported by the current government. Successive governments since Thatcher have unsuccessfully tried to reconcile a speedy planning system with participation.

Current data collected by the Planning Inspectorate shows that 90 English local authorities adopted plans dating from before December 2010.[4] The government stated in 2015 that local authorities whose adopted plans were more than five years old would be subject to intervention:

> In cases where no Local Plan has been produced by early 2017 – five years after the publication of the NPPF – we will intervene to arrange for the Plan to be written, in consultation with local people, to accelerate production of a Local Plan.
>
> (Department of Communities and Local Government, 2015)

Given the resource constraints on local authorities and the strict timescales, extensive public consultation seems more threatened by the current planning regime.

Without a clear rationale for participation, we might ask why resources should be spent on extensive consultation, especially as it is not always clear what influence it has on decisions and policy. Rydin and Pennington (2000) note that participation is based on a variety of overlapping arguments: firstly, that in a democratic society people have the right to be heard; secondly, that it can lead to 'better' policy-making that draws upon local knowledge and values, and that this can be effective in reducing conflict. They go on to question each of these assumptions, arguing that the active minority who participate are often NIMBYs, that public participation is never stable, and that given the difficulties of engaging with a variety of technical forms of information, the quality of participation is poor. These criticisms are reflective of many concerns regarding public participation.

A key argument for increasing public participation is to ensure that a greater variety of perspectives and values are drawn into the planning system. Greater participation may help to ensure greater legitimacy and enable local communities to feel ownership of decisions (Healey, 1997). However, there is no direct line of representation when planning tries to engage with either communities of interest or individual members of the public. While local councillors are elected, there are struggles around attempts to graft on participatory and deliberative forms of democracy to the bureaucracies of the planning system (see Legacy, 2012). Whose voices count, and where does accountability lie?

However, large-scale participation creates new challenges. The Leeds Unitary Development Plan process was extremely time-consuming, given the number of representations made. Planners face difficulties in making sense of large-scale participation if it covers many policy areas. In contrast, representations about development will often have a clear response. We are seeing increased mobilisation by the public against forms of development. Cases such as Stuttgart 21 have revealed that even when planners attempt to build in long-term consultation, public protests can still emerge (Novy and Peters, 2012). Large-scale responses of the public offer no guarantee of significant change to development, as such representations can be quickly dismissed by the planning system (Beebeejaun, 2016). An application for an exploratory well for shale gas development in Lancashire at Preston New Road garnered 18,022 objections from individuals as well as five petitions (32,529 signatories), several representations from non-governmental organisations objecting, and 217 representations in support. The planning officer noted: "3013 of the objections were from within Fylde and this is 4.87% of the adult population (3.99% of the total population of Fylde)" (Perigo, 2015: 71). These are people living within the immediate vicinity of the proposal.

Several planning applications for shale gas extraction received the largest number of objections that Lancashire County Council had ever received. However, in the planning committee, the chief planning officer and others asserted that these were only a small number of the public, and did not represent the viewpoints of the majority. This discounting of public interest in planning raises important questions regarding arguments of deliberative engagement, as without a clear mandate for participation, public voices can be silenced by simplistic arguments because a majority will never participate actively in planning (Rydin and Pennington, 2000).

The Wrong Kind of Public

Arguments regarding the legitimacy of public participation have generally been used to highlight how certain groups, particularly middle-class people, are over-represented in planning. The notion of a lack of an engaged public links to further critique that pits the silent majority against this presumed vocal minority. Here, questions regarding public contributions to knowledge are important to planning become central to participation.

Public participation is a means of bringing new forms of knowledge to planning, particularly local understandings of place (Bickerstaff, 2012). When public participation becomes mobilised against the planning system, often communities are charged with NIMBYism (Inch, 2012). Furthermore, in recent decades, a literature has emerged that is sceptical of the benefits of public opinion in making planning decisions, arguing that mechanisms are needed to overcome or neutralise forms of opposition (see Bell et al., 2005; Metze, 2014). Participation itself is sometimes described as a form of 'tyranny' over legitimate state decision-making (see Cooke and Kothari, 2001). This is further exacerbated in the UK context due to its perceived mundane and bureaucratic nature (Huxley, 2013) and a scepticism that communities themselves are able to promote a viewpoint beyond selfish self-interest (see Inch, 2012). These presumptions of self-interest rely on the notion of an unreflexive public who require education in order to understand planning matters. In many ways, this argument echoes the dispute over scientific and technical decision-making, where for some the public lack the credentials to assess matters. But critics of this perspective note that those who dismiss the public represent science as apart from the social and political sphere, and a form of neutral decision-making. A more sophisticated understanding of science and the public is needed (Keller, 2009; Feenberg, 2010).

A wealth of literature has rejected NIMBYism as providing a too simplistic rebuttal to public concerns. Some critics draw upon environmental psychology to argue that proposals that lead to fundamental changes to local places create anxiety and opposition (see Devine-Wright, 2013) or note that histories are neglected in planning decisions (Bickerstaff, 2012). Others argue that if we assess the actions of so-called NIMBYs using alternate frameworks, we in fact discover strong communities engaged in civic action (McClymont and O'Hare, 2008). The field of citizen science has developed further insights into the limitations of data collection by public bodies and the important role citizens play in developing nuanced data (Corburn, 2003).

Here we return to the contradictions of participation as central to planning, but within a pro-growth agenda and a set of policies with which the public must grapple to render their voice hearable. My research on opposition to fracking in Lancashire revealed a more complex picture of communities (see Beebeejaun, 2016). Objectors encompassed a wide range of different groups that shared concern about shale gas development, but represented several disparate interests. Strategies ranged from direct action and environmental activism to a sustained engagement with councillors and the local authority. However, objectors realised the importance of articulating their concerns following planning guidance. Local groups helped to develop template letters that set out objections in a planning framework, and not addressing wider concerns such as climate change or pollution as these were outside the remit of the planning system. Despite the attempts to engage with planning matters, and an extremely extensive response within the planning report and the assessments produced by the applicant, it was recommended that the site be approved, with conditions being placed on traffic and noise.

Residents were concerned about a range of issues, but were told that these were within the remit of other regulatory agencies. Planning became a proxy arena for the democratic debate. However, there are risks for communities which try to engage in planning debates. In attempting to reframe concerns within the language of planning policy to render themselves hearable, they place themselves within the problematic expert/lay binary. While planners may not hold significant expertise on all areas of the debate, they certainly are expert on the planning system. Thus, it becomes easier to discount community viewpoints due to the superior expertise of officers in understanding the planning system. In some local media, the planning conditions led to reports that characterised communities as NIMBYs, only concerned with local matters such as noise, and not climate change, as their wider concerns were cut out of debate (Beebeejaun, 2016). Engaging in the planning process reframed the voices of these objectors into NIMBY concerns, as issues such as climate change were not dealt with in the planning process (on housing, see Inch, 2012). Thus, participation holds great risks for communities which give their time and resources without charge and may end up not only being misheard, but to some extent misrepresented.

Conclusions

Despite the critique of participation within English planning outlined in this chapter, there remains hope for change. Achieving this will require a significant realignment of the planning system, either within the system itself or through more radical empowerment of civil society – something that the former UK Prime Minister David Cameron's Big Society failed to achieve in the early 2010s. Katie McClymont (2011: 253) is deeply critical of the "hegemony of consensus", arguing that the lack of democratic debate regarding the values of planning creates a context in which those who disagree with government are seen as "acting against the national interest; they are thus denied a legitimate voice in the debate". She argues that development decisions provide a much needed space for debates about the planning values at local level.

Acknowledging the importance of conflict in adding value to participation is an important step that may help reconnect to some of the radical roots of planning. By engaging with conflict, important questions of value can be addressed. However, it does not help us to sufficiently address deep divides in society that cannot be healed through deliberation, and instead may be exacerbated. The political theorist Lynn Sanders (1997) makes some important arguments against deliberation that are echoed in critiques of public participation. Aspects of her argument are well-known, and she draws on examinations of jury deliberations to note the problems of power relations between different identity groups, and the ways that the rules of debate favour some people over others. Her argument is helpful to clarify that while much participatory theory favours the inclusion of marginalised voices, they are simply further disenfranchised through current manifestations of deliberation.

Lynn Sanders (1997) draws on the concept of testimony to argue that we must be open to difference ways of understanding others: "When the perspective of some citizens is systematically suppressed in public discourse, then democratic politics should aim simply and first to ensure the expression of those excluded perspectives" (Sanders, 1997: 372). These criticisms still ring true, and efforts at participation in planning are marred by more fundamental democratic failures within society. Neighbourhood Planning's results are mixed, but do not indicate a radical shift within planning. Participants have to prepare plans that conform to national planning policy, and there is evidence that the process may create disillusionment with the planning system (Brookfield, 2017).

It would seem the tendency for platitudinous statements regarding public involvement and the discounting of public perspectives may be reaching a crisis point. I was astounded when a course I teach on urban politics was very recently criticised by a planning practitioner for insufficiently addressing NIMBYism and how communities are open to bribes, something they asserted everyone knew. Of course, it is important not to fall prey to normative overly romanticised ideas about participation and the community. Even the Skeffington Report (Skeffington Committee, 1969) acknowledged that the community can be bigoted and the local authority authoritarian in attitude. Yet such statements fail to acknowledge how the interests of some sectors of the community, particularly development interests, are deeply intertwined with the ethos and operation of the planning system and the constraint of a pro-growth planning system. Starting from presumptions that communities present problems makes it difficult to shift to meaningful forms of engagement. Equally, the current constraints of the planning system ensure that it is challenging to make positive contributions to the planning arena.

Links between planning theory and practice remain an area of concern. For educators, there remain important advances we can make in linking conceptual insights about participation with empowering professionals to take into account the many barriers between planners and communities, and to try to design engagement that is more sensitive to these power imbalances. At a more basic level, research continues to suggest that planners struggle to create participatory processes that engage or even provide clear information on complex development decisions. This is, in part, due to the continuing under-resourcing of planning services, exacerbated through austerity.

For various reasons, there has been a lack of development of participatory practices from within the planning profession. A large degree of fault can be attributed to successive governments which have constantly changed the legislative framework and have tended to resource and promote community engagement outside mainstream planning. The de-prioritisation of professionals as facilitators of community engagement through putative grassroots initiatives such as Neighbourhood Planning, alongside the intensification of attempts to streamline planning processes, do not aid in developing reflective and often time-consuming participatory practices.

Community campaigns and opposition can build solidarity and valuable forms of civic engagement. While the Lancashire activists mentioned earlier are still engaged with the planning process, many efforts have now been moved to direct action. While their arguments were listened to by local councillors, the planning application was called in and approved by central government. While the capacity that is being built can be seen as positive for civic engagement, it raises concerns regarding the ways in which the planning may become increasingly irrelevant in public campaigns. Some of the basic production of information, arguably the work of the local authority, was developed by opposition groups. While this was subsequently critiqued for being biased, similar scrutiny was not applied to the applicant's material or that of the local authority. It is troubling that some of the basic conditions to enable public participation, namely comprehensible and comprehensive information, are not the norm within the planning system. Greater attention to more robust public engagement, drawing on disciplines outside planning, remains important. Here, perhaps, planners may be able to draw upon lessons from Neighbourhood Planning. How do 'non-specialist' planners seek to engage their own communities, and what kinds of efforts do they make to create legible materials? Currently, the lack of capacity for civic action to be a positive feature of planning system, and the potential for conflict to lead to mutual understanding, are troubling. If public participation is undesirable to the 'silent majority' and the knowledge of the vocal minority is marginal to planning decisions, it may point towards the declining significance of planning.

Notes

1 For studies of these processes, the work of David Madden, Janet, Smith, John Flint, Loretta Lees, Tom Slater and others provides a much-needed critique of the current state of our attitudes towards housing the poor.
2 HC Deb 29 January 1947, vol 432, c 963.
3 The *Equalities Impact Assessment for Neighbourhood Planning* details how groups including ethnic minorities and people in lower-income areas are less likely to participate in planning. However, it concludes: "No groups representing black, Asian and minority ethnic communities or people with disabilities have yet come forward to express concerns about the proposals but, if they do so, we shall discuss their concerns with them and consider how they may be addressed." This demonstrates both how little thought is given to these issues and also how bureaucratic mechanisms to engage with equality can be useless.
4 The Core Strategy is the principal planning document of the Local Development Framework, which also comprises a number of supplementary planning documents. The rationale for moving to this system from the previous production of plans was to streamline the system and increase speed and efficiency.

References

All listed URLs were last accessed on 1 March 2018.

Aitken, M. (2009) Wind power planning controversies and the construction of "expert" and "lay" knowledges, *Science as Culture*, 18(1), pp.47–64.

Baker, M., Hincks, S. and Sherriff, G. (2010) Getting involved in plan making: participation and stakeholder involvement in local and regional spatial strategies in England, *Environment and Planning C: Government and Policy*, 28(4), pp.574–594.

Bedford, T., Clark, J. and Harrison, C. (2002) Limits to new public participation practices in local land use planning, *Town Planning Review*, 73(3), pp.311–331.

Beebeejaun, Y. (2004) What's in a nation? Constructing ethnicity in the British planning system, *Planning Theory & Practice*, 5(4), pp.437–451.

Beebeejaun, Y. (2006) The participation trap: the limitations of participation for ethnic and racial groups, *International Planning Studies*, 11(1), pp.3–18.

Beebeejaun, Y. (2016) Exploring the intersections between local knowledge and environmental regulation: a study of shale gas extraction in Texas and Lancashire, *Environment and Planning C: Government and Policy*. DOI: 10.1177/0263774X16664905.

Bell, D., Gray, T. and Haggett, C. (2005) The "social gap" in wind farm siting decisions: explanations and policy responses, *Environmental Politics*, 14(4), pp.460–477.

Bickerstaff, K. (2012) "Because we've got history here": nuclear waste, cooperative siting, and the relationship geography of a complex issue, *Environment and Planning C*, 44(11), pp.2611–2628.

Booth, C. (1996) Gender and public consultation: case studies of Leicester, Sheffield and Birmingham, *Planning Practice and Research*, 11(1), pp.9–18.

Brookfield, K. (2017) Getting involved in plan-making: participation in neighbourhood planning in England, *Environment and Planning C: Politics and Space*, 35(3), pp.397–416.

Campbell, H. (2012) Planning to change the world: between knowledge and action lies synthesis, *Journal of Planning Education and Research*, 32(2), pp.135–146.

Chapman, R. and Lowndes, V. (2009) Accountable, authorised or authentic? What do faith representatives offer urban governance? *Public Money and Management*, 29(6), pp.371–378.

Clarke, L. and Agyeman, J. (2011) Is there more to environmental participation than meets the eye? Understanding agency, empowerment and disempowerment among black and minority ethnic communities, *Area*, 43(1), 88–95.

Clifford, B. (2016) "Clock-watching and box-ticking": British local authority planners, professionalism and performance targets, *Planning Practice & Research*, 31(4), 383–401.

Cooke, B. and Kothari, U. (2001) *Participation, the new tyranny?* London: Zed Books.

Corburn, J. (2003) Bringing local knowledge into environmental decision making: improving urban planning for communities at risk, *Journal of Planning Education and Research*, 22(4), pp.420–433.

Cullingworth, J.B. (ed.) (1999) *British planning: 50 years of urban and regional policy*. London: Athlone Press.

Dargan, L. (2009) Participation and local urban regeneration: the case of the New Deal for Communities (NDC) in the UK, *Regional Studies*, 43(2), pp.305–317.

Department of Communities and Local Government (2015) Local Plans: written statement – HCWS172. House of Commons Debate, 21 July, col. *86WS*. Available at: www.parliament.uk/business/publications/written-questions-answers-statements/written-statement/Commons/2015-07-21/HCWS172/.

Devine-Wright, P. (2013) Explaining "NIMBY" objections to a power line: the role of personal place attachment and project-related factors, *Environment and Behaviour*, 45(6) pp.761–781.

Doan, P.L. (2015) Why plan for the LGBTQ community? In P.L. Doan (ed.) *Planning and LGBTQ communities: the need for inclusive queer spaces*. New York: Routledge, pp.1–15.

Durose, C., Beebeejaun, Y., Rees, J., Richardson, J. and Richardson, L. (2012) *Towards co-production in research with communities*. Swindon: Arts and Humanities Research Council Connected Communities Programme.

Feenberg, A. (2010) *Between reason and experience: essays on technology and modernity*. Cambridge, MA: MIT Press.

Fung, A. (2009) *Empowered participation: reinventing urban democracy*. Princeton, NJ: Princeton University Press.

Healey, P. (1997) *Collaborative planning: shaping places in fragmented societies*. Basingstoke: Macmillan.

Huxley, M. (2013) Historicizing planning, problematizing participation, *International Journal of Urban and Regional Research*, 37(5), pp.1527–1541.

Inch, A. (2012) Creating "a generation of NIMBYs"? Interpreting the role of the state in managing the politics of urban development, *Environment and Planning C: Government and Policy*, 30(3), pp.520–535.

Innes, J.E. and Booher, D.E. (2004) Reframing public participation: strategies for the 21st century, *Planning Theory & Practice*, 5(4), pp.419–436.

Keller, A.C. (2009) *Science in environmental policy making: the politics of objective advice*. Boston, MA: MIT Press.

Krishnarayan, V. and Thomas, H. (1993) *Ethnic minorities and the planning system*. London: Royal Town Planning Institute.

Legacy, C. (2010) Investigating the knowledge interface between stakeholder engagement and plan-making, *Environment and Planning A*, 42(11), pp.2705–2720.

Legacy, C. (2012) Achieving legitimacy through deliberative plan-making processes – lessons for metropolitan strategic planning, *Planning Theory & Practice*, 13(1), pp.71–87.

Mace, A. (2013) Delivering local plans: recognising the bounded interests of local planners within spatial planning, *Environment and Planning C: Government and Policy*, 31(6), 1133–1146.

McClymont, K. (2011) Revitalising the political: development control and agonism in planning practice, *Planning Theory*, 10(3), pp.239–256.

McClymont, K. and O'Hare, P. (2008) We're not NIMBYs! Contrasting local protest groups with idealised conceptions of sustainable communities, *Local Environment*, 13(4), pp.321–355.

Metze, T. (2014) Fracking the debate: frame shifts and boundary work in Dutch decision making on shale gas, *Journal of Environmental Policy and Planning* 19(1), pp.35–52.

Novy, J. and Peters, D. (2012) Railway station mega-projects as public controversies: the case of Stuttgart 21, *Built Environment*, 38(1), pp.128–145.

Parker, G. and Salter, K. (2017) Taking stock of neighbourhood planning in England 2011–2016, *Planning Practice & Research*, pp.1–13.

Perigo, S. (2015) *Report to the Development Management Committee*, 29 June. Preston: Lancashire County Council.

Raco, M. and Flint, J. (2001) Communities, places and institutional relations: assessing the role of area-based community representation in local governance, *Political Geography*, 20(5), pp.585–612.

Royal Town Planning Institute/Commission for Racial Equality Working Party (1983) *Planning for a multiracial Britain: report*. London: Commission for Racial Equality.

Rydin, Y. (1999) Public participation in planning. In J.B. Cullingworth (ed.) *British planning: 50 years of urban and regional policy*. London: Athlone Press.

Rydin, Y. and Pennington, M. (2000) Public participation and local environmental planning: the collective action problem and the potential of social capital, *Local Environment*, 5(2), pp.153–169.

Sanders, L.M. (1997) Against deliberation, *Political Theory*, 25(3), pp.347–376.

Scottish Government (2017) *Scottish Planning Review: Participation Review*. Edinburgh: Scottish Government.

Skeffington Committee (1969) *Report of the Committee on Public Participation in Planning*. London: HMSO.

Sundaresan, J. (2016) The politics of participation in the land-use planning of Bangalore, India. In Y. Beebeejaun (ed.) *The participatory city*. Berlin: JOVIS, pp.46–53.

Sweet, E.L. and Ortiz Escalante, S. (2015) Bringing bodies into planning: visceral methods, fear and gender violence, *Urban Studies*, 52(10), pp.1826–1845.

Taylor, M. (2007) Community participation in the real world: opportunities and pitfalls in new governance spaces, *Urban Studies*, 44(2), pp.297–317.

Thomas, H. (2004) *Race and planning: the UK experience*. London: Routledge.

Thomas, H. and Krishnarayan, V. (1994a) "Race", disadvantage, and policy processes in British planning, *Environment and Planning A*, 26(12), pp.1891–1910.

Thomas, H. and Krishnarayan, V. (1994b) *Race, equality, and planning: policies and procedures*. London: Royal Town Planning Institute.

Thomas, J.M. (2016) Community organising, planning, and racial marginalization. In Y. Beebeejaun (ed.) *The participatory city*. Berlin: JOVIS, pp.96–103.

Thomas, J.M. and Ritzdorf, M. (eds) (1997) *Urban planning and the African American community: in the shadows*. Thousand Oaks, CA: SAGE Publications

7 The Design Dimension of Planning

Making Planning Proactive Again

Matthew Carmona

A century ago, planning was largely a physical preoccupation, with architects (the master) producing grand visions for cities and neighbourhoods (masterplanning) that were then implemented, often with little political discussion and certainly no citizen engagement in those plans. While this very narrow and top-down type of planning went out of fashion (indeed, was discredited) many decades ago, this chapter argues that in the face of the global and local challenges discussed in earlier chapters, there is a need to remember some of this early vision and to make planning proactive once again. This design dimension of planning requires that planners do more than simply allocate sites, write policies and regulate development; it requires that they bring forward positive visions for change. The chapter discusses some of the conundrums associated with such an approach and considers the best tools to improve practice in the future.

A Bumpy Road

In the UK, as elsewhere globally, planning has been on a journey. From its beginnings as a physical subject, by the 1960s and 1970s it had completely rejected such approaches in favour of systems thinking in which cities and regions were seen as a series of overlapping social and economic systems that could be tweaked through policy in order to manage growth or decline. By this time, few planners were receiving any design training as part of their university education, and the professions of architecture and planning took divergent paths, with disastrous consequences: planning was increasingly divorced from a place perspective and from a sense of its ultimate impact on the built and natural environment, while architecture was increasingly divorced from any serious engagement with the social and economic consequences of design.

While other countries recovered their confidence more quickly and in the 1980s began to systematically address issues of physical planning alongside their social, economic and environmental aspirations (notably parts of Continental Europe), in the UK it took a little longer. Indeed, up until the mid-1990s an unwarranted nervousness persisted within government over conflating design with planning at all, reinforced in the 1980s by a strong concern to avoid what was seen as undue interference in the market (a perspective that has returned to some degree in the austerity years).

A first toe back in the water was the commissioning by the government in 1993 of research that eventually led to the publication of the book *The Design Dimension of Planning* (Punter and Carmona, 1997). The 'Pink Book', as my co-author Professor John Punter (commenting on my design for the front cover – Figure 7.1) christened it, argued first, for the central role of design within the planning system, and second, that this should begin with the comprehensive treatment of design within the new generation of local planning authority development plans – in other words, in planning policy. Today, while I still hold to the first of these principles, I am now far less convinced about the second, precisely because abstract policy can never be a substitute for truly proactive planning that more clearly defines aspirations for how places should be. At the time, however, we argued that design policies within development plans had the potential to:

- establish and articulate the spatial vision of the plan;
- reflect the design aspirations of the local community and other stakeholders;
- guide the 'process' of design as well as the outcomes;
- give designers, developers and the community greater certainty;
- move beyond a narrow aesthetic to a more fundamental place-making view of design;
- deliver a more positive, enabling and even visionary planning process.

During the 1990s and into the 2000s, the government gradually warmed up to the idea of design quality as a political objective, and national policy in Scotland and then in England (and a little later in other parts of the UK) caught up with what we were advocating, moving from a prohibitive to a permissive environment as far as the treatment of design through

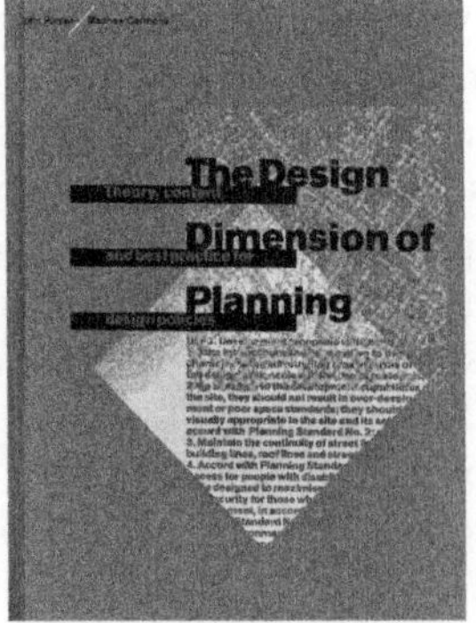

Figure 7.1 The 'Pink Book'

the planning system was concerned. Indeed, following the creation of the Commission for Architecture and the Built Environment (CABE) in 1999 as a body dedicated to moving the national culture away from a 'development at any costs' model to one based on adding value through design, for a time the national policy environment exceeded even our wildest dreams of what might be possible (Carmona et al., 2017). That was until the financial crisis of 2008 hit, leading to the eventual demise of CABE, retreat of the government from engaging with design, a dramatic hollowing out of design skills within local authorities as discretionary activities were quickly cut, and a growing obsession with the quantity of development above all else, and certainly above its quality. Planning in England, perhaps more than any other policy arena, and more so than other parts of the UK (which retained their equivalents of CABE), is and remains a roller-coaster, and nowhere more so than as it relates to design.

So, with all this going on, was our faith in the potential of the statutory development plan to establish and deliver a clear local design vision and agenda justified? Before we get to that, first it is worth considering some of the key themes and problematics associated with any attempt to engage in design, whether in England, elsewhere in the UK, or overseas.

The Problem with Design Governance

> It seems that whatever the system, whatever the governance, no matter what our rules and regulations, however we organise our professions, and no matter what our histories, placeless design seems to be the inevitable consequence of development processes outside our historic city centres. Moreover, this is despite the ubiquitous condemnation of such environments as sub-standard by almost every built environment professional you ever meet.
>
> (Carmona, 2010a)

This was the somewhat damning conclusion from a European research project that focused on the governance of design beyond the Continent's historic city centres. So what do the various systems investigated (and many more beyond Europe) have in common? One aspect is a crude love of standards and regulations as a substitute for design: parking standards, highways regulations, zoning controls, density guidelines, health and safety regulations, construction codes and the like. Typically, these are limited in their scope, technical in their aspiration, not generated out of a place-based vision, and imposed on projects without regard to outcomes. Nobody is consciously designing the places that emerge – just the parts: a housing estate, a road, a cycle track, some signage etc. In a neo-liberal world where the unskilled application of such standards is all there is to safeguard the public interest, the danger is that the work of unscrupulous private developers will largely go unchecked, while the work of enlightened developers will be needlessly and crudely undermined.

All this raises the thorny question of design quality, and what we mean by it? ‘Design quality’ means different things to different actors, and there is often little consensus on the scope of design in the built environment (from a narrow aesthetic perspective to a broad holistic view of place), let alone what, in any given circumstance, qualifies as ‘good’ or ‘bad’ quality design (Carmona, 2016). The endless circular debates that characterise so many of the exchanges between traditionalists and modernists within the architectural profession represent a case-in-point.

Like other aspects of planning, processes of design governance ultimately restrict private property rights, and those who perceive their freedom to design to be most directly affected – typically, designers and developers – often resist such intervention the hardest (Walters, 2007: 132–133). For their part, planners have not always had the confidence and training to define and deliver a positive public design agenda. As one commentator on the state of British planning recently complained: “Vision is something that your average planner simply does not have . . . . Hence noddy box/upvc heaven from one end of the country to the other” (P. Bellay, reader’s comment in Mallett, 2013).

Despite this (perhaps because of it), public authorities (including, but not limited to, planning authorities) have typically been highly adept at applying the sorts of ‘technical’ standards and regulations previously referred to. The question then arises, might it be possible to raise the general standard and expectations in order to focus mainstream efforts more concertedly on higher-order principles, those associated with the making of coherent, sustainable, equitable and life-affirming places? This is the design governance conundrum: can state intervention in processes of designing the built environment positively shape design processes and outcomes, and if so, how? There are certainly plenty of good examples where this has occurred, almost always defined by the public sector playing a far more proactive role in shaping the built environment (Figure 7.2).

The Design Governance Conundrum

Here, we need to be careful. More public intervention might seem to be the most appropriate response to poor place-making (correcting the market failure), but the presumption that more design regulation will, *ipso facto*, lead to better design must be treated with caution:

- In some places there may be no market failure, but instead a failure in governance or regulation.
- Sometimes the solution may be worse than the problem – for example, the creation of a safe street environment, but one that no one wishes to inhabit because it is devoid of character.
- Narrow ‘conservative’ thinking may create barriers to change and innovation in design.

Figure 7.2 Birmingham: the team working on the centre of the city from the late 1980s onwards transformed it from a vehicle- to people-dominated space

Source: Matthew Carmona.

Regulatory economists argue that regulation is inherently costly and inefficient, but difficult to challenge because of what Peter Van Doren (2005: 45, 64) of the right-wing CATO Institute calls: 'bootleggers' (special interests who gain from regulation) and 'baptists' (those who do not like the behaviour of others, and want government to restrict it). Yet even the least regulated places in the developed world impose controls of some sort or other on the use of space. Houston, for example (discussed in Chapter 1 by John Tomaney and Jessica Ferm) is often identified as the only major US city without zoning controls. But even there, ordinances are adopted to alleviate a host of land use problems, including banning nuisances, imposing off-street parking, and regulating minimum lot, density and land use requirements – in other words, zoning by other means (Siegan, 2005: 227).

Two questions arise from this: first, not 'whether', but 'what type of', intervention should occur, and second, at what point will this be most effective? The first question will be determined by the choice of tools available and our ability to use them (and we will come back to that), but taking the second question first, here it is important to make a key conceptual distinction about the role of planning in relation to design, as opposed to private (or public) sector project design.

The 'When' Question

Varkki George (1997: 151–152) makes the important distinction between first- and second-order design processes:

> In first-order design, the designer usually has control over, is involved in, or is directly responsible for all design decisions. . . . Second-order design is appropriate to a situation characterised by distributed decision-making because the design solution is specified at a more abstract level and is, therefore, applicable across a wider range of situations.

He argues that most urban design falls into the second category – characterised by distributed decision-making – as opposed to architecture, which is typically in the first camp.

Design, in the context of planning, needs to deal with shifting and complex economic, social, political, legal and stakeholder environments, and with how places change over very long time horizons. Second-order design is particularly suited to such turbulent decision-making environments because it is more strategic in nature, specifying what is critical to define, and ignoring what is not. The governance of design should therefore be about shaping the decision-making environment within which design decision-making occurs, rather than being concerned with making all of the design decisions.

This in turn should shape an 'opportunity space' within which a creative design and development process can occur (Tiesdell and Adams, 2004) – in other words, establishing the sorts of key parameters and constraints that are necessary for that process to thrive and deliver 'good design'. It follows that in order to be both influential and impactful on design outcomes (and despite the numerical contradiction), this second-order process needs to come before the act of project design – in other words, first. This may raise alarm bells among those seeking to deregulate the development process (as has happened in the UK in recent years), but evidence consistently demonstrates that the increased certainty, coordination and consensus it builds actually helps to streamline the planning process (Carmona and Giordano, 2013).

The 'How' Question

Moving on to the question of what type of intervention, in fact there is a sophisticated toolbox available, as my own research on the work and impact of CABE has demonstrated (see Carmona et al., 2017) (Figure 7.3). Many of these tools operate outside formal regulatory processes and

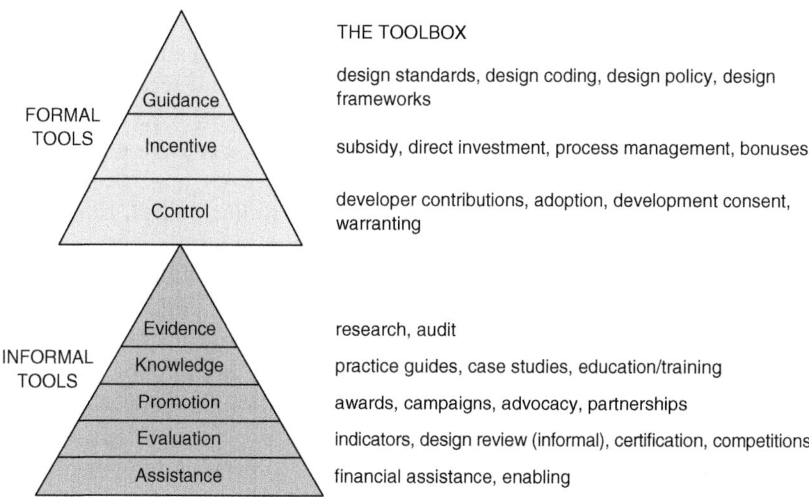

Figure 7.3 The design governance toolbox
Source: Matthew Carmona.

within the realm of informal tools of design governance (Carmona, 2017). They demonstrate the potential and opportunities available to local planning authorities (and others) to work beyond their statutory powers in order to deliver a positive opportunity space within which places can be successfully shaped. This potentially reverses a situation where planners have over-relied on their regulatory powers and have then faced confrontation and delay, instead of consensus and collaboration.

The informal tools can be classified into five categories that move from hands-off and informative to hands-on and proactive, while always advisory, and never statutory:

- *Evidence tools* gather information through focused *research* about design and design processes in order to support arguments about the importance of design, underpin advice about what works and what does not, and as a means to monitor progress towards particular policy objectives or to gauge the state of the built environment. This includes large-scale *audits* of particular development types (e.g. housing) or of particular locations, such as those undergoing rapid change.
- *Knowledge tools* articulate and disseminate knowledge about the nature of successful design, good and poor design practice, and why it matters. This can be expressed through the production of *practice guides* that focus on particular topics or issues (e.g. design for accessibility), the compilation of published *case studies* of best practice, and through *education and training* with a focus on design

knowledge and skills (e.g. design training for local politicians involved in making planning decisions).

- *Promotion tools* make the case for design quality in a more proactive manner by taking knowledge to key audiences and seeking to package messages in a manner that engages attention, wins over hearts and minds, and exhorts particular behaviours. Promotion initiatives include the introduction of local *design awards* (e.g. annually or bi-annually for the best developments in a municipality), *campaigning* around particular issues that undermine environmental quality (e.g. the cumulative impact of minor alterations on local character), *advocacy* work, engaging particular development partners in a more focused fashion in order to advance clear design aspirations (e.g. within the local highways authority), and the building of more formal *partnerships* with like-minded organisations (e.g. developers or housing associations).
- *Evaluation tools* allow systematic and objective judgements to be made about the quality of design by parties external to, and therefore detached from, the design process or product being evaluated. These include the use of *indicators* designed to systemise and structure decision-making processes on design (e.g. the Scottish Government's Place Standard[1]), informal *design review* conducted by an independent design review panel (either within or external to the local authority), the use of external *certification* schemes (e.g. Building for Life[2]); and the use of *design competitions* for specific high-profile sites or projects.
- *Assistance tools* use more proactive means to engage the public sector directly in projects or in otherwise shaping the decision-making environment within which design occurs. They include the provision of direct *financial assistance* to initiatives that act to enlarge the opportunity space for good design (e.g. providing financial support for a local architecture centre) and the use of direct *enabling* within the design process itself. This might encompass the parachuting in of external expert design assistance to advise on, for example, the briefing or commissioning processes associated with an important project, or alternatively the temporary secondment of expertise into a team to help prepare policy, guidance or to provide dedicated design expertise on a challenging planning application.

And That's Not All . . .

While such informal tools can be incredibly powerful for building an informed, responsive and creative design decision-making environment, none are among the most powerful tools in the box. That accolade belongs instead to tools in the formal category that are established in statute and backed by formal regulatory powers. There are three categories here, each with strong place-shaping capabilities (Carmona, 2017) as part of a continuum from advice through to compulsion, or from lesser to greater intervention:

- *Guidance* focuses on the 'positive' encouraging of appropriate development via the production of a range of plans and guides that give a direction for, but not an end solution to, design proposals. In other words, rather than a blueprint (as would be delivered through a fixed masterplan), they provide a trellis up which public design aspirations can grow. They include *design standards* (fixed technical and generic standards), *design coding* (three-dimensional site or area-specific codes), *design policy* (the focus of the 'Pink Book', namely flexible generic policy aspirations requiring case-by-case interpretation), and *design frameworks* (flexible spatial design propositions for particular areas or large sites). Of the formal guidance tools, standards and policy focus on setting out the parameters by which development will be negotiated and assessed, typically under statutory (enforceable) powers, while frameworks and codes are more propositional, shaping change in a more directive manner through advancing place-specific visions for change.
- *Incentive* encompasses the active enabling of development seen to be in the public interest by contributing public sector land or resources to the development process or otherwise making development more attractive to landowners and developers. The critical task is not simply to incentivise development, but to incentivise high-quality development. This can be done by adding 'design strings' to any state *subsidy* for, or *direct investment* within, development – in other words, making the state investment contingent on the quality of the outcomes. *Process management* of regulatory processes can also be used to encourage good design, for example by fast-tracking high-quality schemes, and development *bonuses* can be offered in exchange for particular design outcomes (e.g. higher density in exchange for a high-quality public realm).
- *Control* represents the ultimate sanction of the state, care of the ability to refuse permission for development via regulation and enforcement, typically involving a range of overlapping regulatory regimes (not just planning). The category encompasses the negotiation of *developer contributions*, granting of *development consents* (e.g. planning permission, or listed building consents), *adoption* of highways and other infrastructure by the state, and the *warranting* of construction standards, through building control. Like other tools, control processes can be shaped in a manner that facilitates or hinders better design. Equally, if incentives are viewed as the 'carrots' for good behaviour, then control might be seen as the 'stick', and as a disincentive to bad behaviours. Control is reactive in nature, and often involves managing a complex bureaucracy. But while in

the UK adoption and warranting typically relate to the imposition of fixed, immutable standards, developer contributions and development consents involve the 'discretionary' weighing and balancing of public against private needs (including those relating to design), care of a highly skilled process of interpretation, typically against flexible policy and guidance. The key challenge when designing regulatory systems for design is to make the 'good' easy and the 'bad' arduous.

Moving to a More Propositional System

While the research reported 20 years ago in the 'Pink Book' focused on just one of the tools – design policy – infusing the work was a larger argument around the need for positive engagement in design, reflecting the potential for a more proactive role for the public sector in shaping places, backed by the ultimate sanction of control. After the research finished, I taught for three years at the University of Nottingham, where I explored some of the ideas in the book via a module that required the class to create their own design chapter for a fictitious local authority. My example of 'what not to do' came from the suburban Nottinghamshire borough in which I lived at the time and whose sole design governance tool was a single "Policy HO7: New Housing Development" from their 1994 Local Plan. This very short policy (just seven lines), was even shorter on substance, and open to huge interpretation, with highly subjective statements such as "New development should be laid out so as to provide a high quality of built environment which is in keeping with its surroundings."

There have been two iterations of the plan in the intervening years. In 2004, the policy was re-named "E1: Good Design", and was now part of the Local Development Framework. In terms of substance, it was slightly longer (14 lines), with reference to a broader range of concerns, including aspirations for better accessibility, sustainable water treatment and a high standard of architectural and landscape design. Again, little clue was given about what this might mean in the context of the borough, with catch-all (and largely meaningless) statements such as that planning permission would not be granted without "The creation or retention of a high standard of amenity for all users of the new development". By 2014, Local Plans had returned, and the single design policy was now more ambitiously titled "Policy 10: Design and Enhancing Local Identity". Longer again (now 28 lines), the policy includes statements such as "All new development should be designed to: make a positive contribution to the public realm and sense of place; . . . permeability and legibility", but little more clue than the 1994 document about how this should shape the nature of the borough or what sort of place that should be. The results on the ground reflect this generally low ambition (Figure 7.4).

The case is simply representative of an approach to design that, rather than seeking to enlarge the opportunity space for good design or to

Figure 7.4 This recent infill housing development was listed on the council's website under the title 'The future of housing design'

Source: Amy Tang.

advance a coherent vision for the future, instead remains too focused on the technocratic processes of allocating sites and regulating development in a reactive manner. As one commentator (Mallett, 2013) has argued about contemporary British planning: "Any attempts to re-introduce 'visioning' into planning have not been taken up by the system as a modus operandi." He asks, "Is this because it is too political to draw what is to become of an area?" and concludes: "we need to rediscover the power of design when we plan". I agree, a 'place-based' understanding of the city is almost entirely absent in our development plans, yet we expend huge amounts of resources worrying about and updating policies that in fact change very little from one decade to the next, as the Nottinghamshire example demonstrates all too clearly.

We Need Better Tools to Do the Job

In the 'Pink Book', we argued:

- Design policies in development plans should be the foundation of a system of design governance.
- Policies should be comprehensive and cover all the key design bases – architecture, urban design, landscape, conservation – and cut across all other policy arenas.
- Policies should derive from a profound engagement with and understanding of context.
- Policies should articulate a clear spatial/design vision.

While I still hold to many of the book's conclusions, particularly those regarding the central position of design within the planning process, I now question whether the development plan is the right tool for the job. All the evidence suggests that we continue to struggle to deliver development plans that do most (perhaps any) of these things. They seem incapable of the level of sophistication we ascribed to them in the book. Instead, development plans remain too static, generic, uncontextual and lacking in inspiration or vision to be effective in driving a coherent place-based agenda forward. They are too often what one interviewee at the time of the original 'Pink Book' research called 'barristers' appendices' (designed to get through the long-winded and pseudo-legal process of inspection and adoption) in a vacuum of creativity and propositional planning.

Rather than static, we need plans that are flexible, site- and area-specific. Rather than generic, uncontextual and lacking in inspiration or vision, we need plans that are place sensitive and directive. In other words, planning needs to engage with the sorts of propositional tools that suggest it has something meaningful to contribute beyond its regulatory role – and something that the communities effected (both public and business communities) can engage with and understand.

While the recent introduction of Neighbourhood Planning in England, Place Plans in Wales and community planning in Scotland and Northern Ireland goes some way to engaging communities, these tools are mired in procedural complexity, and tend to add to rather than cut through the policy morass. During the 2000s, by contrast, a proliferation of tools of a more directive nature were increasingly used: urban design strategies, urban design frameworks, design briefs, spatial masterplans, design codes, design protocols, area action plans, design charters etc. In reality, we can narrow these down to two core and essential propositional tools of design guidance, both of which have already been introduced: design frameworks and design codes.

Propositional Tool 1: The Urban Design Framework

Urban design frameworks are particularly valuable for setting out a clear coordinating vision for an area or site, specifying key spatial relationships, a movement framework, density requirements, landscape, land uses, character areas, public amenities, landmarks, parcelisation etc. Crucially, they are also flexible enough to accommodate change. In London, these sorts of flexible frameworks (not fixed masterplans) have been pioneered by the private sector, often working in close cooperation with public authorities, as was the case at the massive King's Cross development (Bishop and Williams, 2017), and are proving successful in delivering high-quality development within an adaptable framework. Outside London, some of the best frameworks have been produced by the consultancy URBED, including the 2007 Liverpool University Urban

Figure 7.5 Extract from the Liverpool Knowledge Quarter, the Climax Plan

Source: URBED.

Design Framework and later its Knowledge Quarter Plan (Figure 7.5), and in the same year, the Nottingham City Centre Urban Design Guide.[3] They can be equally effective in complex historic areas of incremental change, such as the 6km Aldgate to Stratford stretch of arterial street in London that was covered by the High Street 2012 framework. From 2009, when it was produced, and in the run-up to the Olympic Games, this loose framework guided a range of interventions (some successful, some less so) in the street, with a particular focus on conservation, public realm improvement and the provision of cycle infrastructure.

At the same time, the London Olympics Delivery Authority and (post-games) the London Legacy Development Corporation adopted a similar flexible urban design framework in order to debate alternatives and set out a future strategy for the Olympic Park and its surroundings, and this has been very influential in guiding the radical transformation that is happening there. More recently, this has morphed into a whopping 250-page Local Plan, backed by 550 pages of ancillary documents, all of which substitute clarity and vision for obscure policy stodge.

My own research in London's Docklands (Carmona, 2009b) convinced me of the validity of these tools. In the 1980s and 1990s, the area to the south of Canary Wharf (the Millennium Quarter) developed in an ad hoc and incremental manner, and largely without a coordinating plan. Learning from what had worked in neighbouring Canary Wharf, although this time for an area characterised by piecemeal mixed-use development and multiple complex ownerships, the London Borough of Tower Hamlets decided to address increasing pressure for substantial change through the publication of the 1999 Isle of Dogs Millennium Quarter Masterplan. While called a masterplan, in fact this was a very flexible urban design framework within which a coordinating public realm was established, financial contributions agreed from the multiple competing parties, but flexibility allowed over the forms that buildings took in the light of market uncertainty. The framework was successful in helping to coordinate the massive investments that occurred during the 2000s until superseded in 2015 by the South Quay Masterplan (Figure 7.6). This second framework includes a range of more specific three-dimensional prescriptions for the sorts of podium and tower developments that have come to dominate the area, and reflects the drive to deliver more residential development at higher densities than the earlier framework had envisaged.

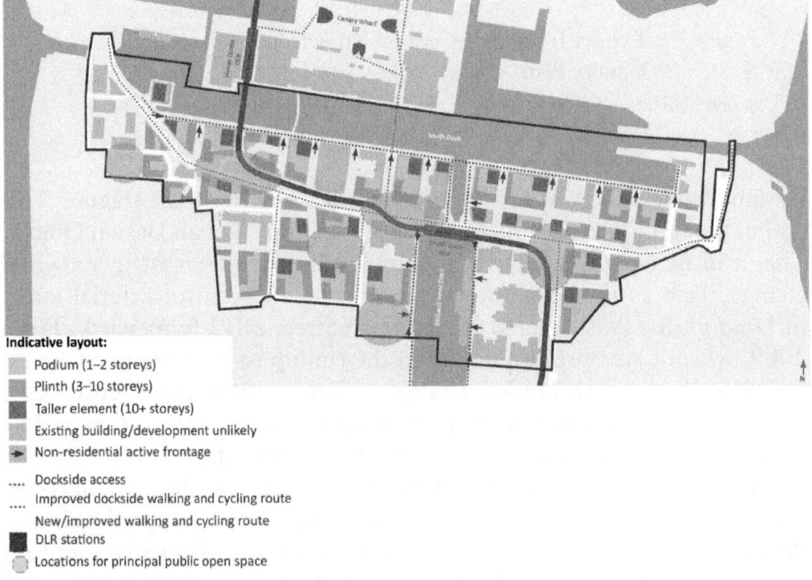

Figure 7.6 Extract from the South Quay Masterplan

Source: London Borough of Tower Hamlets.

Propositional Tool 2: The Design Code

This brings us to the second key tool for a more directive and propositional planning, the design code. Design codes are:

- design guidance for large sites or areas where specification of the whole is coded into parts;
- designed using a limited number of coded components that may be put together in different ways to generate a multitude of final outcomes;
- usually produced to support the delivery of an urban design framework.

They are delivery (not vision-making) tools that are particularly suited to ensuring the coherent delivery of complex multi-phased schemes, which (ideally) focus on establishing and fixing the essential urbanistic components of place (Carmona, 2009a), for example: plot coverage, building lines and setbacks, street widths, frontage treatments, public realm treatments, landscape components, building heights, forms and massing (Figure 7.7).

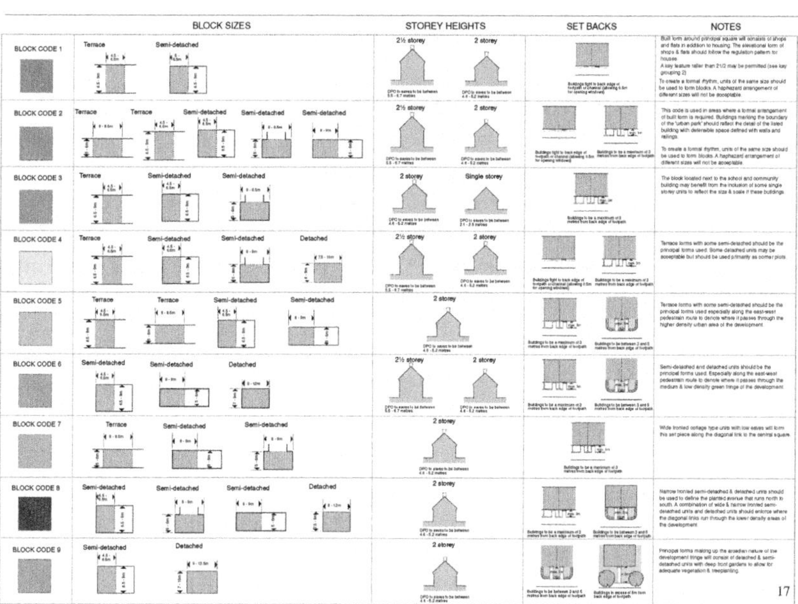

Figure 7.7 Extract from the Fairfield Park Design Code
Source: Mid Bedforshire District Council.

In 2004, the UK Government funded a pilot programme exploring the use and potential of design codes, work I was commissioned to evaluate. The intention of the research was to determine whether codes could help to deliver greater speed, certainty and quality in volume housebuilding, and therefore help to provide an answer to the very poor quality of design in that sector. The research concluded that design codes can play a major role in delivering better-quality development and a more certain design and development process. Also, if properly managed, they can provide the focus around which teams of professional advisors can integrate their activities, delivering in the process a more coordinated and consensus-driven development process. Consequently – in appropriate circumstances – design codes are valuable tools to deliver a range of more sustainable processes and built developments, particularly in connection with large sites built out over many years by different development teams. The findings were captured in the practice manual *Preparing Design Codes*.[4]

Revisiting this work nine years later revealed some surprising results (Carmona and Giordano, 2013):

- Approaching half of local planning authorities had required the submission of or actively commissioned design codes.
- The use of design codes was advocated in policy in a quarter of local planning authorities (rapidly rising).
- Practice was becoming mainstreamed.

The follow-up work confirmed that design codes improve design quality by tying down the 'must-have' design parameters – the urban DNA that holds the scheme together – irrespective of whether traditional or contemporary in character (Figure 7.8). In so doing, they ensure consistency in the delivery of key site-wide design principles between the different phases of development while delivering greater certainty about outcomes and certainty to developers about the process.

What Does This Mean for Contemporary Planning Practice?

As I have already argued, good planning and good design are integral to one another, they are inseparable. Unfortunately, the design middle was long ago squeezed out of British planning, and never made a convincing return in any of the four home nations. Flexible urban design frameworks and design codes offer a potential to become that missing 'urban design layer' in our planning cake. Indeed, if we look internationally, then some of the best international practice brings these two key tools together: for example, Hammarby Sjöstad in Stockholm, which is based on a clear but flexible urban design framework and detailed design codes to 'fix' the key design parameters at each phase. Of course, it is also delivered by a

Figure 7.8 Newhall, Harlow, a high-quality contemporary urban extension, coded by Studio REAL

Source: Matthew Carmona.

public sector team with the means and capabilities to proactively engage through the full range of tools available to them (formal and informal), including powerful incentive vested in enlightened landownership, the use of design competitions at each phase of the development, a rigorous design review and evaluation process, and partnerships between the city and local development teams (Carmona, 2010b) (Figure 7.9).

Here at home, while I now question whether we placed too much faith in the development plan as a tool capable of addressing all (or perhaps any) of the potential ascribed to them at the start of this chapter, we need to remember that the 'Pink Book' came at a time when urban design was still in its prehistoric phase in the UK. Consequently, there were few alternatives to planning policy across much of the country for establishing a local design agenda, and development plans were too often the only game in town!

Today, with the austerity-driven withdrawal of the state at both national and local levels from proactive planning and urban design, in many places the plan is once again the only game in town. As a consequence, even if just as a back-stop, there remains an important role for design policies in development plans backed up by intelligent Development

Figure 7.9 Hammarby Sjöstad, created through a skilled urban design process and now delivering long-term economic, social, health and environmental benefits to its city

Source: Matthew Carmona.

Management to help deliver high-quality places. But we will always need to be realistic about what we can achieve through such limited means, acting alone. Back in 1966 (the year I was born), J. Hope-Wallace, Under Secretary at the Ministry of Housing and Local Government, issued a new Governmental Circular – 28/66 – about the legitimate role of design in relation to planning. Among other sentiments, he stated that the control of design can help to eliminate bad design, but by itself will not deliver good design. This clearly remains the case today.

To achieve good design, let alone great design, we need to engage in a creative, locally responsive design process. If planning is to bring its public interest raison d'être to that party, it needs to engage in the sorts of proactive and propositional tools I have outlined and which suggest that it has something to say. If it doesn't (or can't, because of cuts and timidity), then we deserve everything we get. In such circumstances, planning will continue to be dismissed by the ill-informed as simply irrelevant or as a barrier to progress. That would be profoundly wrong!

Notes

1 www.placestandard.scot/#/home.
2 www.builtforlifehomes.org/go/about.
3 http://urbed.coop/archive/Masterplanning/all.
4 https://matthew-carmona.com/reports-guides/.

References

All listed URLs were last accessed on 1 March 2018.

Bishop, P. and Williams, L. (2017) *Planning, politics and city making: a case study of King's Cross*. London, RIBA Press.

Carmona, M. (2009a) Design coding and the creative, market and regulatory tyrannies of practice, *Urban Studies*, 46(12), pp.2643–2667.

Carmona, M. (2009b) The Isle of Dogs: four waves, twelve plans, 35 years, and a renaissance . . . of sorts, *Progress in Planning*, 71(3), pp.87–151.

Carmona, M. (2010a) Decoding design coding. In C. Clemente and F. De Matteis (eds) *Housing for Europe: strategies for quality in urban space, excellence in design, performance in building*. Rome: Tipographia Del Genio Civile.

Carmona, M. (2010b) Suburban design – sexing it up, *Town and Country Planning*, 79(3), pp.154–156.

Carmona, M. (2016) Design governance: theorising an urban design sub-field, *Journal of Urban Design*, 21(6), pp.705–730.

Carmona, M. (2017) The formal and informal tools of design governance, *Journal of Urban Design*, 22(1), pp. 1–36.

Carmona, M. and Giordano, V. (2013) *Design coding: diffusion of practice in England*. London: Urban Design Group.

Carmona, M., De Magalhães, C. and Natarajan, L. (2017) *Design governance: the CABE experiment*. New York: Routledge.

George, R.V. (1997) A procedural explanation for contemporary urban design, *Journal of Urban Design*, 2(2), pp.143–161.

Mallett, L. (2013) The planner as urban visionary", *bdonline.co.uk*, 18 December. Available at: www.bdonline.co.uk/the-planner-as-urban-visionary/5065218.article.

Punter, J. and Carmona, M. (1997) *The design dimension of planning: theory, content and best practice for design policies*. London: E. & F.N. Spon.

Siegan, B. (2005) The benefits of non-zoning. In E. Ben-Joseph and T. Szold (eds) *Regulating place, standards and the shaping of urban America*. New York: Routledge.

Tiesdell, S. and Adams, D. (2004) Design matters: major house builders and the design challenge of brownfield development contexts, *Journal of Urban Design*, 9(1), pp. 23–45.

Van Doren, P. (2005) The political economy of urban design standards. In E. Ben-Joseph and T. Szold (eds) *Regulating place: standards and the shaping of urban America*. London: Routledge.

Walters, D. (2007) *Designing community: charettes, masterplans and form-based codes*. Oxford: Architectural Press.

Part II

Changing Contexts for Planning Practice

8 Private Consultants, Planning Reform and the Marketisation of Local Government Finance

Mike Raco

Introduction

This chapter examines the ways in which planning systems across the UK are being systematically re-shaped by the twin processes of privatisation and the marketisation of local government finance. It argues that local planning arrangements are being re-fashioned into a growth-led, entrepreneurial mode of governance, designed to maximise financial returns for public and private interests and use planning 'gain' to pay for broader welfare interventions. This systematic *entrepreneurialisation* of local government means that it no longer fulfils its traditional post-war role of acting as a local provider of national welfare programmes, dependent on the re-distribution of centrally allocated funds (see Cochrane, 1993). In its place, local authority planners and planning authorities are being converted into spearheads for a wider governmental programme that prioritises the delivery of growth in the UK's cities and regions. In some instances, as will be discussed below, councils have even become active development agents themselves and established public–private partnerships in an increasingly desperate effort to mitigate the impacts of central government austerity cuts. All of this has taken place in a context of growing social and spatial inequalities, fluctuating and unpredictable welfare demands from increasingly diverse communities, growing pressures on local welfare services brought about by ageing populations, and the constant threat of major governmental shocks, such as the effects of Brexit, de-globalisation and/or another financial crash (see Chapter 1 by John Tomaney and Jessica Ferm; Dorling, 2014).

The chapter will show how the entrepreneurialisation of planning has gone hand-in-hand with fundamental changes in the organisation and management of the UK state. Across the world, governments have undertaken privatisation programmes since the early 1980s as they wrestle with growing fiscal constraints and increasing welfare demands (see Streeck, 2015). Across the UK, the planning system is increasingly subject to processes of privatisation, with private experts becoming active players in the shaping of key policy regulations and outcomes. This, the chapter will argue, has powerful, yet under-researched, implications for understandings of planning practice. Much of the planning literature is still underpinned by assumptions about, for example, the primacy of public planners and/or definitions of a public interest, and has been slow to realise just how significant a change is taking place in how local planning governance is operating. As will be shown, it is increasingly difficult to identify what constitutes a 'public' or 'private' actor, and the chapter concurs with Moore (2012: 593), who argues that "what is of greater significance than the question of what is public and what is private is how and why the dichotomy is normalised and perpetuated in different contexts of development and planning".

The discussion is divided into three sections. The first examines the changing nature of local government finances and the extent of austerity cuts. It argues that a new centralised localism in financial models is being implemented that aims to promote local financial 'self-sufficiency' and the privileging of economic development priorities. The second section examines evidence on the growth of private consultancies, and recent changes in the sector. It reviews published information on the scale and character of the consultancy sector, and draws on the analysis of company documents and strategies to examine how it is changing in the wake of recent reforms. A final section then interrogates the implications of these trends for the future of planning practices, and identifies some of the limitations inherent in recent reforms. It discusses the possibilities for the development of alternative forms of local planning practice and aspects of what this might consist of.

Austerity Urbanism and the Growth of a New Entrepreneurialism

The effects of the financial crisis of 2008, and the implementation of austerity budgets by successive governments since 2010, have had a major impact on the capacities and structures of the UK's planning systems. Under the Coalition (2010–2015) and subsequent Conservative administrations (2015–present), a political project of austerity has been rolled out, premised on the assumption that state bureaucracies had become 'too big' and that a new politics of less top-down and centralist statecraft was required. Reform agendas continue, fuelled by visions of an on-going economic 'emergency' precipitated by the events of 2008 and the perceived need to use state systems and services to generate, where possible, new sources of finance and income (see Wolin, 2008). For former Prime Minister David Cameron (2011), this involved "put[ting] in place principles that will signal the decisive end of the old-fashioned, top-down, take what you're given model of public services. And it is a vital part of our mission to dismantle big government". In order to achieve this end, the government enshrined in law "a new presumption – backed up by new rights for public service users and a new system of independent adjudication – that public services should be open to a range of providers competing to offer a better service".

The practical implications of this approach have been profound, both on local government and the planning system it regulates and oversees. Local authority budgets in England have been cut by £18 billion since 2010, with the burden falling disproportionately on areas of greatest social and economic need. As *The Economist* (2017: 1) notes:

> since 2010 the third of councils that are most dependent on Whitehall [for funding] have had to cut their spending on services by an average of 33%, while the tenth that are least dependent have made cuts of only 9%.

Within this broader picture, spending on local authority planning and development services in England has fallen from £2.197 billion in 2010 to £1.652 billion in 2011/2012, and a new low of £1.059 billion in 2016/2017, an unprecedented reduction of over 50% in just six years.[1] Treasury figures for 2016/2017 show a further 8% cut to come, relative to total budget reductions for local government of only 1% (Department of Communities and Local Government [DCLG], 2016: 4). In other parts of the UK, cuts to local government have been less severe, but still significant. Between 2010/2011 and 2017/2018, central grants to Scottish local authorities will have fallen by 9.2% from £10.5 billion to £9.5 billion at a time of growing demand on services (Accounts Commission, 2017). In Wales, overall budget cuts have been limited to 2.5–3%, but planning and development and housing departments have faced cuts in excess of over 20% (Crawford et al., 2012). The reasons for these reductions are complex, and have resulted from a combination of departmental negotiations among civil servants and ministers, a political aversion to the purpose and principles of government-led planning, and relatively little concerted resistance from local government during the early phases of cuts, with few of the public confrontations about cuts that were seen in the 1980s.[2]

The impacts of resource reductions have been compounded by the mushrooming of statutory regulations under the Labour governments of 1997–2010. Despite the removal of Planning Policy Statements in 2012 and their conversion into a simplified National Planning Policy Framework (NPPF), and the subsequent introduction of the Deregulation Act of 2015,[3] the obligations on local planning authorities continue to be onerous. Recent reforms have introduced significant new demands, such as the production of binding Local Plans, the negotiation of planning gain agreements, and clear strategies for land use and development. Local planners therefore have to act with legally binding 'due diligence' in regard to regulations at the same time as their capacities for action are being seriously eroded by cuts. Meanwhile, many of the core principles that underpinned local government finance in the post-war period are being systematically replaced by an increasingly competitive set of fiscal regimes in which their ability to maintain their budgets will have to be found through local forms of growth-dependent taxation. As the DCLG (2016b: 7) states, by 2020:

> local government will retain 100% of taxes raised locally. This will give local government additional business rates receipts of around £12.5bn to spend on local services. The system will have stronger incentives to boost growth, and areas that take bold decisions to boost growth will see the benefits.

The new arrangements form part of a wider set of central government-led reforms in which qualitative modes of practice, such as 'cooperation' and 'partnership-working' have become converted into legalised *duties* and increasingly quantifiable forms of conduct. The Localism Act 2011, for instance, introduced a new "legal duty to co-operate . . . in preparing plans that relate to 'strategic matters'" (Smith, 2016: 9). Built into these plans are a series of requirements that focus on delivery, planning gain, and the viability and profitability of developments for investors and landowners. These are encapsulated in paragraph 173 of the NPPF (DCLG, 2012), a statement that represents one of the most radical reformulations of planning practice since the Town and Country Planning Act of 1947:

> pursuing sustainable development requires careful attention to viability and costs in plan-making and decision-taking. Plans should be deliverable. Therefore, the sites and the scale of development identified in the plan should not be subject to such a scale of obligations and policy burdens that their ability to be developed viably is threatened.

It goes on to focus on the relationships between the planning system and private developers as:

> to ensure viability, the costs of any requirements likely to be applied to development, such as requirements for affordable housing, standards, infrastructure contributions or other requirements should, when taking account of the normal cost of development and mitigation, provide competitive returns to a willing land owner and willing developer to enable the development to be deliverable.

Good planning is elided with expedited decision-making that will ensure that "pre-commencement planning conditions are only imposed by local planning authorities where they are absolutely necessary" (Smith, 2016: 11). Local planners are told that they must contribute to what central government terms a 'national crusade' to build thousands of new homes (see Forrest and Hirayama, 2015), while reducing the political and socio-economic complexities that exist in local contexts and circumstances. Similar agendas have been rolled out in Scotland in which local authorities are required to draw up Main Issues Reports that identify 'preferred sites' that are "based on a understanding of place, together with consideration of deliverability factors such as site viability and housing land effectiveness" (Scottish Government, 2013: 16). Local planners are required to demonstrate a clear "willingness to explore what scope exists to phase the payment of Planning Obligations to assist the development process" and to actively consider "solutions to reduce costs in order to aid viability . . . and thinking about the scope for revenues to be increased, for example, by increasing the density of the development" (Scottish Government, 2010: 2).

The overall trend is for governments across the UK to apply concerted pressure on local actors to give the go-ahead for developments. In England, for instance, local authorities have been incentivised to build new homes with a New Homes Bonus (NHB).[4] It is a scheme that has faced implementation difficulties, and in the latest round of reforms, the government makes it clear that:

> from 2018/19 we will consider withholding NHB payments from local authorities that are not planning effectively, by making positive decisions on planning applications and delivering housing growth. To encourage more effective local planning we will also consider withholding payments for homes that are built following an appeal.
> (DCLG, 2016a: 9)

This is backed up by the implementation of a 'national baseline' target for anticipated growth that local authorities will have to meet, whatever local market conditions, in order to receive future payments. The NHB is one of a number of similar carrot-and-stick approaches to local government finance that are designed to institutionalise entrepreneurial practices at the local level.

The ethos of the planning system is thus inverted. Its traditional role of ensuring that any new development is only granted permission once it conforms to local, publicly defined needs is replaced by a legal requirement, wherever possible, to prioritise growth and the expansion of new homes and development projects. The role of planning practice is to take the messiness and complexity of places and convert them into spaces ripe for investment. The requirement to become financially self-sufficient will make local authorities increasingly dependent on property market uplift, whatever the wider impacts on marginalised local residents, businesses and places. As Penny (2017) notes, this is leading to a growing correlation between local government in the UK and the entrepreneurial models of 'localism' and growth that have characterised local governance in the United States since the early 20th century (see also Peck, 2017).

However, despite this push from the centre, there is growing evidence that cuts to planning budgets are reducing the capacities of the planning system to deliver its growth targets, no matter what the demand (see Local Government Information Unit and Federation of Master Builders, 2016). Limits on public bureaucracies are being compounded by structural reforms in which local authority services are being compartmentalised and out-sourced in the name of self-sufficiency. Many local government legal departments, for example, now operate as contracted-out business services to other authorities or private clients, whereas in the past their role was principally to provide advice and guidance to their own authorities (see Dobson, 2014). Some authorities have even embarked on the setting up of Special Purpose Vehicles, and in some instances, become directly involved in profit-making development projects, in order to generate income (see Penny, 2017). It is becoming increasingly difficult for many to meet the expected growth in demands for planning services without turning to the capacities found within the private sector.

The combination of these trends is therefore opening up new markets for private actors. As the next section will demonstrate, there is a direct co-evolution between reforms to make the planning system more entrepreneurial and the emergence of an increasingly powerful and influential consultancy sector that is being tasked to 'fill the gap' left in the wake of public sector retrenchment. New mutually reinforcing arrangements are emerging in which private consultancies provide local authorities with the requisite skills and resources to act more entrepreneurially. Forms of inter-dependency are emerging in which local authorities become increasingly reliant on the presence of private consultancies in order to function, and private firms become increasingly reliant on local government restructuring. The result is that private experts have become increasingly involved in the co-regulation of planning policy reforms and in the day-to-day practices associated with the implementation of planning. In the next section, the discussion turns to an assessment of key trends in the structure of the planning consultancy sector and its influences.

The Rise and Rise of Planning Consultancies

Planning Magazine's extensive Careers and Salaries Survey 2016 of 149 consultancies is the most comprehensive overview of the current state of the planning sector in the UK and key trends in its evolution. It found that 44% of planners now work in the private sector and that 20% of remaining public planners are "considering to leave the profession in the next 12 months" (*Planning Magazine*, 2016:3). Professional bodies report a growing trend of low morale, overwork and lack of resources, with the added incentive that wages and working conditions are perceived to be better in the private sector. As an indication of the degree of change, professional organisations have been re-organising their membership structures, with the Royal Town Planning Institute (RTPI), for example, now possessing a private members network called *RTPI Consultants*, consisting of 465 members. It provides a comprehensive online directory that includes details on core activities, competencies and staff. The members tend to be from bigger and more established firms, so the RTPI has also set up a small business association named the Independent Consultants Network, geared up to sole practitioners and those who operate their own small practices. In Scotland and Wales, these networks are supplemented by public–private liaison groups such as the Scottish Forum for Planning[5] and RTPI Cymru's Policy and Research Forum.[6]

The consultancy sector itself is dynamic and undergoing constant reformation. The diverse market opportunities opened up by recent planning reforms have led to a parallel process of consolidation within the sector into bigger companies on the one hand, and the simultaneous mushrooming of small firms specialising in specific niche fields of expertise on the other[7] (see Table 8.1). The latter, in turn, are repeatedly acquired by the former, which are looking to expand their market strength and their market 'offer' to potential local authority clients. In the period 2006–2015, the multinational Capita, for instance, acquired 130 companies, many of which specialise in urban planning in different countries, but mainly in the UK. Established medium-sized specialists are particularly attractive. One recent high-profile purchase took place in 2014, when the biggest UK property market player and planning consultancy Savills acquired Smith Gore Ltd. The latter was an established market player that was founded in 1847 and had 532 staff in 31 UK offices. It was attractive to Savills as it specialised in property development planning in rural locations, a sector the company saw as an area of potential growth, but in which it lacked the specialist skills offered by Smith Gore (see Savills, 2015). Similarly, in 2015, WYG purchased three established firms, FMW consultancy, Taylor Hardy Ltd and Signet Planning, to create an overall team of 135 experts, making it the third largest UK player. It has since formed a Major Project Unit in an attempt to bring in-house all of the regulatory requirements that public or private sector clients might require. This is part of a wider trend in which there has been a push towards the creation of multidisciplinary structures within bigger firms, which are then able to offer public sector clients more 'comprehensive' packages of expertise and knowledge.

As with most forms of privatisation, the marketisation of planning has inflated total costs (see Moran, 2015). The *Planning Magazine* survey shows that companies such as Quod charge their clients a rate of £2,850 per day, and that overall in 2016, "90% of firms charge a maximum rate above £800/day and 52% above £1,200" (*Planning Magazine*, 2016: 4). This has increased from respective figures of 69% and 29%

Table 8.1 The 10 largest UK-based planning consultancies

Rank	*Name*	*Total chartered planning staff*	*Planning fee income 2015/2016 (£m)*
1	Savills	167	24.5
2	Capita	144	Not available
3	Barton Willmore	132	20.29
4	WYG	120	45
5	Nathaniel Lichfield & Partners	112	20.4
6	RPS Group	108	90.6
7	Arup	69	70.949
8	Pegasus Group	65	21.5
9	Indigo Planning	54	7.9
10	Quod	47	14

Source: Adapted from *Planning Magazine* (2016: 13).

in 2015, indicating a rapidly expanding and cost-inflating market for users. The 49 biggest firms reported a total fee income of £498 million, the main growth areas being in advice for activities associated with viability-based planning, such as 'residential planning' and 'brownfield and greenfield planning advice'.[8] Major multinationals have become increasingly active players, responding to and helping to shape a growing market, companies such as Capita witnessing "big increases in its Salford and Barnet offices, where it provides planning services on behalf of local authorities", with the possibility that it might soon also "do the same for North Tyneside" (*Planning Magazine*, 2016: 15). Capita (2015: 9) state explicitly in their accounts to shareholders that cuts have forced local authorities to become "increasingly commercial and open to exploring new service delivery models", from which the company stands to gain. Its single biggest 'business opportunity market' is now the UK public sector, with the most lucrative opportunities emerging in relation to austerity-hit local government and "the ongoing pressure to reduce budgets while maintaining and adapting frontline services" and "increasingly looking to the private sector to find new service solutions . . . from traditional outsourcing to transformational partnerships" (Capita, 2015: 19).

Other major consultancies, such as Barton Willmore (2016: 2), similarly tell potential clients that the company "looks to take advantage of UK growth opportunities, particularly when housing numbers expand . . . as the market eventually responds to the UK's chronic housing need". The message is clear: the bigger the housing crisis and the impacts of austerity, the bigger the market opportunities for private firms. The dilemma for policy-makers is that by introducing new regulations to establish levers of control over the planning process (such as new health and safety measures or Environmental Impact Assessments), planners and regulators are creating new markets for expert private actors and opening up forms of profit-generation that authors such as Levi-Faur (2011) have termed 'regulatory capitalism', or a process in which the implementation of new codes of regulation open up market opportunities for firms that are best able to co-produce and implement them. A good example of how reforms generate market opportunities is provided by the company Pegasus (2015: 2), one of the UK's largest planning consultancies, which tells its investors that:

> by employing specialists we can ensure optimal results and outstanding service. With an acute understanding of the changing nature of planning policy at local and national level, we can inform and advise clients on the implications of emerging planning and environmental planning policy and offer the most informed and sustainable solutions.

Others such as WYG (2016: 7), whose planning arm made a profit of over £10 million in 2015, similarly highlight that their expansion had been "driven by strong demand for service across buoyant planning and infrastructure markets" and a "strategy of delivering future growth by obtaining quality revenues from front-end planning".

The long-term implications of this growing concentration of power in a relatively small number of major consultancies are likely to be profound. Under the NPPF's viability-based arrangements, the (substantial) fees and costs associated with privatisation are recovered by developers/investors through higher property values and future market returns. They form an increasingly important component of negotiations over the subsequent use of land and property. As costs inflate, so the ability of local authorities to impose social obligations on developers becomes more and more limited. There are also spatial implications. Planning practice has traditionally been a local activity, undertaken by local planning authorities which are sensitive to variations in contexts, opportunities and priorities. However, the market opportunities and returns to be found in bigger cities, with thriving property development programmes, is encouraging private firms to gravitate their focus of attention towards major centres, with less interest in areas in which markets are less lucrative. There is already some evidence of major firms concentrating their activities, and establishing a presence, in major centres of 'opportunity'.

The gradual entrepreneurialisation of planning also has implications for territorial competition and patterns of spatial development. The expansion of private expertise is encouraging a competitive growth politics. In Scotland, for example, the Scottish Property Federation, among others, is increasingly drawing on comparative data between different cities and the UK's nations to push for a further streamlining and speeding up of the planning process "if we are to attract and retain global capital to support local jobs and investment" (Melhuish, 2016: 3). Edinburgh City Council, in particular, is criticised for its relatively slow approvals process.[9] The experiences and conditions found in areas of growth are becoming norms of 'best practice' that influence the activities of planning authorities operating under very different market conditions. As Colenutt et al. (2015) have shown, the standard viability 'benchmark' for private sector profits used in negotiations is often set at an approximate rate of 20%, a figure based on the specific experiences of escalating property prices in London and the South East. Reliance on external experts and consultants, when allied to central government directives, will inevitably reduce the 'localness' of planning decisions.

The tendency to increase fees in the private sector shows little sign of abating. Firm accounts and statements repeatedly show that skills shortages are now hampering expansion plans and generating a fierce competition for workers that, in turn, is further pushing up labour costs and fees, while also encouraging further acquisitions. Moreover, as with any field of private practice, there are also wide variations in the ethical outlooks of market players. Since 2012, a new sector has emerged in which consultancies provide expert help to developers to help them reduce their social obligations. Companies such as S-106 Management (2016) market themselves as specialists in reducing the social benefits provided by the planning system:

> If the profit margin for your scheme is pushed to below 17.5% by Affordable Housing or other Section 106 payments, we can help. The demands made by local planning authorities should not jeopardise the viability of any underlying planning permission. In these cases we can prepare a Viability Assessment based on properly documented building costs and sales values, helping you to negotiate a significant reduction in your Affordable Housing provision or Section 106 payments.

They provide examples in which their expertise was used to help developers maximise the building of expensive apartments. In Bexley, London, their assessments helped to 'prove' that the local authority's requirements for 35% to be affordable lacked viability, thereby saving the developer £193,853 in social obligations.[10] In 2016, the site, a former pub, with planning permission for 10 apartments (only one of which had more than two bedrooms for a family), was on sale for "offers in excess of £1million" (see Caldecotte Group, 2016). As market opportunities expand, so inevitably will the presence and influence of such firms.

Where Next for Planning Practice?

This chapter has argued that the very ethos of what the planning system is for and what it should do have been re-imagined and remade in the wake of austerity cuts and the introduction of viability planning regimes. As Peck (2017) notes, such processes represent the extension of a 'late entrepreneurial' mode of local governance, in which local authorities take on new financial risks and activities to maintain their income streams. The introduction of such systems across the UK is truly radical. This situation differs from earlier rounds of property-led urban policy in which well-resourced public bodies, such as Urban or New Town Development Corporations, were set up to promote property development and use market returns to help fund their key infrastructure. In a context of austerity, local authorities increasingly rely on such returns to undertake their basic statutory social duties, making their room for manoeuvre and their ability to promote integrated infrastructures for development all the more limited. This dependency means that planning practices have become intricately bound up with the unpredictability of market conditions and broader shifts in forms of capital investment away from productive uses and into property and rental markets (see Standing, 2016).

Greater reliance on planning gain is also limiting the possibilities for non-market forms of intervention and the types of local programmes that planners have traditionally undertaken, such as the acquisition of land for community uses or the provision of subsidised incubator sites for local entrepreneurs. Innovative activities, such as the re-use or intensification of existing infrastructure, have become less attractive as their levels of viability tend to be lower than those of newbuild programmes. This means that the traditional skills and knowledge(s) that underpinned the practices of post-war planners, such as the ability to negotiate between private and public interests while maintaining a strategic overview of place development, look increasingly outdated. They still haunt contemporary policy imaginations and discussions over the supposedly 'bureaucratic' nature of planning, but as this chapter has argued, these are of less and less significance. In their place, the skills to support contemporary planning practices are now to be found in the fields of contract negotiations, the use of good governance templates, the specification of quantifiable inputs and outcomes, and the empowerment of a new generation of technocratic experts. The capacity to negotiate a 'good contract' with a private developer has taken on a new primacy within local authorities, many of which are now themselves looking for expert help from private consultants.

However, it should also be noted that all models of governance are prone to failures and political challenges. High-profile 'failures' in private provision in sectors such as public transport or the utilities might give a new legitimacy to calls for enhanced public sector control. Some local authorities have also brought in innovative programmes to re-use public assets. In the London Boroughs of Islington and Camden, planners have introduced new models for the delivery of affordable housing that are more exacting on private developers and make full use of their negotiating powers. On a global scale, there exist multiple models of local government practice and financial management that could also be adopted in the UK context. For example, in some parts of Europe and Latin America, there have been strong moves towards the 're-municipalisation' of services and infrastructure, particularly in contexts in which private providers are perceived to have 'failed' to maintain or deliver on their contracted obligations (see Hall et al., 2013; Pigeon, 2012). There are on-going calls from some for the re-municipalisation of public housing and planning policy in the context of governmental shocks such as Brexit or a new financial crisis, and the conditions within which viability planning currently operates may change significantly, necessitating new policy fixes and imaginations (see Shelter, 2017).

At the same time, the growing inter-dependencies between both local authorities and the consultancy sector present new risks and vulnerabilities for all parties. A market crash would leave local authorities with under-priced assets and liabilities, exposing them to the risk of bankruptcy (see Wilby, 2017). The early signs are that new arrangements will entrench existing inequalities between places, but this may, in turn, generate political pressure for reform. Resistance to some of the proposed changes is being mobilised by Conservative-controlled local authorities and the Conservative Party-dominated Local Government Association, as well as at the national level by different political parties. There is much scope for the alteration and amendment of current reforms and proposals. This chapter has argued, however, that the co-evolution of planning reforms and a growing consultancy sector are establishing a powerful dynamic that will take significant political will to re-shape in future.

Acknowledgements

The author wishes to thank Dr Ed Jones for his assistance in compiling materials for this chapter, and Jess Ferm and John Tomaney for comments on the first draft. Thanks also to Sonia Freire-Trigo, Tatiana Moreira de Souza, Joe Penny and Ed at the Bartlett School of Planning for sharing and discussing their stimulating work and insights on contemporary local government reform. Responsibility for the final draft is, of course, the author's alone.

Notes

1 Figures taken from DCLG (2013, 2014).
2 During the 1980s, some local authorities acted as the principal sites of resistance to the Thatcher government's monetarist programmes of reform. Some of the most radical (urban) authorities were eventually abolished by central government (see Cochrane, 1993).
3 The Deregulation Act 2015 abolished some of local government's planning functions, most notably the previous duty to prepare Sustainable Community Strategies and the requirement to create Local Area Agreements and Multi-area Agreements. All were high-profile Labour government interventions.
4 "The New Homes Bonus was introduced by the Coalition government with the aim of encouraging local authorities to grant planning permissions for the building of new houses in return for additional revenue. Under the scheme, the Government matches the Council Tax raised on each new home built for a period of six years. Local authorities are not obliged to use the Bonus funding for housing development" (Wilson et al., 2017: 1).
5 The Scottish Forum for Planning officially "aims to bring together key interests and expertise in planning to: Provide an on-going vision and direction for planning in Scotland through identifying, constructively responding to, and exploring new ways of tackling, emerging issues in planning: Support the delivery of planning reform and performance improvement: Share information activity to maximise joint working and minimise duplication" (www.rtpi.org.uk/the-rtpi-near-you/rtpi-scotland/networks-and-forums/scottish-forum-for-planning/).
6 The Forum "leads on RTPI Cymru policy, practice and research activities and comprises representatives from across Wales with experience in a variety of planning topics" (www.rtpi.org.uk/the-rtpi-near-you/rtpi-cymru/policy-in-wales/policy-and-research-forum/).
7 Small firms are sometimes established by individuals who have left local authority planning departments or major companies.
8 There is also evidence of market consolidation, with the top 10 fee earners alone reporting a total income of £373 million, up from £345 million the previous year.
9 The press release associated with the report is titled "Scottish planning system trailing behind the rest of the UK" (https://www.glhearn.com/news-and-events/news/scottish-planning-system-trailing-behind-the-rest-of-the-uk/).
10 See www.section-106.co.uk/case-studies.

References

All listed URLs were last accessed on 1 March 2018.

Accounts Commission (2017) *Local government in Scotland: performance and challenges 2017*. Edinburgh: Accounts Commission.

Barton Willmore (2016) *Consolidated group financial statements 2016*. London: Companies House.

Caldecotte Group (2016) *Former Fanny on the Hill Public House (freehold)*. Available at: https://media.realla.co/uploads/property/brochures/original/sujFnX0_qDTuNSmw-aYpDw.

Cameron, D. (2011) Cameron unveils privatisation drive, *Health Service Journal*, 21 February. Available at: http://m.hsj.co.uk/5026022.article.

Capita (2015) *Annual report and accounts 2015*. London: Companies House.

Cochrane, A. (1993) *Whatever happened to local government?* Milton Keynes: Open University Press.

Colenutt, B., Cochrane, A. and Field, M. (2015) The rise and rise of viability assessment, *Town and Country Planning*, 84, pp.453–458.

Crawford, R., Joyce, R. and Phillips, D. (2012) *Welsh local government spending: some deep cuts done, but much more to come*. London: Institute for Fiscal Studies.

DCLG (2012) *National Planning Policy Framework*. London: DCLG. Available at: https://www.gov.uk/government/uploads/system/uploads/attachment_data/file/6077/2116950.pdf.

DCLG (2013) *Local authority revenue expenditure and financing: England 2011–12 final outturn (revised)*. London: DCLG.

DCLG (2014) *Local authority revenue expenditure and financing: 2016–17 budget, England*. London: DCLG.

DCLG (2016a) *New Homes Bonus: sharpening the incentive*. London: DCLG.

DCLG (2016b) *The provisional 2017–18 local government finance settlement: confirming the offer to councils*. London: DCLG.

Dobson, N. (2014) What are local authority legal departments for? Available at: https://www.localgovernmentlawyer.co.uk/index.php?option=com_content&view=article&id=18804%3Awhat-are-local-authority-legal-departments-for.

Dorling, D. (2014) *Inequality and the one percent*. London: Verso.

Forrest, R. and Hirayama, Y. (2015) The financialisation of the social project: embedded liberalism, neoliberalism and home ownership, *Urban Studies*, 52, pp.233–244.

Hall, D., Lobina, E. and Terhorst, P. (2013) Re-municipalisation in the early 21st century: water in France and energy in Germany, *International Review of Applied Economics*, 27, pp.193–214.

Levi-Faur, D. (2011) From big government to big governance, *Jerusalem Papers in Regulation & Governance, Working Paper No.35*, Jerusalem: The Hebrew University.

Local Government Information Unit and Federation of Master Builders (2016) *Small is beautiful: delivering more homes through small sites*. London: Local Government Information Unit.

Melhuish, D. (2016) Foreword. In *Annual Planning Survey 2016*. Edinburgh: GL Hearn and Scottish Property Federation.

Moore, S. (2012) Re-evaluating public and private in local development cultures: converging vocabularies of public good and market success in Toronto's new urbanism, *Town Planning Review*, 35, pp.576–595.

Moran, M. (2015) *Politics and governance in the UK*. London: Palgrave.

Peck, J. (2017) Transatlantic city, part 1: conjunctural urbanism, *Urban Studies*, 54(1), pp.4–30. Available at: http://journals.sagepub.com/doi/abs/10.1177/0042098016679355.

Pegasus (2015) *Annual report and accounts, 2014–2015*, London: Companies House.

Penny, J. (2017) Between coercion and consent: the politics of cooperative governance at a time of austerity localism in London, *Urban Geography*, 38(9), pp.1352–1373.

Pigeon, M. (2012) Une eau publique pour Paris: symbolism and success in the heartland of private water. In M. Pigeon, D.A. McDonald, O. Hoedeman and S. Kishimoto (eds) *Remunicipalisation: putting water back into public hands*. Amsterdam: Transnational Institute, pp.24–39. Available at: www.municipalservicesproject.org/sites/municipalservicesproject.org/files/uploads-file/remunicipalisation-chap2-Paris.pdf.

Planning Magazine (2016) Careers and salaries survey 2016, *Planning Magazine*.

S-106 Management (2016) Looking to avoid providing affordable housing? Available at: www.section-106.co.uk/?gclid=CJGV69mdv9ECFcIp0wodKqEMBA.

Savills (2015) Proposed acquisition of Smiths Gore. Available at: www.savills.co.uk/_news/article/55328/187730-0/4/2015/proposed-acquisition-of-smiths-gore.

Scottish Government (2010) *Development viability factsheet*. Edinburgh: Scottish Government.

Scottish Government (2013) *Development planning*. Edinburgh: Scottish Government.

Shelter (2017) Why we need more social housing [England only]. Available at: http://england.shelter.org.uk/campaigns_/why_we_campaign/Improving_social_housing/Why_we_need_more_social_housing.

Smith, L. (2016) *Planning for housing*. Briefing Paper 03741. London: House of Commons Library.

Standing, G. (2016) The corruption of capitalism: why rentiers thrive and work does not pay. London: Biteback Books.

Streeck, W. (2015) *How will capitalism end?* Cambridge: Polity Press.

The Economist (2017) Running on empty; local government, *The Economist*, 28 January.

Wilby, P. (2017) Councils are facing bankruptcy – is this the end of public service? *The Guardian*, 6 March. Available at: https://www.theguardian.com/commentisfree/2017/mar/06/councils-local-authorities-bankruptcy-public-service.

Wilson, W., Murphy, C. and Barton, C. (2017) *The New Homes Bonus Scheme (England)*. Briefing Paper SN05724. London: House of Commons Library.

Wolin, S. (2008) *Democracy incorporated*. Princeton, NJ: Princeton University Press.

WYG (2016) *Annual report and accounts 2016*. London: Companies House.

9 Localism and Neighbourhood Planning

Elena Besussi

Planning for, with and by Neighbourhoods

Six years after the introduction of Neighbourhood Planning through the Localism Act in 2011, the total number of completed and emerging Neighbourhood Development Plans (NDPs) had surpassed the 2000 threshold. The enthusiasm and expectations of those participating in this mass planning exercise have not declined. Positive experiences have encouraged others. Less positive experiences, and especially the lack of grip of NDPs over the scale of development, have not dented its uptake. However, the number of plans produced or in production is not the most useful metric to assess the outcomes of the initiative.

Based on research in two Neighbourhood Forums in London, this chapter probes the connection between Neighbourhood Planning and community-led planning conceptualised here as two different routes that communities use to promote their voice in planning decisions. The objective is to discuss the implications of their co-existence for widening the understanding of and the action over the politics of urban development's dynamics. The chapter argues that Neighbourhood Planning can be better understood when framed as part of a broader set of urban political conflicts and their practices, and that it can become a tool that unveils the politics of development even when it isn't the most effective tool to alter the current neo-liberal form. London, where the pressure of urban development on local communities and their displacement is more tangible and fast-paced than elsewhere in the UK, provides the geographical context for developing this argument more clearly despite the slower uptake of Neighbourhood Planning compared to the rest of the country. However, with over 2000 Neighbourhood Forums now actively engaging in plan-making, the chapter is wary of drawing generalisations from the experiences of a few cases taken from this unique context.

Neighbourhood planning is a manifestation of the government's localist agenda, predicated upon a transfer of some decision-making powers in planning from the state to society and upon a devolution of those powers from central and local government to neighbourhoods. It brings together ideas of the local – here, the neighbourhood – as a functional scale of urban organisation and spatial planning, with the political orientation towards rebalancing the distribution of decision-making powers between state and society in favour of the latter. By doing so, it creates a new and artificial layer of decision-making in planning. But both *neighbourhood* and *community participation* are contested concepts in planning theory and controversial ideas in practice. This chapter presents elements from emerging and adopted NDPs in London to discuss some of the challenges of bringing community-led activism in planning and development into the statutory and institutionalised format of Neighbourhood Planning.

The delineation of neighbourhoods as coherent urban and social entities – and, as such, objects of planning – is not new, and has informed models of area-based interventions focused on neighbourhood renewal as a route to reducing poverty and social exclusion since the 1930s and more widely in the post-war period across diverse planning cultures. The EU 'urban agenda' (i.e. the framework containing the policies and funding streams from the European Union addressing urban development) influenced the development of neighbourhood-based policies in European countries during the 1990s. The Grands Projets de Ville in France, the Kvarterløft ('neighbourhood uplift') programme in Denmark, the Contratti di Quartiere in Italy and the Soziale Stadt ('social city') in Germany are all instances of neighbourhood-level intervention. In the UK, Scotland, Wales and Northern Ireland have all developed legislation or guidance on community planning described as a strengthened base (and in Scotland and Northern Ireland, also a statutory base) for collaboration between community bodies and local authorities for the forward planning of development and services.

The neighbourhood scale has also been contested for its potential disregard of the wider structural, cultural and economic determinants of marginalisation in urban contexts and of the "high rate of mobility and complex social networks" (Mayo, 2000: 2) that characterise communities in urban industrial societies (Colomb, 2017). The possibility of statutory community engagement processes to genuinely confront and challenge existing discourses in planning has also been challenged by critical approaches which see in the logic of deliberation and consensus-building associated with these processes a limit to the formation of political contents more often attributed to community activism and social movements (Legacy, 2017). This can become even more problematic at the hyperlocal scale of the neighbourhood, where mobilised communities might be unable to scale-up their challenges (Inch, 2015: 17).

The combination of these ideas in the principles underpinning a new planning instrument – which carries the same legal weight as the spatial plans prepared by statutory local planning authorities – has raised expectations and led to concerns about the impacts of Neighbourhood Planning on the content of plans and the process for making development decisions.

Critical reviews of the first five years of Neighbourhood Planning have predominantly scrutinised its outcomes against the presumptions that community-led planning offers a more progressive outlook (Parker and Salter, 2016) and have focused on two main questions: can Neighbourhood Planning bring forward a more inclusive route to community participation in planning, and can it lead to the identification and advance of equitable alternatives to the dominant valorisation of economic growth underpinning mainstream planning and development decisions?

The chapter first outlines the key ideas and ideologies that have informed neighbourhood and community delineation, and traces their consequences for past models of urban policy intervention in the United Kingdom in order to highlight what continuities and innovations Neighbourhood Planning has in relation to these practices. It then summarises the key features of Neighbourhood Planning and the scale and scope of its implementation in England, and highlights the main points made by on-going critical reviews of its progress so far. Two cases of Neighbourhood Planning in London are presented and discussed to highlight the complexity and political tensions of bringing together the institutional, deliberative, consensual model of decision-making of Neighbourhood Planning with the commitment to promote community interests in planning. The conclusions discuss the challenges of Neighbourhood Planning to the understanding and advancement of community-led planning.

Neighbourhoods in Planning: Ideologies and Policy Implementations

There is a well-established theoretical tradition challenging the delineation of neighbourhoods as both a unit of analysis for understanding urban social changes and as a site of policy intervention for addressing the impacts of such changes. This tradition is outlined here to contextualise the current academic debates on Neighbourhood Planning and localism which predominantly revolve around the neo-liberal character of its outcomes, the unequal social and geographic distribution of its uptake, and the inherently consensual and deliberative nature of the decision-making process it enshrines. By reproducing neo-liberal politics, Neighbourhood Planning is seen as normalising and institutionalising community activism, and more generally shifting policy-making away from democratic scrutiny and towards the domain of corporations, and private structures of service delivery and procurement (Raco, 2013).

The neighbourhood as an object of study was crystallised by the Chicago School of Sociology in the early 1920s. The Urban Ecologists viewed neighbourhoods as the ecological niche of communities, miniature homogeneous societies with their own history and character, organised around similar collections of institutions and spaces, divided by physical barriers. They were the outcomes of dynamics of invasion, succession and expansion, producing cities as constellations of natural areas organised in a concentric urban structure for which the Chicago School is known (Park et al., 1925).

These concepts have had consequences for the discipline and practice of planning. They have established the use of social survey methods, mapping techniques and descriptive statistics for the definition of urban neighbourhoods. Facilitated by the increasing availability of small-area census data, they have informed the development of methods for the analysis of the geographic clustering of social groups. Geo-demographics is now used in policy-making and commercial practices such as marketing strategies and mortgage-lending redlining. In the UK, area-based indices of social deprivation are used to prioritise areas for urban renewal and anti-poverty investment programmes.

The ideas of the Chicago School have influenced post-war normative criteria for planning of the 'good' neighbourhood (Kallus and Law-Yone, 2016). These included a mix of functional thresholds (e.g. enough population to support an elementary school) and a "sense of community" (Talen, 2006, 2016). The role of planning and design was, and in some ways still is, to engineer the conditions for the formation of good (or sustainable) communities.

"The notion of community in terms of shared locality or neighbourhood" (Mayo, 2000: 2; for a review, see Chisholm and Dench, 2005) is not unproblematic. In sociological terms, interest-based social networks are considered as important in explaining communities and their formation as geographically bounded social ties developed through physical proximity. Political economic traditions in urban studies and planning (Harvey, 1985; Fainstein, 2001; Sassen, 2013; Haila, 2015) have highlighted how political and economic struggles over the production and distribution of resources collectively shape urban development and individuals' experiences of their position in society. These studies investigate neighbourhoods as the place where these conflicts manifest, but question the neighbourhood as a determinant of urban change (Bridge et al., 2012; Slater, 2009, 2017) and the use of spatial segregation and neighbourhood characteristics as determinants of social and economic exclusion. The lack of consideration of broader economic and political forces in the design of urban policy and regeneration programmes has been scrutinised not just for lacking effectiveness, but also for reproducing exclusion (Watt, 2007; Arbaci and Rae, 2013). Neighbourhood approaches to urban policy therefore tend to select some social problems and solutions over others, and to devalue some types of stability and homogeneity over others, particularly when they are perceived as impediments to the implementation of area-based property-led renewal programmes which require the dismantling and reconstruction of physical and social infrastructures.

In the UK, neighbourhoods have played a continuous and important role in both planning and social policy programmes. Localism and Neighbourhood Planning represent the most recent examples in history. This is explored further in the following paragraphs in order to highlight the legacy and influence of 'the neighbourhood' over the current policy landscape.

As a legacy of the ideas of the Chicago School of Sociology, the 1945 Labour government aspired to overcome the failings of single-tenure, single-class mass housing estates built between the wars with the creation of socially balanced and mixed-income communities that would "spark a greater understanding and interaction between members of different social classes" (Homer, 2000: 69). Patrick Abercrombie's Greater London Plan of 1944 identified the need to strengthen and sustain the existing spatial organisation of inter-related and neighbouring communities. Neighbourhood units, as they became known, informed the design and optimal size of urban expansions in London and the new towns built under the New Towns Act of 1946, but by the early 1960s, the model was abandoned and subjected to criticism from both sociologists and the architecture profession. However, area-based policies remained a key feature of urban and social policy programmes in the UK. These programmes found justification in the emergence of studies on the negative impacts of spatially concentrated poverty which mainstreamed the concept of 'neighbourhood effect' as an explanatory factor of life conditions and opportunities.

Area-based policies allowed the Thatcher and Major Conservative governments to establish methods for targeting financial resources at a time when they were effectively withdrawing support from Labour's population-based welfare redistribution approach. Target areas were identified either through competitive bidding, such as in the Single Regeneration Budget model established in the early 1990s, or needs-testing – measured by area-based indices of poverty or deprivation – such as in the Sure Start, New Deal for Communities, Neighbourhood Renewal Funds programmes and the National Strategy for Neighbourhood Renewal, all developed by the New Labour government in the 2000s.

Area-based policies were also used to implement a new model of programme delivery based on governance partnership between local government, private partners, and local residents and community organisations. New Labour's communitarian shift in planning through the Planning and Compulsory Purchase Act 2004 sought to enlist community and neighbourhood interests "as a means of encouraging different forms of [good] behaviour by involving local actors in making decisions about the places in which they lived" (Clarke and Cochrane, 2013: 13). However, strong central control was retained over the definition of good behaviour, the standards and quantitative outcomes of services, including regeneration and planning, delivered through area-based programmes

(Clarke and Cochrane, 2013). In practice, this meant that funding made available to area-based regeneration programmes was managed by partnership structures formed between public agencies, local authorities and self-selected, or at times locally elected, community representatives, but targets and objectives were pre-defined and monitored from the centre, either directly or through a variety of "technologies of performance" (Clarke and Cochrane, 2013: 13) and quangos which proliferated during the New Labour government.

Other planning-related instruments of New Labour's localism applied specifically to rural areas and parish and town councils, and can be seen as precursors to Neighbourhood Development Plans. Village and Community Design Statements, Parish Plans or Community-led Plans allowed rural communities and parish and town councils to identify planning and design expectations for an institutionally defined area and package them into a plan. These plans did not hold statutory planning powers, but could be – and indeed, were – adopted by local planning authorities as part of the Local Plan or used as material considerations in the assessment of applications for development (Parker, 2008, 2017).

Neighbourhood Planning is a central feature of the Localism Agenda brought forward by the UK Government since 2010, but rather than the planning revolution it has been hailed as, shows clear continuities with the planning formats created by New Labour and its aim to shift some political powers to localities as places and to communities as 'big society'. There are, however, some important elements of departure. The Coalition and later Conservative government's localism is committed to the dispersal of power away from Westminster, by which it means a move to free local government from central and regional controls. At the same time, it aims to reduce its role in relation to a 'big society' comprised of a variety of civil society organisations and private sector firms given the task of service delivery. The presumption of localism is that the 'big society' will be predominantly local, but the commitment to communities by the New Labour government was not central to this new version of localism.

The removal of central control and monitoring over local government's activities – exemplified by the infamous 'bonfire of the quangos' (Flinders et al., 2014) – is now counteracted by the dramatic cuts to funding for local authorities and the pressure to become more accountable towards their electorates. The central controls imposed during New Labour's approach to localism, especially the centrally controlled allocation of resources, managed to contain the risk of spreading geographic inequality that instead characterises the implementation of many aspects of the current Conservative government's agenda. The geographical unevenness in the uptake of Neighbourhood Planning is one example, and has been a key concern for practice and research (Parker, 2017).

The Implementation of Neighbourhood Planning in England: Challenges and Limitations

The 2011 Localism Act entitles neighbourhoods to become units of decision-making through Neighbourhood Planning and of service delivery, through the creation of community rights. It gives NDPs legal weight, which was not previously available to Village Statements or Community Plans or to partnership-based initiatives in urban areas (Popple and Quinney, 2009).

Neighbourhood Planning is a package of instruments designed to bring the Localism Agenda into the planning policy arena. NDPs are the most prominent of these; they have legal status, but are non-mandatory, and the decision to produce them rests with the 'neighbourhood'. The voluntary nature of Neighbourhood Planning has led to its uneven take-up, both geographically and socially. There are currently over 2000 parishes and forums, both established and emerging, that have started an NDP, but over 40% of these are located in the South East and South West of England, and only 16% are located in urban areas. Over 75% of NDPs are in the least deprived three quintiles (by local authority area), leading to the concern that Neighbourhood Planning is an exclusive rather than inclusive model of democracy, predominantly taken up in areas dominated by highly educated individuals with above-average earnings and considerable resources (human, time, knowledge, financial) to spare (Parker, 2017).

NDPs are produced by parish councils awarded additional planning powers through the Localism Act, and where a parish is not established, by Neighbourhood Forums (NFs). Members of NFs (21 is the minimum required number) are selected among and by local residents and businesses, and must obtain formal designation by the local planning authority before they can exercise the legal powers to make a plan. Since forums, unlike parishes, are established for the purpose of making an NDP, the area of their jurisdiction must also be selected by the forum and approved by the local planning authority, ensuring that neighbourhood areas do not overlap. These initial stages of Neighbourhood Planning have a foundational role in establishing the democratic credential of an NDP, and can be a source of intense political conflicts. Colomb (2017) has challenged the presumption of the neighbourhood as a coherent and self-aware homogeneous community against the reality of the increasingly diversified social fabric of cities and the co-existence of different types of communities and community ties within one neighbourhood. Similarly, Davoudi and Cowie (2013) have questioned the assumption that forums are automatically representative of their communities. Parker et al. (2015) found that the majority of NDPs are ultimately prepared by a small group of people, rather than by the whole forum, suggesting that even if current regulations require that the forum members be representative of their community, in actual practice the legitimacy of NDPs is not given (see also Cowie and Davoudi, 2015).

After the completion of these initial stages, the preparation of the NDP follows a sequence of steps that mimic the preparation of Local Plans, including elements introduced by the 2004 planning reform: initial consultations and visioning exercises are accompanied by the collection of evidence to justify proposed policies. Once the plan is completed, statutory consultation and independent examination managed by the local authority take place. Finally, NDPs are put through a local referendum before they can be adopted and become material policy. All referendums have delivered overwhelmingly positive results, but turnout is on average below 30% of the locally registered voters.[1]

Since 2011, central government has provided a combined value of £40 million in technical and financial support to Neighbourhood Forums (Parker, 2017), and on 21 September 2017, the Housing Minister announced a further £23 million. Where Neighbourhood Planning takes place, local authorities receive a financial grant to cover the costs of managing statutory public consultation, examination and referendums, but not the costs of additional staff time, despite the duty of local authorities, inscribed in the Localism Act, to collaborate with Neighbourhood Forums. The Ministry of Housing, Communities and Local Government (MHCLG) currently contracts out the management of support for forums and parishes to different delivery partners from the private and non-profit sectors. Financial support through fixed grants of £9000 (with an additional £6000 for neighbourhoods in complex growth areas) is complemented by free or fee-based access to technical support packages provided by delivery partners. Although there are no regulations on how to prepare an NDP, the reliance on a limited number of delivery partners has led to a progressive standardisation of the process and of the kind of support provided. In urban areas, where the relationship between planning and development is more complex than in rural areas, Neighbourhood Forums have struggled to find more targeted support and skills training, prompting the creation of mutual support networks (such as Neighbourhood Planners.London) or collaborations with universities. The cost of making an NDP varies considerably depending on its scope and complexity. Volunteers' time and private resources contribute significantly, and it is not unusual for a forum to appoint a planning consultant to assist in its preparation. This suggests that the aspiration of the proponents of Neighbourhood Planning for remaking planning as a non-technical process, rebalancing the relation between local and technical expertise, has not been achieved (Brownill and Bradley, 2017).

Neither the Localism Act nor the Neighbourhood Planning Regulations 2012 define the content of NDPs, leaving it to communities to decide the scope and detail. However, NDPs must be in general conformity with the strategic policies of the Local Plan (including, in the case of London, the London Plan) and cannot challenge the quantum of development that Local Plans allocate to the neighbourhood area. NDPs must also limit their scope to the statutory definition of development. As the NPPF (DCLG, 2012: para.154) states: "Only policies that provide a clear indication of how a decision maker should react to the development proposal should be included in the plan." These constraints can frustrate non-expert planners who face the task of negotiating communities' propositions and aspirations. The duty to conform to the strategic level raises questions about the real purpose of Neighbourhood Planning and its role in the context of a growth-oriented model of planning and a neo-liberal politics of urban development. For Brownill and Bradley (2017: 32), the purpose of Neighbourhood Planning is to create "spaces oriented to growth", areas where Neighbourhood Planning becomes the tool for creating an acceptance of the politics of economic and housing growth (through, e.g., the promise of a share of developer's contribution to be distributed to NFs). Because of this underlying agenda, only those willing to accept the growth-oriented politics, and the consensual, deliberative format of decision-making that accompanies it, will not be frustrated by Neighbourhood Planning. For Parker, the format and process of Neighbourhood Planning do not allow for alternative, antagonistic content to emerge, and therefore only favour a participation based not just on a degree of consensus with the strategic direction of planning, but on an understanding of participation as deliberative consensus (Parker et al., 2015; Parker and Salter, 2016).

Neighbourhood Planning in London

Against the background of questions raised on the progressive credentials of Neighbourhood Planning, the following two London cases illustrate the complex and symbiotic relationship between community-led initiatives and Neighbourhood Planning in contexts where this co-existence has emerged out of the necessity to combine the progressive nature of the former with the policy credentials of the latter. Both neighbourhood areas are located in Central London Boroughs (Southwark and Camden) where the pressure of property development is highest in the city. Their Neighbourhood Planning experiences differ in their origins: as a continuation of and complement to a long history of community activism in Southwark, and as the policy context to frame the community's response to the threat of displacement in Camden.

'Community-led planning' is here used to mean the type of grassroots activism which seeks to position community interests (whether local or issue-based) at the centre of planning and urban development, either through proactive and independent initiatives of engagement with planning institutions or through the production of alternative community and people's plans and land development models. Community-led planning can be better understood in terms of community development and community organising than as an instance of community participation in planning. While in the latter, planning seeks legitimacy through establishing consensual community voices, in the former, communities seek legitimacy by positioning their voice into, and if necessary disrupting, the process and content of planning.

In May 2017, there were 109 emerging and designated Neighbourhood Forums in London, of which four have successfully passed the referendum and are now part of the Local Plan and an additional nine have completed the preparation of the NDP and are moving through the statutory stages of consultation and examination.[2] These figures confirm the concern that Neighbourhood Planning has made slow progress in London compared to the rest of the country, where about 10% of NDPs have passed referendum.

In contrast to the stereotype that Neighbourhood Planning is dominated by highly educated, wealthy groups, London's Neighbourhood Forums and areas spread across a wide range of incomes, levels of education and tenures (Figure 9.1). Analysis of data from the GLA London Datastore reveals that their internal diversity, measured as the range of incomes, tenures and education levels within the neighbourhood area, also shows significant variation between Neighbourhood Forums, suggesting that Neighbourhood Planning in London might be capable of adopting the city's underlying social and economic diversity. All neighbourhood areas, regardless of size, include different housing tenures in comparable proportions, reflecting the nature of London's housing geography, with social rented housing, owner occupation and, more recently, privately rented accommodation being in close proximity. Income levels within neighbourhood areas also vary, with Dartmouth Park, Norland, Bermondsey, Fortune Green and West Hampstead showing the highest internal diversity, and East Shoreditch, Sudbury, Bankside and Somerstown among those with the smallest variations. The neighbourhoods of Camley Street and Elephant and Walworth (in the London Boroughs of Camden and Southwark respectively) are characterised by a high proportion of households in social rented accommodation and income levels close to the London median. The share of population with a university degree is near the London average in both areas, with the Elephant and Walworth neighbourhood area marginally lower. It is worth highlighting that the Camley Street neighbourhood area and forum include in equal proportion residents and businesses, but the latter are not included in these statistics.

Elephant and Walworth Neighbourhood Forum: Divide and Conquer?

The Elephant and Walworth Neighbourhood Forum was designated by the London Borough of Southwark on 20 September 2016 to prepare the

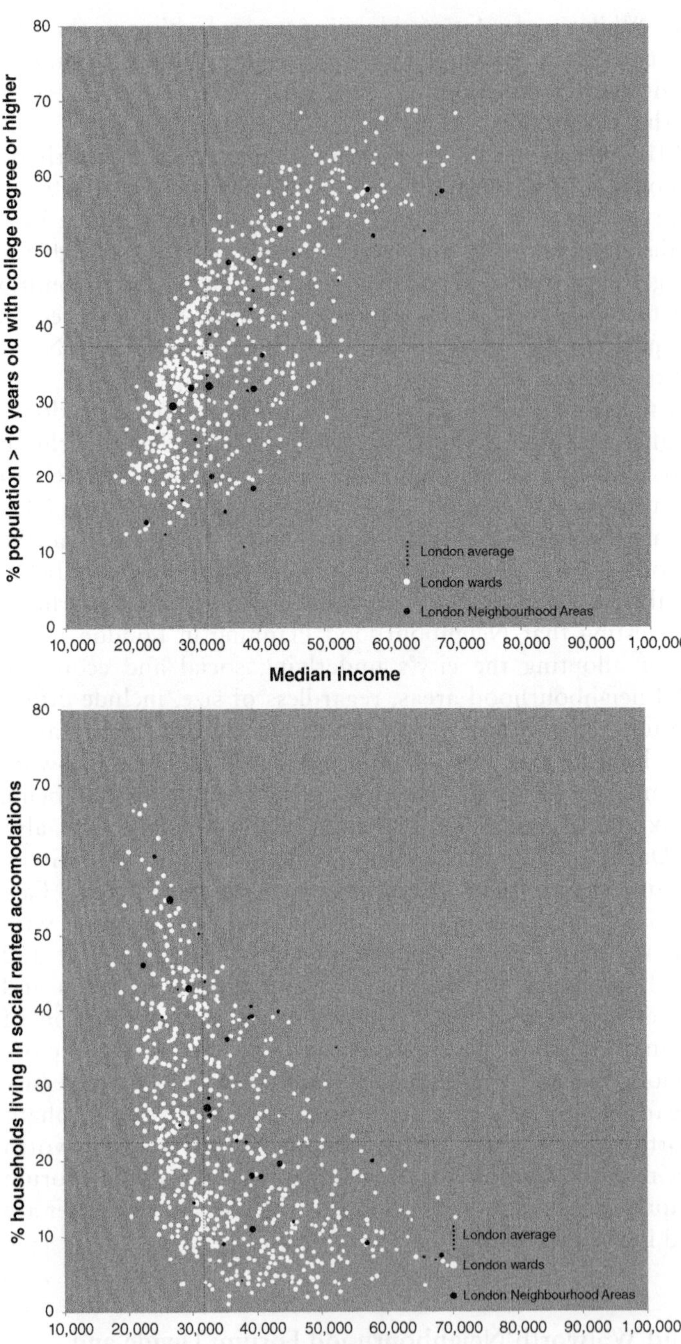

Figure 9.1 Distribution of all London's wards (white) and neighbourhood areas (black) across selected variables

Source: GLA London Datastore.

plan for the Walworth Neighbourhood Area, which had been approved for the purpose of Neighbourhood Planning two weeks earlier. These benchmark decisions came after three years of negotiations between the forum and the council and two unsuccessful applications. While it is standard practice and procedure to submit separate applications for the designation of the area and the forum, the order in which the applications are submitted is often a political decision made case-by-case by the local authority, to exercise control over the process. Examples of this politics can be found in a number of controversial London cases. In Stamford Hill, which is home to London's largest concentration of Haredi Jews, the council chose to not designate either of the two forums competing to represent the area, in order to avoid deepening community divisions (Colomb, 2017). In East Shoreditch, an application for designating an area crossing the boundary between the London Boroughs of Hackney and Tower Hamlets was refused by the former but approved by the latter, with the exclusion of the area falling into the Hackney jurisdiction (London Borough of Hackney, 2015). In the case of the application by the Elephant and Walworth Neighbourhood Forum (EWNF), the justification used by Southwark Council was that designating the area prior to the forum would "ensure the neighbourhood forum is the most appropriate and representative forum for the neighbourhood area" (London Borough of Southwark, 2016).

The solution for the EWNF was to establish a Neighbourhood Forum as a composite network of community groups whose combined geographical reference was significantly wider than the geographical boundaries of the Neighbourhood Plan area. Two parallel political dynamics led to this outcome. First, the negotiation between the emerging forum and Southwark council on the boundaries of the neighbourhood area was in large part influenced by the interest of the council to insulate pre-existing and emerging planning frameworks (the Southwark Plan and the Old Kent Road Opportunity Area) from the influence of the emerging Neighbourhood Plan. During the negotiations, the neighbourhood area boundaries were amended twice. The first proposal in 2013 included the former Heygate Estate and the northern section of Walworth Road, which local community groups had strong political attachment to, having been the object of a long-term grassroots campaign against the council's, and its commercial partner's, regeneration plan for the Elephant and Castle area (Figure 9.2). Council officers and cabinet members initially encouraged the forum to expand the proposed Neighbourhood Plan area, and at the same time, put pressure on the emerging forum to demonstrate its representativeness of the larger area and to complement the geographical expansion with the widening of the network of community groups formally included in the forum. These requests were met through a year-long period of public engagement and community organising which ended with the formal submission of the application for forum and area designation in 2014. However, the emergence of newly contested sites led to the Neighbourhood Forum being advised by the Cabinet Member for Planning and Regeneration that both applications would be turned down, with the recommendations that the neighbourhood area should now be scaled down and exclude not only the former Heygate Estate and shopping centre, but the Old Kent Road Opportunity Area and the area surrounding the Aylesbury Estate. The now-expanded forum, representing over 90 local residents, successfully negotiated the retention of the entirety of Walworth Road and agreed, not without internal debates, to remove the contested sites from its planning area. In addition, the forum agreed that no changes to its composition be made in the application for designation that was submitted in 2015 and finally approved in September 2016.

The second political dynamic is the commitment of the Elephant Amenity Network to maintain and extend a community voice and

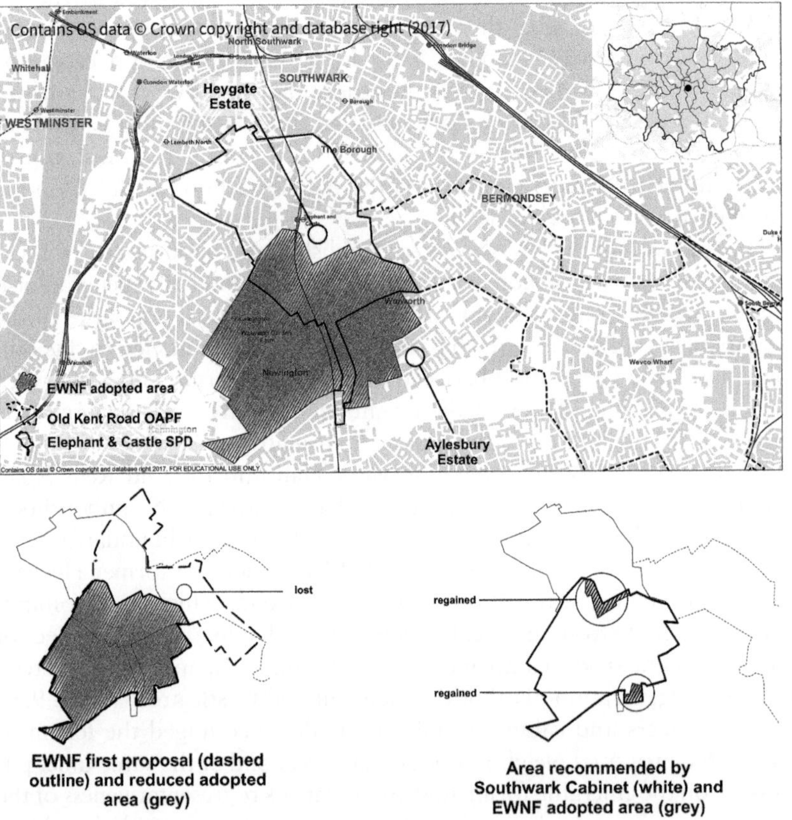

Figure 9.2 Changes in Neighbourhood Planning Area for the Elephant and Walworth Neighbourhood Plan

Source: Basemap: OS VectorMap™ District using EDINA Digimap Ordnance Survey Service, downloaded May 2017.

presence in the planning process of the area. The Elephant Amenity Network (EAN) is a coalition of local community groups which grew from the struggle for the recognition of community interests in the Elephant and Castle regeneration programme. Despite, and in reaction to, the frustration at the failure of the developer-led consultation on the masterplan for the Heygate Estate to generate only minimal community inputs, local communities in and outside the EAN, saw the Neighbourhood Planning format as an opportunity to organise and keep local community groups connected around a shared objective for the Elephant and Walworth area, which had some continuity with previous campaigns and existing expertise. Securing these interests and retaining the momentum of community organising around a community-led agenda are key to explaining the decision of the EAN to experiment with the Neighbourhood Planning format and not to scale back the expanded structure of the forum even when the geographical scale of its planning area was reduced. An important dimension of this process is the commitment of both the EAN and the Neighbourhood Forum to secure the recognition of the interests and accommodation needs of ethnic minority businesses (represented by Latin Elephant), which always had a significant presence and economic role locally and have been central to the struggle over the future of the shopping centre. The NDP and its forum were seen as the viable option to put forward an alternative plan for the area that met the needs of ethnic minority businesses, alongside the EAN campaigning against the proposed development model for the shopping centre.

Camley Street Neighbourhood Plan and Business Activism in Camden

The case of Camley Street in the London Borough of Camden is an important example of grassroots action emerging from the recognition of the potential and limits of Neighbourhood Planning to provide an institutional response to local community interests in the context of neo-liberal urban politics. Camden's Community Investment Programme (CIP) represents the local authority's strategy for coping with capital shortage and housing needs through public land privatisation and private-led housing development. It identifies publicly owned land that can be categorised as surplus to the council's needs and disposed of. The capital receipts of these disposals are reinvested into the supply of housing and social infrastructure. Due to the planning and financial conditions of private-led housing development in the UK (see Chapter 13 by Nick Gallent), the CIP has therefore facilitated the loss of small open spaces, particularly within social housing estates, and of employment land to high-density infill residential developments which offer a very limited affordable housing component.

Camley Street is a cul-de-sac which acts as a shared border between mixed-tenure housing of about 400 homes and 1000 people and a council-owned medium-size industrial estate providing accommodation for around 30 businesses and 500 employees (Figure 9.3). The neighbourhood is adjacent to the King's Cross development, whose near completion has pushed up land values around Camley Street and made the area more attractive to the council's policy to dispose of land for capital receipt and to private development investors seeking to capture the ensuing high land values. The current use as low-density light industrial makes this part of the neighbourhood extremely vulnerable to redevelopment into housing, a change of use which has become so uncontested and frequent as to generate a loss of employment land at three times the target set by the policies in the London Plan and an accommodation crisis for industrial businesses in London (see Chapter 15 by Jessica Ferm, Michael Edwards and Edward Jones; Ferm and Jones, 2015).

In this setting, the Camley Street Neighbourhood Forum emerged as a spill-out from the wider King's Cross Neighbourhood Forum, and was designated in February 2014 as the body responsible for preparing the Neighbourhood Plan for an area which includes both the residential and the industrial sites. The forum included, in equal shares, representatives of the residential community and the business community, but chose not to be designated as a business Neighbourhood Forum, to ensure that both residents and businesses could be included. The main objective of the plan was to secure the retention of the existing mix of residential and industrial uses, and of housing tenures, and to proactively set parameters

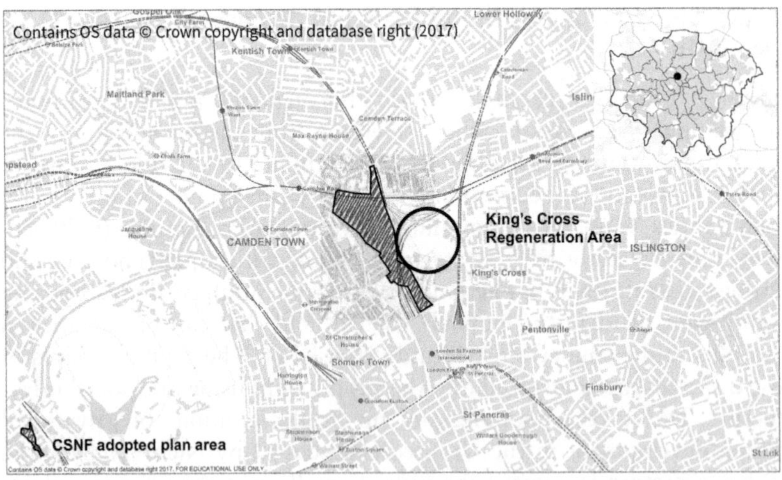

Figure 9.3 Map and location of Camley Street Neighbourhood Planning Area

Source: Basemap: OS VectorMap™ District using EDINA Digimap Ordnance Survey Service, downloaded May 2017.

and conditions on the scale and type of future developments whose inevitability and even necessity had been acknowledged by the forum. In fact, as early as 2011, even before the forum was formed, Camden Council had granted permission for the redevelopment of one of the industrial sites in Camley Street for a high-rise student accommodation building, showing the direction of its strategic interest in the area. In July 2014, two further applications were submitted for the redevelopment of two industrial sites into residential use, both sites located within the boundary of the neighbourhood area. Despite early consultation run by the developer with the wider community in Camley Street, and with members of the forum particularly concerned about how the proposed developments represented an erosion of the industrial character of the area (and therefore a potential threat to the objectives of the forum), the developments were granted permission as originally proposed in March 2015. Acknowledging the limitations of Neighbourhood Planning (and of planning more generally) to recognise diverse interests in the development of the area, the forum sought to gain more power in the decisions on the area and agreed to constitute itself as a Community Land Trust (CLT), at first with the sole intention to acquire the land of the industrial estate owned by Camden, and later, when it became evident that Camden's intention was to redevelop the area for housing, with the purpose to become the landowner and developer of the industrial site and to provide Camden with a vehicle to meet its own policy objectives. The Camley Street Sustainability Zone CLT was established in 2016 to develop a proposal for a mixed-use development for the industrial area, which would retain the existing businesses in new premises (with the least possible disruption to productive activities) and provide up to 1000 heavily discounted housing units for rent under the CLT model of collective community ownership, but with no private individual ownership in the development and the lock-in of profit for community benefits. In early 2017, the proposal found financial backing from institutional investors and maintained open negotiations with Camden Council.

As in the case of the Elephant and Walworth Neighbourhood Plan, the realisation of the limitations of Neighbourhood Planning in the face of dominant planning strategies that transcend the local scale led to a change in community action, organisation and politics. But while the EWNF transferred some of its campaigns into the Neighbourhood Planning format, the Camley Street forum moved some of its action outside the forum format into a structure that would allow for a more proactive campaign for the promotion of the interests of the local business community. However, the NDP was not dismissed, and indeed plays a positive role in setting the planning policy environment that could lock future development to a fixed quantum of non-residential land uses, therefore limiting the escalation of land values, which is the main incentive for Camden Council to dispose of land and for developers to acquire it.

Neighbourhood Planning and the Challenge of Community-led Planning

The Localism Act's commitment to facilitate planning by neighbourhoods has received a number of critiques, which this chapter has highlighted. One of the main concerns is that Neighbourhood Planning is, ultimately, still planning and formally replicates British planning's current model of decision-making, the hegemony of growth and neoliberal politics. Despite its proponents' objective that Neighbourhood Planning would allow communities to plan for their areas according to their needs, the current outcomes make it look like a Trojan horse for a growth-dependent agenda.

But setting aside these conceptualisations of Neighbourhood Planning, how could planning by, for and with neighbourhoods be framed and discussed? The neighbourhood as a scale of politics has always been viewed by different disciplines as problematic, both for its inability to capture the structural processes and dimensions of urban politics and, consequently, its tendency to stifle the identification and practice of progressive planning. And yet neighbourhoods have always been part of the landscape of governments' policies in the UK and in many European countries, and an important practice of community activism.

This chapter has considered these contradictions in two ways: by proposing to frame Neighbourhood Planning not as an instance of participatory planning, but as part of a broader spectrum of practices of community development and community-led planning, and by looking at examples where community activism is not an alternative or in opposition to Neighbourhood Planning, but instead the two approaches combine in a loose symbiotic relation.

The Camley Street and the Elephant and Walworth Neighbourhood Forums illustrate how the ideology of growth, which manifests itself in the incessant need to capture land values through land redevelopment, impacts local communities and their responses. Their experience and actions within and outside the format of Neighbourhood Planning cannot be pigeon-holed as NIMBYism (which would not be possible through the format of Neighbourhood Planning), nor can they be described as a consensual acceptance of the modalities in which growth is delivered.

These aspirations for community-led planning cannot be completely absorbed by Neighbourhood Planning, and Neighbourhood Planning (because it is 'still planning') cannot be used by these communities as the tool to address their needs for progressive development and local politics. This chapter has explored these tensions. Brownill and Bradley (2017) suggest that questioning Neighbourhood Planning for its progressive credentials, for its capacity to give 'power to the people', is the wrong question to ask. What is more important is to continue to explore what Neighbourhood Planning has to offer to less consensual and more radical forms of community development, and how it can help more radical voices in the urban political spectrum become more legible to current statutory planning practices.

Acknowledgements

I thank Richard Lee and Sofia Roupakia of the EWNF and Christian Spencer-Davies and Peter McGinty of the Camley Street NF for allowing me to use their experiences of Neighbourhood Planning as case studies for this chapter.

Notes

1 Author's own calculations from data published in DCLG Notes on Neighbourhood Planning, https://www.gov.uk/government/collections/notes-on-neighbourhood-planning.
2 Author's own research from individual London Boroughs' websites.

References

All listed URLs were last accessed on 1 March 2018.

Arbaci, S. and Rae, I. (2013) Mixed-tenure neighbourhoods in London: policy myth or effective device to alleviate deprivation? *International Journal of Urban and Regional Research*, 37(2), pp.451–479.

Bridge, G., Butler, T. and Lees, L. (2012) *Mixed communities: gentrification by stealth?* Bristol: Policy Press.

Brownill, S. and Bradley, Q. (eds) (2017) *Localism and neighbourhood planning.* Bristol: Policy Press.

Chisholm, M. and Dench, G. (2005) *Community identity: literature review and analysis.* London: Electoral Commission.

Clarke, N. and Cochrane, A. (2013) Geographies and politics of localism: the localism of the United Kingdom's coalition government, *Political Geography*, 34, pp.10–23.

Colomb, C. (2017) Participation and conflict in the formation of neighbourhood areas and forums in "super-diverse" cities, in S. Brownill, S. and Q. Bradley (eds) *Localism and neighbourhood planning.* Bristol: Policy Press.

Cowie, P. and Davoudi, S. (2015) Is small really beautiful? The legitimacy of neighbourhood planning', in S. Davoudi and A. Madanipour (eds) *Reconsidering localism.* London: Routledge.

Davoudi, S. and Cowie, P. (2013) Are English neighbourhood forums democratically legitimate? *Planning Theory & Practice*, 14(4), pp.562–566.

DCLG (2012) *The National Planning Policy Framework.* London: DCLG. Available at: https://www.gov.uk/government/uploads/system/uploads/attachment_data/file/6077/2116950.pdf.

Fainstein, S.S. (2001) *The city builders: property development in New York and London, 1980–2000.* Lawrence, KS: University Press of Kansas.

Ferm, J. and Jones, E. (2015) *London's industrial land: cause for concern?* London: UCL.

Flinders, M., Dommett, K. and Tonkiss, K. (2014) Bonfires and barbecues: coalition governance and the politics of quango reform, *Contemporary British History*, 28(1), pp.56–80.

Haila, A. (2015) *Urban land rent: Singapore as a property state*. Chichester: John Wiley & Sons.

Harvey, D. (1985) *The urbanization of capital: studies in the history and theory of capitalist urbanization*. Baltimore, MD: John Hopkins University Press.

Homer, A. (2000) Creating new communities: the role of the neighbourhood unit in post-war British planning, *Contemporary British History*, 14(1), pp.63–80.

Inch, A. (2015) Ordinary citizens and the political cultures of planning: in search of the subject of a new democratic ethos, *Planning Theory*, 14(4), pp.404–424.

Kallus, R. and Law-Yone, H. (2016) What is a neighbourhood? The structure and function of an idea, *Environment and Planning B: Planning and Design*, 27(6), pp.815–826.

Legacy, C. (2017) Is there a crisis of participatory planning? *Planning Theory*, 16(4), pp.425–442.

London Borough of Hackney (2015) *Key Decision No. LHR K59*. Available at: http://mginternet.hackney.gov.uk/documents/s41422/LHR%20K59_shoreditch_Cabinet_report_Dec_14_.pdf.

London Borough of Southwark (2016) *Neighbourhood planning – designation of a neighbourhood forum (Elephant and Walworth)*. Available at: http://moderngov.southwark.gov.uk/documents/s63897/Report.pdf, last accessed on 4/9/2017.

Mayo, M. (2000) *Cultures, communities, identities*. New York: Springer.

Park, R.E., Burgess, E.W. and McKenzie, R.D. (1925) *The city*. Chicago, IL: University of Chicago Press.

Parker, G. (2008) Parish and community-led planning, local empowerment and local evidence bases: an examination of "good practice" in West Berkshire, *Town Planning Review*, 79(1), pp.61–85.

Parker, G. (2017) The uneven geographies of neighbourhood planning in England. In S. Brownill, S. and Q. Bradley (eds) *Localism and neighbourhood planning*. Bristol: Policy Press.

Parker, G. and Salter, K. (2016) Neo-liberal localisms? Taking stock of neighbourhood planning in England 2011–2016, *Planning Practice and Research*, pp.1–42.

Parker, G., Lynn, T. and Wargent, M. (2015) Sticking to the script? The co-production of neighbourhood planning in England, *Town Planning Review*, 86(5), pp.519–536.

Popple, K. and Quinney, A. (2009) Theory and practice of community development: a case study from the United Kingdom, *Journal of the Community Development Society*, 33(1), pp.71–85.

Raco, M. (2013) *State-led privatisation and the demise of the democratic state: welfare reform and localism in an era of regulatory capitalism*. Farnham: Ashgate.

Sassen, S. (2013) *The global city*. Princeton, NJ: Princeton University Press.

Slater, T. (2009) Missing Marcuse: on gentrification and displacement, *City*, 13(2), pp.292–311.

Slater, T. (2017) Planetary rent gaps, *Antipode*, 49(S1), pp.114–137.
Talen, E. (2006) Design that enables diversity: the complications of a planning ideal, *Journal of Planning Literature*, 20(3), pp.233–249.
Talen, E. (2016) Sense of community and neighbourhood form: an assessment of the social doctrine of new urbanism, *Urban Studies*, 36(8), pp.1361–1379.
Watt, P. (2007) *Understanding social inequality*. Thousand Oaks, CA: SAGE Publications.

10 The Evolving Intersection of Planning and the Commercial Real Estate Market

Tommaso Gabrieli and Nicola Livingstone

Introduction

Urban planning is an active process, operating within fluid, dynamic markets and responding to varied regulatory systems, playing an integral performative role in the continual creation and recreation of the built environment. Harvey (1979) discusses how urbanism reflects spatial patterns and structures, which are mediated by man, with the city as an outcome, as a social product and consequence of many influences. The form and structure of planning and real estate institutions are key influences in this urban city creation, and the case of London today provides us with an opportunity to consider how the active processes of planning interact with commercial real estate investors and developers. It is the evolving intersection of these market actors, their functions and responses to policy and regulation shifts, the circulation of global capital and the increasing stream of international interest in London which are considered here.

This chapter offers original insight into how professional networks and social relationships between planning and real estate actors within an established regulatory system intersect and inherently influence the cityscape of London on the global stage. Rather than considering these professionals as part of a wider institutional framework (see, e.g., Myers, 2016; D'Arcy, 2009), the key objective of the chapter is to examine the evolving, particular experiences of planning and real estate professionals working in the London market today, and to consider how these interconnected roles have adapted in response to globalisation. Although planners and real estate actors interact and influence how cities are created, there has been little academic work which considers *how* their interconnected networks have evolved in the wider context of globalisation and market integration (with the exception of Theurillat et al., 2015, who have examined real estate market 'players' in Switzerland). Specifically, we interrogate the relationships between the planning and real estate industries and their evolution within the London market since the onset of the global financial crisis (GFC) through semi-structured interviews with developers, investors and planning practitioners. We argue that the internationalisation of the commercial real estate sector, combined with deregulation and the resultant growth of private planning consultancies, has manifestly impacted *how* planning practices are expressed in the market, as planners strive to balance sustainable economic, social, and increasingly political interests, in a dynamic and demanding market environment.

The chapter begins by examining London's built environment and considers its present-day position within the global market, from both real estate and planning perspectives. Following the market context, findings from the exploratory empirical research are discussed. These are considered thematically, and reflect on how planning practice has changed post-GFC – the challenges and tensions in relationships between planners and real estate professionals; financialisation and internationalisation – and concludes with thoughts on how the planning and real estate professions will continue to evolve. The final section offers conclusions and recommendations for further research.

Finance, Globalisation and the Built Environment in London

Among world cities, a small sub-set of cities known as international financial centres (IFCs), play a major role in the global system of finance. Those cities act as centres for asset management and product innovation. Economies of scale and agglomeration, which are the benefits that firms obtain by respectively increasing in size and locating near each other, have resulted in an on-going concentration of high-order financial services – such as equity trading, bond trading, foreign exchange activity, derivatives trading and wealth management – in a few key global cities.

In a global economy dominated by the free and fast movement of international funds, IFCs compete with each other in order to attract capital, with London usually being considered one of the most global cities (Sassen, 2001). The attractiveness of London as a destination for both commercial and residential real estate capital has led to the city being been described as a 'safe deposit box' (Fernandez et al., 2016). There are key links between London and other global IFCs, as demonstrated throughout the GFC, where contagion effects were apparent in the global financial and real estate markets (Wojcik, 2013). Such market connections are also demonstrated through cycles, both at local market level and internationally (Weber, 2016; Jadevicius and Huston, 2014; Grover and Grover, 2014) as markets experience 'financialisation'. This relatively new term reflects the "growing influence of capital markets, their intermediaries, and processes in contemporary economic and political life" (Pike and Pollard, 2010: 30), where profit is made "through financial channels rather than through trade and commodity production" (Krippner, 2005: 174). Financial flows into London have been growing steadily over past decades as the city has experienced financialisation, creating new demand for office space and providing funds to transform the built environment, whose features are in turn a central factor in maintaining the capacity of the city to attract more capital. The decisions of investors, developers and planners are related to each other through real estate prices, financial returns and policy constraints.

However, the process of concentration of financial activities in a few cities may not continue as it has done in the recent past, and the future of London and other IFCs is an open topic for debate, even more so after the UK voted to leave the EU. Strands of literature have argued to what extent developments in information and communications technology have transformed the nature of business and removed the need for agglomeration and city locations. In this respect, Lizieri (2009) suggests that one key factor to consider is the distinction between retail and wholesale activity, and between high-volume, low-margin and low-volume, high-margin activities. Retail activity may be less likely to concentrate since it relies on customer knowledge, tastes, preferences and local marketing. By contrast, high-value-added and low-volume businesses (e.g. corporate finance, fund management, mergers and acquisitions) rely on frequent client contact and information from a network of customers, rivals and parallel business, which leads to concentration. This complex interaction of agglomeration benefits, demand for central locations, creation and transformation of office space, which is mediated by market rents and prices, may explain the concentration of very diverse clusters of activities – ranging from the established financial and legal services to innovative start-ups and creative firms – into nearby areas of Central London. The future of the city presents many open questions, ranging from the incentive of innovative firms to relocate away from expensive central areas, as they become more mature and either production- or retail-focused, to the wider impact of Brexit on the optimal location of high-order financial and related services.

The built environment of London has changed a lot in the past 30 years, and has been characterised by significant development of new landmark office buildings as well as the redevelopment of former industrial areas, such as Canary Wharf and other sites in East London, into new mixed office/retail space. This activity is primarily a consequence of the demands for space from international financial service firms and other professional services that cluster around them. At the same time, the availability of adequate and appropriate space for firms is a key competitive attribute of a city. Lizieri (2009) explains that this does not simply mean provision of large, new, technologically sophisticated office complexes. Outsourcing of activities and the need for niche service providers creates demand for a wide range of space, varying in size and quality.

The real estate market is thus an important attribute of the agglomeration economies that promote clustering of financial activity. From this perspective, London has favoured agglomeration through the availability of a wide range of central space, varying in size and quality with new construction and refurbishment of existing buildings, as well as the ability to satisfy the needs of clients in terms of technology, transport, amenities and tailored support to international clients. Nevertheless there are on-going challenges for lower-value businesses and small-to-medium enterprises, which may not be able to afford expensive central locations (see Chapter 15 by Jessica Ferm, Michael Edwards and Edward Jones).

In the complex picture we are describing, real estate is not only a space in which business activities take place, but also an investment asset and a store of value. For this reason, investment in and financing of real estate play a crucial role, since financial resources and expenditures impact the physical dimension. Investment and financing are intrinsically related, and a mix of equity and debt instruments typically finances construction projects and investments in tenanted space. Equity investors in London-based real estate projects or real estate companies are typically foreign and domestic pension funds, or other institutional investors, which have traditionally found it optimal to hold real estate in mixed-asset portfolios because of an attractive risk/return profile or for diversification purposes. The widespread use of debt financing implies that lending to commercial real estate investors forms a significant part of banks' financial activity, and a high proportion of banks' commercial real estate loans are secured on London offices. The size of international investments in London real estate assets has been growing over the last decades, with more than half of offices in the city now being owned by non-UK institutions. In global portfolio allocation strategies, investing in London real estate is often perceived as an expensive but safe option, which implies high asset prices and not necessarily high future returns, but with the benefit of relatively low volatility and low depreciation risk.

The famous Four Quadrant Model of DiPasquale and Wheaton (1992) is an essential analytical tool to understand how the complex interaction between development and investment inevitably creates market dynamics, volatility and cycles (see Miller (2015) for a video lecture on the model). Essentially, the model considers the specific and joint dynamics of property, investment and development markets, where shocks in one market will have an effect – albeit with lags – on other markets through changes in prices and rents. For example, a demand shock in the property market affects property valuations, which in turn will have an effect on investments for new construction, which will ultimately feed back as new supply to the property market, with the possibility of overshooting demand and therefore reversing the cycle. Most IFCs have experienced pronounced development cycles over the last 30 years, and property cycles are a fundamental feature of real estate markets. Office rents are primarily determined by the demand for space that comes from firms. This demand is affected by the state of the economy, as well as shifts in the patterns of employment and changes in ways of working. Supply of new space by developers is also affected by economic and financial dynamics through the cost and availability of equity and debt. Shifts in supply and demand are expected to imply price adjustments: stronger demand causes price increases. Price increases would give an incentive to developers to build new space, but the resulting higher supply would in turn imply a downward re-adjustment of prices. Adjustments are slow because of the lags between a shift in demand, rental movements and the delivery of completed new offices. This contributes to the existence of natural development cycles of demand-driven appreciation and supply-driven depreciation. This natural cycle can be amplified by financial dynamics, since periods of cheap financing would imply stronger demand for assets and higher real estate prices, but also more financing available for new supply that will follow. International capital flows make those linkages even more complex (for a recent analysis of the European office market, see, e.g., McAllister and Nanda, 2016) and prone to systemic risk (see Lizieri and Pain, 2014). There are also several behavioural elements in cycles: if developers, or their funders, are myopic, then they may overreact to short-run upward rental and price trends, hence overbuilding and triggering over-supply that will, in turn, create downward pressure on rents and prices.

Asset market bubbles are defined as rapid price escalations that cannot be explained by underlying fundamental economic factors. The study of asset market bubbles is a widely investigated topic in finance, and this has in turn inspired a sub-field that focuses on cycles and bubbles in real estate markets. Lizieri (2009), among many others, explains that commercial real estate has many characteristics which suggest that it should be prone to bubbles: high transaction costs and illiquidity which contribute to thin trading and lack of transparency, information asymmetry leading to the possibility of common shared errors, as well as heavy reliance on debt in capital structures. Moreover, financial and real estate markets are intrinsically connected. During all recent financial crises, real estate markets have suffered particularly, whereas during recent financial booms, they have been prone to bubbles. This happens because changes in the financial environment have an impact on firms' employment and demand for office space, and therefore on vacancy rates, rents, and ultimately on prices. Real estate market dynamics in turn feed back into the financial system, because the performance of real estate portfolios affects bank lending. Through this type of mechanism, the 2007 sub-prime crisis led to the global financial crisis: a real estate shock triggered a banking crisis, which then spread to other areas of the financial and real economy.

Finance and globalisation in IFCs are linked with debates concerning the ability of the nation state to determine local economic and social activity. O'Brien (1992) and Martin (1994) discuss how financial market regulators no longer have full control over regulatory frameworks within the nation state and cities. As Lizieri (2009) points out, this is related to Castells' (1989: 254) concept of the space of flows "that now dominates and transcends the historically constructed space of places". We can therefore understand that in an economy where global financial flows increasingly affect the built environment, planners may not be able to control such external forces, and therefore have less capacity to influence final outcomes. Indeed, the role of the state in the UK planning system has been increasingly 'hands-off' in recent decades, deregulation of the planning system being an example, as the state is intervening less in the market.

A major challenge for the planning system in a globalised context comes from multi-level pressures. Newman and Thornley (2011) discuss in depth how the formulation of metropolitan strategies takes place within the context of urban politics and is shaped by the degree of power that is brought to bear by different interests. In a global world, the interplay between interests and planning priorities is not confined to the boundaries of city politics, and they analyse the broad pressures from political, economic, environmental and cultural sources that shape a particular strategic planning agenda (see Chapter 1 by John Tomaney and Jessica Ferm). This reveals a complex multi-level interaction between city-level pressures, and the regional and global level. The external forces may take the form of agencies that seek to influence or control the local political decisions and priorities, such as national governments, pressure groups or particular powerful business interests.

This has surely been the case for London over the last three decades, with on-going changes to governance structures, and tensions between the various tiers of government. The flux is illustrated by the dismissal of the Greater London Council in 1986, the consequent fragmentation of responsibilities between lower-tier boroughs with scarce coordination, and the recognised need for strategy and coordination that precipitated the creation of the Greater London Authority in 1997. Questions remain around the tensions between resident groups and business lobbies – such as London First – and their respective impact on plans, as well as tensions created between the right of residents to oppose planning proposals and the central power to order plans with strategic interest, for example the High Speed 2 railway. In all the iterations of the London Plan, there has been a focus on maintaining international competitiveness as one of the primary objectives (or possibly *the* primary objective). Sustaining London's economic success is often interpreted as ensuring growing global financial flows into London, thereby reinforcing the dynamics that have been illustrated in this section.

London: Present-day Professional Reflections

This section of the chapter unpacks the empirical primary research carried out which reflects the 'real-life experiences' (Chang, 2011) of planning and real estate market professionals working in London today. As there is negligible academic precedent for this type of work, semi-structured interviews were used to identify emerging themes in relation to industry networks. Five in-depth semi-structured and exploratory interviews were carried out, providing a qualitative foundation for the development of further work in this area. Each interview represents the perspective of a different market actor (public sector planner, private sector planner, real estate developer, investor, agent), and in essence reflects five detailed and individual case studies of market experiences. From these case study interviews, four key themes emerged, which offer insight into the networks of professionals operating in London and their experiences of the regulatory system, the commercial market, the internationalisation of the city and their evolving, networked roles in the market. When reflecting on the changes in the London market since the GFC and in the longer term, interviewees emphasised the issues faced by built environment professionals in negotiating an increasingly political and deregulated planning system, the shifting roles of public and private actors at play in the market, and London's position in the global market as an IFC. The four emerging themes are discussed in the following sub-sections.

Perceptions of the Evolving Role of Planners: What's Changed?

All of the interviewees discussed how the public sector planning system has become increasingly political – a tool adopted by politicians to meet their own specific needs. Planners are seen as "high up the pecking order for cuts", as "politicians view planning as a negative force, they talk of delays in the system, constraints, lack of flexibility", therefore this acts as a "break on the economy and the growth of London". However, such comments are more directly linked to the overall philosophy of the state itself and its much reduced role in the market.

The withdrawal of the state has left the public sector planning system fulfilling a more reactive rather than proactive role in the networks of actors operating in London. Although the negative perception of the planning sector by politicians in central government is not necessarily a new phenomenon, today it is one that is acutely affecting the operation of the planning system, reflecting "poor political leadership and [a] lack of understanding of how important it is to empower people if you want a professional service". Typically, "delays in the planning system are political, not professional". Indeed, a number of interviewees were keen to strongly emphasise that the role of the public planner "has fundamentally not changed, [but] the role of the state has changed quite dramatically". Indeed, public planners are, across the board, seen to be fulfilling their function to the best of their abilities, and although it would be ideal if planning could be transacted more quickly, most issues experienced by interviewees relate to "resourcing in local authorities and not the professionalism of the planners. Local authorities are respected, but squeezed."

Concomitant to this squeeze in local authority public sector planning, the private sector planning profession has seen significant growth (see Chapter 8 by Mike Raco). Networks of service providers now typically operate as 'consultants', with planners, real estate development and investment agents all working within dedicated global built environment services companies. Some interviewees implied that in part, this move towards the private sector for planners reflects how the public sector professionals are failing to keep up with market shifts and are "almost being caught behind the curve in terms of the wider economy and the Local Plans, there is a need to innovate". Currently, the "private sector does appear to be better at delivering projects, skills in the private sector now seem to be stronger than the public sector" and there is currently "less specialist knowledge in the public sector".

When considering the efficacy of the planning and development process (public and private), the role of the market and its regulatory policies are clearly a considerable influence, one which is impacted by a variety of different networks of individuals and companies in the built environment (construction companies, architects, surveyors). Through such networks, public and private sector actors come together. One interviewee explained that the development process is largely market-driven and the role of public planners is often to select between different proposals from the private sector. Between those different proposals, the planner may choose the one that satisfies most of the – or rather, the preferred – policy objectives. Indeed, "a lot of developments that have been supported have been because the local planning staff have been supportive and interpreted those developments within the Local Plan context and their localities objectives". However, due to such interpretation, it is very rare that all the policy objectives will be satisfied; the planners (and often other actors involved) are likely to have to accept a compromise and trade-offs between different policy objectives. Planning consultants for private developers potentially have a greater impact on the outcome because they have the responsibility to present the trade-offs and argue for compromises:

> There are so many policies and they are so far reaching in terms of car parking spaces, building materials, height of the building, affordable housing targets, uses that are protected, uses that are encouraged . . . it would be almost impossible to design a scheme that ticks every single policy box . . . there is no situation where you are not going to have to compromise on some of those big policy issues . . . And it is the role of the applicant to set out the compromises.

In these circumstances, the role of public and private planners today is clearly very different. One interviewee commented that agents acting for developers are "toughening up their act, in parallel with public sector services being disenfranchised in some ways and losing resources", reinforcing the perspective that private sector planners active in the market today potentially play more powerful roles than public sector planners. In particular, when it comes to compromises and trade-offs, the private sector planner is seen as having greater leverage. However, both the public and private sector actors are playing an essential role in the development process; their motivations and positions may be contrasting, but they are each working towards a successful, potentially compromised outcome. One interviewee suggested that these contrasting motivations may prove to be problematic if antagonisms between actors are exacerbated in the longer term, and that although:

> drivers of public and private sector [actors] are very different, it is a bad thing if the balance goes too far in the direction of the private sector, because the public sector is what gives changes in the [planning] environment a credibility, and a kind of legitimacy.

Public sector planning continues to embody the 'democratic foundation' of the planning system in the United Kingdom.

Active Challenges and Embedded Tensions in Relationship Networks

It has already been established that planning is becoming increasingly political, and is today a "relatively unsettled profession which has been exploited by the politicians" – a profession which, in the public sector, is perceived to be falling behind the curve and not adjusting quickly enough to market shifts. It can also be argued that the political orientation of the planning committee is often the factor that may strike the balance in one direction or another:

> Politics plays a major role in the decisions over policy objectives. Ultimately reasonable sized applications are decided by local planning committees, made up of locally elected representatives, who are members of political parties; so it is about their policy objectives more than anything else. The planner knows to an extent what is viable, but the reality is that he/she says "If I can only do this or that, I will only do what is politically acceptable, or desirable."

Therefore, when it comes to reaching an agreement on an application through the consultation process, there are expected trade-offs between communities, planners and policy-makers, trade-offs which are inherently influenced not only by built environment professionals, but also the local politics. When planning applications are submitted, there is typically "huge cynicism towards developers . . . you are starting at square one with [most] of the local community". Often when interacting with the local community to consult on a development, there is clearly "a lack of knowledge and education of the people on the planning committees, the members of the local authority who will often push back against the [planning] officer's recommendations because they have simply not understood the product". It was suggested that real estate developers who adopt a more long-term approach to creating a successful development, and who intend to retain the development moving into the future rather than selling on, approach the consultation process in a more successful and proactive way with local communities.

However, whether the developer has a short- or long-term interest, an additional challenge that was identified was the consultation and application process itself (for perspective on this, see Chapter 6 by Yasminah Beebeejaun). Across a number of interviews, there was generally thought to be a "lack of good consultation at the start of the planning process", a need for local authorities to be more proactive and for an earlier start to consultation. Interacting with the local community and planning committee earlier in the process would ensure that the community feel their opinions are valued as "people need to play a role and have ownership of the plan making process". This could potentially help to diffuse the issues faced by developers in overcoming conflict in local areas, but also potentially speed up the planning process itself and improve those all-important networked relationships.

The 'Financialisation' and 'Internationalisation' of the City

This section reflects a shift from discussing the more localised networks of actors in manoeuvring the planning system, and moves to more of a global narrative, which considers the role London currently plays in the world market as "huge amounts of capital are attracted to London, it is seen as a safe haven, and hugely experienced people use the best consultants and joint ventures" to facilitate and execute their real estate activities in the city.

The London "real estate sector is a global stage, and a significant amount of capital is coming in from different jurisdictions across the world", and there is "nothing at all wrong with inward investment, as long as it is active. But if it isn't realising its potential, if it is being used as a security deposit box, then that is a bad investment." Interviewees emphasised the need for real estate investors and developers to take a longer-term approach and interest. The capital flowing into the city should deliver additional benefits to the local community, and not just maximise profits. Many real estate investors already take that approach, and it is recognised that part of the seemingly perpetual negative rhetoric surrounding international investors in the last decade is not an accurate representation of the reality. In this respect, "perhaps in the past there hasn't been enough emphasis on the overall, non-monetary benefits that are delivered through development, and perhaps too much emphasis on extracting the maximum value of the land". Private sector actors have been seen to provide clear community 'value add' in a number of developments across London, such as Capco's interest in Covent Garden and the public–private partnership active in redeveloping the Woodberry Down estate in Hackney. One interviewee discussed Argent, which redeveloped and transformed King's Cross from a neglected to regenerated area of the city as an obvious example of successful private development, influenced by the international market. Argent is owned by Hermes Investment Management, which is a UK-domiciled company operating on a global scale. Although viewed as a success in urban design terms and putting King's Cross 'on the map' in terms of investment, the development attracted controversy due to the displacement of residents and businesses, as well as issues surrounding 'publicly owned private spaces' and affordable housing provision. These issues are not unusual in the London market, and scepticism persists in relation to international flows of capital coming into the city, specifically from the East, with questions raised over "whether the new owners will have as much interest in the future interest and vibrancy of the surrounding areas". A clear example of how investments from the East currently affect surrounding areas is the Olympic Village at Stratford. Prior to the Olympic Games in London in 2012, the Athletes' Village was sold to Qatari Diar (Qatar's real estate investment company) and Delancey Estates (UK investors). Even with wider concerns over the internationalisation of London, it is not a case of international developers profiting exclusively to the detriment of local communities; rather, the antagonisms persisting in the London market are nuanced and complex. The planner's role in mediating between investor and developer requirements and community and social needs in culturally specific contexts reflects the need for balanced and careful application of specialist knowledge between all involved parties.

Developers and investors want a well-informed "route to knowledge, [with] speed and certainty", and they depend upon the specialised knowledge of the planners involved in achieving the overall aim of spreading capital across London's built environment. There is clearly an element of trust in a planning consultant's capacity to provide appropriate professional advice and information on, for example, market-specific planning practices, policies and regulations. However, there is also an element of market competition, because if services provided are not deemed efficient, or effective enough, then the real estate developers and investors can find another planning consultancy which replicates the services provided. Therefore, the financialisation and internationalisation of the real estate market in London has both stimulated growth in private sector planning due to increased demand for services and fuelled competition between private planning consultancies.

As London's perception as a 'safe deposit box' has emerged, the city has become consistently attractive to potential developers and investors, with the private sector planning knowledge initially, combined with the public sector interaction latterly, influencing progress and potential success. Although the public sector planning system has been squeezed, the private sector planning and real estate consultancies have continued to grow significantly, becoming key to executing developments and investments. In this respect, international actors especially rely on the local professional planning and real estate services to accurately inform and support their decision-making process. As a corollary, if the so-called route to knowledge is clear, then such actors are "likely to be much more flexible, likely to adapt their schemes and negotiate in all sorts of ways", in order to spread their capital into London. So, on the flipside, rather than local planning officers considering accepted policy-related compromises, the real estate developers and investors are also often willing to consider making concessions. Such is the appeal of London as an IFC with an established global real estate market. These international developers and investors are seen as more able to "manoeuvre the system over time", as due to the capital under their command, they have the luxury of being able and willing to be patient, waiting for the best opportunities to emerge in line with their strategic needs in the capital. From such comments, it is clear that there are temporal, strategic and power relations at play in London, as international investors and developers seek to achieve particular objectives in a highly competitive market. The roles of both public and private sector planners are critical to achieving these objectives and providing reliable, up-to-date professional knowledge and counsel.

Market Processes and Public Land Use

The final key theme of the interviews was related to the future, and how planning may continue to evolve across the structures of the built environment profession and regulatory environment. Much was discussed about the lack of effective use of public land, and the potential benefits that could emerge from blending public and private responses to market-driven built environment processes in London. The market-driven process of development is described as an efficient process in terms of the use of resources:

> One can look at the past and see mistakes, for example a lot of regeneration schemes from the 90's have built two-storey buildings in areas that are now central and prime, which would be considered today to be a very inefficient use of land . . . but one can argue that at the time, given those market conditions, that was an efficient use of land.

The advocated reason is that in London, the land market is so competitive that inevitably a developer is forced to optimise the site to get the most benefit out of it for all involved parties, and sites which were developed historically are not providing at their optimal potential today (from residential, commercial or density perspectives). Having said that, one of the major inefficiencies seems to be the use of public land. One interviewee argued that councils can often acquire land for development at nil cost or borrow money relatively cheaply, whereas it is very expensive for the developer. However, local authorities rarely use this as an opportunity for public-led development, and in general could use and manage land more efficiently, given the policy objectives. One interviewee provided a hypothetical example, reflecting on current practice:

> A council could take land and develop it itself and achieve a 100% affordable housing rate, rather than selling the land to the private developer, or it could develop it with better quality materials . . . [But] the way that public land has been managed is disposal to the open market, because of a perceived statutory obligation to achieve best consideration . . . and best consideration has been interpreted as highest capital receipts . . . and the way to obtain highest capital receipts is to dispose of it to the highest bidder who pays the highest land value . . . and the reason that they can pay the highest value is because they have been more bullish on the assumptions that they make, which often implies that they will build less affordable housing and build more cheaply.

It is also argued that even this is largely a political decision, and that if best consideration was interpreted as that which achieves the best social benefits, as well as profits, the council could enter into a joint venture or partnership, or covenant the land. This has started to happen with some recent schemes, for example the construction of Bernard Wetherill House through the Croydon Urban Regeneration Vehicle, which partnered Croydon Council and John Laing (2008–2016). As another interviewee noted, certain local authorities in addition to Croydon, such as Ealing and Barking, are beginning to develop more strategic visions in relation to what they do with their land and emerging potential development opportunities. There is a need for local authorities to become more proactive in the planning process once more and to approach opportunities by 'thinking outside the box'. In looking to the future and striving towards a more fluidly functioning market of both global and local networks of actors, "the answers lie . . . with building bridges to bring groups together to achieve the best we can deliver and be positive".

Concluding Thoughts

This chapter has reflected on how professional networks and social relationships between planning and real estate actors within an established regulatory system intersect and inherently influence the cityscape of London on the global stage. It emphasised the role of global financial flows, how those are the main drivers of real estate activity, how this implies the need for a planning system that facilitates the capacity of a global city to continue to attract new global flows, and how this implies new challenges for planners. Despite our inevitable focus on London, this being one of the most global IFCs, our reflections could inspire or guide further research on other IFCs and competitiveness in regional cities.

The clear message that emerges from our research is that the built environment in London functions as a myriad of networked institutional roles. These reflect the regulatory 'rules of the game' and the interpretation of policies (such as Local Plans), and demonstrate how the state, although influential and key to the creation of the city as an important IFC, is inclined to let the market be interpreted by specialised professionals and adopt more neo-liberal approaches to planning and the economy. However, specific politicians and parties active on the ground, and in localities, are now adopting planning as a mechanism they can use to affect change in the real estate market – depending on whether it is interpreted as positive or negative, and funded by domestic or international capital. It is clear that politics now plays a significant role in the market, and affects how both local and national politicians and perceived.

Both public and private sector planners are key to the successful completion and integration of new developments into local communities and the wider city. Although the private sector is viewed as being more proactive, compared to the more squeezed and now reactive public sector, each play important roles in the development process. There is some beauty in this difference, as it reflects how the planning system as a whole has adapted and responded to the needs of both investors and developers, and the state. There appears to be, at present in the London market, a precarious balance between the functions of different actors and companies, which are operating within the rules of the game, but representing varied perspectives and points of view. The importance of communicating these points of view to the local communities through an effective consultation process cannot be understated. There appears to be a need to integrate local community perspectives earlier in the planning process, to ensure a smoother, more successful negotiated outcome for all parties involved. The activities of the local community and local planning committees can clearly have an impact on how a development proceeds and is perceived. The impact of the 'local' cannot be understated, as consultation can affect outcomes for small-scale, capital-light local companies and large-scale international, capital-heavy investors. Although London as an international market is seen as accessible, transparent and a 'safe haven' for many, the notion of market convergence can be somewhat contradicted due to the realities of planning and developing in local authorities.

The market dynamics of real estate and planning actors, as well as other built environment professionals active in London today, are flexible and fluid (although change may come more quickly in the private than the public sector). Networked relationships play a significant role, as each tries to achieve the best outcome under 'best consideration' and 'highest and best use' for burgeoning developments in the city. The companies themselves are competitive and strategic in their approach to clients and the demands on their services, especially within the private sector. However, moving forward, there may be a need for both public and private planners to 'think outside the box' and continue to evolve their roles in order to successfully respond to the new challenges arising from their networked and increasingly intersected relationships. As cities continue to develop and become increasingly 'financialised', planners and real estate professionals must continue to adapt and effectively respond to both investors and developers in a highly competitive market, which inherently incorporates perspectives from the local to the global.

References

All listed URLs were last accessed on 1 March 2018.

Castells, M. (1989) *The informational city: information technology, economic restructuring, and the urban-regional process*. Oxford: Blackwell.

Chang, H. (2011) Institutions and economic development: theory, policy and history, *Journal of Institutional Economics*, 7(4), pp.473–498.

D'Arcy, E. (2009) The evolution of institutional arrangements to support the internationalisation of real estate involvements: some evidence from Europe, *Journal of European Real Estate Research*, 2, pp.280–293.

DiPasquale, D. and Wheaton, W. (1992) The markets for real estate assets and space: a conceptual framework, *Journal of the American Real Estate and Urban Economics Association*, 20(2), pp.181–197.

Fernandez, R., Hofman, A. and Aalbers, M. (2016) London and New York as a safe deposit box for the transnational wealth elite, *Environment & Planning A*, 48(12), pp.2443–2461.

Harvey, D. (1979) *Social justice and the city*. London: Edward Arnold.

Grover, R. and Grover, C. (2014) Property bubbles – a transitory phenomenon, *Journal of Property Investment & Finance*, 32(2), pp.208–222.

Jadevicius, A. and Huston, S. (2014) A "family of cycles" – major and auxiliary business cycles, *Journal of Property Investment & Finance*, 32(3), pp.306–323.

Krippner, G. (2005) The financialization of the American economy, *Socio-Economic Review*, 3, pp.173–208.

Lizieri, C. (2009) Towers of capital: office markets and international financial services. Oxford: Wiley-Blackwell.

Lizieri, C. and Pain, K. (2014) International Office Investment in Global Cities: the production of financial space and systemic risk, *Regional Studies*, 48(3), pp.439–455.

Martin, R. (1994) Stateless money, global financial integration and national economic autonomy: the end of geography. In S. Corbridge, R. Martin and N. Thrift (eds) *Money, power and space*. Oxford: Blackwell.

McAllister, P. and Nanda, A. (2016) Do foreign buyers compress office real estate cap rates? *Journal of Real Estate Research*, 38(4), pp.569–594.

Miller, N. (2015) *Explaining the Four Quadrant Model by Miller*, YouTube educational video. Available at: https://www.youtube.com/watch?time_continue=586&v=kVwHvliV1pA.

Myers, D. (2016) *New economic thinking and real estate*. Chichester: Wiley.

Newman, P. and Thornley, A. (2001) *Planning world cities: globalization and urban politics*. London: Palgrave Macmillan.

O'Brien, R. (1992) *Global financial integration: the end of geography*. London: RIIA.

Pike, A. and Pollard, J. (2010) Economic geographies of financialization, *Economic Geography*, 86(1), pp.26–51.

Sassen (2001) *The global city: New York, London, Tokyo*. Princeton, NJ: Princeton University Press.

Theurillat, T., Rerat, P. and Crevoisier, O. (2015) The real estate market: players, institutions and territories, *Urban Studies*, 52(8), pp.1414–1433.

Weber, R. (2016) Performing property cycles, *Journal of Cultural Economy*, 9(6), pp.587–603.

Wojcik, D. (2013) The dark side of NY-LON: financial centres and the global financial crisis, *Urban Studies*, 50(13), pp.2736–2752.

11 Planning for Diversity in an Era of Social Change

Claire Colomb and Mike Raco

This chapter focuses on the relationship between the planning system and the ethnic, cultural, religious and demographic diversity which has arisen as a result of post-war waves of migration to the UK. It examines the ways in which perceived forms of 'difference' arising from this diversity have been addressed in planning and urban policy. We first outline how 'ethnicity' is conceived in the UK, before assessing how planning theorists and practitioners have advocated new forms of 'planning for diversity' since the 1980s, driven by a politics of recognition of difference. Such concerns have first been addressed through national legislative anti-discrimination and equality provisions. We then show how local planning authorities (LPAs) have encouraged the participation of ethnic minority groups in planning processes and sought to address their specific needs through both minority-targeted policies and area-based urban policies. Finally, the role of planning in creating spaces of (multicultural) encounter is addressed. The chapter concludes by contrasting normative calls for 'planning for diversity' with the ambiguities, contradictory outcomes, dilemmas and challenges of doing so in practice.

Conceptions of Ethnic Diversity in the UK

Between 1948 and 1970, nearly half a million Caribbean migrants came to the UK, followed from the 1960s onwards by migrants from India, Pakistan, Bangladesh and East Africa. First mainly composed of Commonwealth citizens filling labour shortages, those migratory waves later became more diverse in terms of national origin and migration status. In the 2000s and 2010s, substantial migration from Central and Eastern Europe was facilitated by the accession of 10 new countries to the European Union, with just under one million Polish nationals residing in the UK in 2016. In 1991, a question on 'ethnic group membership' was introduced in the census, in contrast with most European countries, which do not collect ethnic or racial data. The categories used to capture differences of origin in social statistics and public policy do not take stock of "true and authentic" identities, but are "socially constructed, influenced by existing (and shifting) power relationships, national images and stereotypes, legal procedures and historical paths" (Simon and Piché, 2012: 1358). Collecting such data raises a dilemma: does "distinguishing and characterizing populations according to their ethnic origins constitute a risk of stigmatisation or is it, on the contrary, an asset for measuring and explaining discrimination and for demanding more inclusive policies" (Simon and Piché, 2012: 1358)? The acronym Black and Minority Ethnic (BME) is used here to refer to individuals who self-describe as not 'White' British" in the UK census (they may be British citizens or foreign nationals). The terms 'ethnicity' and 'race' are thus not used as objective categories, but as social and relational constructs which structure public action (Thomas, 2000). Acknowledging the critiques of these analytical categories (e.g. Brubaker, 2004; Vertovec, 2007), we later reflect on the problems posed by their use in planning and urban policy.

In 2011, the BME population (see Figure 11.1 for a breakdown) represented just under 20% of the population of England and Wales, but was unevenly distributed across the territory: half of them lived in three cities – London, Birmingham, and Manchester. London's BME population reached 55% in 2011. There is thus a particularly *urban* dimension to the challenges of a more diverse society – although not exclusively.[1] Within cities, BME households tend to be concentrated in particular areas where the proportion of BME population is higher than average, something referred to by sociologists – in a descriptive, non-normative way – as ethnic 'segregation': the unequal distribution of a particular kind of attribute, in this instance ethnicity, among spatially defined population aggregates. In British cities, however, areas of BME concentration are usually ethnically mixed.

The ways European states have dealt with the integration of migrants into their national society have differed significantly, reflecting different 'public philosophies of integration' (Favell, 1998) which evolved over time. In the UK, there was a gradual 'racialisation of immigration' in British politics: non-White immigration was increasingly portrayed as problematic and in need of controls, introduced in 1962. Since then, successive national governments have combined (variable degrees of) restrictions on the entry of new migrants with the promotion of 'race equality', 'anti-discrimination', and later 'equal opportunities' for the resident BME population (Thomas, 2008). At the local level, from the 1970s onwards, several local authorities began to develop 'pluralist' or 'multiculturalist' policies (e.g. in Birmingham, Leicester, Sheffield and London), often more progressive than those of the national government. Indeed, some of the most significant and effective forms of 'planning for diversity' have been developed at the local level, more specifically in super-diverse cities (Raco et al., 2017). In London, the ethnic and cultural diversity of the population have been embraced and marketed in positive terms by successive Mayors. This ostensible celebration – often underpinning

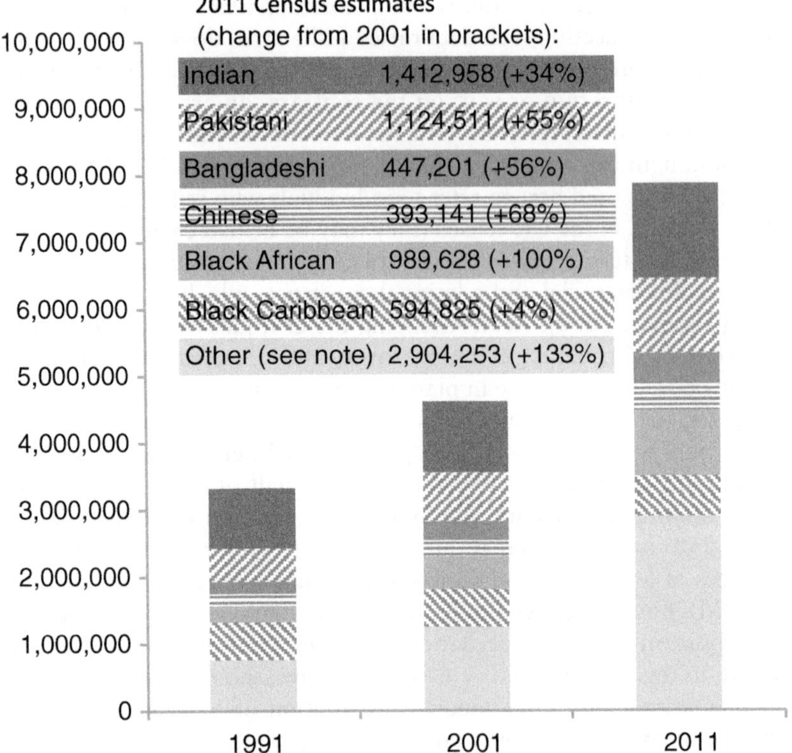

Figure 11.1 Ethnic groups other than White in England and Wales, 1991–2001–2011 census data

Source: Jivraj and Simpson (2015: 21), reproduced with permission.

Note: The 'Other' groups are: Mixed – 1,224,400 (+82%); Other Asian – 835,720 (+238%); Other Black – 280,437 (+186%); Arab – 230,600 (not measured before 2011); Other – 333,096 (+46%) (this excludes White Irish and White Other categories).

an agenda of economic competitiveness – has recently stood in stark contrast with the national government's increasingly negative views on migration and diversity, in particular in the wake of the Brexit referendum and increased anxieties about terrorism.

The Politics of Difference and the Case for Diversity-sensitive Planning

In the 1960s, critical voices began to challenge the post-war 'rational comprehensive planning' consensus which dominated Western planning practice. Planning, as an instrument of state power, was criticised by Marxist and neo-Weberian scholars for reproducing patterns of inequalities or discrimination against particular groups (e.g. ethnic minorities or low-income groups) and for marginalising their needs. In the UK, Rex and Moore's (1967) study of housing and race relations in Birmingham showed how bureaucratic procedures for council housing allocation systematically disadvantaged BME individuals. Pahl (1975) further investigated the role of 'urban gatekeepers', such as planners or estate agents, who through the allocation of urban resources can favour or disadvantage particular individuals. This was compounded by portrayals of 'authoritarian' and 'insensitive' planners who destroyed communities through top-down slum clearance (Dennis, 1970, 1972) – practices which became increasingly challenged by grassroots mobilisations. Thomas (2000), in his extensive work on the topic, argues that British planning practice has historically been 'socially conservative', with key planning ideas such as urban containment, rural conservation and New Towns contributing to sustaining racial segregation in inner cities and a 'White' view of Englishness.

In the 1970s and 1980s, concerns for the 'politics of recognition' and 'difference' took centre stage in both critical social theory and progressive political debates. Post-structuralist, post-colonial and feminist thinkers shifted the traditional focus on class inequalities towards the need for recognition and empowerment of individuals and groups marginalised because of their ethnicity, gender, age, culture, religion, (dis) ability or sexuality (Young, 1990). In this context, the built environment and planning practices were shown to reflect dominant power structures and reproduce systemic inequalities (Sandercock, 2003). In the UK a minority of activist planners began to push the Royal Town Planning Institute (RTPI) to work on issues of gender and racial equality. The RTPI, in partnership with the Commission for Racial Equality (CRE), published an extensive report which highlighted how planning had been an arena for unwittingly discriminatory practices or colour-blind approaches deemed inadequate (RTPI/CRE, 1983). In the decade that followed, however, little progress was made in implementing its recommendations (Krishnarayan and Thomas, 1993). A further study of LPA practices with regard to BME groups (Loftman and Beazley, 1998) showed that only 3% of LPAs in England, Scotland and Wales monitored the impact of planning policies on BME groups, 10% undertook research on BME planning needs, 14% had mechanisms for direct contacts with BME group, and 13% had specific planning policies (for a similar review in Northern Ireland, see Ellis, 2001).

The Evolution of Anti-discrimination and Equality Legislation and Its Application to Planning

The Race Relations Act (RRA) – the first legislation of its kind in Western Europe – was first passed in 1965 and later revised in 1968, 1976 and 2000. It made it unlawful to discriminate against anyone on grounds of race, colour, nationality (including citizenship), ethnic or national origin,[2] and the 1976 version referred explicitly to land use planning. This legislation has helped to fight against direct racial discrimination in planning – for example, the refusal to grant planning permission to an Indian applicant for a takeaway restaurant due to concerns over the smell of food (Thomas, 2000), or against racist representations in public consultations (RTPI, 1996). Yet it has been of "little practical use in preventing the application of planning regulations in ways that are blind to differences of culture and ethnicity" (Gale and Naylor, 2002: 390).

The Equality Act of 2010 brought together 116 separate pieces of anti-discrimination legislation. Article 149 reiterates the so-called 'public sector equality duty' to actively promote equality of opportunity and tackle *direct* and *indirect* discrimination in relation to nine 'protected characteristics': age, disability, gender, race, religion and belief, pregnancy and maternity, marriage and civil partnership, sexual orientation and gender reassignment.[3] This duty is reflected in the RTPI Code of Professional Conduct and Statement of Ethics and Professional Standards, to which all chartered planners must pledge. In the case of planning, indirect discrimination may occur "when a criterion, requirement or condition is applied to everyone, but in practice a much smaller proportion of some groups can comply with it than is the case for others" (Office of the Deputy Prime Minister [ODPM], 2005: 31), for example by imposing a requirement to write representations on planning applications in writing and in English. Indirect discrimination "does not imply that individuals in an organisation are necessarily evil or racists", but reveals an ignorance about the real effects of policies and procedures (Thomas, 2000: 16).

Public bodies have used various tools to demonstrate how they meet the public sector equality duty, for example through 'Race Equality Schemes' and 'Race Equality Impact Assessments' (both created by the Race Relations (Amendment) Act 2000). Such assessments aim to encourage public bodies, including LPAs, to anticipate the impact of proposed plans and policies on BME groups (although they are no longer a compulsory legal requirement under the Equality Act 2010). There is no systematic study of the application of such assessments in the field of local planning. They seem to have been used unevenly, with some uncertainty, often as a tick-boxing exercise within a broader 'politics of documentation' in which 'doing the document' rather than 'doing the doing' is more important (Ahmed, 2007). In 2012, the Conservative government announced a review of the public sector equality duty, viewing such assessments as time-consuming and often unnecessary bureaucratic exercises.

Nevertheless, the legally enshrined 'public sector equality duty' has opened the possibility for individuals and organisations to challenge public bodies through judicial reviews in front of the courts. There are only few examples of this process of 'judicialisation' in the planning field (Halford, 2010). In the case *R (Harris)* v. *London Borough of Haringey (Equality and Human Rights Commissions intervening)* [2010] EWCA Civ 703, the Court of Appeal quashed the decision of Haringey Borough Council to grant planning permission for the development of a site (known as Wards Corner) on the grounds that the council failed to discharge its duty to "promote equality of opportunity and good relations between persons of different racial groups" (Section 71 of the RRA). The court ruled that an LPA must prove it has properly assessed the likely impacts of a proposed scheme on different racial groups (even if it would still be able to grant planning permission if, on balance, the proposals were deemed acceptable).

Legislation is a necessary but insufficient step for change, and needs to be complemented by the integration of equality opportunities and diversity principles into everyday policies and practices at a range of spatial scales (Reeves, 2005). It was not until the arrival of New Labour into government in 1997 that the word 'diversity' appeared in national planning guidance, with the publication of a research report (Booth et al., 2004) and good practice guide (ODPM, 2005: 14) which stated that "the culture of planning should recognise, respect, value and harness difference". The guide encouraged LPAs to recognise diversity through research and data gathering, effective community engagement, the integration of diversity objectives in planning policies and procedures, and changes in organisational culture. The government additionally called for increasing the recruitment of under-represented categories into planning. In 2000, the proportion of planners from a BME background was less than 2% (Chartered Association of Building Engineers, 2005). In 2010, only 3.3% of RTPI members defined themselves as non-White (Ellis et al., 2010); as of May 2017, this share had increased to 7.87%.[4] The Tomorrow's Planners initiative was set up in the early 2000s by the Planning Inspectorate, (then) ODPM and RTPI, with the aim to bring 500 BME individuals into the planning profession through a placement and educational programme developed in partnership with LPAs, planning consultancies and universities. The scheme benefited approximately 90 BME planners, but was stopped in 2007.[5] However, in 2015/2016, 21% of UK-domiciled students enrolled on RTPI-accredited courses were from a BME group.[6]

Engaging the BME Population in Participatory Processes

As calls for public participation in planning became stronger in the 1970s, so too were efforts to include BME groups, often referred to as 'culturally' distinct, 'hard-to-reach' or marginalised (Beebeejaun, 2006). Some of the barriers that prevent BME individuals from engaging with planning include language, lack of educational capital to navigate the complexity of the system, time pressures due to multiple employment and care responsibilities, or feelings of disenfranchisement. LPAs have used a variety of means to encourage BME participation, such as translating information materials into foreign languages, inviting BME representatives to participate in public events, organising BME-targeted participatory activities, setting up a forum of 'representative' BME organisations, or more rarely, appointing a BME liaison officer.[7]

While this is preferable to a situation which ignores BME voices, such participatory approaches are often fraught with ambiguities, flaws and unintended adverse effects. The adoption of ethnic categories to structure consultation approaches on the basis of the census classifications and the 'protected characteristics' of the 2010 Equality Act naturalises identity categories which are in reality changing, complex, mixed, hybrid, or even irrelevant for the individuals concerned. Members of an ethnic group are assumed to have culturally distinctive and relatively homogeneous needs, values and lifestyles which are stable over time and shared by all members (Thomas, 2008). Such assumptions may reinforce stereotypes in the policy-making process and ignore internal group differences (Beebeejaun, 2006). Recent research has indeed shown that there is a significant diversification of the BME population in terms of class, income, age, disability, gender or lifestyles – captured by the notion of 'super-diversity' (Vertovec, 2007). However, public policies and service delivery are still framed by a simple ethnicity-focused approach that neglects new relevant variables such as "differential immigration statuses and their concomitant entitlements and restrictions of rights, divergent labour market experiences, discrete gender and age profiles, patterns of spatial distribution, and mixed local area responses by service providers and residents" (Vertovec, 2007: 1025).

Moreover, BME voices are often channelled by 'advocacy agents' (e.g. non-governmental organisations fighting for particular groups) or by representatives who claim to speak on behalf of a supposedly cohesive 'community'. Such an approach has been criticised for unwittingly fostering separation and for giving disproportionate power to older 'community leaders' who can silence particular voices within an ethnic 'community'. Beebeejaun's (2006) analysis of BME engagement in two LPAs shows that male, business-oriented and socially conservative voices dominated the process, at the expense of women and younger people. Finally, there is often a problematic shortfall between "initial participatory discussions involving ethnic minorities and concrete inclusion of their views and opinions in either the policy or the built environment" (Beebeejaun, 2012: 546), because the discretionary nature of the UK planning system allows planners to determine whether particular matters are planning-related or not.

Responding to the Needs of Spatially Concentrated BME Populations: Planning and Urban Policy Responses

BME households exhibit clear patterns of spatial concentration in particular areas, which are explained by a combination of structural-economic factors (e.g. lower incomes), discrimination and ethnic-cultural preferences (Phillips, 2007; Phillips and Harrison, 2010). In those areas, the impact of migrants and BME groups on the demand for services and amenities has been a central aspect of debates on planning for diversity. In the immediate post-war era, no attention was paid to the specific needs of new migrants. Various dispersal initiatives sought, on the contrary, to 'dilute' the presence of BME households (Phillips and Harrison, 2010), for example through the planned dispersal of East African Asian refugees in the early 1970s. Birmingham City Council applied a dispersal strategy in social housing allocation between 1969 and 1975, eventually outlawed under the 1976 RRA. Dispersal-oriented approaches were gradually abandoned, with the exception of the mandatory dispersal policy still imposed on asylum seekers.

From the 1970s onwards, attempts were made to address the needs of spatially concentrated BME populations through two main types of approaches. Firstly, a number of Labour-led cities committed to anti-racist and multiculturalist agendas (such as the Greater London Council or Leicester) sought to respond to the *qualitatively different* needs arising from the cultural or religious practices/values of specific ethnic groups, through targeted – and at times controversial – policies. In the field of housing, for example, the prevalence of multi-generational households among Bangladeshi or Pakistani groups and of large family units in Haredi Jewish communities were addressed through the modification of local planning policies to facilitate larger housing units (as in the London Borough of Hackney, where house extensions were conditionally allowed in residential areas where the Haredi community is concentrated). In parallel, the growth of BME-run housing associations was encouraged from the 1980s onwards[8] – an almost internationally unique example of state-funded institutionalised self-management on ethnic or religious lines (Flint, 2010). Another area of adaptation of local planning policy has been the provision of non-Christian places of worship. Following evidence of significantly higher rates of refusal for applications for the construction of, or conversion of, residential buildings into mosques (Gale, 2008), some LPAs (e.g. Leicester City Council in 1977) changed local policies to help faith communities gain planning permission for suitable premises.

However, some of the needs of BME groups do not arise from different cultural features per se, but rather from their socio-demographic profile – often on average younger or poorer than the rest of the population (Thomas, 2000). In areas of high concentrations of deprivation, such needs have been addressed by a second type of approach: 'area-based' urban policies targeting deprived neighbourhoods defined on the basis of statistical indicators measuring deprivation or unemployment. As such areas are often those with a high rate of BME residents, the latter were indirectly supposed to benefit from such policies. In 1968, two weeks after Enoch Powell's infamous 'River of Blood' speech, the Labour government launched the Urban Programme to support deprived inner-city areas – the first of a long series of urban policy initiatives set up by successive governments. Such interventions are anchored in debates about so-called 'neighbourhood effects': whether where people live affects (in a positive or negative way) their opportunities and life chances above and beyond individual characteristics, and whether public policy should intervene to dissolve concentrations of deprived (and/or BME) households in particular neighbourhoods. With few exceptions,[9] however, no urban policy initiative was ever formulated with an explicit focus on BME populations, for fear of alienating the White electorate (Atkinson and Moon, 1994). The focus was on concentrations of deprivation.

The property-led urban regeneration initiatives set up by the Conservative governments in the 1980s (e.g. urban development corporations) paid scant attention to BME needs, and their supposed 'trickle-down effect' failed to materialise for low-income groups (Brownill et al., 1996). In 1997, the New Labour government set up new initiatives to address social exclusion in the poorest neighbourhoods of England (the New Deal for Communities), acknowledging that addressing racial discrimination in such programmes was essential, although this aspect was found to be lacking in practice (CRE, 2007). In parallel, the policy objective of 'mixed communities' became central to the 'Urban Renaissance' agenda, based on the assumption that mixing different types of housing tenure would lead to greater social mix and positive effects for deprived neighbourhoods and their residents (Lupton and Fuller, 2009). This was to be achieved through the redevelopment of low-income areas of private housing in northern English cities (Housing Market Renewal) and the partial demolition and redevelopment of social housing estates seen as 'problematic'. Such programmes have generally not led to greater social interaction or significant positive socio-economic effects for deprived neighbourhoods and residents (Cheshire, 2009; Tunstall and Lupton, 2010). They have often had negative impacts on low-income and/or BME populations through the direct displacement of households and businesses (Lees, 2014).

Debates on BME concentrations took a new turn in 2001, after episodes of urban unrest between young people from different ethnic groups in Bradford, Burnley and Oldham. Official reports attributed those 'riots' to divisions created by the 'self-segregating tendencies' of working-class British Asians and Whites, depicted as living 'parallel lives' (Cantle, 2001). This took place in the context of a growing backlash against 'multiculturalist approaches' (Vertovec and Wessendorf, 2010) by both conservative and progressive commentators. The terrorist attacks perpetrated in the USA in 2001 and in London in 2005 further compounded public anxieties about the supposed self-segregation of Muslims (Phillips, 2006) and led New Labour to promote a new policy agenda for 'community cohesion' and 'national integration'. After 2010, Conservative-led governments stopped funding national urban policy initiatives in deprived neighbourhoods. In the context of public anxieties about the socio-economic impacts of globalisation and migration on cities and regions, the rise of far-right political parties and the fear of terrorism, the government has strengthened its discourse on national identity, integration and shared 'British values'.

Four decades of area-based urban policies in the UK have altogether had a small effect on the reduction of inequalities between places and people, and have not significantly addressed the way racial discrimination adversely affects the life chances of BME groups (Brownill and Thomas, 2001), who still suffer from stigmatisation and higher rates of deprivation. This points to a crucial challenge at the heart of planning and regeneration practice: the extent to which one can produce positive local socio-economic change through physical, area-based interventions which do not always address the root causes of socio-economic or racial inequalities (Cheshire, 2009).

Planning for Spaces of (Multicultural) Encounter

For Sandercock (2003), the co-existence of different cultures requires engagement between people who perceive themselves as different, the recognition of the porosity and internal heterogeneity of cultures, and openness to the possibility (and reality) of mutual influence between them. This is only possible in particular spaces of encounter and interaction. This includes open and green spaces (parks, allotments and sports grounds), publicly owned facilities (libraries or schools) or community-run facilities. Privately owned, but publicly accessible, commercial or leisure spaces such as cafés, cinemas, restaurants or shops and services for daily needs also play a key role. A common and often unchallenged assumption in planning practice is that the provision of, and improvements to, such spaces will lead to more and better social interactions. There is indeed an abundant literature on the role of urban design in fostering (or hindering) positive behaviours and social interactions (e.g. New Urbanism). Moreover, in cities such as Leicester, Birmingham or London, local authorities have purposefully used public spaces to celebrate expressions of 'difference' by supporting "world cultures, minority voices, ethnic pluralism, and alternative local histories" (Amin, 2002: 968), for example through festivals. In some areas, particular markers of ethnic 'culture' or entrepreneurship, such as restaurants, have been marketed as assets for neighbourhood branding and revitalisation (on London's 'Banglatown', see Shaw et al., 2004). The commodification of ethnic cultures that this entails is not without critics, who note that a 'Steel Band, Sari and Samosa' approach can superficially celebrate difference without addressing questions of inequality (Perrons and Skyers, 2003).

Yet public spaces are not exempt from conflicts and exclusions, as they accommodate multiple users who may clash with one another. In a city like London, daily encounters with 'commonplace diversity' (Wessendorf, 2014) in public, institutional and associational spaces are usually experienced and valued positively, although some groups (women, older people, BME youth) often have negative perceptions of safety. More broadly, the transformation of public spaces under multiple processes of privatisation, commodification, exclusionary zoning, surveillance and policing has had significant impacts on the social diversity allowed in such spaces – a process compounded by contemporary fears about crime, social disorder and terrorism. While safer spaces may encourage greater social interactions, strengthened practices of surveillance and policing through closed-circuit TV, police controls or defensive urbanism are shown to disproportionally affect certain (already vulnerable or discriminated against) groups, for example young Black or Asian males.

For those reasons, planning should not solely be concerned with providing 'grand public spaces' where strangers can mingle (Amin, 2002). It should also resource "situations and institutions through which people can make contact on the basis of shared activities and interests which might transcend fixed identities such as gender, race, and class" (Iveson and Fincher, 2011: 413). Ideally, these are sites of 'convivial encounters' (Neal et al., 2013) where 'prosaic negotiations' are compulsory (Amin, 2002), such as the workplace, schools, universities, sports clubs, public libraries and drop-in centres. The UK planning system plays a key role in the delivery of such spaces through the plan-led allocation of sites for social infrastructure, development control decisions, and mechanisms for planning gain. Yet in an era of austerity and deregulation, LPAs are increasingly limited in this task. Many have had to close down public facilities such as libraries, or cut subsidies and stop the lease of public buildings to community organisations which perform key services for particular social groups. More generally, in a city like London, planners have lacked powers to control the rapid transformation of the built environment in the face of strong development pressures. The combination of market-led gentrification and state-led regeneration often threatens existing patterns of socio-economic and ethnic diversity. This has generated grassroots struggles to preserve sites central to the life and identity of particular BME groups (e.g. Afro-Caribbean culture in Brixton or Latin American culture in Elephant and Castle).

Conclusion

This chapter has discussed how UK planning and planners, at the national and local level, have responded to the diversification of British society which arose from waves of migration. The examples of planning for a more diverse society mentioned here show that there are significant challenges between normative calls for 'planning for diversity' and the reality of actually doing so in practice, with difficult, politically and socially contentious decisions to be made by planners and policy-makers. In law-making, public policy design and resource allocation, there is a tension between the universal and equal treatment of all citizens and the need to 'recognise' difference (especially when it is a source of inequality) by targeting specific groups. An equal distribution or treatment may be 'unfair', and a fair distribution or treatment may be 'unequal'. Planning practitioners cannot simply 'accommodate' or 'embrace' diversity as such, they have to distinguish between 'desirable and undesirable', 'just or unjust' forms of diversity and homogeneity (Fincher and Iveson, 2008: 2–3). According to Fincher and Iveson (2008), this means combining three social logics of 'planning for a just diversity': *redistribution*, to plan for the redress of disadvantage and inequality rooted in class; *recognition*, to define the attributes of (diverse) groups of people so that their needs can be met; and *encounter*, through which the interaction of individuals are 'planned for' in order to offer opportunities for increased sociality.

The increasing focus on the recognition of 'difference' and 'diversity' in public policy should not mask fundamental questions of socio-economic and class inequalities (Benn-Michaels, 2008). There is a danger that privileging 'identity politics' shifts attention away from some of the key processes that generate contemporary inequalities, such as the functioning of labour and housing markets and/or the promotion of development programmes that prioritise economic returns and the creation of gentrified urban environments. Moreover, a focus on ethnicity as marker of 'difference' may underplay the *intersections* between class, ethnicity, culture and place that shape the lives of individuals and communities, and the need to shift towards a relational, rather then essentialist, approach to identity. A stronger emphasis on understanding such intersectionalities may therefore provide a fruitful way of thinking about future planning priorities, so that they become more focused on the root causes, rather than the symptoms, of inequality (Valentine and Sandgrove, 2012).

Acknowledgements

The authors would like to thank the editors, Jamie Kesten, and Tatiana Moreira de Souza for their comments on earlier versions of this chapter. The chapter draws on research funded by the European Union's Seventh

Framework Programme for research, technological development and demonstration under Grant Agreement No.319970 – DIVERCITIES. The views expressed in this publication are the sole responsibility of the authors, and do not necessarily reflect the views of the European Commission.

Notes

1 The greatest relative growth in the BME population between 2001 and 2011 was in rural parts of England and Wales (Jivraj and Simpson, 2015).
2 Northern Ireland has separate legislation (see Ellis, 2001).
3 It is worth noting that 'affirmative action' or 'positive discrimination' (e.g. minimum quotas of BME individuals), as used in the USA, are unlawful in Britain. However, 'positive action' measures are allowed, to meet training, education or welfare needs.
4 Data supplied by the RTPI, 2 May 2017.
5 Thanks to Chris Shepley (former head of the Planning Inspectorate) for sharing his recollections about the initiative he was instrumental in setting up.
6 Data supplied by the RTPI, 2 May 2017.
7 Beyond LPAs, a number of organisations have worked to assist disenfranchised groups in making their voice heard in relation to planning, such as Planning Aid, the (now defunct) Black Planners' Network, and the London Just Space network.
8 There were over 100 such associations in the mid-1990s, supported between 1986 and 1996 by funding from the Housing Corporation.
9 Exceptions were Section 11 of the Local Government Act 1966, which created central government grants to support local authorities hosting high numbers of immigrants, and a small portion of funding created within the Urban Programme in 1974 for BME social and cultural projects.

References

Ahmed, S. (2007) You end up doing the document rather than doing the doing: diversity, race equality and the politics of documentation, *Ethnic and Racial Studies*, 30(4), pp.590–609.

Amin, A. (2002) Ethnicity and the multicultural city: living with diversity, *Environment and Planning A*, 24, pp.959–980.

Atkinson, R. and Moon, G. (1994) *Urban policy in Britain*. Basingstoke: Macmillan.

Beebeejaun, Y. (2006) The participation trap: the limitations of participation for ethnic and racial Groups, *International Planning Studies*, 11(1), pp.3–18.

Beebeejaun, Y. (2012) Including the excluded? Changing the understandings of ethnicity in contemporary English planning, *Planning Theory and Practice*, 13(4), pp.529–548.

Benn-Michaels, W. (2008) Against diversity, *New Left Review*, 52, pp.33–36.

Booth, C., Batty, E., Gilroy, R., Dargan, L., Thomas, H., Harris, N. and Imrie, R. (2004) *Planning and diversity: research into policies and procedures*. London: ODPM.

Brownill, S. and Thomas, H. (2001) Urban policy deracialized? In O. Yiftachel, J. Little, D. Hedgcock and I. Alexander (eds) *The power of planning*. Dordrecht: Kluwer, pp.189–203.

Brownill, S., Razzaque, K., Stirling, T. and Thomas, H. (1996) Local governance and the racialisation of urban policy in the UK: the case of UDCs, *Urban Studies*, 33(8), pp.1137–1155.

Brubaker, R. (2004) *Ethnicity without groups*. Boston, MA: Harvard University Press.

Cantle, T. (2001) *Community cohesion: a report of the independent review Team*. London: Home Office.

Chartered Association of Building Engineers (2005) *Black and Minority Ethnic representation in the built environment professions*. London: Centre for Ethnic Minority Studies, Royal Holloway, University of London.

Cheshire, P. (2009) Policies for mixed communities: faith-based displacement activity? *International Regional Science Review*, 32(3), pp.343–375.

CRE (2007) *Regeneration and the race equality duty: report of a formal investigation in England, Scotland and Wales*. London: CRE.

Dennis, N. (1970) *People and planning*. London: Faber.

Dennis, N. (1972) *Public participation and planners' blight*. London: Faber.

Ellis, G. (2001) The difference context makes: planning and ethnic minorities in Northern Ireland, *European Planning Studies*, 9(3), pp.339–358.

Ellis, G., Murtagh, B. and Copeland, L. (2010) *The future of the planning academy*. London: RTPI.

Favell, A. (1998) *Philosophies of integration: immigration and the idea of citizenship in France and Britain*. Basingstoke: Macmillan.

Fincher, R. and Iveson, K. (2008) *Planning and diversity in the city: redistribution, recognition and encounter*. Basingtoke: Palgrave.

Flint, J. (2010) Faith and housing in England: promoting community cohesion or contributing to urban segregation? *Journal of Ethnic and Migration Studies*, 36(2), pp.257–274.

Gale, R. (2008) Locating religion in urban planning: beyond "race" and ethnicity? *Planning Practice and Research*, 23(1), pp.19–39.

Gale, R. and Naylor, S. (2002) Religion, planning and the city: the spatial politics of ethnic minority expression in British cities and towns, *Ethnicities*, 2(3), pp.387–409.

Halford, J. (2010) *The Equality Act and its impact on planning law*. London: Environmental Law Foundation.

Iveson, K. and Fincher, R. (2011) "Just diversity" in the city of difference. In G. Bridge and S. Watson (eds) *The new Blackwell companion to the city*. Oxford: Blackwell, pp.407–418.

Jivraj, S. and Simpson, L. (2015) How has ethnic diversity grown? In S. Jivraj and L. Simpson (eds) *Ethnic identity and inequalities in Britain: the dynamics of diversity*. Bristol: Policy Press, pp.19–31.

Krishnarayan, V. and Thomas, H. (1993) *Ethnic minorities and the planning system*. London: RTPI.

Lees, L. (2014) The urban injustices of New Labour's "new urban renewal": the case of the Aylesbury Estate in London, *Antipode*, 46(4), pp.921–947.

Loftman, P. and Beazley, M. (1998) *Race equality and planning*. London: Local Government Association.

Lupton, R. and Fuller, C. (2009) Mixed communities: a new approach to spatially concentrated poverty in England, *International Journal of Urban and Regional Research*, 33(4), pp.1014–1028.

Neal, S., Bennett, K., Cochrane, A., and Mohan, G. (2013) Living multiculture: understanding the new spatial and social relations of ethnicity and multiculture in England, *Environment and Planning* C, 31(2), pp.308–323.
ODPM (2005) *Diversity and equality in planning: a good practice guide*. London: ODPM.
Pahl, R. (1975) *Whose city? And further essays on urban society*, 2nd edn. Harmondsworth: Penguin.
Perrons, D. and Skyers, S. (2003) Empowerment through participation? Conceptual explorations and a case study, *International Journal of Urban and Regional Research*, 27(2), pp.265–285.
Phillips, D. (2006) Parallel lives: challenging discourses of British Muslim self-segregation, *Environment and Planning D*, 24(1), pp.25–40.
Phillips, D. (2007) Ethnic and racial segregation: a critical perspective, *Geography Compass*, 1(5), pp.1138–1159.
Phillips, D. and Harrison, M. (2010) Constructing an integrated society: historical lessons for tackling Black and Minority Ethnic housing segregation in Britain, *Housing Studies*, 25(2), pp.221–235.
Raco, M., Kesten, J., Colomb, C. and Moreira de Souza, T. (2017) *DIVERCITIES: dealing with urban diversity: the case of London*. Utrecht: Utrecht University, Faculty of Geosciences.
Reeves, D. (2005) *Planning for diversity*. London: Routledge.
Rex, J. and Moore, R. (1967) *Race, community and conflict: a study of Sparkbrook*. London: Institute of Race Relations.
RTPI (1996) *Planning authorities and racist representations*. London: RTPI.
RTPI/CRE (1983) *Planning for a multi-racial Britain*. London: RTPI.
Sandercock, L. (2003) *Cosmopolis II: mongrel cities in the 21st century*. London: Continuum.
Shaw, S., Bagwell, S. and Karmowska, J. (2004) Ethnoscapes as spectacle: reimaging multicultural districts as new destinations for leisure and tourism consumption, *Urban Studies*, 41(10), pp.1983–2000.
Simon, P. and Piché, V. (2012) Accounting for ethnic and racial diversity: the challenge of enumeration, *Ethnic and Racial Studies*, 35(8), pp.1357–1365.
Thomas, H. (2000) *Race and planning: the UK experience*. London: UCL Press.
Thomas, H. (2008) Race equality and planning: a changing agenda, *Planning Practice and Research*, 23(1), pp.1–17.
Tunstall, R. and Lupton, R. (2010) *Mixed communities: evidence review*. London: Department of Communities and Local Government.
Valentine, G. and Sandgrove, J. (2012) Lived difference: a narrative account of spatiotemporal processes of social differentiation, *Environment and Planning A*, 44, pp.2049–2063.
Vertovec, S. (2007) Super-diversity and its implications, *Ethnic and Racial Studies*, 30(6), pp.1024–1054.
Vertovec, S. and Wessendorf, S. (eds) (2010) *The multiculturalism backlash*. London: Routledge.
Wessendorf, S. (2014) *Commonplace diversity: social relations in a super-diverse context*. Palgrave Macmillan.
Young, I.M. (1990) *Justice and the politics of difference*. Princeton, NJ: Princeton University Press.

12 Sustainable Development and Planning

Catalina Turcu

Introduction

The complexity of global challenges that shape the context for planning has been discussed elsewhere (see Chapter 1 by John Tomaney and Jessica Ferm). It is worth mentioning here, however, five megatrends that provide the framework for delivering sustainable development (SD). *The world population is ageing, in both expanding and shrinking cities and regions*. This has seen new planning models coming of age, such as planning for healthy cities, compact cities and low-growth cities. *The world is urbanising at a fast pace, and cities are at the front of delivering SD*. Cities are forming urban networks and are powerful global actors. From the C40 Cities Climate Leadership Group to United Cities and Local Governments, these organisations reach beyond the boundaries of cities and nation states to project influence on planning for SD. *The global economic power is shifting*. Planning for SD is increasingly seen as a lever for delivering new models of growth, such as the green economy, the circular economy and the transition economy. *Climate change and resource scarcity* have also prompted planning responses around the world. These include planning for climate change mitigation and adaptation, low-carbon cities and eco-cities. *Rapid technological advance* means that real-time urban data is plentiful and increasingly available. For the first time, planning can employ large-scale urban modelling across the economic, social and environmental areas of our lives to aid decisions and improve outcomes. Planning for the smart city is such an example.

In addition to global forces, British planning has also been shaped by national conditions (see Chapter 1). Among these, at least three are relevant to planning for SD and for what follows in this chapter. First, the British planning system is devolved in the context of a discretionary planning model. This means that England, Scotland, Northern Ireland and Wales have their own national planning policy and guidance and subsequent SD agendas (see Chapter 2 by John Tomaney and Claire Colomb). Second, UK planning has been through successive rounds of deregulation, which in England have been paralleled by a view that planning inhibits growth. However, planning for SD seems to distance itself from this view under the promise of delivering new, sustainable growth. Third, following the global financial crisis, local authorities have experienced stringent austerity measures, impacting especially upon planning departments. Emerging evidence suggests that in some local authorities, human and financial 'sustainability resources' have been first to be cut. This has had an impact on the capacity of local planning to deliver SD on the ground.

With these global and national challenges in mind, this chapter looks at how planning for SD is framed by policy and delivered in practice in the UK. SD is a long-contested concept (Turcu, 2012). However, there is agreement among scholars that it represents the intersection of three spheres (economic, environmental and social), which need to be balanced over time (to ensure intergenerational equity) and across scales (to consider planetary boundaries). This chapter deploys this understanding of SD. It also acknowledges the intersections of planning for SD with other concepts and models discussed in the sustainability literature, such as sustainable, green, ecological or low-carbon urbanism, and smart, circular or healthy cities. There are two main sections to the chapter following this introduction.

The first section considers how the planning system at the various levels impacts on SD. It makes three claims: First, the national planning frameworks of the four nations – in particular the English one – do not provide a clear framework for the delivery of SD, hence, room for 'manoeuvre' is large; the current English focus on Neighbourhood Planning (which puts communities in the driving seat) can be challenging for the delivery of SD in practice; and third, UK-wide austerity measures have hit local authorities unequally, limiting the ability of planning to consistently guide the delivery of SD on the ground.

The second section looks at planning practice in the case of North West Bicester, the first eco-town in England, to illustrate some of the claims made in the first section. It finds that: the challenge posed by the ambiguity of framing of SD in the National Planning Policy Framework (NPPF) in England is bypassed by drawing on previous planning policy; local communities are instrumental in the delivery of SD on the ground, but also 'feared' by planners because of their new Neighbourhood Planning powers; and the local planning department has not been affected much by austerity cuts because of the project's flagship status and location. The chapter concludes by drawing wider lessons, of national and international relevance.

Policy, Legislative and Fiscal Context

Planning has been under societal and political pressure to protect the 'common good' by ensuring the development of sustainable cities and communities (Polk, 2010). We live in a world that is increasingly challenged by its environmental limits and resource scarcity. Planning as a discipline provides ideas about how spatial arrangements and patterns are manifested and processes are managed in order to achieve an optimum balance of needs or demands within available resources, with public interest at its heart. These are key issues for SD. It has been argued, however, that planning theory fails to fully problematise planning from a SD perspective (Næss, 1994), because planning is traditionally associated with boundary-delimited and relatively short-term fixed goals and outputs, while SD implies cross-boundary thinking and a long-term process of shifting goals and outcomes (Næss, 2001; Bagheri and Hjorth, 2007).

SD is also a challenge for planning practice, especially in relation to its operationalisation on the ground. Planners have to implement the concept in practice, because "turning concepts into reality must lie at the very heart of what planning is about", and somehow make sure initiatives do not merely "pay lip-service to the words but do justice to the original concept" (Campbell, 2000: 259). This is a challenging task. Moreover, delivering SD is not legally binding at the European level, and with the exception of countries in Scandinavia, where important strides have been made to mainstream SD into planning policy, in most other European countries, planning for SD has relied on moral commitments and political resolve. Environmental and economic concerns dominated political agendas in the late 1980s and early to mid-1990s, while it was only in the late 1990s that the social agenda associated with SD started to emerge. The early to mid-2000s saw a relatively equal balancing of the three dimensions of SD and the addition of a fourth – the institutional/cultural dimension – due to a growing interest in governance processes. However, the aforementioned global trends are changing the balance yet again, and in most European countries, the SD agenda has returned to a primary emphasis on economic development, with an environmental and social secondary focus in European countries such as Sweden and Germany.

SD has been a central theme of British urban policy since the late 1980s, and this has been complemented by a substantial body of academic research. However, it was only in the mid-2000s that a SD policy agenda crystallised through a series of policy papers, built on earlier initiatives since 1999, including the 2004 Egan Review (Office of the Deputy Prime Minister [ODPM], 2004) and two complementary 2005 Sustainable Communities five-year plans (ODPM, 2005a, 2005b). This culminated with the UK's Department for Environment, Food and Rural Affairs (DEFRA) re-launching its new Sustainable Development Strategy: Securing the Future (DEFRA, 2005), which provided five guiding principles of SD: living within environmental limits; a strong, healthy and just society; a sustainable economy; good governance; and sound, responsible science. The strategy also named building sustainable communities as one of four UK priorities and suggested a set of SD indicators (Office for National Statistics, 2014). This strategy is still in place today.

Delivering the UK's SD strategy required new policy frameworks, and planning policy is perhaps one area of British policy which has been strongly shaped by it. This had to be framed within the UK's devolved and discretionary planning system. Although the basic structures of the four planning systems in the UK's four countries are similar (see Chapter 2), there are differences in their detail and delivery on the ground. All national planning policy in the UK introduces a presumption in favour of development that contributes to SD; however, there is variation in the way it is framed. This is to say that while England's 2012 National Planning Policy Framework relies on planning's three roles (as driver for economic, social and environmental development), which are discussed in greater detail below; Scotland's 2012 National Planning Framework 3 (NPF3) places a strong emphasis on place-making; Wales's 2014 Planning Policy Wales uses a well-being perspective; and Northern Ireland's 2015 Strategic Planning Policy Statement employs a focus on climate change adaptation and mitigation, and eco-system services.

The changes introduced by the UK Coalition government (2010–2015) have since seen a greater divergence between the planning system in England and the other three countries, especially in relation to England's specific focus on cities. Before 2012, planning policy in England was stated in 25 different Planning Policy Statements (PPSs), with four of them having a strong relation to sustainable development: PPS1, which looked at overall planning for sustainable development (2005); PPS1 Supplement, framing zero-carbon newbuild (2007); PPS11 Microgeneration (2008); and PPS22 Renewable Energy (2004). This was replaced by the NPPF in 2012, which "underpins sustainable development and planning in England" (Her Majesty's Government, 2016) and offers England's view on the economic, social and environmental role of planning in SD (Box 12.1).

The NPPF is part of a wider reform in English planning, enshrined in the 2011 Localism Act. It introduces Neighbourhood Planning and aims to curtail the planning powers of local government by delivering 'sustainable localism'. This means that communities in England are given powers to challenge municipal planning decisions and draw up their own Neighbourhood Plans. Neighbourhood Planning rests on an ideology of 'stakeholder citizenship' with ideals of civic duties and rights, and appeals to individuals' responsibilities for social well-being (Scerri and Magee, 2012). As a statutory tool that promises communities the autonomy to shape local development and realise local ambitions, it has the potential to allow the advancement of pro-environmental action from the grassroots level in an age of eco-awareness. In other words, it can be seen as a way to achieve SD via community-led planning.

Box 12.1 The NPPF's view on the economic, social and environmental role of planning

- an **economic** role – contributing to building a strong, responsive and competitive economy, by ensuring that sufficient land of the right type is available in the right places and at the right time to support growth and innovation; and by identifying and coordinating development requirements, including the provision of infrastructure;
- a **social** role – supporting strong, vibrant and healthy communities, by providing the supply of housing required to meet the needs of present and future generations; and by creating a high quality built environment, with accessible local services that reflect the community's needs and support its health, social and cultural well-being;
- an **environmental** role – contributing to protecting and enhancing our natural, built and historic environment; and, as part of this, helping to improve biodiversity, use natural resources prudently, minimise waste and pollution, and mitigate and adapt to climate change including moving to a low-carbon economy.

Source: Department for Communities and Local Government [DCLG] (2012: 2–3).

A full critical discussion of the NPPF and its implementation is still to emerge. However, there is emerging criticism on at least two counts: its loose definition of SD, and its over-reliance on the powers of communities at the local level. On the first count, the NPPF provides little guidance for the operationalisation of SD in planning practice (NewsForum, 2011). Box 12.1 is a good illustration of this, showing how planning's three roles lend themselves to multiple interpretations. On the second, it is argued that the NPPF's enthusiastic promotion of community participation in planning (via localism and Neighbourhood Planning) has its caveats. That is to say, planning knowledge that is co-produced with local communities can be 're-scripted' to ensure conformity with already existing forms of planning practice which contravene the 'representative democracy' claims made under Neighbourhood Planning (Parker et al., 2015; Bradley, 2015; Davoudi and Cowie, 2013). Moreover, Neighbourhood Planning is a form of 'liberal institutionalism', drawing on community participation, but also existing local institutions, and so opens up for discussion the geography of civic infrastructure and capacity in England (Wills, 2016).

Communities have been an area of debate in planning for SD; while their merits and achievements have been much praised, they have also been associated with a number of challenges in relation to the delivery of SD. SD appeals to common responsibilities and goals, and Campbell and Marshall (2000) have questioned the ability of individuals to work for collective interests, positing that individuals favour self-interests in decision-making, due to differences in opinion and conflicting needs. Communities in planning tend to associate themselves with physical boundaries, and that challenges the interconnected and cross-boundary thinking prevalent in SD debates. They also argue that "expanding the opportunities for public participation in environmental planning is not always the best option" (Campbell and Marshall, 2000: 153) because of the limits of collective action (such as free-riding and shirking) associated with environmental goals (i.e. air/water pollution), which potentially affect larger sections of the population (Rydin and Pennington, 2000). Finally, the interest in Neighbourhood Plans has been particularly strong in rural and commuter belt regions with affluent communities (Matthews et al., 2015), areas that traditionally have a history of 'local protectionism', but also experience of community planning in its previous guises – Parish Plans or Community Design Statements (Matthews et al., 2015; Inch, 2012). This means that communities can lobby against SD goals that contravene local interests, but also that some communities start at an advantage in influencing planning processes.

Austerity measures resulting in public expenditure cuts together with wider changes in the political landscape have challenged the effectiveness of English planning to deliver the social and economic role of planning for SD outlined in the NPPF. For example, many efforts towards the integration of SD in mainstream policy have been curtailed since 2010 (Rydin and Turcu, 2014), and substantial reductions in local authority budgets have seen planning and/or sustainability capacity and resources reduced or eliminated (Jane, 2013). In addition, Brexit negotiations may greatly impact the environmental dimensions of planning. Planning is a system through which the state controls and manages space, and the European Union does not have a direct role in national planning. However, some areas of EU policy do have a big impact on shaping national planning policy and the spatial distribution of people, industry and commerce. The EU has a series of key goals, including the promotion of economic and social cohesion, conservation of natural resources and cultural heritage, which help to achieve a more 'sustainable' economy across Europe. As such, much of the UK's environmental legislation is transported from EU directives. One example is the requirement for an Environmental Impact Assessment (EIA) for larger developments and developments with potentially significant environmental impact (airports, motorways, power plants etc.), whereby predicted impacts of the development on people, flora, fauna, soil, water, air, climate, landscape and cultural heritage are investigated and reported.

It is unclear what EU-level regulation and legislation will mean in a post-Brexit era. While the UK remains a full member of the EU, with all corresponding obligations, and it is expected that these will be maintained via various 'deals', following Brexit, there is no guarantee that this will happen, and it is uncertain what will happen to EU legislation and regulation, which fall just within the transitional period. This includes various amendments to air quality (an area for which London has been sanctioned more recently), transport, energy and water legislation – all areas of relevance to spatial planning.

There are at least three changes which are of particular importance to planning for SD in the period of Brexit negotiations: EIAs, maritime planning and energy planning. First, all member states will have to strengthen the quality of EIA procedures by July 2018 by enhancing links with other EU-level actions and developing further strategies and policies in areas of national competence. Second, by March 2021, all member states will have to transport into national policy the Maritime Spatial Planning Directive. This is a new directive which establishes a framework for maritime spatial planning in order to promote the sustainable growth of the maritime economy, spatial development and natural/maritime ecosystems. Third, there will be a series of changes in the EU's Internal Energy Market (IEM) and Emissions Trading System (ETS), which will require joint compliance with relevant EU rules on energy, environment and competition. It is rumoured that the UK will want to stay in the IEM but will leave the ETS, which charges power plants and factories for every tonne of CO_2 they emit. All this uncertainty will have an impact on how existing and new development is planned for and built, and adds to wider concerns regarding the current government's position on environmental issues. In fact, the 2017 Spring Budget was seen as 'a missed opportunity' to tackle green problems such as energy efficiency and air pollution, with generally little space and funding allocated to the environment and sustainability agenda (Aid, 2017).

Planning for SD in Practice

This section examines planning practice in the delivery of North West Bicester (NWB), and draws on a range of publicly available data and five interviews with representatives of the planning, development and consultancy sectors involved in its delivery. NWB is the first eco-town in England, and an extension to the market town of Bicester. Bicester is located in Cherwell District, Oxfordshire, and is a 'growth' town with large housing targets in the South East of England, 10 miles from Oxford. In 2007, a government initiative was set up to develop eco-towns in

England in response to a wider and acute housing shortage in the UK. These were seen as an opportunity to achieve exemplary sustainability standards in at least one of the following areas: deployment of environmental technology; building low-carbon homes; achieving social and spatial integration; and delivering 30–50% affordable housing (DCLG, 2007). In 2008, 15 locations were selected, and in 2009, four winning locations, including NWB, were announced and identified in *PPS: Eco-towns*, a supplement to the then *PPS1: Sustainable Development*, as 'exemplars' for SD. The local authority supported the idea, and in 2010, Eco-Bicester: One Shared Vision was formulated, working closely with a social landlord (A2Dominion) and sustainability think-tank (Bioregional), and using One Planet Living (OPL) principles to flesh-out the characteristics of an eco-town (BioRegional, 2015). This was adopted by the council and subsequently included in its Core Strategy 2011–2031 Part 1 (or Local Plan) as Policy Bicester 1, a strategic allocation for up to 6000 new homes (Cherwell District Council, 2016).

When the NPPF came into force in 2012, a masterplan and supporting vision documents for NWB, drawing on the previous *PPS: Eco-towns*, was approved by the council in 2014. In 2015, *PPS: Eco-towns* was annulled for all areas except NWB through a ministerial statement. Concerned that this 'exception' would be cancelled in time, the council decided in 2016 to bring the NWB eco-town standards into a supplementary planning document (SPD). The SPD sets out the minimum standards for NWB and supports the implementation of the Local Plan. Arguably, the SPD bypasses the NPPF by drawing heavily on previous planning policy and OPL principles. It reportedly takes into account advice in the NPPF, but that is difficult to map bearing in mind the NPPF's loose definition of SD and direction for implementation. The SPD also offers a strong SD framing for any Neighbourhood Planning process and ensuing Neighbourhood Plan that may be adopted in the future. When fully delivered, NWB is planned to provide (Cherwell District Council, 2016: 3):

- up to 6,000 "true" zero carbon homes;
- employment opportunities providing at least 4,600 new jobs;
- up to four primary schools and one secondary school;
- 40% green space, half of which will be public open space;
- pedestrian and cycle routes;
- new links under the railway line and to the existing town;
- local centres to serve the new and existing communities;
- integration with existing communities.

NWB's first phase started on-site in 2012, with intended completion in 2018. Elmsbrook is a 'sustainability exemplar' for NWB, following OPL principles (BioRegional, 2015) – see Table 12.1. It has an OPL

Action Plan which is reviewed annually and sets up SD targets such as a 30% reduction in embodied CO_2, zero waste to landfill during construction, reducing car usage to 50% (from 65%), and 40% of its area to be dedicated to open space. In addition, it aims to achieve a net biodiversity gain, climate change adaptation, and a combination of zero carbon and Level 5 Code for Sustainable Homes[1] for housing across the development. By 2017, Elmsbrook had built some 400 homes, one energy centre, a nursery, a community centre, an eco-business centre, an eco-pub and primary school, and some 1500m^2 of commercial space (BioRegional, 2016).

Table 12.1 Ten OPL principles guiding the delivery of Elmsbrook

1 Health and happiness
It is easy, attractive and affordable for people to lead healthy, happy lifestyles within a fair share of the earth's resources.
2 Equity and local economy
Thriving, diverse and resilient local economies support fair employment, inclusive communities and fair trade.
3 Culture and community
A culture of sustainability and community has been nurtured, building on local cultural heritage to foster a sense of place and belonging.
4 Land use and wildlife
Communities contribute to an increase in biodiversity and biological productivity, and support beautiful landscapes.
5 Sustainable water
Water is used efficiently in buildings and in the products we buy, and water is managed to support healthy land use and avoid flooding and pollution.
6 Local and sustainable food
People are able to eat healthy diets high in local, seasonal and organic produce and lower in animal protein.
7 Sustainable materials
Goods and materials – for construction or consumer goods – are sourced locally and made from renewable or waste resources with low embodied energy.
8 Sustainable transport
It is easy for people to walk and cycle, and low- and zero-carbon modes of transport are provided.
9 Zero waste
Resources are used efficiently, waste levels are close to zero, and ultimately zero waste is sent to landfill.
10 Zero carbon
All buildings will be energy-efficient and run completely from renewable energy.

Source: BioRegional.

Planning for SD at Elmsbrook has meant achieving 'exemplary sustainability standards', such as maximising potential for affordable housing, walkable neighbourhoods, water/energy/waste efficiency, job creation and community governance. This has been facilitated by political support and planning standards adopted by all levels of government, and 'strong partnerships based on like-minded individuals' representing the local authority, A2Dominion and Bioregional.

Communities have been involved in planning at Elmsbrook mainly via community involvement and community capacity-building initiatives, rather than the new powers of localism and Neighbourhood Planning. Extensive consultation has been carried out with the existing and surrounding communities under a town-wide strategy, to respond to community needs. This has involved creating opportunities for community capacity-building such as Bicester Green – a centre for skills, sustainability and recycling, where "people from all walks of life come together to share and engage in the art of repair" (interviewee) – and the Community House for "residents' own use and enjoyment" (interviewee), as well as providing demonstration homes, a school extension and self-build programmes.

Planners, however, have worked under the assumption that under the new powers of Neighbourhood Planning, communities could challenge their decisions in the future, so they have been seen as important to have on board. It would be interesting to monitor in the coming years whether any of these mechanisms will materialise and what their interaction will be with the strong framing provided by the SPD, OPL and the example set by Elmsbrook. Community boundaries were clearly delimited at Elmsbrook, which can be seen as a barrier to planning for SD. However, planners used the OPL framework as a tool to think across boundaries and address this.

Cherwell District Council is situated in the wealthy South East of England, and this made it less likely to be hit as hard as other areas by the austerity cuts imposed on English local councils since 2010. Budget cuts have been made, but the council has managed by changing the way it operates via sharing management and services with adjacent councils. Increases in council tax have also been used to bump up the reduced local budget and to fund services, including planning and economic development (*Banbury Guardian*, 2015). Planners at Cherwell District Council noted that this, together with NWB flagship project status and its location (in a growth area), have spared cuts in the planning department. Following from this, the case of NWB demonstrates that current planning practice for SD depends on: the ability of the local authority to 'internalise' austerity cuts and so sustain planning departments and institutional sustainability knowledge/skills, the 'visibility' of the project, and a capacity to reach out to partners beyond planning to both define what SD means in practice and partner for delivery. All these are a long way from mainstream planning practice for SD in England at the moment.

Conclusions

This chapter has looked at SD within the wider framework for planning policy in the UK, and focused on one example of planning practice for SD in England. It has found that the planning policy and guidance for SD in the UK, and particularly in England through the NPPF, does not provide a clear framework for the delivery of SD in practice. It has also claimed that the current English framing of Neighbourhood Planning and communities in planning can be challenging for the ideas and goals purported by SD, and that the consequences of current austerity cuts, which have seen sustainability resources diminished at the local level, and the uncertainty surrounding Brexit, have been additional barriers to planning for SD in the UK.

Indeed, some evidence of this has been found in practice, as in the case of North West Bicester. The development of NWB/Elmsbrook has caused controversy from the beginning by evading normal planning control routes. In other words, planning for SD at NWB has drawn on planning policy that pre-dates the NPPF and an additional SPD, which have been 'accommodated' within NPPF's loose framing of SD. NWB is an exceptional planning practice example due to its special eco-town status; however, it stands as testimony for the significant amount of 'interpretation' (and documentation) that planning practice in England has to undertake in order to deliver SD in practice. One can argue that the rather prescriptive SPD and OPL framing adopted at NWB can be seen as a source of tension within the context of current Neighbourhood Planning and future Neighbourhood Plans. At least two lessons can be inferred from this discussion. They refer to the emerging institutional innovation in an austerity climate, and communities in planning for SD.

First, emerging evidence suggests that the changing nature of planning frameworks in the UK, together with austerity cuts and uncertainty brought by Brexit, have resulted in institutional innovation at the local authority level, including revenue-generation, financialisation of assets, pro-growth mechanisms and alternative models of service delivery. How sustainable this is going to be in the long term is questionable. However, in the short term, some local authorities have found ways to keep afloat. NWB shows that current planning policy and austerity measures have provided impetus for the council to 'do things differently', and in terms of planning for SD, there is evidence of shared services, particularly in terms of economic and transport strategies. Multi-authority approaches to such endeavours seem sensible and likely to promote holistic thinking and consideration of extra-local impacts and priorities, which fit very well with the broader aims of SD. This, however, raises questions about how planning responsibilities for SD are framed, located and delivered in practice, and how they intersect with responsibilities which lie beyond the influence of planning (Turcu, forthcoming).

Second, the focus on communities in planning for SD can be challenging, both across the UK and internationally. While engaging communities in planning has been seen as an important step in the democratisation of planning processes, some literature points to the tensions between the wider aims of SD and community priorities, particularly in the form of anti-development sentiment (Matthews et al., 2015) and perceptions of local identity, also fostered by an awareness of environmental impacts on a local scale (Seyfang and Smith, 2007; Mitchell, 2001). Arguably, this gives credence to the argument that deep-seated SD requires significant strategic action from higher levels (Robbins and Rowe, 2002), and challenges previous assumptions about the benefits of involving communities in planning, such as raising sustainability awareness and co-producing knowledge (Healey, 1992; Healey, 1997; Seyfang, 2010; Middlemiss and Parrish, 2010). Moreover, the ability to pursue SD at the local level by engaging communities in planning in the UK is heavily dependent on the skills, resources and awareness of communities involved in the process. That is to say, some areas and communities may start at an advantage at the cost of others. Despite the fact that the Neighbourhood Planning model in England does not create a planning system that exclusively relies on public initiatives, it is nevertheless a model which, by indirectly relying on community resources and infrastructure, directs one's attention to the geography of such initiatives.

Note

1 The Code for Sustainable Homes is a voluntary standard in England which allows councils to adopt their own sustainability levels (1–6) as a planning requirement for new residential development. The Code was abolished by the government in 2015.

References

Aid, C. (2017) The green reaction: "a missed opportunity", *The Guardian*, 12 March.

Bagheri, A. and Hjorth, P. (2007) Planning for sustainable development: a paradigm shift towards a process⊠based approach, *Sustainable development*, 15, pp.83–96.

Banbury Guardian (2015) Cherwell freezes council tax for sixth successive year, *Banbury Guardian*, 24 February.

BioRegional (2015) *One Planet Action Plan*. Wallington: BioRegional Development Group.

BioRegional (2016) *North West Bicester One Planet Action Plan*. Wallington: BioRegional Development Group.

Bradley, Q. (2015) The political identities of neighbourhood planning in England, *Space and Polity*, 19, pp.97–109.

Campbell, H. (2000) Sustainable development: can the vision be realized? *Planning Theory & Practice*, 1, pp.259–284.

Campbell, H. and Marshall, R. (2000) Public involvement and planning: looking beyond the one to the many, *International Planning Studies*, 5, pp.321–344.

Cherwell District Council (2016) *Adopted Cherwell Local Plan 2011–2031 (Part 1)*. Available at: https://www.cherwell.gov.uk/info/83/local-plans/376/adopted-cherwell-local-plan-2011-2031-part-1.

Davoudi, S. and Cowie, P. (2013) Are English neighbourhood forums democratically legitimate? *Planning Theory & Practice*, 14, pp.562–566.

DCLG (2007) *Eco-towns prospectus*. London: DCLG.

DCLG (2012) *National Planning Policy Framework*. London: DCLG. Available at: https://www.gov.uk/government/uploads/system/uploads/attachment_data/file/6077/2116950.pdf.

DEFRA (2005) *The UK Government Sustainable Development Strategy*. London: Department for Environment, Food and Rural Affairs.

Healey, P. (1992) Planning through debate: the communicative turn in planning theory, *Town Planning Review*, 63, p.143.

Healey, P. (1997) *Collaborative planning: shaping places in fragmented societies*. Basingstoke: Macmillan.

Her Majesty's Government (2016) *Department for Communities and Local Government's consultation on national planning policy*. London: The Stationery Office.

Inch, A. (2012) Creating "a generation of NIMBYs"? Interpreting the role of the state in managing the politics of urban development, *Environment and Planning C: Government and Policy*, 30, pp.520–535.

Jane, D. (2013) Agency, sustainability and organizational change, *Anthropology in Action*, 20(2), pp.37–45.

Matthews, P., Bramley, G. and Hastings, A. (2015) Homo economicus in a big society: understanding middle-class activism and NIMBYism towards new housing developments, *Housing, Theory and Society*, 32, pp.54–72.

Middlemiss, L. and Parrish, B. (2010) Building capacity for low-carbon communities: the role of grassroots initiatives, *Energy Policy*, 38, pp.7559–7566.

Mitchell, D. (2001) The lure of the local: landscape studies at the end of a troubled century, *Progress in Human Geography*, 25, pp.269–281.

Næss, P. (1994) Normative planning theory and sustainable development, *Scandinavian Housing and Planning Research*, 11, pp.145–167.

Næss, P. (2001) Urban planning and sustainable development, *European Planning Studies*, 9, pp.503–524.

NewsForum (2011) *The NPPF – a disaster or an opportunity?* London: London Forum.

ODPM (2004) *The Egan Review: skills for sustainable communities*. London: ODPM.

ODPM (2005a) *Sustainable communities: homes for all: a five year plan from the Office of the Deputy Prime Minister*. London: ODPM.

ODPM (2005b) *Sustainable communities: people, places and prosperity: a five year plan from the Office of the Deputy Prime Minister*. London: ODPM.

Office for National Statistics (2014) *Sustainable development indicators*. London: Office for National Statistics.

Parker, G., Lynn, T. and Wargent, M. (2015) Sticking to the script? The co-production of neighbourhood planning in England, *Town Planning Review*, 86, pp.519–536.

Polk, M. (2010) Sustainability in practice: the interpretation of sustainable development in a regional planning arena for dialogue and learning in western Sweden, *Planning Theory & Practice*, 11, pp.481–497.

Robbins, C. and Rowe, J. (2002) Unresolved responsibilities: exploring local democratisation and sustainable development through a community-based waste reduction initiative, *Local Government Studies*, 28, pp.37–58.

Rydin, Y. and Pennington, M. (2000) Public participation and local environmental planning: the collective action problem and the potential of social capital, *Local Environment*, 5, pp.153–169.

Rydin, Y. and Turcu, C. (2014) Key trends in policy for low-energy built environments: a 20-year review, *Local Environment*, 19, pp.560–566.

Scerri, A. and Magee, L. (2012) Green householders, stakeholder citizenship and sustainability, *Environmental Politics*, 21, pp.387–411.

Seyfang, G. (2010) Community action for sustainable housing: building a low-carbon future, *Energy Policy*, 38, pp.7624–7633.

Seyfang, G. and Smith, A. (2007) Grassroots innovations for sustainable development: towards a new research and policy agenda, *Environmental Politics*, 16, pp.584–603.

Turcu, C. (2013) Re-thinking Sustainability Indicators: local perspectives of urban sustainability, *Journal of Environmental Planning and Management*, 56(5), pp.695–719.

Turcu, C. (forthcoming) Responsibility for sustainable urban development in Europe: what does it mean for planning theory and practice? *Journal of Planning Theory & Practice.*

Wills, J. (2016) Emerging geographies of English localism: the case of neighbourhood planning, *Political Geography*, 53, pp.43–53.

Part III

Planning in Practice

13 Planning for Housing

The Global Challenges Confronting Local Practice

Nick Gallent

Introducing the Global Frameworks

Planning practice in relation to housing seems always to be in the dock, accused of clumsily attempting to direct the market, but ending up impeding the supply of new homes, thereby inflating prices and restricting access. Planning is a market inhibitor, and generates the housing crisis that is now all-too-visible in London and the wider South East of England. But this world-view supposes that the crisis – expressed in rising property prices, declining affordability (relative to earnings), falling rates of homeownership and rising levels of long-term renting, homelessness and general housing inequality (Edwards, 2016) – is one generated largely by low levels of new housing supply, with that supply reduced by land use policy (e.g. restrictions on building in the Metropolitan Green Belt) and local planning practice.

This seems to be a strangely local and closed view of the demands on housing supply (i.e. the supply of *existing second-hand properties* coming onto the market plus *newbuild*, the latter representing less than 1% of supply each year in England). Either that, or it supposes that additions to the total housing stock can satiate a composite demand for housing that comprises: (1) the 'requirement' arising from new household formation; (2) households migrating permanently to the UK for work or other reasons; (3) households trading up (or down) through the market as their needs change; (4) households trading up through the market for reasons of investment; (5) domestic buyers seeking investment properties (including 'buy-to-let') or second homes; and (6) overseas buyers acquiring residential property for its capital appreciation potential. There are also sub-sets of the above, including parents purchasing homes for their children to live in while studying at UK universities. Like items 5 and 6, such purchases subtract from housing available for items 1–4 and are driven by the investment motive: if capital appreciation is strong, then it makes sense to put one's children (and capital) in a purchased flat for three years rather than specialist rented accommodation. What all this means is that the demand for housing far exceeds the requirement arising from demographic change. Over the last five years or so, the projection of newly arising demand (in England) has been fairly stable: around 240,000 households forming and 'needing' homes each year. This is then taken to be the 'target' for housing completions, which came close to 140,000 in England in 2015/2016.[1]

Planning should be 'facilitating' this level of new supply by allocating land for housing in the right places and speedily granting development permission, attaching as few conditions on development as possible. Nationally, the planning system is viewed as a hindrance to this level of delivery because it insists on constraining supply where 'demand' is thought to be greatest – in and around London – through its Green Belt policy (Mace et al., 2016). Locally, the sorts of big schemes needed if supply is to be increased seem forever mired in local conflict and often fail to get off the ground (Gurran et al., 2016), at least not on the scale that was originally envisaged. Local planning authorities are accused of having too much power and too little interest in seeing development succeed (Barker, 2004). The response has been sustained criticism of Green Belt policy and planning more generally as major causes of the housing crisis (Hilber, 2015). Simultaneously, government seeks to demonstrate its commitment to increasing housing supply by launching new programmes every few years: Growth Areas (2003), Growth Points (2006), Eco-towns (2008), Garden Cities (2012) and Garden Villages and Towns (2016). Often the programmes try to breathe new life into failed or stalled schemes. Some of the 2008 eco-town candidate sites have now re-emerged as prospective garden villages. Government has also trimmed back local authority budgets and tied funding to housing supply through the New Homes Bonus (Department for Business, Innovation and Skills, 2010), which is the latest of a string of attempts to incentivise local support for development.

But analyses of the wider political economy of the crisis suggest that it is not all down to a troublesome planning process. Because housing's function has changed over the last 50 years or so, demand for it has soared, and that demand is not always predicated on the need for somewhere to live. Reflecting again on the 240,000 figure quoted above, it seems simplistic that this should be taken as an annual building target. Others (including Cheshire et al., 2014) have long argued that economics (and earnings) have a greater effect on the demand for housing (and its price – see Meen, 2012) than the mere 'aspiration' of households to form and secure a home. For that reason, economic drivers need to figure in projections of housing demand. This point is emphasised by Whitehead (2016: 419), who shows that stability in real house prices in England will be achieved only when new annual supply of 400,000 homes is achieved. At that point, earnings and house prices will rise at the same rate. But this does not mean that housing will become more affordable, as the ratios between earnings and property prices are already extremely stretched in some places. To achieve increased affordability – that is, close the gap between earnings and prices – the sustained rate of building will need to greatly exceed 400,000 homes per year. In light of recent and historic building rates, achieving this figure through speculative development alone seems unlikely. And if the required build rate is far greater that the conventional *need for housing*, then two questions arise: what is driving this demand (just earnings?), and what is housing really for?

Post-war public housing programmes have been reined back since the 1970s. Housing is once again a private matter, both in terms of how it is produced (by either a contract or speculative housing industry) and how it is consumed (by individual purchasers, with cash or credit). This process of privatisation (and marketisation of housing as exchange good) paved the way for a re-functioning of housing as asset, and coincided – in Western Europe, North America and Australasia – with weakening manufacturing bases and a new reliance on profit-taking from fixed assets (Edwards, 2002) as a mainstay of post- or late-industrial economies. In short, housing gained a broader economic function in the late twentieth century. Demand in excess of need and supply, and therefore upward pressure on house prices, boosts consumer confidence, drives consumption across the economy, and helps sustain tax revenues in support of the state (directly through property transaction taxes, and indirectly through taxes on other forms of consumption). Public finances are increasingly dependent on house price growth (Royal Institution of Chartered Surveyors, 2014). Housing has gained the status of high-quality collateral (Aalbers, 2016). It is that status which has fuelled investor demand, sometimes – but not always – supported by less restrictive bank lending practices and by the deregulation of lending and the creation of 'new money' in support of housing consumption. These two 'global frameworks' – credit flow and investment, which have re-shaped the housing market – are now briefly examined.

In the years following the 2009 Global financial crisis, there has been heightened concern about the impact of credit availability (and the flow of money into housing) on housing demand and house prices. More attention has been given to the channels by which credit affects price (Duca et al., 2010) and how easier access to loans (as banks prioritise lending on real estate) resulted, in the years leading up to the crisis, in a pattern of 'over-investment' (initially in the US sub-prime market) that raised personal debt to the point where it was unsustainable and banks were unable to retrieve the cost of 'bad loans' from foreclosure and onward sale (the Bank of England has warned of a return to this situation in England today). Housing had become 'financialised' to the point where the value of the fixed asset bore a diminishing relationship to the size of the debt attached to it. The results are well known: this level of over-investment had global ramifications, and underscored the vulnerability of banks and national economies which 'implicitly treat housing markets as liquid and efficient' (Duca et al., 2010: 204). Bank lending contributed significantly to this situation, as lending practices decoupled the value of property from earnings. Moreover, the deregulation of those practices (specifically, the removal of rules requiring a balance between money lent and deposits; Wainwright, 2009) resulted in new money being 'created' on spreadsheets to match the supposed value of a house: "Whenever a bank makes a loan, it simultaneously creates a matching deposit in the borrower's bank account, thereby creating new money" (McLeay et al., 2014: 1). It is the deregulated supply of money to the economy by banks (at the start of the global financial crisis, just £1.25 was held in deposit by UK banks for every £100 advanced as credit; Ryan-Collins et al., 2012) and therefore the rapid supply of that money relative to the slow (and seemingly difficult) supply of homes that underpins systemic risk. In this sense, it is the movement of capital into housing – rather than people – that drives the housing market. At the beginning of 2017, the UK's housing stock was valued at £6.8 trillion, with London and the South East accounting for half of that value (Evans, 2017).

Lending practices and credit liberalisation have, to a large extent, shaped a new relationship with housing. That relationship has been manifest in solid house price growth and then in new patterns of housing consumption: from domestic buyers moving their capital into bricks and mortar (and levering loans from rental income) to overseas buyers 'parking' money in key investment destinations. Barker (2014) makes the important point that the prospect of 'reasonable investment return' is a motivating factor in all private housing consumption. The investment motive is not new, and underpins the preference for homeownership. But in some forms of consumption, the investment motive is more conspicuous and dominant. There is currently burgeoning interest in foreign investment in globally connected cities – including London – not necessarily because that investment is seen as an over-riding driver of *national* housing outcomes, but because it is emblematic of the change in the function of housing, and the way it is consumed, suggested above. That said, although foreign investment appears localised, there is now evidence that prices in the London housing market track investment behaviour to a greater extent than earnings (Meen, 2011). At the same time, the link with earnings has changed: while it makes intuitive sense that movement in incomes should underpin housing demand and prices, the reality in recent years has been one of significant increases in house prices (a 41% increase since 2008 across the UK; Office for National Statistics, 2016) running alongside declining incomes (a drop of 10% in median real weekly earnings over the same period; Machin, 2015).

The decoupling of housing demand (and house prices) from earnings (in some areas) provides part of the evidence to suggest that the movement of wealth into housing is becoming a key market driver. But that wealth is not only sourced overseas. The purchase of second, third and further homes has been a feature of many Western housing markets for decades, motivated by the recreational opportunities and by the investment potential that such purchases offer (Gallent et al., 2005). Amateur landlordism – manifest in the UK as the 'buy-to-let' phenomenon – is also an important expression of housing's attraction to domestic investors (Turner, 2008; Bank of England, 2015a) beyond the asset growth that individual homeowners enjoy. Although foreign buyers are also involved in this segment of the market, buy-to-let is principally a business or income supplement for UK buyers, some of whom worry about the future value of their pensions (Edwards, 2015), given the reliance of those pensions on the performance of stock market assets. The rapid expansion of amateur landlordism is a peculiarity of the UK housing system. This expansion began in the late 1980s with the creation of more flexible (and short-term) tenancy arrangements. Further deregulation of mortgage lending in the 1990s fuelled growth in the market.

Through the 1990s and into the 2000s, much of the capital flowing into housing was released by bank and credit liberalisation. Today, access to credit, like wealth in general, is more concentrated in the hands of existing homeowners or propertied interests who sustain high levels of market transaction through cash-buying (Bank of England, 2015b) and out-compete less prosperous groups, consigning a growing section of the population to a largely unregulated and unstable rental sector (Kemp and Kofner, 2010).

In short, housing has been recast as a market and economic good. Profit-taking from fixed assets is a new economic corner-stone, vital to service sector growth and the consumption of imported goods. Because of this economic role, the housing market has become untouchable. Government does not seek to control demand in any serious way (unless it clearly conflicts with growing homeownership, hence recent moves against buy-to-let and second homes), but deals with market externalities – including declining affordability – through specific product interventions, with these increasingly designed to support *market* access (hence the move from social to affordable rents and from part-ownership models to full-ownership 'starter' home initiatives). Government's focus is on delivering market entry for the majority (an economic priority), rather than working for broader access to decent homes. The worst-off households are placed in short-term accommodation, often in the private sector, with subsidy in the form of Housing Benefit directed to buy-to-let owners. Planning's role in all this is to primarily work for, and with, the market.

Local Frameworks in a Global Context

The practice of planning for housing is not solely concerned with allocating land for new development. Land use planning may also form part of the response to declining housing demand (also known as 'market restructuring'), as it did in the Housing Market Renewal Initiatives in the Midlands and North of England in the 2000s (Gallent and Tewdwr-Jones, 2007). Likewise, those calling for a comprehensive 'plan' to deal with the current housing crisis are concerned as much with fiscal as land use policy (see Barker, 2014; Edwards, 2015, 2016). But the way in which planning facilitates or impedes land supply has long been the primary concern of national policy. It is also this issue that has dominated recent academic and political debate, so it provides the focus in this section. Two main questions are addressed. First, how is land for housing allocated, and how has that process sought to connect with the complexities of the market? And second, because the process of allocating land for housing has both technical and political dimensions (being about analysis of opportunities – see Box 13.1 – the bureaucracy of site selection *and* decision-making by elected representatives) and is sometimes fraught with conflict, how has the localisation of planning in England sought to deliver a more acceptable allocations process?

Box 13.1 Identification of sites for development

1. Formulate a spatial vision and set objectives for the distribution of housing sites in support of that vision.
2. Review evidence of housing need and demand between different locations, linking this to the spatial vision (revising that vision as necessary).
3. Give regard to broader planning goals, including reducing carbon emissions (arising from spatial dislocation and potential travel patterns between homes, jobs and services) and achieving efficiencies in land use through land recycling.
4. Give regard to existing infrastructure capacities and how these will shape viability and create opportunities for development.
5. Give regard to neighbourhood context and the goal of enhancing well-being through mixed development and service improvement.
6. Undertake a sieving of specific sites, including or discounting according to site constraints that might be physical, ownership-based or determined by access, contamination, stability, flood risk, biodiversity or restrictive designation.
7. Work with the development industry and landowners to ascertain market interest and the achievability of development within envisaged timescales.

Land Allocations and the Market

The allocation of land for housing is a key purpose of development planning practice. Practical advice to local authorities on how they might achieve that purpose procedurally was provided by the Department of the Environment (DoE) in 1984 (DoE, 1984) (building on earlier instructions to maintain a five-year land supply and work with the building industry on housing land availability studies; DoE, 1980). Authorities were tasked with maintaining a 'sufficient' supply of land for new housing, to be formally allocated within Local Plans. Four years later, that same advice was rolled into new 'planning policy guidance' (PPG) on housing, and a few years after that – in 1992 – a broader view of what planning should seek to achieve through its regulation of housing development was set out in a revision of that guidance. Negotiation for the inclusion of 'affordable housing' in private schemes joined a shopping list of planning functions: to seek and support design quality, achieve housing mix and type (and 'balanced communities'), set appropriate parking standards, and strike a balance between land recycling and the use of greenfield sites through appropriate allocations.

But throughout the 1980s and into the 1990s, maintaining an 'effective' or sufficient five-year supply became a key point of contention. Despite the involvement of housebuilders in the land availability studies preceding allocations, those allocations seemed rarely to suit the aspirations of private enterprise. Local practice therefore entered a period of 'planning by appeal', in which local authorities unable to demonstrate 'effective supply' regularly saw their decisions overturned by successive Secretaries of State (Adams, 2011: 954). The narrative from this point was one of strengthening the status of plans in decision-making (through the Planning and Compensation Act 1991) and the replacement of Housing Availability Studies with a series of alternative tools for selecting and allocating sites for development. Urban Capacity Studies (set out in the revision of PPG3 in 2000) sought to deliver more housing on brownfield land and were introduced in tandem with a 'sequential approach' to land allocations, enabling authorities to resist development on 'greenfields' until all previously developed sites were exhausted. Adams (2011: 954–956) provides a detailed account of this transition, as well as the switch back to Housing Land Availability Studies – in the form of Strategic Housing Land Availability Assessments (SHLAAs) – which were re-designed to deliver closer collaboration between local planning and the development industry. The SHLAAs were part of a new planning approach that would be more alive to market conditions and signals, largely because of the input provided by Strategic Housing Market Assessments, which "were intended to provide local authorities with the necessary market data and information for decision making" (Adams, 2011: 955).

Development Planning's 'clumsy' attempts to connect with market information, and the economic impacts of the planning system, have figured prominently in academic debate for several decades (from Bramley, 1993, to Hilber, 2015). Planning by appeal in the 1980s is often presented as the eruption of an inherent friction between regulation and enterprise that can be papered over – as it was in 1991 – but is always manifest in costs to developers and housing under-supply. Planning practice has moved on since the 1990s, and now focuses on finding and allocating 'deliverable' (viable) sites (Department for Communities and Local Government [DCLG], 2012), keeping allocations under constant review.

The transition from sufficiency of allocations to deliverability of development, based on more sophisticated market intelligence, can be traced back 25 years, but the impetus to transform local planning practice came from the 2004 Barker Review of Housing Supply. Barker presented existing practice as unresponsive to market change. She claimed that, for reasons of local politics (popular resistance to specific land releases justifying political rejection), allocations were not always sufficient (and effective), and sites allocated not deliverable within the timeframes envisaged. Authorities needed greater incentive to proactively pursue (and promote the case for) development with partners, and therefore contribute to meeting national housing targets (making the right allocations and actual delivery should be rewarded, according to Barker). And finally, large strategic allocations – in the form of new settlements and urban extensions – were likely to be the right responses to market signals in some places. The Barker Review was instrumental in linking housing growth to affordability and set in train a number of key shifts, including:

> commissioning and publishing a controversial affordability model and establishing the controversial National Housing and Planning Advice Unit, which in 2008 produced a much-disputed target range for future housing growth in each English region. Significantly, both were predicated on macro-economic modelling, which sought to link house prices, earnings, migration patterns, household formation and employment to land release at the regional level. This reflected the increasing role of economics in driving spatial policy, to the extent that the Department for Communities and Local Government had begun to think of itself as an 'economics department'.
>
> (Adams, 2011: 957)

A subsequent Planning Policy Statement on Housing (PPS3) published in 2006 required local planning to take market information into account when identifying land for development and managing supply. How this should be done was not immediately apparent. But a later *Housing Market Information Advice Note* issued by the DCLG made it clear that simple demand indicators (e.g. price spikes) were inadequate to the task, and allocations should be guided by Strategic Housing Market Assessments undertaken at a sub-regional level. This became the 'affordability-led' approach to planning for housing, predicated on the view that regional, and therefore national, housing affordability is achievable through market-responsive planning practice and higher rates of housebuilding.

This approach supposes that increases in earnings – of new and existing resident households – drives housing demand, and therefore house prices (see the earlier discussion). More recent analysis has queried the extent to which essentially local trends – in demography and earnings – are able to explain patterns of demand and price-setting. The global frameworks detailed earlier in this chapter – credit flow and investment – impact on demand either directly (through the consumption of new housing) or indirectly (through the consumption of existing housing and by pushing 'local demand' to the newbuild segment). Conventional models, including those constructed in the 2000s for government, match earnings and household formation to required building rates, but assume that, by and large, housing functions as home. Models that acknowledge the asset function of housing – and factor in the attractiveness of residential property to investors – point to a level of demand far in excess of household formation rates underpinned by earnings. As noted above, stability in real house prices (relative to earnings) will be achieved when the current level of new housing supply in England is tripled, and greater affordability (the stated objective of planning for housing in the 2000s) will require building rates even higher than that (Whitehead, 2016).

The task for planning practice, if responses to the housing crisis are all to be on the supply side, is to get to grips with a much broader array of market evidence (that quantifies new patterns of housing function, use and consumption), and then help achieve a step-change in housing supply through a much faster, flexible, streamlined and incentivised development planning process. But of course, many will doubt whether this increase in supply is desirable or achievable – or whether residential property should be viewed, in the main, as an economic infrastructure: a commodity sold in the global marketplace to sustain tax yields and economic growth.

This broader question is returned to at the end of this chapter. Another important aspect of planning for housing is its political or governance dimension – the democratic practice that underpins land allocations for housing and the level of engagement with community interests. While the Barker Review and PPS3 initiated an 'affordability-led' approach to planning for housing, the combined effect of the Localism Act 2011 and the National Planning Policy Framework 2012 was to deliver at least the potential to localise allocation decisions to 'neighbourhoods'.

Localisation and the Acceptability of Allocations

Barker (2004) was critical of the 'parochialism' of local development planning, attributing an implementation gap against housing targets to the uncertainties and vagaries of local decision-making. Localism since 2011 has turned this argument around, with the same implementation gap re-presented as an outcome of the 'democratic deficit' that grew during the years of Labour government as a result of its regional experiment (Gallent, 2016). Too many plans were made and decisions taken at remote regional centres, fuelling local objection to development proposals and turning reasonable people – who might otherwise see the case for new housing in their neighbourhoods – into NIMBYs (Gallent and Hamiduddin, 2012). More local democracy – achieved by dismantling the regional apparatus, returning power to town halls, and integrating a new process of neighbourhood development planning into Local Plan-making – was *presented* as part of the answer to lifting housing supply. The DCLG would return to being a *communities* rather than an economics department. But the case for dealing with housing stresses mainly on the supply side had already been made, and in promoting localism, government was offering its own formula for a step-change in the rate of housebuilding. That step-change was to be achieved through local *consensus* and incentive and through a continuation of market responsiveness (joined by creeping deregulation since 2011 in the form or changes to permitted development and permission in principle measures).

The counter-balance to the DCLG's communities focus has been the distillation of accumulated planning guidance into the National Planning Policy Framework. The NPPF handed Local Planning the task of not merely allocating a 'sufficient' quantity of land for development, but of maintaining – and keeping under annual review – a pool of 'deliverable sites' for new housing (DCLG, 2012: para.47). The broader concepts of 'sufficiency' and 'effectiveness' in allocations were displaced by the specific goals of 'availability' (sites being available now), 'suitability' (sites offering a suitable location for development now) and 'achievability' (there being a realistic prospect of housing being delivered on the site within five years and of the site being viable). Past prescriptions on density and restrictions on windfall allowances were scrapped, and recast as matters to be determined by the local market. Similarly, the framework signalled a new approach to negotiating on-site contributions of 'affordable housing'. 'Flexible' policies were to be the order of the day, to be revisited in light of market shifts that might alter the capacity of sites to remain viable under the weight of planning gain. This more flexible approach to Section 106 Agreements was then clarified in the Growth and Infrastructure Act 2013. The market alignment sought in PPS3's approach to housing land allocations remains strong in the NPPF, and sits alongside a presumption in favour of 'sustainable development', cast as development that helps achieve the need for growth (DCLG, 2012: 2–5).

The freedom of the market to determine housing outcomes (respected by local planning in the ways noted above) needs to be reconciled with community interest. An improved technical process needs to be allied with a better political process. These are the respective concerns of the NPPF and the localisation of planning brought about by the Localism Act. The technical process followed in the past – sketched in Box 13.1 – sieved for possible housing sites before a political process took over that required public *consultation* on fixed options. Communities tended to be consulted on professional advice, and had little influence over local detail. Neighbourhood development plans potentially hand communities much more direct control over the siting of housing, although the amount of housing that needs to be planned for is set within a district or borough plan, and will still be determined by market evidence and analysis.

One recent example of community input into general allocations can be found at Thame in the District of South Oxfordshire. Thame Town Council was faced, in 2010, with a Core Strategy from the District Council which proposed that 600 new homes should be built on a single site on the edge of the town (of a total allocation of 775 homes over 15 years). In the same year, the town council approached the district to express its desire to become one of England's first Neighbourhood Planning front-runners. This was accepted, and the town became an early recipient of a grant to produce a neighbourhood development plan. In the summer of 2011, the process of putting together the plan began, and the town engaged the assistance of private consultants. The consultants worked towards the production of a residents' vision. Initially, the plan for a single site with 600 homes was opposed. Eventually, the residents identified enough land for 2000 homes in and around the town; seven sites were eventually designated in the neighbourhood development plan, for 775 homes. The plan went to referendum, was approved by 75% of voters, and went before the district council in the summer of 2013 (Cook, 2013). The town council's website notes that originally an allocation was "decreed", that "protests fell on deaf ears", but the Localism Act gifted an "opportunity for self-determination".[2] Other neighbourhood groups have been reviewing the Thame experience, and it may happen that 'community-led' site allocations become a key feature of future neighbourhood development plans.

Early in the localisation process, Ellis (2011: 17) warned of a probable shift of the "tension inherent in planning from between regional and local to between local and neighbourhood". It was envisaged that prescriptions within Local Plans, determined by national policy, would run contrary to community ambition. In the case of Thame, a path around this tension seemed to have been found. However, intra-neighbourhood tensions remain. Despite approval from three-quarters of voters, more than 800 residents have since signed a petition to 'Save the Elms': one of the allocated housing sites in the Neighbourhood Plan. In a move which is reminiscent of the tactics of other planning protests in England, usually against 'top-down' allocations decided in regional planning (including the Campaign Against the Stevenage Expansion or Keep Chilmington Green in Ashford; see Gurran et al., 2016), a website has been set up (see http://elmspetition.org.uk) on which the unfolding story of protest, and the injustices of this localised planning process, are relayed and updated.

Despite such conflicts, an altered democratic practice of allocating land for new housing (integrated in some way with the technical process) undoubtedly offers potential to smooth the path of some development. But to what extent will winning over the local opponents of development – through localised engagement – help accelerate and achieve a step-change in housing output? Put another way, how important are community actors in generating the tensions now observed in the housing market, and what contribution can they realistically make to delivering answers to the big housing questions now confronting local practice?

Conclusions – an Alternate Reality for Planning Practice

Among this chapter's many blind spots is the issue of comprehensive and high-quality place-making. It has not been possible in the space available to detail the key role of planning practice in the arrangement of infrastructure, services and spaces that contribute to liveable residential places. Fortunately, there are many excellent reviews of planning's role in helping achieve housing design quality (see Carmona, 2001) within desirable and functional environments (see Adams and Tiesdell, 2013). The principal focus of this chapter has been the global challenges confronting local planning practice – the recasting of housing as an economic good, and the tensions this generates within housing markets and for wider housing access. The observable housing crisis is deeply embedded in our changed relationship with property, and with housing in particular. I return to this point below. But first, if planning were called upon to help resolve this embedded crisis, what actions might it take in some alternate reality in which governments and their politicians sought to decouple housing from economic performance?

Perhaps local planning practice could be tasked to allocate land for housing that is needed before allocating for openly tradable property of the type desired by investors. Government might redefine and therefore re-function housing, distinguishing in planning law between 'resident' and 'investment' housing. Under such a system, no household would be permitted to purchase more than one 'resident' home, and all such homes would be subject to capital gains tax on onward sale. The value of land allocated for resident housing would be depressed, but not to the same extent as land restricted to building for target groups. Resident housing would be accessible to all households needing to live and work anywhere in the country who did not own another home of this type – so all newly forming households or those seeking to move from the rental sector. There is no reason to imagine that selling land for resident housing, or building such homes, would not be an attractive proposition for private enterprise. However, attached tax and ownership rules would limit the accumulation and concentration of wealth in such housing. But given the current needs of the economy (which might change in the future), that displaced wealth might look for a new home, which would be provided by investment housing permitted and built on surplus land not needed for resident housing. Investment housing in the new-build segment of the market would assume greater scarcity value, being tradable across the existing global market.

While it might also be possible to vary housing classes to a greater extent, creating new opportunities for professional investment in private rental, the point here is that planning practice might be engaged to limit the concentration of wealth in housing, which is central to the housing crisis. Depending on tax rules, some potential for equity growth could be maintained, providing households with the means to cover transaction costs once they need to move home (or recover the costs of home improvement). Similarly, expectations from ownership would change, opening the door to a great many housing models – including mutual and pooled ownership – that have struggled to get a foothold in the current open-market system. One of the many dangers of this planning remedy is that ingrained expectations of ownership would drive investment to the second-hand market, pushing up prices there and depressing demand for new housing, and therefore its supply. For that reason, any reformed approach to newbuild must be coupled with incremental capital gains and council tax changes applied to second-hand housing.

Such measures, while unimaginable to many, and certainly full of risk, acknowledge that the current crisis in England is embedded in our relationship with housing – and in the recasting of housing's function in the 20th century. Through planning, it might be possible to challenge that function and change embedded attitudes and aspirations, though we may not survive the economic shock of doing so. This is the global dilemma that local practice faces, or rather renders such practice impotent. It can emerge victorious from local battles – delivering a few 'affordable' homes here and there, gaining acceptance for a new development or supporting some local innovation – but the war in unwinnable. Like all genuinely 'wicked problems', the housing crisis is a symptom of another more pervasive crisis – in this case, a crisis of production afflicting post-industrial economies, hooked on growth, but now struggling to fuel that growth with anything other than disruptive housing consumption.

Notes

1 DCLG Live Table 209, available at: https://www.gov.uk/government/uploads/system/uploads/attachment_data/file/669003/LiveTable209.xlsx.
2 www.thametowncouncil.gov.uk.

References

All listed URLs were last accessed on 1 March 2018.

Aalbers, M. (2016) *The financialisation of housing: a political economy approach*, London: Routledge.

Adams, D. (2011) The "wicked problem" of planning for housing development, Housing Studies, 26(6), pp.951–960.

Adams, D. and Tiesdell, S. (2013) *Shaping places: urban planning, design and development*. London: Routledge.

Bank of England (2015a) *Financial stability report: Part A: the UK housing market*. Available at: www.bankofengland.co.uk/publications/Documents/fsr/2015/fsr37sec4.pdf.

Bank of England (2015b) *Inflation report Section 1: money and asset prices*. Available at: www.bankofengland.co.uk/publications/Documents/inflationreport/2015/may1.pdf.

Barker, K. (2004) *Review of housing supply*. London: Her Majesty's Treasury.

Barker, K. (2014) *Housing: where's the plan?* London: London Publishing Partnership.

Bramley, G. (1993) Land use planning and the housing market in Britain, the impact of housebuilding and house prices, *Environment and Planning A*, 25(7), pp.1021–1051.

Carmona, M. (2001) *Housing design quality*, London: Routledge.

Cheshire, P., Nathan, M. and Overman, H.G. (2014) *Urban economics and urban policy: challenging conventional policy wisdom*. London: Edward Elgar.

Cook, B. (2013) How we did it – allocating sites through a neighbourhood plan, *Planning Resource*, 14 June.

DCLG (2012) *National Planning Policy Framework*. London: DCLG. Available at: https://www.gov.uk/government/uploads/system/uploads/attachment_data/file/6077/2116950.pdf.

Department for Business, Innovation and Skills (2010) *Local growth: realising every place's potential*. London: Department for Business, Innovation and Skills.

DoE (1980) *Land for private house-building*, Circular 9/80. London: HMSO.

DoE (1984) *Land for housing*, Circular 15/84. London: HMSO.

Duca, J.V., Muellbauer, J. and Murphy, A. (2010) Housing markets and the financial crisis of 2007–2009: lessons for the future, *Journal of Financial Stability*, 6(4), pp.203–217.

Edwards, M. (2002) Wealth creation and poverty creation, *City*, 6(1), pp.25–42.

Edwards, M. (2015) *Prospects for land, rent and housing in UK Cities*. London: Government Office for Science.

Edwards, M. (2016) The housing crisis and London, *City*, 20(2), pp.222–237.

Ellis, H. (2011) Questions of far-reaching reform, *Town and Country Planning*, 80(1), pp.15–20.

Evans, J. (2017) UK housing stock value soars to a record £6.8tn, *The Financial Times*, 18 January.

Gallent, N. (2016) England's turn to localism and planning at the "neighbourhood scale", *Territorio*, 78, pp.148–158.

Gallent, N. and Hamiduddin, I. (2012) Housing and growth under the new regime. In M. Ward and S. Hardy (eds) *Changing gear – is localism the new regionalism*? London: The Smith Institute, pp.108–117.

Gallent, N. and Tewdwr-Jones, M. (2007) *Decent homes for all*. London: Routledge.

Gallent, N., Mace, A. and Tewdwr-Jones, M. (2005) *Second homes: European perspectives and UK policies*. Aldershot: Ashgate.

Gurran, N., Gallent, N. and Chiu, R. (2016) *Politics, planning and housing supply in Australia, England and Hong Kong*. London: Routledge.

Hilber, C. (2015) *UK housing and planning policies: the evidence from economic research*. London: London School of Economics.

Kemp, P.A. and Kofner, S. (2010) Contrasting varieties of private renting: England and Germany, *International Journal of Housing Policy*, 10(4), pp.379–398.

Mace, A., Blanc, F., Gordon, I. and Scanlon, K. (2016) *A 21st century metropolitan greenbelt*. London: London School of Economics.

Machin, S. (2015) *Real wage trends*. London: Bank of England. Available at: https://www.ifs.org.uk/uploads/Presentations/Understanding%20the%20recession_230915/SMachin.pdf.

McLeay, M., Radia, A. and Thomas, R. (2014) Money creation in the modern economy, *Quarterly Bulletin*, Q1, London: Bank of England.

Meen, G. (2011) A long-run model of housing affordability, *Housing Studies*, 26(7–8), pp.1081–1103.

Meen, G. (2012) House price determination. In S.J. Smith (ed.) *International Encyclopaedia of Housing and Home*, Vol. 3. Amsterdam: Elsevier, pp.352–360.

Office for National Statistics (2016) House Price Index September 2016, Figure 2: average UK house price, January 2005 to September 2016. Available at: www.ons.gov.uk/economy/inflationandpriceindices/bulletins/housepriceindex/sept2016.

Royal Institution of Chartered Surveyors (2014) *RICS policy position: help to buy*. Available at: www.rics.org/Global/RICS%20Policy%20Position%20-%20Help%20to%20Buy.pdf.

Ryan-Collins, J., Greenham, T., Werner, R. and Jackson, A. (2012) Where does money come from? Available at: www.neweconomics.org/publications/entry/where-does-money-come-from.

Turner, G. (2008) *The credit crunch: housing bubbles, globalisation and the worldwide economic crisis*. London: Pluto Books.

Wainwright, T. (2009) Laying the foundations for a crisis: mapping the historico-geographical construction of residential mortgage backed securitization in the UK, *International Journal of Urban and Regional Research*, 33(2), pp.372–388.

Whitehead, C. (2016) Using projections of household numbers – tensions between planning and economics, *Town and Country Planning*, 85(10), pp.415–421.

14 Planning for Infrastructure

John Tomaney, Peter O'Brien and Andy Pike

Introduction

The provision of infrastructure is a key objective of the planning system. This chapter examines the challenge confronting planners in providing the physical infrastructure, especially at the strategic scale. The chapter begins by tracing the involvement of the planning system in the development of urban infrastructure and the shifting context within which planning objectives are achieved. It examines the reasons for the resurgence of interest on the part of the state and private interests in the creation of infrastructure, especially at the strategic scale. Central to understanding the planning of strategic infrastructure is its contemporary transformation from public good to private asset class. In this context, the chapter illustrates the complexity and contradictions of large-scale infrastructure developments at the UK scale and in Scotland, London and Northern England.

Modern British planning might be said to have its origins in the effort to provide urban infrastructure. As Britain urbanised in the 19th century, governments began to legislate to create local governments and other structures, empowering them to improve streets, water, sanitation and housing, and later to provide public transport within and between cities and regions. Infrastructure has traditionally been regarded as a public good, although in recent years, financial actors have begun to see infrastructure as a new investment class. Even so, the state still plays a key role in infrastructure at different spatial scales because of its large capital requirements and strong association with statutory planning and property and landownership issues that require regulation, negotiation and resolution. It retains an integral and enduring role in collective infrastructure provision because of its interests in establishing the conditions for capital accumulation, managing externalities and other market failures, its long-term time horizon, and monopoly and competition issues that call "for some combination of finance capital and state engagements" (Harvey, 2012: 12). In addition, some major infrastructure schemes incur substantial risks during construction phases that only governments are either able or willing to bear and underwrite. This is increasingly evident as the costs of building new infrastructure rise (Her Majesty's [HM] Treasury, 2010). The planning system is deeply implicated in these processes.

Planning for Infrastructure

Infrastructure can be defined as "a long-lasting network connecting producers and service providers with a large number of users through standardised (while variable) technologies, pricing, and controls that are planned and managed by coordinating organizations" (Neuman, 2006: 6). These can take a variety of forms (see Box 14.1). Much infrastructure was developed at the local scale in the 19th century, often by public authorities, or later acquired by local government when private provision failed. In the mid-20th century, much existing infrastructure was nationalised (electricity, gas, water, railways etc.) and new infrastructure such as New Towns and motorway networks were developed, justified on principles of universal provision and equal access, which Graham and Marvin (2001: 88) define as the "modern infrastructural ideal". After 1979, most of this state-owned infrastructure was privatised, reflecting an ideology that claimed the private sector was better able to raise finance for investment and more efficiently build and manage assets though the discipline of competition. But increased levels of investment in newly privatised infrastructure were slow to materialise, and privatisation was achieved at the cost of 'splintering' previously integrated networks, inhibiting strategic spatial planning. Moreover, conceiving of infrastructure as a means to deliver financial returns to private capital leaves gaps in provision, especially in disadvantaged localities and regions. Infrastructure endowments are geographically uneven, and are related to differences in market conditions and economic performance. Strongly performing urban economic agglomerations attract the most private capital and public funding, often bolstered by cost benefit analyses that support existing investment patterns. More generally, by providing and denying access, through both connecting and separating (segregating) users spatially, infrastructures play vital roles in producing (in)equitable and (un)just cities and societies (Neuman, 2006).

Box 14.1 Defining infrastructure

Infrastructure refers to structures and networks – on, above or below ground and water – that support health, safety and welfare. This broad but not exhaustive take has traditionally included categories of systems such as:

(continued)

(continued)

- utilities – energy, water supply and sewerage, waste collection and disposal;
- public works – roads and bridges, dams and canals, ports and airports, railways;
- community facilities – prisons, schools, parks, recreation, hospitals, libraries;
- telecommunications – telephony, internet, television, satellites, cable, broadband, wireless, mobile, the cloud;
- green infrastructures – interconnected networks of vegetated and riparian habitats: parks, rivers, corridors, swales, green roofs and walls and porous paving that provide ecosystem services.

Source: After Neuman (2006).

Recently, against a background of stagnant growth, historic low interest rates and burgeoning capital surpluses, there has been renewed interest on the part of government and private actors in the provision of infrastructure in countries such as the UK, which poses new challenges for planning practice. Several factors have prompted this resurgence of interest. First, in many parts of the Global North, infrastructure first developed in the 19th century is now ageing and in need of replacement, producing an "infrastructure emergency" (Neuman, 2006). According to *The Economist* (2016), for instance, in Britain:

> Roads are more clogged: the percentage of journeys on main routes that are classed as "on time" has fallen by six percentage points since 2010. Trains are getting more crowded, too: a quarter of trains arriving in London in rush hour are overcrowded, up from a fifth in 2010. Commuters are putting up with creaky carriages: in 2005–15 the average age of the rolling stock rose from 15 to 20 years. The number of local buses has fallen by 2.5% since 2010, even though the population has grown by 3%. The World Economic Forum ranks the quality of Britain's overall infrastructure 24th in the world, down from 19th in 2006, and behind Iceland and America (which is 13th).

Second, these problems are exacerbated by broader social, economic and environmental changes (see Box 14.2). Fast-growing cities and regions like London and the South East have experienced rising populations, requiring additional infrastructure. Elsewhere, investments in infrastructure are deemed necessary to accelerate growth in lagging cities and regions. Climate change calls forth new types of infrastructure to mitigate and adapt to its impacts.

Box 14.2 Structural characteristics that affect infrastructure

- population and economic growth;
- increasing mobility of people, goods, information, capital;
- increasing speed of movement of people, goods, information, capital;
- growing size of cities;
- growing complexity of cities;
- increasing impacts of, and uncertainty due to, growing size and complexity;
- increasing global energy consumption, carbon dioxide production and climate change;
- increasing per capita costs and risks of infrastructure projects and networks;
- the telecommunications and networking revolutions that are underpinning many of these characteristics;
- increasing neo-liberalism of politics, with reduced government, reduced taxes and revenues, increased deficits and debts.

Source: Neuman (2006).

Third, infrastructure provides an outlet for capital seeking long-term returns, leading to a shift in the designation of infrastructure from public good to private asset class. *The Economist* (2017: 76) has argued that:

> Linking public-sector need with private-sector capital ought to be a perfect match . . . . When public finances start to creak, capital spending is often the first thing to go. Meanwhile, the pitiful yields on government bonds, plus longer lifespans, mean pension funds are desperate for fairly safe assets that offer a stable, inflation-plus return to provide the income they have promised to the retired. The steady, fee-based revenue generated by airports, toll roads, seaports and utilities seems ideal . . . . PPP [Public–Private Partnership] thus promises to deal with a host of shortages: of infrastructure; of fiscal space; of long-lived and safe securities; and of aggregate demand and jobs.

From a more critical perspective, urban development (including infrastructure renewal) is a mechanism for addressing the problem of surplus capital which Harvey (2012) attributes to over-accumulation. Under these conditions, capital invests in asset values (i.e. the secondary circuit) rather than production (i.e. the primary circuit), sparking the search for 'innovative' means of increasing asset values, using new (and often riskier and speculative) financial innovation (practices and mechanisms), drawing in institutions and actors with a specific interest in shaping urban development. This process is defined as *financialisation*. The state is often an active agent in seeking to attract private investment to increase property and/or tax yields. Local governments are encouraged to adopt entrepreneurial approaches to local economic development through urban growth coalitions and heightened inter-urban competition, and aligning themselves more closely with business and mimicking commercial strategies and traits. These processes entrench the power of large corporations, which are mainly concerned about the value of their assets and the returns they generate rather than the fairness, equity, efficiency and sustainability of the services they deliver (for a fuller discussion, see O'Brien et al., 2018). Although often resting on claims about their wide benefits, according to *The Economist* (2017: 76), "the shortish history of PPP is littered with examples where private provision did not live up to its promises".

The provision of sewerage services in London demonstrates how these processes come together. London's system was built for the Metropolitan Board of Works (MBW), established by Act of Parliament in 1855, to capture rainwater and sewage produced by four million people. Led by Sir Joseph Bazalgette, the MBW built 57 combined sewer outflows that allowed sewage to enter the Thames during periods of high rainfall. By the 21st century, London's population had grown to eight million and storm flows were increasing, flushing 39 million tonnes of raw sewage straight into the Thames annually, conflicting with obligations arising from the EU's Waste Water Treatment Directive. A 25km tunnel was built under the tidal section of the river in Central London; it captures, stores and conveys almost all the combined raw sewage and rainwater that previously was discharged into the river. The financing, building, maintenance and operation of the Tideway Tunnel is undertaken by a private consortium, regulated by the Office of Water Services. Tideway Tunnel is a separate company from the local utility, Thames Water, itself a private organisation with a fiendishly complex ownership structure (including Chinese and Abu Dhabi investors) run by Macquarie, an Australian fund manager, ultimately located in the Cayman Islands (*Financial Times*, 2017). The total cost of the project was £4.2 billion in 2012 prices (rising from initial estimates of £1.7 billion), raised from Thames Water customers and the capital markets. Such opaque private structures and complex financial engineering test the planning system (and regulators) in guarding the public interest.

Since 2011, to address infrastructure deficiencies, the UK government has set out its infrastructure priorities and re-stated its overall approach in annual National Infrastructure Plans, since 2016 called the National

Table 14.1 The 'four sublimes that drive megaproject development'

Type of sublime	*Characteristic*
Political	The rapture politicians get from building monuments to themselves and their causes, and from the visibility this generates with the public and media
Technological	The excitement engineers and technologists get in pushing the envelope for what is possible in 'longest-tallest-fastest' types of projects
Economic	The delight business people and trade unions get from making lots of money and jobs from megaprojects, including for contractors, workers in construction and transportation, consultants, bankers, investors, landowners, lawyers and developers
Aesthetic	The pleasure designers and people who love good design get from building and using something very large that is also iconic and beautiful, like the Golden Gate Bridge

Source: Flyvbjerg (2014).

Infrastructure Delivery Plan. In 2013, the UK government announced a pipeline of major infrastructure investments of £375 billion (later raised to £383 billion), mainly in the energy and transport sectors. Among Organisation for Economic Cooperation and Development countries, the UK is unusually dependent on the private sector to fund, finance and operate key infrastructure. Some two-thirds of the proposed pipeline is expected to be privately financed, with the balance coming from public sources (HM Treasury, 2010). Most of the projects contained in the National Infrastructure Delivery Plan correspond to Flyvbjerg's (2014: 6) definition of megaprojects as "large-scale, complex ventures that typically cost a billion dollars or more, take many years to develop and build, involve multiple public and private stakeholders, are transformational, and impact millions of people". Moreover, Flyvbjerg (2014: 11) identifies the "'iron law of megaprojects': Over budget, over time, over and over again". Although justified by use of 'objective' techniques, such as cost benefit analysis, in practice, according to Flyvbjerg, they are driven by the pursuit of 'the four sublimes' (see Table 14.1). Planners are both susceptible to and potential promoters of these sublimes. But the analysis presented in this chapter stresses the relative dominance of economic and financial factors in explaining the contemporary trajectory of infrastructure development in the UK.

Shifts in the ownership, finance and funding of infrastructure are closely linked to changes in the planning system. 'Fast-track planning' is considered critical to accommodate the leading role of the private sector in infrastructure projects and to guarantee investment returns. The National Infrastructure Delivery Plan states:

> The delivery of effective, timely and high value for money infrastructure projects requires a transparent planning and consents regime which is able to respond quickly to the need for new infrastructure at both the national and local level. An efficient planning regime is vital to encourage private sector investment.
>
> (HM Treasury, 2010: 17)

It is assumed that planning delays impact upon the private sector's assessment of the commercial viability of projects. But the National Infrastructure Delivery Plan sets out a spatial framework which seeks to integrate land use, transport and environmental policies nationally. Most large infrastructure decisions are taken on a case-by-case basis, in which cost benefit analysis plays a key role. At the same time, reflecting arguments that cities are the sources economic growth, attention has focused on the development of infrastructure at the city-region scale to support urban growth (Glaeser, 2011; Katz and Bradley, 2013; for a critical review of these arguments, see Pike et al., 2017).

The planning of large-scale infrastructure is highly susceptible to political conflict because it often involves the exercise of government and corporate power and the clash of values. The adversarial culture of the Westminster system of government does not lend itself to careful deliberation. The ability of citizens to influence the outcomes of large-scale infrastructure can appear limited, while "conflicting views about data, methods, system boundaries and optimisations, are more likely to become polarised and to undermine the quality of the political debate" (Coelho et al., 2014: 5). We discern a shift from a traditional approach to governing infrastructure, which tended to be centralised, top-down and project-focused, to an emergent approach which is decentralised, bottom-up and system-focused (see Table 14.2).

Multi-level Governance and Planning for Infrastructure

UK Infrastructure

Planning for infrastructure occurs within a framework of multi-level governance (see Chapter 2 by John Tomaney and Claire Colomb). At the UK scale, the Planning Act 2008 introduced a new development consent process for Nationally Significant Infrastructure Projects (NSIPs), typically megaprojects (relating to energy, transport, water, waste water or waste) which require 'development consent'. A Development Consent Order (DCO) removes the need to obtain several consents that would otherwise be required for development, including planning permission and compulsory purchase orders. This is intended to be a quicker process for megaprojects to get the necessary planning permission and other related consents they would require, rather than having to apply separately to multiple planning authorities for different consents. Originally, the final decision on whether

Table 14.2 Transitions in approaches to governing and planning infrastructure funding and financing at the city/city-region scale

Dimension	*Traditional approaches*	*Emergent approaches*
Rationale(s)	Economic efficiency (and social equity) Market failure	Unlocking economic potential (e.g. gross value added, employment) Expanding future revenue streams and/or tax base Releasing uplift in land values Market failure
Focus	Individual infrastructure items (e.g. roads, bridges, rail lines)	Infrastructure systems and interdependencies (e.g. connectivity, telecommunications, district heating)
Timescale	Short(er), 5–10 years	Long(er), up to 25–30 years
Geography	Local authority administrative area	'Functional Economic Area'/'Travel to Work Area', city-region, multiple local authority areas
Scale	Small, targeted	Large, encompassing
Lead	Public sector	Public and/or private sectors
Organisation	Projects	Programmes
Funding	Grant-based (e.g. from taxes, fees and levies)	Investment-led (e.g. from existing assets and revenue streams, grants, borrowing)
Financing	Established and tried and tested instruments and practices (e.g. bonds, borrowing)	Innovative, new and adapted instruments and practices (e.g. value capture, asset leverage and leasing, revolving funds)
Process	Formula-driven allocation, (re) distributive, closed	Negotiated, competition-based, open
Governance and planning	Centralised Top-down National government- and single local authority-based	(De)centralised Bottom-up and top-down National government- and multiple local authority-based (e.g. Combined Authorities, Joint Committees)
Management and delivery	Single local authority-based, arms-length agencies and bodies	Multiple local authority-based, joint ventures and new vehicles

Source: O'Brien et al. (2017).

development consent should be granted rested with the Infrastructure Planning Commission (IPC), a non-departmental public body which would take decisions in line with National Policy Statements designated by government. The Localism Act 2011 abolished the IPC. Responsibility for decisions on NSIPs now lies with the Secretary of State, on the advice of the National Infrastructure Directorate of the Planning Inspectorate.

The Thames Tideway Tunnel referred to above was one of the first and largest schemes to secure a DCO under the Planning Act 2008 as an NSIP. Achieving planning consent was complex, in part because the scheme involved 14 local authorities and more than 900 community groups with which to consult and engage. Moreover, the project was controversial and generated significant opposition. The consultation concerned the need for the project and whether a tunnel was the most appropriate solution, the preferred route and alignment, and the impact of construction. An Application for Development Consent was made to the Planning Inspectorate in February 2013, and following an examination, the government gave its consent in September 2014, overriding some of the concerns of the Planning Inspectorate, notably relating to the impact of construction on local communities. The speed with which the DCO was approved might be judged a success for the system. But doubts have been expressed, in addition to lingering uncertainties about its costs. Critics, including Sir Ian Byatt, the former water regulator, have questioned whether the tunnel was needed at all, suggesting that environmental and customer benefits could be achieved by smaller, less expensive projects and that the case for the tunnel option rested more on the benefits that would accrue to its owners rather than consumers (*Financial Times*, 2015). Evaluating the project, the National Audit Office (2017) suggested the government did not fully explore the uncertainty in its modelling before endorsing the tunnel option, while correcting for inaccurate predictions could have resulted in a smaller, lower-cost tunnel.

Some megaprojects are authorised by Act of Parliament, rather than the Planning Act 2008. Hybrid Bills consider projects that would affect the public, but would also have a significant impact for specific individuals or groups. In this process, a committee of Members of Parliament assesses the evidence and receives representations in relation to a proposed development. This mode of approval was used for the Channel Tunnel, the Dartford Crossing, the Severn Bridges, the Cardiff Bay Barrage, the Channel Tunnel Link, Crossrail ('The Elizabeth Line') and, most recently, High Speed 2 (HS2). Various degrees of controversy attended these projects. A highly contentious piece of legislation was the High Speed Rail (London–West Midlands) Act 2017, which was enacted by a Hybrid Bill. First, the costs and economic impacts of a high-speed rail line (HS2) from London to Birmingham (and later Sheffield, Leeds and Manchester) were contested. The House of Lords Economic Affairs Committee reported in March 2015 posing a series of questions to the government, and querying the supporting cost benefit analysis and the anticipated net benefits of the scheme (House of Lords Economic Affairs Committee, 2015; see also Tomaney and Marques, 2013). Second, the Act gives the government the power to acquire land and property for the purposes of building the railway affecting individual business and households. Questions of compensation loomed large in the concerns of petitioners. These anxieties were debated in the House of Commons, but in the House of Lords the government challenged the right of half of the petitioners to make their case on grounds which the House of Lords HS2 Select Committee (2016: para.33) considered "arcane, opaque and unhelpful".

Scotland

Below the UK level, infrastructure planning takes place in increasingly diverse jurisdictions (see Chapter 2). The Scottish Government's Economic Strategy sets out its Infrastructure Investment Plan, with a strong emphasis on developing natural resources and underpinning a shift to a low-carbon economy founded on increased use of renewable resources (Scottish Government, 2015). The Third National Planning Framework (NPF3) "is the spatial expression of the Government Economic Strategy, and of our plans for infrastructure investment" (Scottish Government, 2014: iii). NPF3 sets outs statutory spatial development priorities for cities and towns, rural areas, the coast and islands, and national developments. The NPF designates these 'national developments'. Fourteen of them (selected from 200 proposals) are contained in the NPF3 – with scope for others to be added, including, a carbon capture and storage network, thermal generation, a high-voltage energy transmission network, pumped hydroelectric storage, the Metropolitan Glasgow Strategic Drainage Partnership and a National Digital Fibre Network. Scottish Ministers take decisions on these national developments. Inclusion in NPF3 does not imply funding on the part of the Scottish Government, but to support their delivery, priorities identified in NPF3 will be considered when future spending programmes are developed or reviewed (Scottish Government, 2014). There are some similarities between the UK system and the Scottish system, insofar as they allocate responsibility for decisions about megaprojects to ministers. (Similarly, under the Planning (Wales) Act 2015, applications for 'Developments of National Significance' are dealt with by the Planning Inspectorate on behalf of the Welsh Government, while the Planning Act (Northern Ireland) 2011 stipulated that regionally significant planning applications remain the responsibility of ministers in the executive.) But, in contrast to the UK Government's approach, the Scottish Government has produced a spatial framework for its whole jurisdiction which aims to integrate its different urban and regional and infrastructure priorities into a single plan (Scottish Government, 2014: 61).

London

The London Infrastructure Plan 2050 (LIP) (Mayor of London, 2014) sets out proposed investments in transport, housing, green infrastructure, digital, energy, water and waste infrastructure totalling £1.3 trillion, which London is expected to require between 2016 and 2050. The creation of a pipeline of infrastructure projects and programmes mirrors that of the UK's National Infrastructure Plan, and is designed to instil and sustain investor confidence in projects and programmes and attract private investment while adopting more strategic and planned approaches to urban infrastructure renewal. Unlike London's spatial, transport, housing and economic strategies, the LIP is not a statutory document. The London Plan (as altered) sets out the Mayor's spatial development priorities (Mayor of London, 2014, 2015). Population growth – and attendant pressures on housing, transport, education and health systems – presents a special challenge for the planning, governance, funding, financing, operation and maintenance of infrastructure in the London global city-region. London's infrastructure and utilities have proved attractive to international investors, as noted above in the discussion of the Thames Tideway Tunnel. But the rapid appreciation in value of commercial and residential real estate assets has generated policy concerned with how some of this can be captured to support the provision of infrastructure. The Mayor's Community Infrastructure Levy aims to raise up to £600 million to help finance the Crossrail project by seeking contributions from developers for additional floorspace they create across London. The size of the contribution is calculated once a planning application is submitted to the local authority, and is based on the amount of floorspace created, the location and how the development is to be used (Greater London Authority [GLA], 2016). Efforts to capture value from appreciating private assets for publicly funded infrastructure are likely to remain central to planning practice in London.

The 3.3km Northern Line Extension (NLE) is a major feature of the redevelopment of the Vauxhall, Nine Elms, Battersea Opportunity Area and nationally designated Enterprise Zone (EZ), which is defined in the London Plan as a new employment and residential district located on the edge of Central London. It extends the existing London Underground Northern Line to Nine Elms and Battersea (including two new stations) by 2020. The NLE is estimated to cost £1.04 billion, financed through a £480 million long-term loan from the European Investment Bank, £200 million of finance drawn from an index-linked bond issue, and the remaining £300 million of capital raised from developers. The GLA will repay the finance and fund project costs using developer contributions collected by Wandsworth and Lambeth Boroughs. Business rate growth above a defined baseline in the new EZ will be retained by the Boroughs and the GLA. Once the NLE is operational, fare income will pay the operational costs of the extension as part of a 'bespoke' funding and financing model. But this form of funding and financing infrastructure has implications for planning objectives set out in the London Plan. High levels of housing densification and reduced levels of affordable housing were required in Nine Elms in order to secure rates of return to international investors which are majority-owned by the Malaysian Government through a Sovereign Wealth Fund. Bringing this complex array of different public and private sector actors together in a coherent and cohesive planning framework is a difficult and fraught process. The NLE demonstrates how the state and private interests in London are seeking new forms of investment in infrastructure against a background of national austerity, limited local fiscal autonomy and London's continued dominant 'national champion' role within the UK political economy, forging innovative, untried and relatively risky arrangements.

London's planning is complicated further by the lack of formal strategic planning framework covering the entire global city-region (i.e. the travel to work area), which extends beyond the Mayor's jurisdiction. There are noticeable differences in the institutional capacity, statutory responsibilities and resources between the GLA, London Boroughs and local authorities and Local Economic Partnerships in South East England, which makes governance, long-term planning and assembling public and private (particularly international) infrastructure funding and financing difficult.

Northern England

If capturing value arising from the growth is the priority in London, investing in infrastructure to promote growth shapes planning in the Midlands and North of England. The Northern Powerhouse represents the latest episode in efforts to mitigate the longstanding regional disparities between North and South in England, albeit influenced by economic theories that stress the relationship between agglomeration and productivity and cities as the supposed motors of economic growth (Lee, 2017; Northern Powerhouse, 2016; Parr 2017). Devolution to Metro Mayors in some regions also forms part of the context for the policy. The Northern Powerhouse strategy is heavily focused on making investments in transport infrastructure that contributes to the potential for allegedly transformational agglomeration benefits from a more integrated economy, and on planning and decision-making to enhance the economic potential of the North. Transport for the North, an agency created to promote the agenda, commissioned the Northern Powerhouse Independent Economic Review to provide the underpinning evidence base for decision-making on transport investment priorities across the North of England. The government claims it is committed to £13 billion of transport infrastructure investments in the North, but Lee (2017: 483) suggests that the Northern Powerhouse is characterised by "geographical fuzziness, vagueness about leadership and responsibility, drift from the theoretical idea and unclear financing". Funding and financing infrastructure in the North of England in an era of austerity and in a context where private investment is expected to take a leading role is especially challenging. The UK Government has developed a prospectus for international investors (Department for International Trade, 2016). Greater Manchester has attracted significant recent foreign investment in infrastructure. In 2013, the Beijing Construction Engineering Group agreed a joint venture with Manchester Airports Group, Carillion and the Greater Manchester (local government) Pension Fund for a new £800 million development at Manchester airport, known as 'Airport City', which it is hoped will create up to 16,000 new jobs (see O'Brien et al., 2016). But at least two challenges face planning of infrastructure in the North. First, it is unclear whether adequate resources exist outside the very largest cities to make significant investments in infrastructure. Second, outside those city-regions which have devolved strategic plan-making powers, there is "a policy gap in terms of strategy-making, intelligence collection and wider economic development coordination" (Wong and Webb, 2014: 698).

Conclusion

This chapter has considered planning for infrastructure, with a principal focus on the strategic scale. Its main aim has been to show how the planning system interacts with systems of funding and finance to create megaprojects. Private sector investment plays an increasingly important part in the development of infrastructure. In this context, the planning system is increasingly concerned with ensuring returns to private investors rather than producing public goods. There are obvious dangers here. Contemporary planning practice can end up favouring corporate and governmental interests, creating "an unholy alliance between politicians and capital markets", in the words of Sir Ian Wyatt, former Director General of the UK water industry regulator (quoted in *Financial Times*, 2017). Major dangers include a lack of integration between different infrastructures because these do not suit private interests, and gaps in provision where needs are high but commercial returns are limited. These will affect different places and social groups in different ways, and represent a central challenge to contemporary planning practice.

References

All listed URLs were last accessed on 1 March 2018.

Coelho, M., Ratnoo, V. and Dellepiane, S. (2014) *Political economy of infrastructure in the UK*. London: Institute for Government. Available at: https://www.instituteforgovernment.org.uk/sites/default/files/publications/Political%20economy%20of%20infrastructure%20in%20the%20UK%20final%20v1.pdf.

Department for International Trade (2016) Northern Powerhouse investment opportunities. Available at: https://www.gov.uk/government/uploads/system/uploads/attachment_data/file/595701/NPH_pitchbook_2016_Brochure_English_low_res_version.pdf.

Financial Times (2015) OFWAT accused of failing to protect customers over "supersewer", 7 September. Available at: https://www.ft.com/content/927de830-54aa-11e5-8642-453585f2cfcd.

Financial Times (2017) Thames Water: the murky structure of a utility company, 4 May. Available at: https://www.ft.com/content/5413ebf8-24f1-11e7-8691-d5f7e0cd0a16.

Flyvbjerg, B. (2014) What you should know about megaprojects and why: an overview, *Project Management Journal*, 45(2), pp.6–19.

GLA (2016) Crossrail funding: use of planning obligations and the Mayoral Community Infrastructure Levy. Supplementary planning guidance. Available at: https://www.london.gov.uk/sites/default/files/crossrail_funding_spg_updated_march_2016v2.pdf.

Glaeser, E. (2011) *The triumph of the city*. London: Pan.

Graham, S. and Marvin, S. (2001) Splintering urbanism: networked infrastructures, technological mobilities and the urban condition. London: Routledge.

Harvey, D. (2012) The urban roots of financial crises: reclaiming the city for anti-capitalist struggle, *Socialist Register*, 48, pp.1–35.

HM Treasury (2010) *National Infrastructure Plan 2010*. London: Her Majesty's Treasury.

House of Lords Economic Affairs Committee (2015) *The economics of High Speed 2. 1st report of Session 2014–15*. HL Paper 134, 25 March. Available at: https://www.publications.parliament.uk/pa/ld201415/ldselect/ldeconaf/134/134.pdf.

House of Lords HS2 Select Committee (2016) *High Speed Rail (London–West Midlands) Bill: special report of Session 2016–17*, HL Paper 83, 15 December. Available at: https://www.publications.parliament.uk/pa/ld201617/ldselect/ldhs2/83/83.pdf.

Katz, B. and Bradley, J. (2013) *The metropolitan revolution: how cities and metros are fixing our broken politics and fragile economy*. Washington, DC: Brookings Institution.

Lee, N. (2017) Powerhouse of cards? Understanding the "Northern Powerhouse", *Regional Studies*, 51(3), pp.478–489.

Mayor of London (2014) *London Infrastructure Plan 2050: a consultation*. London: Greater London Authority.

Mayor of London (2015) *London Plan 2015*. London: Greater London Authority.

National Audit Office (2017) *Review of the Thames Tideway Tunnel: report by the Comptroller and Auditor General*. HC 783 Session 2016–17. Available at: https://www.nao.org.uk/wp-content/uploads/2017/03/Review-of-the-Thames-Tideway-Tunnel.pdf.

Neuman, M. (2006) Infiltrating infrastructures: on the nature of networked infrastructure, *Journal of Urban Technology*, 13(1), pp.3–31.

Northern Powerhouse (2016) *Northern Powerhouse strategy*. Available at: https://www.gov.uk/government/uploads/system/uploads/attachment_data/file/571562/NPH_strategy_web.pdf.

O'Brien, P., Pike, A. and Tomaney, J. (2016) Beyond the northern pitchbook. In M. Raco (ed.) *Britain for sale? Perspectives on the costs and benefits of foreign ownership*. London: Smith Institute. Available at: www.smith-institute.org.uk/wp-content/uploads/2016/05/Britain-for-sale.pdf.

O'Brien, P., Pike, A. and Tomaney, J. (2018) Governing the "ungovernable"? Financialisation and the governance of transport infrastructure in the London "global city-region". *Progress in Planning*, DOI: 10.1016/j.progress.2018.02.001.

Parr, J.B. (2017) The Northern Powerhouse: a commentary, *Regional Studies*, 51(3), pp.490–500.

Pike, A., Rodrìguez-Pose, A. and Tomaney, J. (2017) *Local and regional development*, 2nd edn. London: Routledge.

Scottish Government (2014) *Ambition, opportunity, place: Scotland's Third National Planning Framework*. Edinburgh: Scottish Government. Available at: www.gov.scot/Resource/0045/00453683.pdf.

Scottish Government (2015) *Infrastructure Investment Plan 2015*. Edinburgh: Scottish Government. Available at: www.gov.scot/Resource/0049/00491180.pdf.

The Economist (2016) Life in the slow lane, 5 March. Available at: www.economist.com/news/britain/21693936-government-trumpets-its-ambitions-roads-railways-and-airports-fact-infrastructure.

The Economist (2017) How and when to use private money in infrastructure projects, 22 April. Available at: www.economist.com/news/finance-and-economics/21721229-public-private-partnerships-their-promise-and-their-pitfalls-how-and-when-use.

Tomaney, J. and Marques, P. (2013) Evidence, policy, and the politics of regional development: the case of high-speed rail in the United Kingdom, *Environment and Planning C*, 31(3), pp.414–427.

Wong, C. and Webb, B. (2014) Planning for infrastructure: challenges to northern England, *Town Planning Review*, 85(6), pp.683–670.

15 Planning for Economic Progress

Jessica Ferm, Michael Edwards and Edward Jones

Introduction

The introduction to this book discussed the dominant neo-liberal view of planning as a hindrance to economic development – as state interference in an otherwise competitive and efficient market. This negative perception of state 'interference' has meant that national government has over the years moved away from 'rebalancing the economy' and achieving inter-regional equity. Although its recent Industrial Strategy (Department for Business, Energy and Industrial Strategy, 2017) aspires to foster growth in all parts of the UK, doubt has been cast on its ability to meet this challenge (Bailey et al., 2017). State strategy has on the whole emphasised economic competitiveness, working with rather than against the forces of inter-regional and intra-regional inequality. This has given local authorities and regional bodies (where they exist) a more explicit role in supporting the economic development of their localities in pursuit of competitiveness.

However, for many planning practitioners, the economy is somewhat of a 'black box'. It is increasingly the domain of economists, and planners rely rather uncritically on evidence prepared by economists to inform their plans. This division of intellectual labour between 'economists' and 'planners' has worsened since the 1960s, when planning in Britain was re-defining itself within social science, the economist Nathaniel Lichfield was president of the Royal Town Planning Institute (RTPI), and the Regional Studies Association was founded. The 1970s and 1980s saw a blossoming of regional and local economic development teams within public service and a rich set of policy-development initiatives, some of them seriously challenging the burgeoning neo-liberal regime of the 1980s (Eisenschitz and Gough, 1993; Greater London Council, 1985).[1] The journal *Local Economy*, edited by Sam Aaronovich, was the lively in-house magazine of this branch of planning. As planning was weakened in the late 1980s and 1990s, economic planning initiatives were suppressed, and by the end of the century, planning had re-defined itself as much closer to urban design, reinforced by the report of the Urban Task

Force (1999). Now we have rather few planners equipped and confident to challenge the economic orthodoxies coming down to them from government, from Local Enterprise Partnerships and, in the London case, from GLA Economics.

This chapter's title refers to planning for economic progress, rather than economic growth. This is intentional. We would hope that planners would want to support an economy that represents 'progress' for its people, not an economy that increases inequality and environmental degradation. However, their reliance on mainstream economists for their analysis reinforces the influence of neo-liberalism on planning. The overall message of this chapter is that planning in the UK is reliant on a limited framing of the economy, one that focuses on specialisation, economic competitiveness and agglomeration as driving forces for economic growth, and underplays the role of diversity as a driver for economic progress – let alone more radical approaches to an economy that question growth (as measured by Gross Domestic product [GDP]) as an overarching objective.

The first section of this chapter reviews the dominant theoretical framing of the economy, evident in the various reports used as the evidence bases for local, regional and, in the case of Wales and Scotland, national plans. This framing, we argue, overemphasises the role of specialisation and agglomeration as growth strategies, underplaying the potential role of diversity as a driver for economic growth, and the costs (as well as benefits) of agglomeration. The second section considers the framework guiding the way planners approach planning for the economy, looking at what is stipulated in national government guidance and how this has changed over recent years, with increasing emphasis on market imperatives, and the implications of this. Here we consider the nature of the 'evidence' on the economy that is prepared and used to inform planning policy, and what this evidence typically includes and excludes. Finally, we conclude and reflect on what future political and economic changes might mean for planning for economic progress.

Framing the Economy: Specialisation versus Diversity

The idea that countries[2] should specialise in the production of the goods for which they have the greatest relative labour productivity advantage dates to David Ricardo's *Principles of Political Economy*, published in 1817. The logic is that total production is expanded if each place specialises in what it can do best – where it has a 'comparative advantage' – and is prepared to trade its products freely with others. With globalisation and the opening up of trade, it further pays to specialise. Openness to trade increases market size and brings greater competition, encouraging innovation and driving efficiency. It also allows economies to benefit from access to new technology. This all drives productivity in the economy, and encourages places with high land and labour costs to shift from less productive to more productive economic activities. This is often described rather misleadingly as a shift from a manufacturing to a service-dominated economy.

In geographical terms, the concentration of high-wage, service sector employment in the centre of larger cities has become more pronounced over the past 10–15 years, and has been witnessed across cities in the UK (Swinney and Bidgood, 2014). As Cheshire et al. (2014) show, service sector businesses benefit the most from agglomeration, despite their growth in an era of expanding telecommunications. This underpins the renewed enthusiasm for cities – that 'cities matter' – reflected in new political structures and the appointment of Metro Mayors in several of the UK's large metropolitan cities (see Chapter 2 by John Tomaney and Claire Colomb). Theoretically, this has led to a revival of interest among economic geographers in Marshallian theories of agglomeration originally used to explain industrial districts. In the late 1800s, Alfred Marshall argued that agglomeration of specialised industrial firms arises because of (1) the potential for 'knowledge spillovers' or the informal transmission of knowledge facilitated by proximity, (2) the advantages of 'thick' labour markets for specialised skills, and (3) proximity to suppliers, customers and other businesses in the co-production chain, which primarily reduces transport and transaction costs. It is the importance of knowledge transfer that has received the most attention when explaining agglomeration in the service industries in the contemporary age. As Peter Rees, former Chief Planning Officer at the Corporation of London, told the *Financial Times*: "the gossip hotspots, restaurants and pubs are just as important as the offices – it's that which keeps the City going" (Allen, 2014).

Proposals for a Northern Powerhouse were based on a (rather simplistic) logic of agglomeration: if connectivity between geographically proximate cities in the North (particularly focused on the 'core cities' of Manchester, Liverpool, Sheffield, Leeds and Newcastle) could be improved, then together they could create one large agglomeration to rival London and redress the North–South economic imbalance: "Agglomeration effects are crucial; sustainable UK growth will rely increasingly on our major cities doing for the North West, North East, West Yorkshire and Midlands – for example – what London does for the South East – driving investment, productivity and growth" (City Growth Commission, 2014: 11).

The economic analysis underpinning the Northern Powerhouse proposals has focused on identifying the North's relative specialisation and comparative advantage. As stated in the Independent Economic Review (SQW and Cambridge Econometrics, 2016: 11), the analysis:

> draws on "Smart Specialisation" principles, where places are encouraged to select a limited number of priorities for investment that focus on their strengths and comparative advantages, and the concept of 'capabilities' which encompass assets, expertise and competences which cut across sectors.

In Wales, there is also a focus on Welsh 'comparative advantage' in the renewable energy sector: "Just as the City of London and south east England exploit their comparative advantages of financial muscle, political power and geographical location, we in Wales must leverage our own comparative advantages" (Institute of Welsh Affairs, 2015: 39).

Although pursuit of comparative advantage and specialisation might lead to an increase in total global production, Watson (2017) argues that this does not mean that 'everyone is a winner'. On the contrary, Ricardo's theory and modern competitiveness discourse ignore the political realities, power dynamics and inequalities that make it work in practice.

The mainstream literatures and strategies tend to treat the pursuit of GDP growth as axiomatic, disregarding the environmental, equity and conceptual critiques. GDP is part of the apparatus of national income accounting in which, broadly, activity is valued through market prices of products, disregarding environmental and other externalities and distributional considerations. It also values housing services through estimated imputed rents, which is especially problematic for a rentier economy like the UK. There are strong critiques of the concept (Fioramonti, 2013), and some innovative alternative measures have been championed for the UK by the New Economics Foundation (NEF, 2013).

A similar disregard for negative consequences is found in the mainstream treatment of the concept of agglomeration, which is concerned overwhelmingly with its benefits:

> The downside of London's fabled agglomeration economies is largely borne by citizens in the form of high rents and prices for housing, high travel costs, air quality which seriously breaches the law, displacement and disruption of communities and enterprises and the dispossession of tenants and leaseholders in erstwhile social housing.
>
> (Edwards, 2016)

The negative consequences are not limited to London's citizens. There are negative consequences for the rest of the country, too. As Edwards (2015: 34) explains:

> Massive investments are made to contain and mitigate these negative effects, notably through the state's provision of transport, sewerage and other infrastructure improvements without which the growth would be impossible. Insofar as the benefits accrue privately and

> the costs are socialised, we have no possibility that ordinary market processes will bring the city's growth to a halt when it passes some optimum level. We can thus expect that, on current trends, London will continue to pre-empt the UK's major infrastructure budgets as it has done in recent years, and probably long after it would have been better to invest elsewhere. Indeed that point may well already have passed. Landed, property, construction and financial interests have a vested interest, however, in keeping London's ascendancy growing.

The framing of the specialisation discourse also ignores an alternative understanding, which is that economic diversity can equally (or alternatively) be an engine for urban growth (Duranton and Puga, 2000; Jacobs, 1969; Buck et al., 2002). The counter-argument to the specialisation-drives-growth theory was encapsulated by Jane Jacobs in *The Economy of Cities*, where she wrote: "a city grows by a process of gradual diversification and differentiation of its economy" (Jacobs, 1969: 126). Although large firms might be more economically efficient and productive, this does not – she argued – lead to economic growth, which arises from the process of adding new work to old work: "the period when an organization is most fertile at adding new work is while it is still small" (Jacobs, 1969: 75). Jacobs agreed that knowledge transfer is an important driver of agglomeration, but argued that cross-sectoral spillovers between heterogeneous businesses drive innovation.

The empirical evidence on diversity as a source of growth is inconclusive, but indicative. In a comparison of New York and Pittsburgh in the early 1960s, Chinitz (1961) concluded that an urban environment dominated by a few large firms or a single industry leads to less economic growth than an environment with many smaller heterogeneous industries, which foster more competition. Later, a larger comparative study found the same: Glaeser et al. (1992) examined the 170 largest cities in the US (between 1956 and 1987) and found that diversity and local competition fostered employment growth, whereas specialisation reduced it. Feldman and Audretsch (1999) specifically focus on knowledge spillovers as drivers of agglomeration, and question whether an increased concentration of a specific industry facilitates knowledge transfer, or whether the exchange of knowledge across diverse firms is what leads to new knowledge (and thus innovation), as suggested by Jacobs. In their empirical work on US cities, Feldman and Audretsch found more support for the so-called 'diversity thesis'.

Glaeser et al.'s original study has prompted a large empirical literature on this subject: some studies provide more support for the specialisation thesis, some the diversity thesis. In an attempt to navigate this vast literature, de Groot et al. (2015) conducted a statistical meta-analysis of 73 scientific articles on the subject and found that the heterogeneity among studies is huge. However, overall, they concluded that the support for Jacobs' hypothesis is relatively most convincing and Glaeser et al.'s (1992) overall conclusion of the importance of competition and diversity "has not been overturned". Of course, large cities can be both specialised and diversified (Duranton and Puga, 2000), and understanding their historical trajectories over time is important (Krugman, 1991). Buck et al. (2002) argue that London's economic diversity underpins its long-term success, despite the emergence of sectors of specialisation.

This is under-recognised in the Economics Evidence Base (EEB; GLA Economics, 2016) underpinning the emerging London Plan, where a discussion of London's economic specialisation and comparative advantage forms the bulk of the first chapter and frames the discussion for the whole document. A critique was prepared by Just Space Economy and Planning[3] (JSEP, 2016), which includes some of the present authors, following an invitation to attend a series of meetings with GLA Economics during the preparation of the EEB. Following these meetings, amendments were made to acknowledge in the executive summary that "London is a diverse economy", but this diversity is discussed solely in terms of the broad range of economic sectors that exist. As argued in JSEP's critique, there is a lack of analysis of the inter-dependencies between different parts of the economy, in particular the dependencies between the global sectors and the 'ordinary' businesses that make the city work and provide goods and services to other businesses and residents. There is very limited reference to the social and cultural diversity of London's enterprises, the significant proportion of start-up business owners who are from Black and Minority Ethnic backgrounds, and insufficient emphasis on the importance of diversity (more generally, cultural, social and economic) to London as such a success story. Importantly, the consideration of London as a diverse economy does not then translate into an analysis that considers this diversity as a driver of growth.

These gaps in the evidence base are then likely to translate to weaknesses in the emerging London Plan itself. The framing of the 2016 EEB is very similar to the previous one, despite updates and improvements. Looking at the spatial translation of this in previous versions of the London Plan, we have seen a prioritisation of employment in the Central Activities Zone and centripetal transport infrastructure, with a lack of emphasis on, provision for, or understanding of the role of employment elsewhere – in town centres, high streets and on industrial land, where more than half of London's jobs are (JSEP, 2014).

Failing to acknowledge the importance of London's economic diversity is likely to have consequences. In their report *Future Proofing London*, Atkins and Oxford Economics (2015: 39) suggest that London's economy becoming unbalanced is one of the four risks to London's competitive advantage, and that "the economy is in danger of losing the diversity that has enabled it to prosper". They elaborate as follows:

> As the structure of the economy changes towards increasingly high value sectors, with the associated loss of industrial land to commercial uses, there is a danger that London is losing its ability to accommodate businesses that not only provide jobs for the lower skilled, but also help the economy to function properly. It is also important to ensure that the economy is not overly reliant on footloose multinational companies but also meets the need for space for small SMEs and companies. This will help to ensure that the economy remains diverse and is adaptable to changing global economic conditions.

The work of Gibson-Graham (2006) emphasises the power of economic and common language to be 'performative' in actually having material consequences: defining our perceptions and actions, and thus changing the world of economic activity.[4]

In the statements released by the Mayor of London, Sadiq Khan, in the preparation of his new London Plan and associated strategies, there is a strong emphasis on 'economic fairness'. Although the Mayor of London supports London's role as a global city, he has included a new policy (GG5) on 'Growing a good economy' in his draft London Plan, which amongst other things seeks "to ensure that London's economy diversifies and that the benefits of economic success are shared more equitably across London" (Mayor of London, 2017: 21). This suggests some scope for progress.

Similar optimism can be found looking outside England. In the spirit of breaking from the dominant approach in Westminster, Scotland's Economic Strategy (Scottish Government, 2015: 8–9) puts emphasis on a diverse economy and 'sharing' growth:

> A strong, vibrant and diverse economy is essential to our national prosperity and in creating the wealth to support high quality public services. Ensuring that growth is shared and sustainable is the key to unlocking all of Scotland's potential and strengthening our greatest asset – the people of Scotland.

It also states: "There is growing international evidence that promoting competitiveness and addressing inequality are important interdependent ambitions" (Scottish Government, 2015: 11).

This section has considered the dominant framing of the economy, which directly provides the intellectual context for planning. However, planners working in their day-to-day jobs are likely to be largely unaware of the extent to which this framing influences their work. Rather, they follow the policies and procedures within a hierarchical planning framework, which involves direction from national government guidance on the way in which they plan locally for their economies. The next section turns to this framework.

Planning for Economic Development: From National Guidance to Local Practice

The practice of planning for economic development in the UK is strongly influenced by the requirements and prescriptions of plan-making defined by central government. Here, we examine the role of planners in seeking to govern local economic development. We review the key drivers shaping policy-making and practice, and critically reflect on the understandings underlying these attempts to foster conditions amenable to economic growth.

Over the last two decades, planning for economic development has been influenced by ideas around the 'compact city' and opportunities to reinvigorate urban life through an 'urban renaissance'. From the 1990s, concerns about social and economic issues in inner city areas, the environmental quality of city centres, and beliefs around post-industrial urbanism coalesced into a renewed enthusiasm for area-based physical regeneration as a solution to a range of problems. The influential Urban Task Force report viewed sites protected for uses such as factories and offices (known as 'employment land') as likely candidates for redevelopment to deliver an improved public realm and housing-led mixed-use regeneration.

These ideas were soon reflected in policy. From 2004, government guidance recommended that planning authorities identify and protect only the 'best' employment sites, mindful of 'market realism' (Office of the Deputy Prime Minister, 2004: 5, 25). This approach has been reiterated in generations of guidance. The guidance in *Planning for Sustainable Economic Growth* (Department for Communities and Local Government [DCLG], 2009) and the *National Planning Policy Framework* (NPPF) (DCLG, 2012) both stress that employment sites should not be protected unless there is a 'reasonable prospect' of use.[5] Significant weight is therefore placed on assessments of the potential utility of employment land, and the overarching need to release sites for redevelopment to other uses.

In England, local authorities are required by the NPPF to conduct regular reviews of employment designations with due regard to market and economic 'signals' (paras 22 and 158). In assessing economic development needs, councils are required to adopt an evidence-based approach, translating employment forecasts and projections into anticipated land requirements, and in so doing provide a robust basis for appraising individual sites (DCLG, 2015). This methodology places great emphasis on extrapolations of top-down statistical data in deciding whether specific sites should be protected for employment uses or released for redevelopment. Any protection of employment sites has to be justified with reference to technical assessments, grounded in economic forecasts and projections.

It must be recognised, however, that employment land assessments (while crucial to Local Plan-making) are not the only types of economic studies that are commissioned by planning authorities. Office policy reviews, retail assessments and town centre audits are used to understand various dimensions of local economies, but in doing so, they create 'silos' of evidence that neglect the inter-dependencies and relationships which characterise the economic whole. Taking these studies at face value risks cementing a partial and constrained understanding of local economies into planning practices, leaving little room for bottom-up articulation of collectively defined local economic needs and aspirations.

Since 2010, prompted by development pressures and threats to existing economic activity and livelihoods, a number of local economic studies in London have been prepared. These have sought to 'get under the skin' of local economies and understand the inter-relationships between businesses and their locales and populations. However, there is little consistency in methodologies to enable the patchwork of studies to form a whole picture and inform strategic policy. A recent review of the range of studies conducted to date, the methodological challenges they face and remaining gaps in knowledge was undertaken by the authors (under the UCL London 2034 programme) and is now accessible online (Ferm et al., 2017). The recent proliferation of such studies is welcome, but these tend to be the exception rather than the rule. In general, the economic evidence bases of Local Plans fail to address the diversity of economic practices and the spatial inter-dependencies which underpin the operations of firms. For example, one of the Royal Town Planning Institute's professional competencies[6] is an understanding of the 'economic context'. In this framing of the economy, economic and financial factors are conflated, with a strong emphasis on development viability and deliverability as key components of economic knowledge (RTPI, 2015: 44). The locus of action for planners is drawn at the scale of an individual development site, rather than the wider local economy of which sites form a part. This requirement neglects useful skills and areas of knowledge, such as (for example) understanding the complex interactions and inter-dependencies which characterise local and regional economies, or eliciting and delivering a democratic and collectively conceived vision for the future development of local economies as part of the plan-preparation process.

Market imperatives have also been felt in recent years through the curbing of the powers of local authorities to control the loss of employment sites and premises to other uses. This commitment to deregulation has resulted in changes to permitted development rights, which have allowed the conversion of offices and light industrial buildings to residential use without the need for planning permission, leading to the loss of office stock, particularly for small businesses (CBRE, 2015; see Chapter 4 by Ben Clifford in this volume).

Financial resourcing, as well as centrally defined policy prescriptions and agendas, shape the room for manoeuvre available to planning authorities in seeking to plan for local economies. Economic evidence bases of plans are commonly prepared by consultants because councils typically lack planners with the necessary specialist skills to prepare robust assessments. Cuts to local authority funding since 2008 have focused resources on forms of evidence that meet the minimum requirements of central government. Opportunities to conduct in-depth investigations of local economic dynamics are therefore difficult to resource.

The continuing context of austerity also affects local authorities' remits outside their spatial planning competencies (see Chapter 1 by John Tomaney and Jessica Ferm). Many councils hold stocks of employment land, thereby occupying multiple roles – as landlords as well as planning authorities. The potential to generate funds through increased revenue and capital receipts has prompted councils to explore options for the potential intensification of sites and redevelopment for new uses, particularly on council-owned industrial estates (see Ferm and Jones, 2016). Local authority economic development capacities have also diminished through austerity measures. One local authority officer characterises their economic development section as a 'promotional team' whose efforts focus on the creative and digital industries, rather than in providing day-to-day practical support to a wider range of businesses. They reflect that:

> We can't provide that support any more. Back in the day, the government used to provide a lot of business support, paid for everything from staff training, cheap and easy loans, hiring new people, figuring out how to do profit and loss, all of that stuff. All of that money's gone, Business Link has long gone.
>
> (authors' research)

In addition, certain sectors are prioritised:

> In an ideal world, [we] would subsidise workspace, provide incentives for universities to relocate to the borough, and invest in telecommunications infrastructure. The financial reality in local government means that the council acts instead as a partner in several projects to support tech and creative businesses, local talent and local creative organizations.
>
> (extract from undated Hackney Council document, quoted in Jones, 2017: 147)

The funding squeeze experienced by local authorities has in numerous ways affected their ability to plan effectively for economic progress. As planning authorities, landlords and economic development/regeneration agencies, councils have been forced to explore means of raising funds to pay for core services, as well as scaling back existing economic development activities. Yet there is potential for the planning system to better grasp the dynamics and functioning of local economies. Improved ways of understanding local economies would be valuable in helping to unpack and illuminate the 'black box' of the economy, and enable planners to effectively articulate and plan for collective economic aspirations. Current means of evidence-gathering fall short of this ambition.

The broader implications of a focus on viability and deliverability in national guidance were discussed in the earlier chapters in Part I. Coupled with the imperative to increase the supply of housing, allied with high and rising residential land values in London and the South East, this has resulted in pressure for residential-led redevelopment of employment sites, even on employment sites nominally protected by planning policy (Ferm and Jones, 2016). One of the consequences of this has been a widespread loss of employment land in London. A study for the GLA (AECOM, 2016) has revealed that between 2001 and 2015, the total stock of industrial land decreased by 15.8% in London and 4% in the inner South East, and that this loss has been more than double the London Plan target. The economic health of an area is not necessarily best served by the untrammelled operation of real estate market forces. The redevelopment of sites for ever more affluent occupiers presents obstacles to London's businesses and workforce, limiting choice in accommodation and leading to displacement and dispersal. Existing planning policies and practices have proved to be of limited utility in preventing or mitigating these deleterious consequences of market-led development, with implications for the economic sustainability of the region.

In current practice, the function of planners is to smooth the way for the operation of market forces, rather than attempt to elicit and shape a democratic future for local economic development. Implicit in generations of government guidance is the axiom that market forces deliver optimum outcomes and the role of the planning system is to make modest adjustments to a market-led system to enhance the sustainable credentials of the resulting developments. However, the market-led nature of the system is rarely challenged. In England, the NPPF's pro-development emphasis within this ideological envelope reflects the economist Edward Glaeser's argument that state agencies "shouldn't try to stop the great course of urban change. Those currents are just too strong to hold back, and there's no reason to try" (Glaeser, 2011: 256) and Cheshire et al.'s (2014: 13) call for 'market realism' in policy, which means recognising that "it is difficult (if not impossible) for policymakers to erase spatial disparities and transform the economic fortunes of places".

Conclusions

This chapter has reviewed and analysed the dominant framing of the economy, and the policy frameworks that shape and guide the way in which planning for the economy takes place in the UK. Although we have drawn mainly on London examples, its dominance in the national economy justifies specific consideration, and across the UK we find a dominant narrative of the economy being driven by specialisation and comparative advantage, with a lack of consideration of the role of economic diversity and diverse economies. An overemphasis on the benefits of agglomeration, rather than the costs, furthermore has negative implications for social equality and the health of diverse, economic activities and jobs in London, but it also makes it difficult to plan for and support diverse and dispersed economic activity across the wider UK. This is not economic progress.

In this chapter, we have, on the whole, been telling a dispiriting story. The ascendancy of neo-liberal discourse and policy through recent decades has weakened the will and the capacity of local authorities and agencies to plan proactively for the development of their economies. It has shifted the emphasis of their work to a narrow concern with facilitating real estate development, attracting 'inward investment' and checking the 'viability' of plans and projects in ways which prioritise private profitability. Part of this story has been a weakening and narrowing of the economic skills available in-house in typical local planning authorities and the consultancies they are able to commission. It seems that there is a lack of capacity, and indeed foresight and courage, to engage in serious and broad-based discussions on what the economy is (and what it could be) as part of plan preparation processes.

We have not, in this chapter, paid much attention to the future. There may, however, be grounds for some optimism that planning for economic progress at sub-national levels may experience a renaissance. Britain seems likely to have to deal with the dislocations occasioned by Brexit: industrial structural change, shifts in the terms of trade, and barriers to labour and student mobility. That is likely to pose major challenges in most localities. Even if the UK backs away from Brexit or negotiates a very 'soft' version, the country will be seeking ways of recovering from a decade or more of the 'austerity' which has so weakened the economy, brought us falling real median household incomes (similar to the experience of Greece) and very severe in-work poverty. Although now postponed, proposed changes to business rates and local government finance (with or without devolution) would entirely upset local fiscal systems for every local authority, as well as boosting some businesses and threatening others. The years ahead will be interesting times, and will call for radically improved local economic development capacities for which public authorities, professionals and universities now need to prepare.

Acknowledgements

We are hugely indebted to members of Just Space Economy and Planning for insights and discussions over the past three to four years. In particular, the thinking of the group and the focus on diverse economies in this chapter has been inspired by the PhD research of Myfanwy Taylor, whom Michael Edwards has been privileged to supervise, and we have worked with them all closely.

Notes

1 Some of the radical creativity in local economic thinking has survived, however, in the work of the Centre for Local Economic Strategies (2017), based in Manchester.
2 Ricardo never dealt with cities or regions, but the concept of comparative advantage and specialisation is often used in these contexts, as examples later in this chapter show.
3 JSEP was set up in 2013 to give a boost to Just Space capacity on economic issues in London Planning, and was supported in its first two years by Myfanwy Taylor as part of her action-based PhD research (Taylor, 2017). For a discussion of JSEP's influence on London Planning since its inception, see Taylor and Edwards (2016).
4 This idea is central to the PhD research of Myfanwy Taylor (2017, ch.1), who would have been a co-author of this chapter had she not been prioritising the thesis. Her work is part of an alternative performance.
5 This phrase can be found in Policy EC2 of Planning Policy Statement 4 (DCLG, 2009) and paragraph 22 of the NPPF (DCLG, 2012).
6 Planners in the UK chartered by the RTPI must undergo a comprehensive accreditation procedure, including an 'assessment of professional competence'.

References

All listed URLs were last accessed on 1 March 2018.

AECOM (2016) *Industrial land supply & economy study 2015*. Available at: https://www.london.gov.uk/sites/default/files/industria_land_supply_and_economy2015.pdf.

Allen, K. (2014) City planner Peter Wynne Rees on the love of his life: London, *Financial Times*, 18 July. Available at: https://www.ft.com/content/803fe9ba-0786-11e4-8e62-00144feab7de.

Atkins and Oxford Economics (2015) *Future proofing London*. Available at: www.atkinsglobal.co.uk/en-GB/group/sectors-and-services/services/future-proofing-cities/london.

Bailey, D. et al. (2017) *Regional Studies Association response to the Industrial Strategy Green Paper consultation*. Available at: www.regionalstudies.org/uploads/documents/Regional_Studies_Association_FINAL-5.pdf.

Buck, N. et al. (2002) *Working capital: life and Labour in contemporary London*. London: Routledge.

CBRE (2015) *Office-to-residential conversion: establishing the impacts of the prior approval regime*. London: British Council for Offices. Available (to members) at: www.bco.org.uk/Research/Publications/Office-to-residential_conversion.aspx.

Centre for Local Economic Strategies (2017) *What needs to be done: the manifesto for local economies*. Available at: https://cles.org.uk/wp-content/uploads/2017/05/What-Needs-to-be-Done_The-Manifesto-for-Local-Economics.pdf.

Cheshire, P.C., Nathan, M. and Overman, H.G. (2014) *Urban economics and urban policy: challenging conventional policy wisdom*. Cheltenham: Edward Elgar.

Chinitz, B. (1961) Contrasts in agglomeration: New York and Pittsburgh, *The American Economic Review*, 51(2), pp.279–289.

City Growth Commission (2014) *Unleashing metro growth*. Available at: https://www.thersa.org/globalassets/pdfs/reports/final-city-growth-commission-report-unleashing-growth.pdf.

DCLG (2009) *Planning Policy Statement 4: planning for sustainable economic growth*. London: DCLG.

DCLG (2012) *National Planning Policy Framework*. London: DCLG. Available at: https://www.gov.uk/government/uploads/system/uploads/attachment_data/file/6077/2116950.pdf.

DCLG (2015) *Planning practice guidance: housing and economic development needs assessments*. Available at: https://www.gov.uk/guidance/housing-and-economic-development-needs-assessments.

de Groot, H., Poot, J. and Smit, M. (2015) Which agglomeration externalities matter most and why? *Journal of Economic Surveys*, 30(4), pp.756–782.

Department for Business, Energy and Industrial Strategy (2017) *Consultation outcome: building our industrial strategy*. Available at: https://www.gov.uk/government/consultations/building-our-industrial-strategy.

Duranton, G. and Puga, D. (2000) Diversity and specialisation in cities: why, where and when does it matter? *Urban Studies*, 37(3), pp.533–555.

Edwards, M. (2015) *Prospects for land, rent and housing in UK cities*. Working Paper 18, Foresight Future of Cities Project. London: Government Office for Science. Available at: https://www.gov.uk/government/uploads/system/uploads/attachment_data/file/440527/15-28-land-rent-housing-uk-cities.pdf.

Edwards, M. (2016) Rebalancing the UK economy and the role of citizens' organisations, *Town and Country Planning*, 85(8), pp.324–326.

Eisenschitz, A. and Gough, J. (1993) *The politics of local economic development: the problems and possibilities of local initiative*. Basingstoke: Macmillan.

Feldman, M.P. and Audretsch, D.B. (1999) Innovation in cities: science-based diversity, specialization and localized competition, *European Economic Review*, 43(2), 409–429.

Ferm, J. and Jones, E. (2016) Mixed use "regeneration" of employment land in the post-industrial city: challenges and realities in London, *European Planning Studies*, 24(10), pp.1913–1936.

Ferm, J., Jones, E. and Edwards, M. (2017) *Revealing local economies in London: methodological challenges, future directions*. London: UCL. Available at: http://discovery.ucl.ac.uk/1566799.

Fioramonti, L. (2013) *Gross domestic problem: the politics behind the world's most powerful number*. London: Zed Books.

Gibson-Graham, J.K. (2006) *A postcapitalist politics*. Minneapolis, MN: University of Minnesota Press.

GLA Economics (2016) *Economics evidence base for London*. Available at: https://www.london.gov.uk/what-we-do/research-and-analysis/economy-and-employment/economic-evidence-base-london-2016.

Glaeser, E.L. (2011) *Triumph of the city: how our greatest invention makes us richer, smarter, greener, healthier and happier*. London: Pan Macmillan.

Glaeser, E.L., Kallal, H.D., Scheinkman, J.A. and Shleifer, A. (1992) Growth in cities, *Journal of Political Economy*, 100, pp.1126–1152.

Greater London Council (1985) *London Industrial Strategy*. London: Greater London Council.

Institute of Welsh Affairs (2015) *An economic strategy for Wales?* Cardiff: Institute of Welsh Affairs. Available at: http://iwa.wales/wp-content/uploads/2016/01/IWA_EconomicStrategyforWales.pdf.

Jacobs, J. (1969) *The economy of cities*. New York: Random House.

Jones, E.M. (2017) *Tech city: exploring the operation and governance of inner East London's digital cluster*. PhD thesis, University College London.

JSEP (2014) *Response to the further alterations of the London Plan*. Available at: https://justspacelondon.files.wordpress.com/2014/04/falp-jsep-response.pdf.

JSEP (2016) *Review of GLA economic evidence base*, May 2016. Available at: https://justspacelondon.files.wordpress.com/2016/05/160523b-jsep-comments-on-eeb-final.pdf.

Krugman, P. (1991) Increasing returns and economic geography, *Journal of Political Economy*, 99, pp.483–499.

Mayor of London (2017) *The London Plan: Draft for Public Consultation, December 2017*. London: Greater London Authority. Available at: https://www.london.gov.uk/what-we-do/planning/london-plan/new-london-plan/draft-new-london-plan/.

NEF (2013) *Five headline indicators of national success*. Available at: http://b.3cdn.net/nefoundation/1ff58cfc7d3f4b3fad_o4m6ynyiz.pdf.

Office of the Deputy Prime Minister (2004) *Employment land reviews: Guidance Note*. London: Office of the Deputy Prime Minister.

RTPI (2015) *Assessment of Professional Competence (APC) guidance: licentiate guide to RTPI chartered membership*. Available at: http://www.rtpi.org.uk/media/1283765/apc_guidance_2015.pdf.

Scottish Government (2015) *Scotland's Economic Strategy March 2015*. Available at: www.gov.scot/Publications/2015/03/5984/0.

SQW and Cambridge Econometrics (2016) *The Northern Powerhouse independent economic review: executive summary*. Available at: https://transportforthenorth.com/wp-content/uploads/Northern-Powerhouse-Independent-Economic-Review-Executive-Summary.pdf.

Swinney, P. and Bidgood, E. (2014) *Fast track to growth: transport priorities for stronger cities*. London: Centre for Cities.

Taylor, M. (2017) *Contested urban economies: representing and mobilising London's diverse economy*. PhD thesis, University College London.

Taylor, M. and Edwards, M. (2016) Just Space Economy and Planning: opening up debates on London's economy through participating in strategic planning. In Y. Beebeejaun (ed.) *The participatory city*. Berlin: JOVIS, pp. 76–86.

Urban Task Force (1999) *Towards an urban renaissance: final report of the Urban Task Force*. London: SPON.

Watson, M. (2017) Historicising Ricardo's comparative advantage theory, challenging the normative foundations of liberal international political economy, *New Political Economy*, 22(3), pp.257–272.

16 Planning for Public Transport

Applying European Good Practice to UK Regions?

Iqbal Hamiduddin and Robin Hickman

Introduction

Transport planning faces many challenges over the coming decades. Projected population growth in many areas of the UK needs to be reconciled with the need to reduce car-based travel on multiple grounds, including energy depletion, carbon dioxide emissions, traffic casualties, local air quality, obesity and health impacts of inactivity, and the loss of street space to the car (Hickman et al., 2017). In the UK, urban public transport often suffers from large under-investment, certainly relative to practice found in countries such as France, Germany, the Netherlands and Switzerland. Yet an even larger problem is found in public transport provision beyond the main cities – connections tend to diminish considerably at the metropolitan boundary, which is described by Sloman (2003) as a 'cliff edge'. Investment in public transport is difficult to justify in many contexts, but particularly in dispersed rural populations, market towns and small, former industrial urban centres (Hickman, forthcoming). In many of these areas, depopulation, economic decline, low incomes and high levels of social deprivation are combined with relatively high levels of private car usage. Smaller urban centres of under 250,000 inhabitants and their regions struggle to attract funding for public transport. In these areas, car usage often follows a self-reinforcing spiral of diminishing public transport supply compounded by slackening demand. Car use is 'forced' when it becomes the only realistic means of access to employment, education, health and other opportunities necessary to achieve basic living standards and lifestyle quality. If left unchecked, transport under-investment can become a major social equity issue (Lucas, 2012; Mattioli et al., 2017). Recently, however, developments in Light Rapid Transit (LRT) systems across mainland Europe have created high-quality rail-based transport services that attract high levels of ridership, and at lower capital and operating costs – meaning that there are stronger cases for investment.

This chapter examines the problems of providing public transport services in the UK, comparing this to the provision of innovative LRT systems in mainland Europe. Two case studies are explored: the Valenciennes Line 2 single-track tramway system in France[1] and the Kassel RegioTram, an integrated, regional tram-train system in Germany. Both cases serve low-income areas, are associated with urban regeneration, and help create a positive image of city and region. There appear to be many lessons to be learnt for smaller urban and regional centres in the UK, where high-quality rail-based public transport systems could provide many benefits, but seem very difficult to justify and implement. The lessons for transferring good practice are considered, including how the integrated territorial planning and transport approaches, transport appraisal and funding approaches in France and Germany support the provision of public transport services.

Providing Public Transport Services in the UK

For many people in smaller urban areas and rural areas in the UK, the provision of public transport is critical to accessing employment, services and activities. A quarter of the UK population have no access to a private car, and this is disproportionately concentrated on low-income households. Yet the key problem is that funding for public transport has been woefully inadequate over recent decades, and in recent years has suffered from major budget cuts. The private sector delivery of bus services (outside London), supplemented by public funding for 'socially necessary' services, has not worked – it doesn't provide the quality and extent of services necessary to attract high mode shares (Sloman, 2003; Campaign for Better Transport, 2016). In some areas, public transport has ceased entirely, leaving people unable to access essential facilities and activities. Since 2010–2011, funding for supported bus services in England has been reduced by over £70 million, a reduction of 25%, and similar reductions have been experienced in Wales and Scotland. Beyond London, the bus system is essentially in crisis (Campaign for Better Transport, 2016).

In parallel, the current inadequacy of rail provision in the UK can be traced to decisions made during the 1960s and 1970s, notably with the publication of *The Reshaping of British Railways* (Beeching, 1963). This led to the closure of approximately one-third of Britain's rail network, predominantly across rural areas, ostensibly justified through declining passenger ridership and the loss of coal freight with the advent of domestic central heating – but implemented largely as a result of the aspiration to support the growth in private car ownership. Although some of the closed railway alignments were safeguarded and have since been re-utilised, many were subsequently destroyed, with cuttings used for development or landfill refuse. Some of the protected alignments, including the Borders Railway between Edinburgh and Melrose, have been reinstated as a consequence of the recent rail revival. Similarly, funding to reinstate part of the abandoned 'Varsity Line' between Oxford and Cambridge has been announced (BBC News, 2016). Yet the extent of the rail network still remains very inadequate relative to coverage in the 1950s and earlier.

In terms of LRT, the UK remains frustratingly behind mainland Europe in developing projects. The high point of initiative was in the late 1990s, when John Prescott envisaged 25 new LRT lines (Department for Transport, Local Government and the Regions, 2000), but ultimately few were given funding to progress implementation. In the UK, there are only nine operational tramway networks, compared with 25 in France and over 50 in Germany. In the UK, we cannot seem to move beyond very poor bus provision as the only public transport offer beyond the large cities.

There are a number of reasons for this intransigence. At the most basic level, too much money is spent on highway schemes and too little on public transport. A contributory issue here is the way funding is prioritised. The centralised appraisal system used in the UK means that projects are dependent on funding from the Department for Transport (DfT). Investment is prioritised using cost benefit analysis (CBA), emphasising the economic aspects of the case presented, within which travel time savings are strongly valued. CBA is carried out within multi-criteria analysis (MCA), as part of the DfT's WebTAG (Web-based Transport Appraisal Guidance) process. Proposed projects are assessed against national transport objectives – and decisions often made with only limited knowledge of the local context. There is much debate on the limitations of this approach and the need to give greater weight to social and environmental objectives, and indeed local policy priorities (Hickman and Dean, 2017). There are major questions about the legitimacy of this centralised approach – why should the decisions on investment be made in this way? The current CBA-based approach makes expenditure on regional transport infrastructure around smaller cities and more rural regions difficult to justify, for a number of reasons: there are often few time savings to be found as there are limited patronage levels, certainly when compared to investment in public transport in larger urban areas or in highway schemes, and the social and environmental benefits of regional public transport are given little weight in CBA or in WebTAG. Many of the benefits of tram-based systems are difficult to quantify, and are ignored in project appraisal. Hence, the estimated project 'benefits' compare poorly relative to the perceived high capital costs. An alternative project appraisal approach is, of course, not straightforward to develop, but a step forward would be to test projects against multi-criteria, locally derived, and to incorporate multi-actor views – hence a wider range of project impacts could be considered against local policy priorities. This would better incorporate views beyond those of the project promoter and Whitehall (Dean et al., forthcoming).

Funding also remains a significant obstacle to project delivery – not simply because of budget constraints and available public funds – but also arrangements and responsibility for budget control. There are some interesting moves towards devolution, such as through City Deals

(O'Brien and Pike, 2015). For example, Greater Manchester has gained significantly more influence over the allocation and control of transport funding in recent years, and hence an increase in freedom to spend against local policy priorities – the continuing extension of its tramway network being a visible symbol of its relative power (Coleman et al., 2015). However, Manchester remains an exception in the relative autonomy of its control of transport investment.

The administrative boundaries between urban areas and their surrounds present further barriers to the development of integrated strategies and projects at the regional level, particularly when little effective support for regional and sub-regional planning exists and the mechanisms to develop cross-border strategies are limited. Very few regional public transport projects are currently being progressed in the UK. The South Cambridgeshire busway and South Hampshire bus rapid transit are rather conspicuous exceptions, but have been built to very modest specifications, and present very limited networks overall. There are a host of other areas that would benefit from tram- or bus-based public transport schemes, including the West of England, Blackpool–Preston, Belfast, Cardiff, Cambridge, Hampshire, Manchester–East Lancashire, Merseyside, Oxford, Sheffield–Rotherham–Doncaster, suburban London, and many others. But, as yet, there is no real impetus to invest in a significant new series of public transport projects in the UK. By far the better practice in developing public transport is found in mainland Europe, and two case studies are considered which offer much potential for the UK.

Case Study 1: Valenciennes' Single-track Tramway System

Located in the north-east of France, close to the Belgian border, Valenciennes is a small city of 42,000 inhabitants serving a relatively built-up former industrial metropolitan region with a population of 400,000. Building on the success of the Line 1 tramway, a conventional double-track system that opened in 2006, Valenciennes planned to upgrade transport links to the north-east of the metropolitan area into the Pays de Condé. The only feasible route for a new Line 2 was to use an arterial street corridor that also formed a major traffic route out of the city (Figure 16.1).

The concept for a single-track tramway system emerged as a solution to reducing land take on a route with limited space and to serving a limited potential patronage. The Valenciennes Line 2 tramway runs for 15.5km of single-track and 2.5km of conventional double-track tramway. It is unique in becoming the first new tramway to be designed and operated almost entirely as a single-track, bi-directional system over a significant length in an urban context, making it the longest single-track tramway system in Europe. The passing loops at stations allow trams

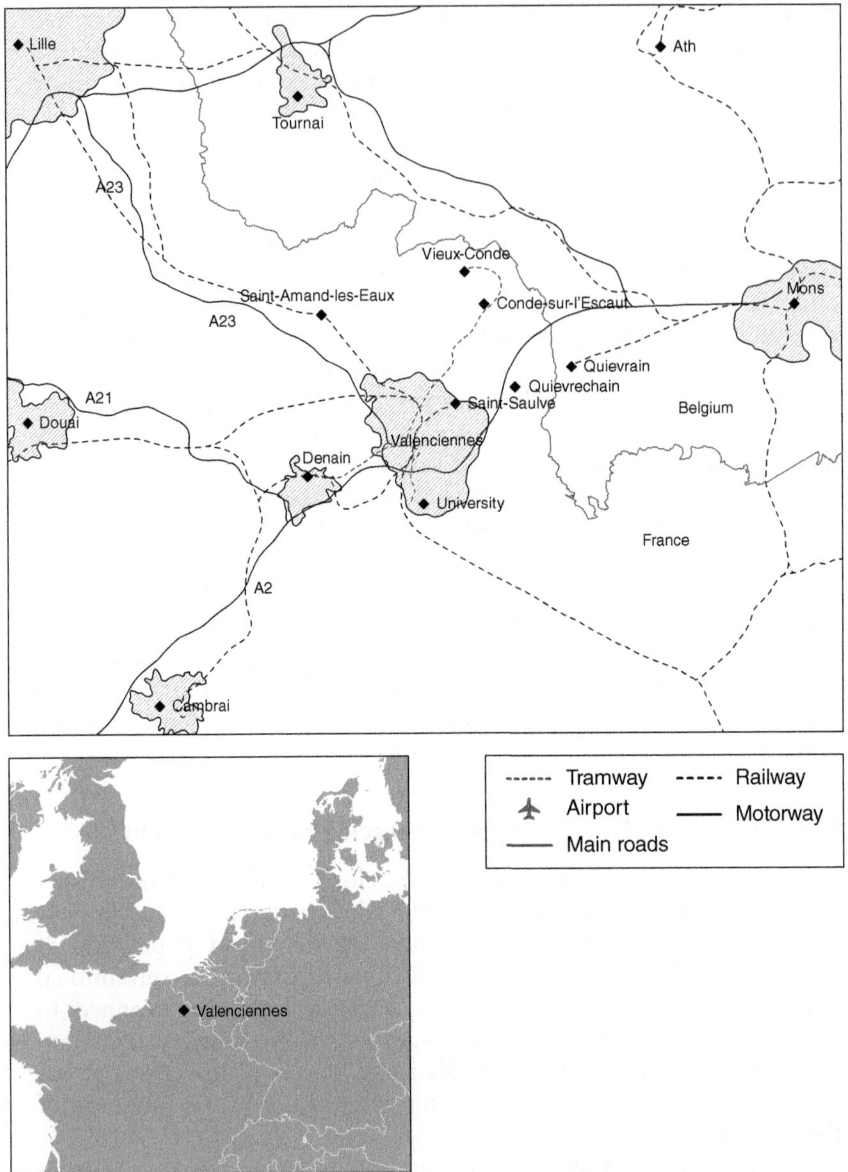

Figure 16.1 Valenciennes – the region and location in France
Source: Hamiduddin et al. (2015).

to cross, and advanced signalling and control technology has enabled bi-directional operation of urban tram services with high frequency (Figure 16.2). A conventional double-track tram system would typically

Figure 16.2 Valenciennes, tram double-tracking at stations, and single track beyond

Photo credit: Robin Hickman.

require a 20m-wide street corridor, whereas only an 18m corridor was available for most of the extent of Line 2. The single-track option required a clear routeway in the region of 4.2m outside the stations, compared with an average of approximately 6.6m for a conventional double-track system.

The key technical and planning features of the Valenciennes tramway Line 2 (single track) relative to Line 1 (double track) are summarised below:

- Design characteristics: The cross-sectional footprint of the single track is usually considerably less than a conventional double-track system, at 6.6m relative to 11.5m, except where island-style stations are used in a double-track system, where the land take is the same at 10.6m. Between stations, the single-track route occupies 4.2m in width, compared to 6.6m for a double track.
- Operating performance: Both systems achieve similar maximum performance speeds, at 70kph, and average speeds across the route at around 30kph. But the average commercial speed of the Line 1 Phase 2 (regional running) is significantly higher than Line 2 Phase 3C (regional running) at 32kph against 18.7kph. This reflects the

higher operating speed of the double-track system in the regional running phase. Both lines operate a peak time service interval of 10 minutes.

- Capital costs: Those for the single-track system are approximately one-third less than the double-track system, at €10 million/km, compared with €15 million/km. Costs indicated do not include the preparatory relocation of utilities away from the track bed.[2]

In the UK, a number of tramway systems, such as Croydon (in London) and Nottingham, include extended sections of single-track line, but there is limited use of passing loops to maintain bi-directional services, and none approach the 15.5km system created in Valenciennes. The Valenciennes system should be of significant interest to smaller urban areas and their regions in the UK. The project has been very important in helping to improve public transport accessibility in a former coal mining region, linking and helping to regenerate the centre and region of Valenciennes. The system has strong social objectives, with investment in high-quality public transport not prioritised in terms of economic efficiency, but for wider urban planning goals, seeking to help residents access employment and other activities by public transport rather than the private car, and to help redevelop the region. The tramways have been introduced into a spatially constrained physical setting, with the design modified to reflect the narrow street widths. The potential savings in capital costs over comparable double-track systems are also attractive, although it is not yet clear (because of the recent commencement of operations) whether any increases in operating and maintenance costs have been introduced due to the operation of points at each of the passing loops. The reliance on points to direct tram vehicles into passing loops does carry a risk of failure compared with conventional double-track systems, although no significant incidents were reported in the first year of full service operation.

Much of the Valenciennes Line 2 tramway lies beyond the city boundary. It was designed to be a regional transport system, serving a predominantly peri-urban settlement pattern outside the city and larger rural settlements beyond, with a primary objective of encouraging mode shift away from the private car, therefore reducing the impact of traffic entering the city. An important element of the plan has been the re-organisation of some regional bus routes away from providing direct services into the urban area and instead into feeder services for the tramway. While this has reduced bus traffic and added tram ridership, it has also, somewhat contentiously, increased journey times on some routes and introduced the requirement for those passengers to interchange between transport modes. However, the overall effect is positive, and although there is not yet an ex-ante evaluation of the scheme, ridership levels have exceeded original projections.

Case Study 2: Kassel's RegioTram System

Karlsruhe was the first city in the world to deploy tram-train vehicles capable of interoperability between heavy and urban light rail networks, but Kassel can also claim a pioneering role in the development of regional light rail, having developed an extensive tram-train system linking Kassel to neighbouring towns and villages. The system includes a fleet of diesel-electric tram-train vehicles capable of using unelectrified regional railway lines. The objectives of tram-train include extending the reach of the urban light rail network into the surrounding region, reducing urban traffic through regional mode shift towards public transport, improving the regional economy through improved urban–regional accessibility, and enhancing mobility for all social groups. In Kassel and Karlsruhe, the regional tram-train services are known as RegioTram.

Kassel RegioTram began operating in 2007, after almost two decades of preparation and development. The first and perhaps crucial stage of this was the creation of a single transport authority for the Kassel region to develop and manage regional transport operations – the Nordhessischer VerkehrsVerbund GmbH was created in 1995. The new transport authority began to take an interest in Karlsruhe's newly established RegioTram network and the success this was having in attracting modal share from traffic by offering direct rail connections from outlying villages to the city. Several important factors made tram-train a potentially viable option for the Kassel region. First, the key components were already in place in the form of an established urban tram network within Kassel and regional rail lines passing through outlying settlements. Second, a pilot project to use tram vehicles on a seldom-used freight line – the Kurhessenbahn – had established a working relationship between the urban tram operator and Deutsche Bahn, the owner of Germany's railway infrastructure; and had proved the principle of sharing track infrastructure between light tramway and conventional heavy rail vehicles. Third, Kassel had a pattern of regional settlements that created sufficient demand for RegioTram regular services directly into the urban tramway network, but not such a high demand as would cause capacity problems (Figure 16.3).[3]

One of the key challenges confronting Kassel was the low Wolfhagen tunnel on the regional line proposed for RegioTram, where overhead electrification was not deemed to be viable. Options included using a third rail system or attempting to lower the tracks to provide sufficient overhead clearance, but both were very costly. Instead, diesel-electric tram-train

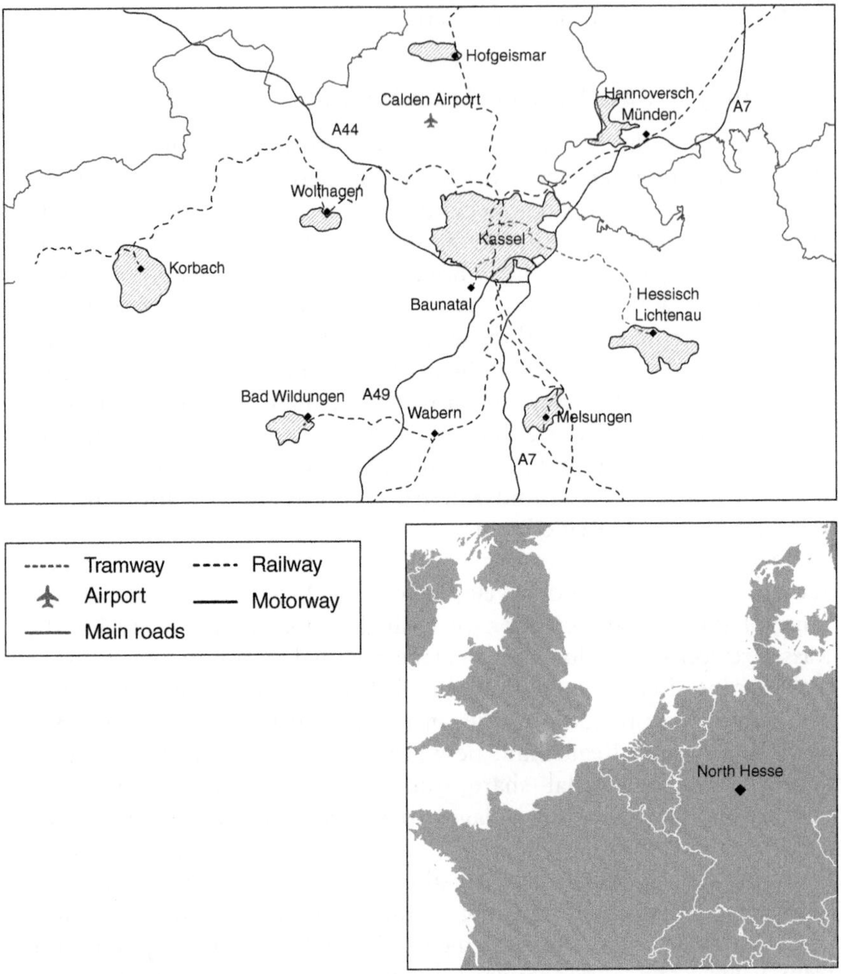

Figure 16.3 Kassel – the region and location in Germany
Source: Hamiduddin et al. (2015).

vehicles were commissioned from Alstom to use on the Wolfhagen line at a cost of approximately €6 million per vehicle. This was nearly double the cost of a standard tram-train vehicle and had a greater operating overhead, offset against capital cost savings as the entire line remained unelectrified.

An important section on the network is Kassel Hauptbahnhof (the central rail station; Figure 16.4), where the connection between the urban tram network and regional railway lines has been made to allow the tram-train vehicles to interoperate between both systems. This required a tunnel under the Hauptbahnhof, and the station was also refurbished as a 'cultural'

Figure 16.4 Kassel Königsplatz – the tram and tram–trains interchange in the city centre

Photo credit: Robin Hickman.

station, with two cinemas, an art gallery, exhibition space, an architectural centre, restaurants and retail facilities. Regional trains still operate on lines served by the RegioTram to provide express services, while RegioTram provides a greater stopping frequency and services onto the urban tram network. In 2017, RegioTram covered over 120km and was marketed as a regional network, operating routes RT3 (to Hümme), RT4 (to Wolfhagen) and RT5 (to Melsungen). The tram-train project cost €180 million, with federal and state governments funding 90% of the total.

Although the improvement of the city and regional economy formed one of the aims for RegioTram, more specific objectives were not specified at the outset. Nevertheless, Holzapfel (2012: 138) argues that:

> There is no question that the Regiotram and the overall expansion of the Kassel tramway system have had a major influence on the city's economic development and these economic benefits have been felt across the region too. This is a by-product of a regional economy that has grown over the years, with a 43 per cent overall growth in a five-year period between 2008 and 2013.

In other words, RegioTram has helped to strengthen the urban economy of Kassel by improving accessibility from the surrounding region.

The tram-train network has also been responsible for some positive economic effects across regional settlements, including:

- station improvements, new retail units and employment opportunities;
- patronage of retail and services in the vicinity of RegioTram stations;
- new housing and commercial developments in the proximity of stations;
- support for businesses and local retail economies in regional settlements, with improved population and employment catchments.

Of these effects, the uplift in the regional real estate sector has perhaps been the most significant secondary effect of RegioTram – with the region becoming more accessible to both employees and students alike, and hence becoming more attractive. As Holzapfel (2012: 138) notes:

> The new network supports the development of trade and business in the metropolitan centre as well as connecting the University with the surrounding area. Without the expanded capability of the tram system, it would hardly have been possible for all of the 20,000 students and 2,800 employees of the University to reach their various destinations in the centre of the city. The Regiotram increases the attractiveness and the value of homes close to a line in the surrounding area, and improved overall regional accessibility has certainly had a positive influence on the Kassel area's growing economic success.

The Karlsruhe region has recorded similar effects. In Bretten, a small town 30km west of Karlsruhe, land prices have traditionally been low. With the introduction of RegioTram services, property prices in Bretten rose from €160 per m^2 in 1988 to €230 per m^2 in 2004, although still less pronounced than in other villages such as Gölshausen and Bauerbach that have experienced a doubling or tripling in real estate values over the same period. Other towns and villages in the region have not seen such property price increases, hence the tram-train appears to have significantly contributed to the uplift in land prices. This issue requires further research, in Kassel and elsewhere, to identify the impact of transport investment, alongside other factors, on property value increases. There are many dimensions to be explored, including issues of gentrification and affordability. In transport appraisal, development and land value increase is treated as a 'benefit' associated with transport investment, irrespective of the type of development – yet clearly, this is a position that can be challenged and requires further consideration (Hickman and Dean, 2017).

In Kassel, the tram-train has enabled a regional light rail system to be built with a modest capital cost. Of the 120+ kilometres of RegioTram, only 3.7km were entirely new sections of rail infrastructure to link the regional rail and urban tramway systems, modify routes and extend the tracks at a number of settlements. Other cities in Germany, Netherlands and France have recognised the potential cost-effectiveness of this approach, while the UK has begun trials of the vehicles between Sheffield and Rotherham in 2017. In general, the approach may be considered to be suitable for cities and regions with the following characteristics:

- An urban tramway system exists with an appropriate track gauge and a loading gauge sufficient to accommodate tram-train rolling stock; exclusive rights of way can maintain services with fixed schedules and designate access slots on regional rail lines.
- The regional rail network has existing and anticipated demand for conventional rail services (passenger or freight) which precludes conversion from heavy to light rail.
- Sufficient spare capacity is available on urban tramway and regional networks for additional tram-train services with a different operating profile compared to conventional heavy rail vehicles.
- Existing high levels of passenger interchange between regional rail and urban tram services are evident, caused by the separation of rail hub and central activity zone.
- Sufficient demand exists to and from regional destinations for direct rail access to the central activity zone and other key urban destinations which can be met within the vehicle capacity and scheduling limitations of tram-train.

The costs of introducing tram-train will depend both on the condition of existing heavy and light rail infrastructure and the type of rolling stock required. Some instances may require a trade-off between higher infrastructure expenditure (e.g. on electrification) but lower vehicle and operating costs, and vice versa. Tram-train vehicle costs can vary considerably, depending largely on power arrangements, including power sources (diesel-electric being most expensive), traction distribution (hilly terrain may require all bogies to be powered), internal specifications and overall order size. The small number of vehicles required for a limited system can create high vehicle costs, despite the large degree of commonality between tram-train and regular tram vehicles and recent efforts by manufacturers to encourage coordinated purchases. This requires strong levels of cooperation between a range of different agencies, including the urban tramway operator, regional rail track owner, local and regional governments, and the national licensing body. The operating costs of tram-train can also be significantly higher than conventional tram or light rail services, because of tariffs charged for access onto heavy rail lines and the costs of training and employing dual tramway- and railway-qualified drivers (Hamiduddin et al., 2015; Naegeli et al., 2012).

Conclusions: Transferring Good Practice to the UK?

Public transport provision in the UK is suffering from major problems, particularly beyond London and the major cities. Bus provision is inadequate, and LRT systems have not been developed to any significant degree. The EU Sintropher project (Hickman and Osborne, 2017) has examined these issues, seeking to make the case and to provide improved regional public transport networks. Blackpool is the smallest conurbation with a working tram system by a considerable margin, having retained its seafront tramway largely for tourist use, deploying a fleet of heritage vehicles. Plans for new tramway systems have been largely restricted to expansions of existing networks, with an exception in Preston, which is currently pursuing plans for a new lightweight system. The current situation means that the scope for tram-train deployment in the UK, following the Kassel or Karlsruhe model remains very limited. Beyond the current Sheffield–Rotherham tram-train trial, only the following three areas have expressed an interest in operating the vehicles:

- Greater Manchester, for use on services to and from Stockport;
- West Midlands, for potential use on the Wednesbury–Stourbridge, Walsall–Wolverhampton and Walsall–Wednesbury routes;
- Blackpool, for use on the South Fylde Line to Preston.

The tram-train pilot for Sheffield–Rotherham is spending £70 million for the trial of the system, and it is hoped this will lead to much greater use of this technology. The low levels of funding over the trial period show the limited aspirations at the national level in the UK. Much greater ambition, and funding, are required. There are some opportunities – the potential impact of the HS2 North–South rail link means that Birmingham, Manchester, Preston and Sheffield will become important hubs. A considerable challenge will be to ensure that positive economic impacts are distributed for the benefit of the wider region, and it is here that wider tram-based networks can be used to 'irrigate' the region (Hickman et al., 2013). Without this, the benefits of HS2 are likely to fall to the larger cities, and in particular to London. Indeed, it should be noted that both Kassel and Valenciennes introduced RegioTram and the regional tramway as part of a regional development programme that included connections to the high-speed rail network. The Blackpool tramway perhaps offers much potential to be developed as a tram-train system, and was recently modified to be able to accept tram-train vehicles as part of its upgrade project in anticipation of Preston becoming a hub on HS2. Feasibility studies have also been undertaken as part of the EU Sintropher project, with options assessed to connect the Blackpool tramway to the South Fylde Line, and beyond to Preston and Manchester. However, blockages remain in the limited powers for transport decision-making at the local level and availability of funding.

A related aspect is the on-going devolution in sub-national transport governance, with support for local funding priorities to be developed. This is part of a more widespread reform of sub-national and local transport management that, from 2015, has seen the devolution of powers and budgetary responsibilities to new Local Transport Bodies. These organisations now co-exist with Local Enterprise Partnerships to shape spatial strategy over functional economic areas. In some areas of the country, the advent of combined authorities has placed further emphasis on the reinforcement of local and regional transport connections by enhancing rail services. As yet, however, the devolution of powers has not been matched with suitable levels of funding, even in the more progressive regions such as Manchester. As ever, transport planning is intensely political – developing an effective public transport system requires sufficient local autonomy, power and funding. Without these, the public transport system will remain inadequate in reducing transport energy consumption, carbon dioxide emissions and traffic casualties.

In terms of potential regional tram systems, including single-track variants, the combination of capital cost-effectiveness, high level of service frequency and suitability for constrained urban environments, as demonstrated by Valenciennes' tramway Line 2, ought to be of great interest in the UK. Some discussions continue in historic, congested smaller cities, such as in Oxford and Bath, over the merits of different public transportation schemes – but very little progress is being made. There has been recent interest in the use of bus-based systems to provide lower-cost high-quality public transport in smaller cities and regions. In some circumstances, a high-quality bus service can provide an optimal approach, or even an intermediate step prior to the introduction of a tramway, as some smaller French cities have developed, such as Nantes. However, bus systems alone generally struggle to attract or convey levels of ridership, generate development impacts, or offer as high an image quality as tramway systems do (Hall, 2012; Hensher and Mulley, 2015). Again, the story from the UK is of little progress – there are too few resources available for strategic planning and the development of new public transport projects.

In both Valenciennes and Kassel, rising car use and the overall decline of public transport from the 1970s onwards has led to innovative approaches being developed, each focused on radically improving the public transport network. Both cases used devolved governance arrangements and budgetary responsibilities to open the potential for innovative public transport investment. Projects have been appraised against local policy objectives, rather than relying on CBA to prioritise funding in a centralised manner. Subsequently, it has been found that the projects developed have much wider impacts than envisaged, as other developments have been used to capitalise on the investments. The process of project development has been both iterative and incremental.

Lastly, it is often stated that an influential advocate or 'champion' is required to help define and implement the project. This, of course, is self-evident, but doesn't really help us in understanding how more innovative tram-based systems can be developed across more of the UK. We cannot simply wait for our champion to arrive. The intriguing issue is how advocates appear in some countries, cities and regions, and not others. The conditions for leadership appear easier in some contexts relative to others. Usually, it is the technical experts who develop the strategy and sell this to the politicians – hence there is an important role for a competent technocracy. But many problems remain: where institutional structures are fragmented, where different organisations are required to cooperate to facilitate progress; where funding is limited and prioritised on a competitive basis; where funding is centralised; where appraisal is carried out largely against notions of economic efficiency, and not against wider-ranging, local policy objectives. All of these issues militate against the development of innovative public transport projects. This framing of the decision-making process can be revised – but involves quite radical changes to the decision-making process. As Wolmar (2016) reminds us: it is the investment given to the private car that has been the great story of transport subsidy over the last 100 years. It is time for us to switch the investment priority given to different modes, and to include the city-region and peripheral areas in a huge increase in public transport spending. To do this requires quite fundamental changes in our approaches to transport planning – Valenciennes and Kassel offer us a glimpse of what is possible, and what the process might entail.

Notes

1 This chapter draws on work carried out in the EU Sintropher project (Hickman and Osborne, 2017; Hamiduddin et al., 2015), part of the Interreg IVB programme; see http://sintropher.eu/.

2 In France, the utility providers are expected to cover the cost of relocating services – a significant expense that can account for much of the discrepancy in capital costs between UK and French tramway systems.

3 Tram-train services are constrained by a unique set of circumstances that include the availability of slots on feeder regional railway lines, the capacity of the urban tram network itself, and limitations on the vehicles themselves. It is often not possible to attach multiple vehicles together because of the short urban tramway platforms and out of consideration for other street users.

References

All listed URLs were last accessed on 1 March 2018.

BBC News (2016) Oxford-Cambridge rail link gets £110m funding, 23 November. Available at: www.bbc.co.uk/news/uk-england-38082338.

Beeching, R. (1963) *The reshaping of British Railways*. London: British Railways Board.

Campaign for Better Transport (2016) *Buses in crisis: a report on bus funding across England and Wales, 2010–2016*. London: Campaign for Better Transport.

Coleman, A., Segar, J. and Checkland, K. (2015) The devolution project in Greater Manchester: introduction to the special issue, *Representation*, 51(4), pp.377–384.

Dean, M., Hickman, R. and Chen, C.-L. (forthcoming) Testing the effectiveness of participatory MCA: the case the South Fylde line, *Transport Policy*.

Department for Transport, Local Government and the Regions (2000) *Transport ten year plan 2000*. London: The Stationery Office. Available at: www.railwaysarchive.co.uk/documents/DTLR_10YearPlan.pdf.

Hall, P. (2012) Lifestyle lines and dynamic decentralisation, *Town and Country Planning*, 81(3), pp.114–115.

Hamiduddin, I., King, C. and Osborne, C. (2015) *Connecting European regions using innovative transport: investing in light rail and tram systems – technological and organisational dimensions*. EU Sintropher Project Report, Interreg IVB. London: UCL.

Hensher, D.A. and Mulley, C. (2015) Modal image: candidate drivers of preference differences for BRT and LRT, *Transportation*, 42(1), pp.7–23.

Hickman, R. (forthcoming) Transport appraisal: thinking beyond the CBA? In I. Docherty and J. Shaw (eds) *The inside track: why transport matters and how we can make it better*. Bristol: Policy Press.

Hickman, R. and Dean, M. (2017) Incomplete cost – incomplete benefit analysis in transport appraisal, *Transport Reviews*. Available at: https://doi.org/10.1080/01441647.2017.1407377.

Hickman, R. and Osborne, C. (2017) *Sintropher executive summary, Interreg IVB*. London: UCL.

Hickman, R., Hamiduddin, I., Hall, P., Jones, P. and Osborne, C. (2013) *S-MAP 2030. North West of England case study: irrigating the region*. EU Interreg IVB, Synaptic Project. London: UCL.

Hickman, R., Smith, D., Moser, D., Schaufler, C. and Vecia, G. (2017) *Why the automobile has no future: a global impact analysis*. Hamburg: Greenpeace Germany.

Holzapfel, H. (2012) The city that came out of the shadows, *Town and Country Planning*, 81, pp.135–138.

Lucas, K. (2012) Transport and social exclusion: where are we now? *Transport Policy*, 20, pp. 105–113.

Mattioli, G., Philips, I., Anable, J. and Chatterton, T. (2017) Developing an index of vulnerability to motor fuel price increases in England. Paper presented at *UTSG 49th Annual Conference*, Dublin.

Naegeli, L., Weidmann, U. and Nash, A. (2012) Checklist for successful application of tram-train systems in Europe, *Transportation Research Record*, 2275(1), pp.39–48.

O'Brien, P. and Pike, A. (2015) City deals, decentralisation and the governance of local infrastructure funding and financing in the UK, *National Institute Economic Review*, 233(1), pp.14–26.

Sloman, L. (2003) *Rural transport futures: transport solutions for a thriving countryside*. London: Campaign for Better Transport.

Wolmar, C. (2016) *Are trams socialist? Why Britain has no transport policy*. London: London Publishing Partnership.

17 Planning for the Regeneration of Towns and Cities

Claudio de Magalhães and Nikos Karadimitriou

Introduction

Defining what 'urban regeneration' is and what interventions and policies that term encompasses is not straightforward. The term has been applied equally to any significant redevelopment of rundown urban sites, as well as to complex sets of strategies to tackle structural, social, and economic urban problems. As with most practice-based policy fields, the definition of what 'urban regeneration' is has been built over the years, as understandings of what the urban problems that need regeneration solutions are have evolved and changed.

Gripaios (2002) suggests that urban regeneration problems could be classified roughly into two categories. The first comprises deteriorated areas within otherwise relatively prosperous cities, whose economy and population have persistently failed to benefit from the surrounding prosperity. The second encompasses those cities and areas of cities situated in regions with a depressed economy, which require interventions that go well beyond the locality and the city.

However defined, a constant element in urban regeneration interventions is the use of large-scale changes in the built environment through redevelopment operations, as a way of revitalising the local economy and changing the dynamics of social relations in a locality. If, in the past, those large-scale redevelopment projects were led and funded by the public sector as part of state-led comprehensive strategies, they have become dependent upon private initiative, private funding and the dynamics of real estate markets for the delivery of the social and economic policy goals expected from them. Moreover, as discussed in Chapter 1 by John Tomaney and Jessica Ferm, private initiative and funding are increasingly global in nature, creating a complex link between localities and global flows of capital.

This chapter focuses on the built environment dimension of urban regeneration – where planning is of paramount importance – and looks at the challenges facing practice. The first section examines the concept of urban regeneration, and looks at the role property development has assumed in it. Urban regeneration has evolved as a policy field concerned with solving localised social and economic problems, mostly through changes in the built environment. From the 1980s, those changes have increasingly taken the form of private-led property development projects. Emblematic of that are the large private-led but state-supported flagship projects such as Canary Wharf in London, Salford Quays in Greater Manchester, the Quayside in Newcastle-upon-Tyne, or more recently, the London Olympic Park, which were meant to redefine the economic role of their locations and create the wealth that would ultimately address problems of social need and deprivation. Whether or not they have achieved this goal, or were even inherently capable of doing so, is still a contentious point (see Swyngedow et al., 2002; Imrie et al., 2009). Turok (1992) pointed out early on the limits of regeneration strategies based on an excessive reliance on property development and the weakness of the claims made in their favour. Moreover, the existing evidence is inconclusive as to whether regeneration programmes based on physical restructuring and redevelopment have been the main determinant of long-term structural changes in the economy and social well-being of the areas where they have been applied, and whether change was in the intended direction and the benefits were received by those for whom they were meant (see Cheshire, 2006; Ball and Maginn, 2005; Webber et al., 2010). Nevertheless, as the involvement of the public sector in the funding and delivery of those projects recedes even further, more of the task of achieving broader policy goals is left to the property market. The nature of urban regeneration practice changes accordingly as it becomes preoccupied with configuring and influencing property markets, capturing part of the value they create and using that value for broader policy goals.

The second section of the chapter then looks at the challenges property-led urban regeneration presents to those involved in its delivery. If urban regeneration is about addressing problems of economic decline, social exclusion, dereliction and lack of sustainability through physical, property-related interventions, we need to understand how physical change impacts on social and economic processes, and how this can be utilised in policy delivery. Moreover, if urban regeneration interventions produce benefits that are broader than just local improvements in the built environment, how are they distributed? The reliance on property markets to deliver regeneration outcomes entails the risk that left to their own devices, markets will distribute those outcomes through price mechanisms, and more often than not, those communities regeneration seeks to benefit will be outbid by others. There is therefore a distributional challenge, as witnessed, for example, in the debates around gentrification and the capture of regeneration benefits by wealthier in-comers. This reliance on markets also means that urban regeneration is, as a rule, delivered in partnerships with private actors, which have the power to fund and develop those interventions.

Balancing private and public interest is always difficult. Imbalances of power within regeneration partnerships and the sometimes conflictive nature of the interests represented in them require strong accountability mechanisms that are responsive to all those who should have a say in a regeneration intervention. Finally, as regeneration has come to depend on property markets, the issues of risk management and value capture come to the fore. Property development is a risky business, and more so if it is required to deliver public goods and other policy objectives. Ensuring successful regeneration means that the different risks facing private, public and community actors in the different stages of an intervention are managed adequately so that expectations are met and the project does not stall. Capturing the value created by those interventions and apportioning it appropriately to meet policy objectives is an essential part of the challenge.

The chapter concludes this brief summary of the challenges facing urban regeneration practice with some reflections on what they mean and the implications for practitioners.

Urban Regeneration: a Shifting Concept

The basic idea that urban areas are in need of regeneration (and not simply of redevelopment) comes from a particular understanding of the causes of the problems of economic and social decline in advanced capitalist cities and of the appropriate policy responses to those problems. That understanding has at its core the proposition that the economic decline of a locality, with its attending social and environmental problems, could be more effectively addressed as problems *of* that locality rather than as economic, social or environmental problems that happen to take place *in* that locality.

From its emergence as a distinct policy field in the 1970s to today, urban regeneration has come to signify that field of public policy that deals with the restoration of economic activity, the promotion of social cohesion and the re-establishment of environmental quality in localities where those elements have deteriorated (Couch and Fraser, 2003).

However, this multi-dimensionality of the concept of urban regeneration begs the question of what the causal links connecting those dimensions might be, how they work, and how policy could act upon them. The notion of urban regeneration is based on the assumption that economic and social problems are not a-spatial, and that the character of a location can determine the nature of those problems and compound them. Extensive areas of physical dereliction or inadequate physical infrastructure are likely to deter investment in a locality and may exacerbate downward spirals, making spontaneous renovation far more difficult. The spatial concentration of socially disadvantaged groups might compound their problems by weakening their interactions with the rest of society, thus reinforcing patterns of social exclusion. It should be noted that some of these causal links have been assumed rather than demonstrated (see, e.g., Cheshire, 2006).

Another element in the notion of urban regeneration is that the decline (physical, social or economic) is often of a structural nature, and will not be reversed spontaneously as part of the normal process of change and adaptation that is part of the life of cities. In this case, change requires purposive action by the state through policy and direct intervention, as market forces in themselves cannot trigger and ensure adaptation or transformation, and may well be causal factors of the decline itself (Jones and Evans, 2013).

The problems addressed by urban regeneration are often described as examples of 'wicked issues' (Clarke and Stewart, 1997). They are policy problems that seem intractable, persistent and not amenable to simple solutions. Moreover, they are multi-faceted; their consequences span over the areas of competence of many different government agencies; they are not amenable to solutions coming from a single powerful governmental actor, rather they require the involvement of actors beyond government; and it takes much longer than conventional programme horizons and electoral cycles for solutions to have an impact.

The multi-dimensionality of the problems addressed by urban regeneration interventions underpins the complexity of the objectives those interventions seek to achieve. These are marked by tensions, not just between different views of what a better city or city quarter might be, but also between different perceptions of the role of those different dimensions in bringing about the desired outcomes. The conflicts between physical redevelopment and environmental improvement, on the one hand, and social and economic benefits, on the other, are well documented (Turok, 1992; Swyngedow et al., 2002). Similarly, Butler and Hamnet (2009) point out to a longstanding tension between economic competitiveness, physical transformation and social inclusion.

All that complexity makes urban regeneration foremost an empirical policy field, which grapples with the complex connections between the built environment, the economy and society at different scales, and tries to intervene in processes and phenomena for which causality has not always been clearly established. Urban regeneration practice has often tried to replicate 'what works', even if it often cannot explain why it works or whether it would work in a different context.

Nevertheless, the problems of urban decline are real, and they can dramatically affect the economic and social well-being of neighbourhoods and put considerable pressure on governments. Because of its inherent complexity, over the nearly four decades in which urban regeneration policies have been pursued in the UK, their objectives have varied. This is not only because of the changing nature of the problems associated with urban decline, but also because of changing understandings of how the dimensions of regeneration relate to one another and how that relationship could be mobilised towards desired outcomes. Changing ideological perspectives from successive governments and shifts in the balance of power of the potential beneficiaries and losers of regeneration policies have also affected regeneration programme objectives (De Magalhães, 2015).

Two related elements, however, have become characteristic of regeneration practice, no matter what the aims of particular regeneration interventions might have been. The first is a close relationship between urban regeneration and property development – which has a long tradition in planning thought. The second is a reliance on public–private partnerships, which emerged in the 1980s and gained substantial ground with the dominance of New Public Management approaches to government, with their emphasis on introducing private sector management practices into the running of the state (Leach and Percy-Smith, 2001).

After an early period where the focus was on property development for its own 'virtues' of employment creation and economic multiplier effects (for early critiques, see Turok, 1992, or Swyngedow et al., 2002), the key focus of such policies eventually shifted towards a more complex treatment of the built environment. This includes the creation of mixed communities in terms of income and tenure, the return of middle-class households to the city and the introduction of mixed-use developments in formerly single-use areas. As before, private developers and private capital were meant to play a major role in these processes.

This type of engagement with markets and the private sector means that the final combination between private and public goods of all sorts, on which the delivery of policy objectives depends, is determined by a mix of policy directives and market signals. Brandsen and Pestoff (2006) have used the term 'co-production' to define this approach to shaping policy goals when it comes to the relationship between the state and voluntary sector organisations. That term could also describe how public sector and private sector actors engage in contemporary urban regeneration. In this field, societal goals are to be met by a process of partnership and negotiation with (and transfer of a wider range of decision-making powers to) developers, third sector providers, financial agents, and the beneficiaries and users. Therefore, in urban regeneration, the boundaries between the state and private interests, state and civil society, between producers and users of policy are increasingly shaped by contractual relations and partnership mechanisms, which attribute rights and responsibilities in a way that makes the distinction between client and contractor, provider and user or policy-maker and policy beneficiary rather tenuous (Sullivan and Skelcher, 2002).

This shift from a 'provider' state to an 'enabling' one (Sullivan and Skelcher, 2002) and the move towards co-production have not been smooth processes. Organisational forms, skill sets and routines that might have been useful under one governance mode have proven to be inadequate under the other. For the public sector, the restructuring that has accompanied that shift is well documented (see Anderson and van Kempen, 2001; Stoker, 2004; Leach and Percy-Smith, 2001; Stewart and Walsh, 1992).

Similarly, private sector players in regeneration have had to adapt their business strategies to take into account the introduction of a multiplicity of new policy objectives into their business environment (Karadimitriou, 2005). Policy objectives have been factored into property development for quite a while. However, in more recent times, an increasingly complex set of societal objectives is required from private developments, well beyond those implicit or explicit in land use planning and related policies. For example, the delivery of affordable housing, of forms of mixed use and mixed tenure, an attractive public realm, local employment initiatives, amenities and social facilities are now almost standard requirements in private-led and privately funded large development projects in the UK (Figure 17.1). Planning gain, the developers' obligations under Section 106 of the Town and Country Planning Act 1990, was originally a way to provide mitigation for the impacts of a development, but it has progressively become the main instrument of delivery of a broad array of policy objectives, especially affordable housing (see Burgess et al., 2011).

Figure 17.1 The Olympic Village in London, regeneration through property development. The built environment outcomes are clear, but how can it produce the desired social outcomes?

Source: EG Focus CC BY 2.0.

An important consequence of this redefinition of the relationships between state and market actors in development is that the problems of urban and regional decline and its physical consequences have often been read from the perspective of the property market (Turok, 1992; Colenutt, 1999; Adams et al., 2005; MacLaran, 2003). This has affected the way these problems are perceived and defined, and consequently the solutions proposed to tackle them. From this perspective, the consequences of the decline of a locality suffering from the loss of economic activity – including the existence of rundown houses, derelict buildings and vacant spaces – can be interpreted as a problem of land and property prices in that area, associated with falling demand for that location. The assumption that a healthy property market is a precondition for economic and social regeneration has affected urban policy and regeneration initiatives since the 1980s (see Turok, 1992).

Under this light, the problems of declining urban areas are often recast as relating to a lack of demand in the property market. This lack of demand would mean that no private investment would come forward to provide the new or refurbished spaces that could attract and accommodate more dynamic economic activities or the housing and amenities for the labour force coming to serve them. Making available the 'right' kind of public and private goods, such as commercial buildings, parks, facilities, homes and infrastructure, would therefore be an important element in attracting those businesses and an adequate pool of labour, provided that other economic, social and institutional parameters were favourable.

There has been a long debate as to what the relationship between a dynamic property market and a growing economy and prosperous society is (Turok, 1992; Adams et al., 2005), and the current consensus is that the relationship is more complex than one of constant unidirectional causality between property investment and economic development. However, few deny the importance of investment in the built environment in reversing declining urban areas. In a context in which a large proportion of this investment has had to come from actors other than the state, the problem and its solutions have been formulated, at least in part, in terms of property markets and their functioning.

According to this logic, therefore, in order to achieve such objectives, policies are needed to restore the function of the property market in problem areas, which in the long run will secure their regeneration. Thus, various constraints to development have been identified in the form of, for example, fragmented landownership, costs of land decontamination, poor transport access, lack of adequate infrastructure, costs of and access to development finance, lack of confidence and excessive risks, uncertainties and low profitability (Jeffrey and Pounder, 2000; Syms, 2002; Adair et al., 2003). State involvement aiming to secure the provision of buildings and infrastructure is largely predicated on the premise that these constraints have to be lifted.

Moreover, given the significant household investment function of homeownership, increasing dwelling prices often create a substantial 'wealth effect', whereas lack of demand and falling prices inevitably lead to a decrease in the price of many households' most important asset, their homes, affecting their mobility and consumption (Barker, 2004; Gregory, 2011). Saddled with mortgages for homes whose price drops significantly, homeowners can be trapped in increasingly more derelict locations where declining consumption creates self-reinforcing spirals of decline (Nevin and Leather, 2006). Thus, securing a buoyant housing market has been seen as important for public policy. This rationale underpinned government-funded regeneration programmes tackling housing market weakness through supply-side measures such as selective demolition, stock transfers, refurbishment and reconstruction in order to establish and inflate a housing market (Nevin and Leather, 2006). This perhaps oversimplistic view of the role of housing markets in regeneration has begun to change only very recently with the crisis of housing affordability, especially acute in London and the South East of England. An excessively buoyant housing market can be as much of an urban regeneration problem as a stagnant or declining one.

What the paragraphs above try to do is to describe what urban regeneration in the UK has become: a way of addressing issues of decline, social exclusion and a host of other public policy objectives through private-led property development operations, which are expected to provide the spaces, the public goods and the kind of built environment that will turn those policy objectives into reality. This, of course, presents several challenges to practitioners, which are discussed in the next section.

The Challenges for Practice

From the discussion above, it is clear that urban regeneration is about more than just ensuring that the redevelopment of derelict areas results in places that are liveable, environmentally sustainable and of high design quality. That is very important, but what makes a redevelopment 'regeneration' is that it should also help to deliver a series of social and economic policy goals as well as places that are liveable and sustainable. Employment, economic growth, affordable housing, poverty, social exclusion, education, skills etc. are all potential target areas of urban regeneration, to be acted upon with the help of built environment interventions. Because of that, although the remit of urban regeneration is in a sense wider than that of planning, it is still essential to engage with planning as a policy field in which decisions about the built environment are taken, which ultimately will or will not deliver all other policy objectives.

However, as suggested above, those regeneration targets are to be delivered primarily through privately funded and private-led property development interventions, which are structured around profitability and financial viability. In the past, public sector subsidies in various forms ensured the desired balance between profitability and the delivery of non-profitable policy objectives (public spaces, affordable housing, schools, health facilities, training etc.). Over the years, however, and especially with reductions in public spending, which preceded but were made more drastic in the wake of the 2007 financial crisis, subsidies and public investment have dwindled. Securing broader regeneration objectives has become increasingly dependent on the ability of governments – national and local – to influence the workings of property markets through regulating them and trying to re-shape the decision-making context of market players or the factors that determine profitability and viability (for a discussion on the relationship between planning and markets, see Adams and Tiesdell, 2010).

As mentioned earlier, partnerships of all sorts have been used to try to bring public, private and occasionally community actors together to try and align interests and shape the context for outcomes. In the recent past, instruments such as Urban Development Corporations created the framework for a partnership between the public sector, local authorities and – albeit belatedly – communities. Today, apart from the two Mayoral Development Corporations in London, ad hoc partnership arrangements prevail. In some cases, local authorities have used their ownership of land to influence the outcomes of developments and secure public goods and other policy objectives. In others, the use of regulatory powers has been the main instrument to secure those outcomes: Compare, for instance, the regeneration of New Islington in Manchester, where the city council was a major landowner and used its holdings to secure large public spaces and social facilities, and King's Cross in London, where public land was residual and public goods had to be negotiated in a protracted planning permission application, or the controversial regeneration of the Heygate social housing estate in London, in which local authority landownership does not seem to have been used to its full potential apart from facilitating the hugely profitable private redevelopment (see Lees and Ferreri, 2016) (Figure 17.2).

In this context, the role of planners is different from that of proposers of urban regeneration plans, or of just arbiters of private development proposals, making sure they respond to the needs of a place in a way that meets the public interest. For that to happen, there is a need for complex arrangements in which public sector actors use their legal powers to authorise development, or their leverage as infrastructure providers or regulators, or their powers as landowners (where possible), to influence and shape the dynamics of the property market in a particular location and make sure private developers create a financially successful development and, at the same time, deliver the public goods and the kind of place local communities and planners want. These arrangements need to be at once firm enough to secure public goods are delivered, but also flexible to

Figure 17.2 The Heygate Estate in London: landownership could have given the local authority a powerful tool to shape the outcomes of the redevelopment towards the aspirations of the existing community, but many argue this has been wasted

Source: London SE1 Community Website CC BY 2.0.

cope with the uncertainty and cyclicality of property markets. Successful regeneration projects are those that have managed to keep all key stakeholders (developers, landowners, local authorities, communities), with their different aims and motivations, in a constant dialogue so that risks and benefits are shared in acceptable ways.

Implicit in this often uneasy combination of public, private and community actors is an effort to ensure that the different types of uncertainties and risks faced by the different actors are considered and reduced as far as possible. Urban regeneration is inherently uncertain and risky. This includes financial and market risks for private partners, financial and political risks for public bodies, and risks to the welfare of the communities involved. The delivery of goods, services and facilities such as affordable housing, health, education and public spaces is therefore a key element in the negotiation between public, private and third sector actors around the apportionment of risks and rewards. The way this is done shapes the nature of urban regeneration as public policy. Aligning the interests of all those parties requires negotiating and arranging how risks and rewards are distributed (Karadimitriou et al., 2013; Karadimitriou and Manns, 2016).

What, then, is the role of planning and planners in this process? This chapter discusses two main challenges associated with that role: the issue of how to ensure that what is primarily a private development operation produces public goods and social and economic policy goals, and that of ensuring that the necessary negotiations that lead to development outcomes are as transparent and accountable as possible.

The traditional planning instruments such as Local Plans and area-based planning frameworks certainly play a part here, by outlining a vision for areas to be regenerated through redevelopment. However, achieving regeneration outcomes relies on extracting all sorts of public goods and social and economic benefits from private-led development operations, some of which might come as a natural consequence of development itself (e.g. a renewed built environment, active land uses where previously there weren't any, valorisation of the surrounding area), but many will need to be manufactured through negotiation, imposition and bargaining.

The challenge is how to capture part of the uplift in land value created by redevelopment and regeneration, the benefits and positive externalities they generate, and utilise them to pay for public goods that will benefit the intended beneficiaries of regeneration. The topic of value capture has featured high in the agenda of planners and municipal administrators worldwide, who are trying to find ways of devolving to society some of uplift in value generated through development, which is socially created and would otherwise be captured privately, to help fund public goods and key infrastructure (see, e.g., Ingram and Hong, 2012; Alterman, 2012). For historical reasons, UK local governments and the planning system have never had strong instruments for the capture of land value uplift, unlike some of their European neighbours. In absence of betterment taxes, municipal land banking, pre-emption rights or intermediary public landownership, UK local authority planners have had to rely on weaker mitigating instruments such as planning obligations under Section 106 of the Town and Country Planning Act 1990, more recently on a fixed-value Community Infrastructure Levy, and on time-consuming negotiating and bargaining (discussed in Chapter 5 by Patricia Canelas).

In those circumstances, planners need to have the relevant skills to allow them to understand the dynamics of development, to capture value without compromising viability, to direct the benefits to the intended recipients, to be flexible in adjusting to market cyclicality, to tie the parties together, all of which are not normally part of what is typically associated with their professional profile. The private development companies involved in urban regeneration will have multidisciplinary teams with appropriate sets of skills. However, local authority planners working in urban regeneration can no longer rely on equivalent teams in their own authority, as these have more often than not been decimated by budget cuts. There is therefore an imbalance in the ability to capture development value to secure policy outcomes; how to overcome it is where the real core of the challenge lies.

That brings forth the second of the challenges discussed in this section. The process of negotiation and bargaining required to allocate benefits and risks and secure value uplifts that are shared among private developers and communities requires complex negotiation. Occasionally, but not always, this is under the institutional umbrella of a public–private partnership, in which compromises and adaptations have to be made, both with regard to the development itself and the requirements of the local authority. Urban regeneration, as a rule, is likely to produce winners and losers. We should remember that a common critique of urban regeneration through property development projects is that its benefits are more likely to be appropriated by development interests and incoming residents than by existing residents and businesses, whereas the losses are more likely to fall to the latter (Imrie and Thomas, 1993). However, in democratic societies, the process whereby decisions are made about who loses and who wins matter.

The point is how the public interest and the interests of deprived communities might be protected in urban regeneration interventions. For much of the history of urban policy in representative democracies, this was seen as the natural role of the state and public sector. However, British regeneration policy objectives have been predicated upon interventions in which the state is only one, and not necessarily the dominant, partner. An abundance of mechanisms have been employed, with different configurations of relative power between public and private sector actors and different levels of accountability to the communities affected. While there are several examples of partnerships that have been effective in representing the interests of a wide range of stakeholders and in managing conflicts well, there are also plenty of examples of contested arrangements, in which stakeholders felt unrepresented, and which were seen as biased towards development interests to the detriment of local residents or the public interest (see Imrie et al., 2009).

Again, the way different views are taken into account, the way decisions are made, and how the balance between different aspirations and needs is struck, does matter. The challenge for urban regeneration and those involved in it is therefore participation and accountability – more so as many decisions about the shape, timing and outcomes of urban regeneration projects are taken within public–private bodies outside the normal rules of accountability of local governments. The issue is therefore how to secure accountability and representativeness in partnerships and other similar governance mechanisms. Ensuring that all those with a stake in the regeneration intervention are represented and managing the conflicts that are unavoidable in that sort of policy action are key in ensuring that regeneration takes place, that it is supported, and that the social and economic outcomes are genuine and fairly distributed. And this is no easy task.

Conclusions

This brief overview of urban regeneration describes what this field of policy is in practice, and the challenges it poses for those – planners or other professionals – in charge of delivering it. For a start, one would expect that after decades of urban regeneration policies, we would be able to offer a much more decisive account of what works and what does not, and therefore what urban regeneration should be about and how it should operate. However, even the question of whether regeneration policies and programmes themselves actually make any difference has not been settled. It may sound evasive to say 'it depends', but the truth of the matter is that the impact of any such initiatives actually does depend on contextual and other factors which often are beyond anyone's control. There are brilliant examples of regeneration initiatives that have turned entire cities around, and there are an equal number of programmes which have thrown good money after bad, year upon year. Early 21st-century globalised capitalism and its ever-increasing speed of change in the social and spatial arrangements of production relationships make it exceedingly hard for governance systems to respond to the challenges and the opportunities that are often thrust upon them.

This requires institutional arrangements that can bring together different parties with an interest in the regeneration of an area, accommodate diverse interests and negotiate conflict, and above all, be flexible in adapting to the contextual changes and the various challenges and risks those changes will bring over the typically long run of a regeneration intervention.

Faced with this context, planning practitioners engaging in regeneration have to develop skills which span a breadth of disciplines, and which traditionally have not been part of their education. Urban design or policy-making skills are, of course, indispensable, but not enough to deal with the multiple layers of complexity and the fuzzy nature of the process. The management of the risks inherent in this process and the sensitive nature of the negotiations about risk and return require lateral thinkers who can understand regeneration through the eyes of a wide range of actors and manage conflicting interests. Financial literacy is now required more than ever, coupled with negotiation and communication skills, as well as a focus on human well-being and a strong commitment to the cause of creating liveable, sustainable communities.

References

Adair, A., Berry, J. and McGreal, S. (2003) Urban regeneration and property investment performance, *Journal of Property Research*, 20(4), pp.371–386.

Adams, D. and Tiesdell, S. (2010) Planners as market actors: rethinking state–market relations in land and property, *Planning Theory and Practice*, 11(2), pp.187–207.

Adams D., Watkins, C. and White, M. (eds) (2005) *Planning, public policy and property markets*. Oxford: Blackwell.

Alterman, R, (2012) Land use regulations and property values: the "windfalls capture" idea revisited. In N. Brooks, K. Donaghy and G.-J. Knaap (eds) *The Oxford handbook of urban economics and planning*. Oxford: Oxford University Press, pp.755–786.

Anderson, H. and van Kempen, R. (eds) (2001) *Governing European cities: social fragmentation, social exclusion and urban governance*. Aldershot: Ashgate.

Ball, M. and Maginn, P. (2005) Urban change and conflict: evaluating the role of partnerships in urban regeneration in the UK, *Housing Studies*, 20(1), pp.9–28.

Barker, K. (2004) *Review of housing supply – delivering stability: securing our future housing needs – final report*. Norwich: HMSO.

Brandsen, T. and Pestoff, V. (2006) Co-production, the Third Sector and the delivery of public services, *Public Management Review*, 8(4), pp.493–500.

Burgess, G., Monk, S. and Whitehead, C. (2011) Delivering local infrastructure and affordable housing through the planning system: the future of planning obligations through S obligations through Section 106, *People, Place & Policy*, 5(1), pp.1–11.

Butler, T. and Hamnet, C. (2009) Regenerating a global city. In R. Imrie, L. Lees and M. Raco (eds) *Regenerating London: governance, sustainability and community in a global city*. Abingdon: Routledge, pp.40–57.

Cheshire, P. (2006) Resurgent cities, urban myths and policy hubris: what we need to know, *Urban Studies*, 43(8), pp.1231–1246.

Clarke, M. and Stewart, J. (1997) *Handling the wicked issues: a challenge for government*. Birmingham: INLOGOV.

Colenutt, B. (1999) Deal or no deal for people based regeneration? In R. Imrie and H. Thomas (eds) *British urban policy: an evaluation of the urban development corporations*. London: SAGE Publications, pp.233–245.

Couch, C. and Fraser, C. (2003) Introduction: the European context and theoretical framework. In C. Couch, C. Fraser and S. Percy (eds) *Urban regeneration in Europe*. Oxford: Blackwell, pp.1–16.

De Magalhães, C. (2015), Urban regeneration. In J.D. Wright (ed.), *International encyclopaedia of the social and behavioural sciences*, 2nd edn, Vol. 24. Oxford: Elsevier, pp.919–925.

Gregory, J. (2011) *Can housing work for workers?* Fabian Society Touchstone Pamphlet No.11. London: Trades Union Congress.

Gripaios, P. (2002) The failure of regeneration policy in Britain, *Regional Studies*, 36, pp.568–577.

Imrie, R. and Thomas, H. (1993) The limits of property-led regeneration, *Environment and Planning C: Government and Policy*, 11, pp.87–102.

Imrie, R., Lees, L. and Raco, M. (eds) (2009) *Regenerating London: governance, sustainability and community in a global city*. Abingdon: Routledge.

Ingram, G. and Hong, Y.-H. (eds) (2012) *Value capture and land policies*. Cambridge, MA: Lincoln Institute of Land Policy.

Jeffrey, P. and Pounder, J. (2000) Major themes and topics: physical and environmental aspects. In P. Roberts and H. Sykes (eds) *Urban regeneration: a handbook*. London: SAGE Publications, pp.86–108.

Jones, P. and Evans, J. (2013) *Urban regeneration in the UK*. London: SAGE Publications.

Karadimitriou, N. (2005) Changing the way UK cities are built: the shifting urban policy and the adaptation of London's housebuilders, *Journal of Housing and the Built Environment*, 20(3), pp.271–286.

Karadimitriou, N. and Manns, J. (2016) Our common estate: planning for land in large scale urban development, *Journal of Urban Regeneration and Renewal*, 9(2), pp.139–148.

Karadimitriou, N., De Magalhães, C. and Verhage, R. (2013) *Planning, risk and property development: urban regeneration in England, France and the Netherlands*. Abingdon: Routledge.

Leach, R. and Percy-Smith, J. (2001) *Local governance in Britain*. Basingstoke: Palgrave.

Lees, L. and Ferreri, M. (2016) Resisting gentrification on its final frontiers: learning from the Heygate Estate in London (1974–2013), *Cities*, 57, pp.14–24.

MacLaran, A. (ed.) (2003) *Making space: property development and urban planning*. London: Arnold.

Nevin, B. and Leather, P. (2006) Understanding the drivers of housing market change in Britain's post-industrial cities. In P. Malpass and L. Cairncross (eds) *Building on the past: visions of housing futures*. Bristol: Policy Press, pp.97–126.

Stewart, J. and Walsh, K. (1992) Change in the management of public services, *Public Administration*, 70(4), pp.499–518.

Stoker, G. (2004) *Transforming local governance: from Thatcherism to New Labour*. Basingstoke: Palgrave.

Sullivan, H. and Skelcher, C. (2002) *Working across boundaries: collaboration in public services*. Basingstoke: Palgrave.

Swyngedow, E., Moulaert, F. and Rodriguez, A. (2002) Neoliberal urbanisation in Europe: large-scale urban development projects and the New Urban Policy, *Antipode*, 34(3), pp.542–577.

Syms, P. (2002) *Land, development and design*. Oxford: Blackwell.

Turok, I. (1992) Property-led urban regeneration: panacea or placebo? *Environment and Planning A*, 24(3), pp.361–379.

Webber, C., Larkin, K., Tochtermann, L., Varley-Winter, O. and Wilcox, Z. (2010) *Grand designs? A new approach to the built environment in England's cities*. London: Centre for Cities.

18 Conclusion

Beyond Reflective, Deliberative Practice

Jessica Ferm and John Tomaney

Introduction

The world of planning practice is under-researched and under-theorised. Despite some important past contributions, the domain within which planners find themselves is undergoing rapid and constant change, which affects how planners go about their practice. We have sought to capture some of this change and critically reflect on how this is affecting planning practice, in terms of the tools and processes within planning, the skills and knowledges of planners, as well as the outcomes of planning interventions (quality and quantity of housing, economic progress, sustainable development etc.). The contributions to this book have been rich and varied. Collectively, they build a picture of the key challenges facing planning practice – and the dilemmas practitioners face – in the contemporary age. Each chapter includes its own detailed reflections on the challenges for its area of focus. Here, we reflect on our original guiding questions to highlight the overall contributions of this book.

We began in Part I with an exploration of how planning is being practised today, whether this differs from the past, and perhaps also differs from the theory of that practice. A related question is what skills and knowledges contemporary planners require. In seeking to answer these questions, in Part II the contributors investigated the various aspects of the work that fall under 'planning practice', ranging from plan-making, managing development, development value capture, public participation and place-making. In Part III, we investigated planning practice with a view to looking at the various outcomes of planning, such as housing, transport, and urban regeneration. In some cases, practising planners fall into distinct silos, such as policy planners, Development Management officers, urban designers, transport planners, urban regeneration specialists etc. However, in practice, these distinctions are much more fluid, and many functions and areas of expertise interweave and overlap. One danger of this approach is that we might replicate the various 'silos' of the profession in structuring the discussion in the way we have. Ultimately, we have adopted a pragmatic stance on this, so the structure reflects rather traditional categories and distinctions. However, one conclusion of the book is that the problem of strategic coordination is a key challenge facing planning practice – between various parts of the splintering state, between different actors implicated in the planning process, and between planners working within silos – which undermines a holistic approach to solving some of the pressing problems of our age.

In the next two sections of this chapter, we reflect on this question of how planning practice has changed and explore the extent to which existing theoretical work helps us to understand what we observe in the contemporary context. We argue that the linked theoretical contributions around deliberative practice and communicative planning have been hugely influential in guiding practitioners in their work, and continue to be so. However, there are limits to communicative planning, and tensions between it and other structural changes, which we explore. On the other hand, the concept of reflective practice – although often dismissed as placing too much evidence on individual actions – deserves renewed attention given the increasingly complex and varied structural constraints within which planners work. The communicative planning moment has given way to two further *regime* shifts: a revival of evidence-based planning and – as an extension to this – the formalisation (in policy) of viability-based planning. Neither of these regimes entirely replace the previous, but are layered on top of previous practices, requiring new and additional expertise of practising planners and creating greater complexity in terms of the balancing of interests and inputs into the planning process. So planners are now required to be creative, work collaboratively, make decisions based on up-to-date evidence *and* be mindful of market realism in their decision- and plan-making. We explore this issue in more detail below.

In Chapter 1, we set out some of the global and national contexts and trends that provide the framework for planning practice – from globalisation, deregulation of markets, financialisation of urban development, privatisation, austerity, demographic shifts, climate change, devolution and planning reforms. Another key guiding question for the book is therefore how these changing contexts and trends affect planning practice? Part II of the book addressed this question directly, exploring some of these contexts in greater depth, but each chapter has touched upon it to some degree, and we draw out some conclusions below (see 'Structure Matters'). Later, we explore further two changing frameworks of planning practice that have emerged as critically important in this book: the changing nature of the state, and the rising influence of the private sector in planning. Here, 'change' has now become part of the problem, to which planners are struggling to adapt. Alongside the splintering state, the increasing role of the private sector in planning represents challenges, raising important questions around who plans and who shapes planning, and fundamentally challenging long-held assumptions that planning is a public sector activity, whose purpose is promote the 'public good'. This leads us, in the last section, to reflect on the very purpose of planning: Why do we plan? What should planning seek to achieve? Here, we expose a fundamental disagreement in perspectives on this question, which needs to be resolved if planning is to continue to have relevance in the future.

The Limits of Reflective and Deliberative Practice

Despite some notable biographical accounts and memoirs, Fischler (2012) argues that *The Reflective Practitioner* by Donald Schön (1991, first published in 1983) – a culmination of decades worth of work on the nature of professional knowledge and action – represented one of the first comprehensive attempts to provide evidence on the way planners thought in daily practice. *The Reflective Practitioner* emerged at a time when many were criticising the male-dominated technocracy and the rational-scientific model. Schön was "a critic of dominant planning practice, particularly its pretence of mastery and control" (Fischler, 2012: 319), arguing that professional practice in the postmodern era was different, and must deal with greater complexity, uncertainty and instability, requiring professionals to both reflect *in* action and reflect *on* action. But few planning scholars have engaged critically with Schön's work, possibly because "the theory of reflective practice is very much a theory of individual behaviour, in which larger economic and political factors receive little attention" (Fischler, 2012: 323).

In *The Deliberative Practitioner*, John Forester addresses this challenge, stating that his work extends "the individual work of reflection-in-action towards the more social and political work of practical deliberation" explaining that "reflecting alone, a practitioner learns; deliberating with others, practitioners learn together and craft strategies to act collaboratively" (Forester, 1999: 4). This contribution followed *Planning in the Face of Power* (Forester, 1989), where he argued that planning is deeply argumentative and planners are constantly engaged in disagreements about desirable and possible futures. Forester's theoretical work was informed by a teaching tool he used throughout his career, whereby he brought into the classroom various planning practitioners to recount stories of their practice, highlighting to students the range of value-laden choices and ethical dilemmas faced by planners (Forester, 2017).

The studies of Forester and Schön, revealing more about how planners actually worked in practice and challenging the traditional modernist approach to planning, followed radical citizen-led protests in the 1960s and 1970s, in response to top-down planning interventions; high-profile examples include protests in the US against the redevelopment of the historic Penn Station and Jane Jacobs' condemnation of the proposals to drive a highway through her beloved Greenwich Village in Manhattan, and in the UK, campaigns in London to prevent the demolition of Covent Garden and the extension of the A40 (following the unpopular Westway overpass). These citizen-led protests provided fuel for the emergence of what we now know as 'communicative planning', led most notably by Judith Innes and John Friedmann (in the US context) and Patsy Healey (in the UK), who looked to philosophers Habermas and Foucault, and derived their insights from in-depth studies of practice. Writing as de Neufville (1983), Judith Innes claimed that planning theory based on the rational model did not mesh with practice and was alienating practitioners. She proposed an agenda for planning theorists to confront the dilemmas, grounding theorising in research on practice, use holistic, interpretive methods, and create new imagery of what planning is and what planners do. In *Planning in the Public Domain*, John Friedmann (1987) referred to a new mode of 'transactive' planning, which emphasised the importance of "face to face transactions and dialogue" for radical practice. In an essay on communicative planning, Patsy Healey (2012) charts its emergence from these tentative beginnings in the 1980s, to a widely known 'label' in the 1990s so, by the 2000s, it was well established and on planning theory reading lists. She argues that the main contribution of the communicative perspective has been to direct attention to the fine grain (or 'micropractices') of planning work, to challenge the broad stereotypes of what planning is and how it is done, and to highlight the significance of bringing together different forms of knowledge, communicative competence, technical skill and ethical attention. The contributions in this book acknowledge the positive changes this communicative turn in planning has brought, but at the same time argue that there are limits to this perspective, which are becoming increasingly evident through examining contemporary practices and experiences.

Healey (2012: 353) warned that communicative planning as an intellectual perspective cannot "be neatly turned into the promotion of forms of collaborative practice that will somehow move polities along a trajectory towards an ideal of a better participatory democracy". The contributions to this book raise some more fundamental concerns with the trajectory of community planning. In Chapters 6 and 9, Yasminah Beebeejaun and Elena Besussi – focusing on public participation and Neighbourhood Planning respectively – both come to the same conclusion: that the focus on the deliberative model and consensus-building in communicative planning theory has stifled more radical action. More radical elements, which wish to disrupt the status quo, are forced outside the planning system. Under localism in England, Besussi argues that aspirations for community-led planning cannot be completely absorbed by Neighbourhood Planning. The requirement for Neighbourhood Planning to comply with the broader government agenda for growth means that only those willing to accept the growth-oriented politics and the consensual, deliberative format of decision-making that accompanies it will not be frustrated by Neighbourhood Planning. Beebeejaun's focus is on public participation in mainstream planning, where she argues that despite nearly 50 years having passed since the publication of key works emphasising the reciprocal benefits of public participation for both planners and communities, little progress has been made. Although communicative planning is generally seen to be a 'good thing', reinforced through localism, and in some cases it has prompted better engagement with communities in Local Plan-making (see Chapter 3 by Jessica Ferm), Beebeejaun argues that the presumption in favour of development in the National Planning Policy Framework means that public participation in plan-making is now framed around development, particularly engagement with increased housebuilding – and has thus narrowed the issues of concern. In this context, communities' objections to development are too easily represented as self-interested or NIMBY, and many issues of concern raised by communities are dismissed as not being 'planning matters'. More than being a problem for public participation in planning, ultimately this "may point towards the declining significance of planning", says Beebeejaun. Both chapters provide some empirical material to support already-existing theoretical reflections on the application of the geographical literature on the post-political condition to spatial planning (see Allmendinger and Haughton, 2012) and to complement other empirical studies on the place for disagreement in consensus-oriented planning (Özdemir and Tasan-Kok, 2017). Their observations resonate with the argument made by Allmendinger and Haughton (2012) that the promotion of spatial planning as 'progressive' contains the danger that rather than offering an empowering arena for debating future development priorities, it offers only choreographed processes with clear limitations on what is open for debate. In practice, there is only superficial engagement, offering weak legitimacy, while focusing on delivering narrowly defined 'growth', while dissent is presented as parochial or regressive.

Many of the decisions on the built environment that impact upon local communities are made outside the planning and local government framework. As Claudio de Magalhães and Nikos Karadimitriou show in Chapter 17, participation and accountability present a major challenge for those involved in urban regeneration since many of the key decisions on urban regeneration projects are taken within public–private partnerships outside the normal rules of accountability of local government. What all this points to is that the real limits of the communicative turn arise from the inequities of power that are endemic in society, and that planners' and communities' influences are limited by structural constraints. On the issue of power, it is not just the power dynamics between property interests and local communities (which are all too evident), but that in focusing on micro politics and micro practices, communicative planning ignores the macro politics of planning – for example, geopolitical shifts in power on a global scale, which in turn impact upon the local.

In emphasising process, communicative planning turns attention away from the unequal interests of the groups concerned, and the domination of powerful material interests. We will return to the importance of structure later.

In terms of their use as theoretical constructs, reflective and deliberative practice are still useful concepts. However, whereas a huge amount of energy and attention have been devoted to the implementation and critique of deliberative practice in the last two decades, reflective practice deserves some renewed attention. Hitherto dismissed as focusing too much on individual agency, the observations of Schön (1991) remain relevant to contemporary planning practice. As is evident from the contributions in this book, the world within which planners are practising today is even more complex than it was, the profession is even more insecure, and there is arguably greater global instability than there was in the 1980s. So Schön's call for more reflective practice to deal with these increasingly complex, uncertain and unstable situations – which present planners with value conflicts – is surely as relevant today as it was then, albeit they must be understood in relation to the structural constraints bearing on the planning system.

From Evidence-based to Viability-based Planning and Beyond

Despite the attack on rational-scientific modes of planning by the critical pragmatists (e.g. Forester) and communicative theorists, the 1990s (in the UK, under New Labour) saw a revival of evidence-based policy-making, which signalled a renewed interest in the research–policy interface (see Young et al., 2002). The impetus to reconnect policy and evidence might be understood as part of New Labour's 'Third Way' stance, or as an attempt to construct a shared understanding (and thus potential for consensus) among diverse stakeholders in partnerships, and should be seen in the context of the transition from government to governance discussed in more detail later (for an overview of the role of evidence in England's spatial planning system, see Lord and Hincks, 2010). But Davoudi (2006) argues that this turn suffers from the same misconceptions as the earlier rational-scientific approach to planning, where simplistic assumptions are made about the linear and direct relationship between evidence and policy. This time enshrined in legislation through the required 'tests of soundness', evidence-based planning had little time to embed in planning practices before the onset of the recession and incoming Coalition government, which abolished regional planning and introduced requirements for viability testing.

In Chapter 3 on plan-making, Jessica Ferm reveals that the introduction of tests of soundness represented a transformative shift in the way planners made plans, but the austerity context has made it harder for local planning authorities to keep up with the extensive requirements of evidence-based planning. The ever-increasing pressure on them to speed up the plan-preparation process – under a drive for 'efficiency' – also means there is less clear progression from evidence-gathering to plan-making. In Chapter 15, Jessica Ferm, Michael Edwards and Edward Jones examined the use of evidence on the economy in planning, arguing that the narrowing and weakening of the in-house economic skills available in local authorities – exacerbated under austerity – and a reliance on consultancies or independent studies of the 'economic evidence' results in a narrow framing of the economy focused around specialisation and agglomeration, underplaying the importance of economic diversity and diverse economies, and overemphasising the benefits of agglomeration over the costs.

Other critiques revolve around the tensions between evidence-based planning and participation in planning. The sheer volume of evidence (and lack of clarity in progression according to a hierarchy of plans) is confusing, and undermines participation in the planning process. There is also the question of how 'lay' knowledge is considered alongside commissioned evidence in the process of evidence-based planning. Questions concerning the construction of knowledge, what counts and what doesn't count, spur a fertile debate in planning theory (see Rydin, 2007). More fundamentally, we might observe that despite talk of evidence-based planning, planning seems to happen despite, rather than because of, evidence. The commitment to building a high-speed rail link between London and the North of England, connecting to the west coast mainline to Glasgow (High Speed Rail 2) is a prime example of this. Despite fairly convincing evidence that high-speed rail is likely to deepen inequalities between the regions in the UK (and provoke substantial public opposition), the government is pressing ahead with building it on the grounds that it will 'rebalance' regional economies (Tomaney and Marques, 2013).

The revival of evidence-based planning, together with the extensive requirements for technical reports that developers are obliged to meet when submitting planning applications, have provided fuel for the private consultancy sector in planning. In Chapter 8, Mike Raco points out that this has been further compounded by the impacts of austerity cuts and the mushrooming of regulations – most recently under the Coalition government – to support a viability-based planning regime, which has led to further growth of the consultancy sector. The increasingly technical nature of the assessments required under new regulations means that in-house skills and abilities are stretched, and planners are having to outsource these assessments to meet the requirements, leaving officers and politicians in local authorities with limited ability to challenge the evidence. Viability-based planning has thus given greater control to the private sector (more on this below), which has in turn fuelled consultation apathy and community tensions, as citizens rally against the lack of transparency associated with decision-making based on confidential viability assessments. There are many cases where viability planning has been used to reverse commitments to the provisions of affordable housing. The homelessness charity Shelter found that because of viability assessments, 2500 affordable homes were lost in one year in just 11 council areas in England, representing some 79% of the affordable homes that should have been delivered through Section 106 (Grayston, 2017). This is, however, starting to change, with some individual local authorities demanding public access to developers' viability assessments, and the leadership shown by the Mayor of London (2017) in publishing affordable housing and viability Supplementary Planning Guidance, which demands greater transparency.

Under viability-based planning, which places an emphasis on *flexibility* (of plans and policies) and *deliverability* (of plans and development proposals) in order to support development and growth, this inevitably shifts power away from the development plan and local government. Although evidence-based planning implies a linear progression from higher-tier plans (based on evidence) to lower-tier site plans and proposals, under viability-based planning, the influence is in the opposite direction: developer-led site proposals (demonstrated to be viable) inform higher-tier area action plans or Local Plans.

Whether or not the viability-led (rather than creative-led) nature of forming development proposals also has implications for design and quality remains underexplored. However, there is certainly frustration among practising planners and urban designers in the private sector that their work has been reduced to a technical calculation exercise (see Chapter 3). In Chapter 7, Matthew Carmona argues that the design dimension was long ago squeezed out of British planning, and under austerity, any consideration of design (in strategic planning) is limited to design policies in local development plans. But, as he warns, "the control of design can help to eliminate bad design, but by itself will not deliver good design", suggesting a need to bring forward more positive visions for change and rediscover some of the visioning potential that was an integral part of planning a century ago (Bowie, 2016; Ellis and Henderson, 2014). Such a rediscovery could align well with the need – argued by Catalina Turcu in Chapter 12 – for "significant strategic action from higher levels" if planning is to deliver sustainable development and better outcomes, which do not always align with communities' priorities and the self-interest of individuals within those communities who participate in planning.

Structure Matters

One of the key objectives of this book has been to bring attention to the structural constraints under which planning occurs, something we argue has been neglected or underplayed by existing bodies of planning theory – notably, communicative planning theory, which has, in bringing attention to 'agency' and the social and political dimensions to planning practice, diverted attention away from the structural forces that shape the production of the built environment. Part of the lack of attention to structure might well be due to a determination to 'act' despite the constraints faced, and a sense of resignation that structural constraints are by their very nature difficult to affect. Several chapters in this book have reflected on the nature of these structural constraints and the limits planners face acting within them.

The impact of deregulation was explored by Ben Clifford in Chapter 4 in the case of Development Management (DM). Most of the focus for planning deregulation has been on DM, portrayed (most negatively in England, but across the UK) as being slow and inefficient, and a barrier to growth. As Clifford observes, rather than confront broader issues of political economy, successive governments have become obsessed with 'tinkering' with planning, reflecting a view that implies it does not add (economic) value. This creates tensions for planners in managing development. On the one hand, there are constant pressures and reforms to increase speed and efficiency in processing planning applications, plus an expectation that planners should be involved more proactively in shaping development (up-front pre-application discussions, planning performance agreements etc.). All this puts more pressure on planners, but with fewer resources, and the onus is on DM, through fees, to act as a service to provide financial resources for other planning services (policy-making, enforcement), putting most pressure on DM planners. On the other hand, the ability of planners to exercise control (and deliver public benefit and sustainable outcomes) is being stripped and constrained through extensions to permitted development rights, proposals for permission in principle, the brownfield register and further privatisation of core planning services. Increased housebuilding comes at the cost of increased pressure on local infrastructure while neglecting other potential goals and outcomes that we might want from DM, such as democracy, community engagement and social justice. Nevertheless, DM planners strive to continue to deliver public benefit, reflecting their professional and ethical dispositions. However, as Patricia Canelas points out in Chapter 5, as austerity bites, development value is captured, not so much to get public benefit, but to fund core services.

Together, the impacts of deregulation and decentralisation provoked changes to local government financing under what Mike Raco refers to in Chapter 8 as a "new centralised localism" that promotes local financial self-sufficiency. These changes have been on-going, and pre-date austerity measures. The impact of changes that promote financial self-sufficiency at the local level are the privileging of economic development priorities and 'growth' and the locking of local authorities into a dependence on property market uplift (and thereby private sector actors) to deliver basic services and facilities, which then impacts on the financial resources left over for adequate infrastructure to support new development. Chapter 15 by Jessica Ferm, Michael Edwards and Edward Jones provides an illustration of how structural constraints in a deregulated environment are narrowing the sphere of influence and action of planners over economic development. Whereas the state's strategy previously focused on 'rebalancing the economy' (i.e. minimising the impact of negative externalities and market failures), planners have become increasingly reluctant to get involved in directing economic activity, as planning is portrayed as 'interfering' in the economy. Rather, planners today are encouraged to work with rather than against market forces, supporting (e.g. through facilitation of new infrastructure) agglomerations of businesses to boost local economic competitiveness. But rather than planning proactively, local authority planners' role in the economy is narrow – facilitating real estate development, attracting 'inward investment' and checking the financial 'viability' of plans and projects.

The actions of planning practitioners are also severely constrained in the context of financialisation. In Chapter 14, John Tomaney, Peter O'Brien and Andy Pike expose the challenges facing infrastructure planning, where private sector investment plays an increasingly important role and financial actors see infrastructure as a new asset class. In this context, planning's role becomes to support the market and facilitate returns to investors, rather than produce public goods. One of the negative aspects that arises is that there remain gaps in provision, where needs are high but commercial returns are limited, resulting in geographical imbalances or lack of integration between distinct types of infrastructure provision (due to fragmentation). In the case of transport provision, in Chapter 16, Iqbal Hamiduddin and Robin Hickman provide an example of the problems of such models of financing infrastructure, which is resulting in patchy geographical coverage and reinforcing inequalities. In housing, similar processes mean a lack of investment in and development of affordable housing and housing types/sizes that are less profitable. Whereas planning's role previously would have been to address such market failures, the scope for planners to adopt such a position is now limited, and planning increasingly reinforces existing inequalities rather than addressing them.

While the political consensus is that the UK's planning system is the main cause of the housing affordability crisis, in Chapter 13 Nick Gallent exposes the limits of viewing the housing crisis as a problem of a lack of supply, and therefore of local planning practice. This view fails, he argues, to consider a fundamental change in the function of housing, away from residential use primarily for occupation and towards a vehicle for investment and wealth accumulation. This is the case across the whole of the UK, where the proportion of people owning their own homes rose through credit liberalisation, but it is particularly the case in strong markets where foreign investment in housing is significant – although the affordability crisis means ownership rates have fallen. Housing has thus gained a broader economic function – that of driving economic growth through consumption in a context of declining production in post-industrial economies. In this context, it becomes very difficult to identify alternative approaches to planning for housing. Gallent argues that the risk of an economic shock inhibits government action, but a fundamental change to the process of allocating land for housing could be envisaged, whereby different land use categories are established for land that is for housing occupation (directly meeting housing need) and land that is for housing investment.

In *Rethinking the Economics of Land and Housing*, Ryan-Collins et al. (2017: 112) point to mortgage credit being the "elephant in the room" when it comes to understanding the behaviour of housing and land prices and the broader imbalances in the economy. Property is now the single largest source of wealth in the UK, making up half of all total household assets and net wealth. Mortgage debt comprises the majority of bank lending and household liabilities. Maintaining these asset values is now the overriding macroeconomic policy concern. Although the global financial crisis had exposed the limits of this model, basic trends remain unaltered. The authors suggest that the growth in wealth inequality, charted by Thomas Piketty and others, derives principally from housing rather than other assets and reflects underlying land values. They suggest further that the financialisation of housing is the root cause of the UK's poor productivity performance – housing crowds out more productive investment. As Gallent warns, if we don't tackle this problem head-on, then we will never solve the housing crisis, no matter how many additional homes we build.

With major structural shifts and transformations globally, new challenges are presented to planners, who are faced with much greater uncertainty – for example, planning for very uncertain population projections because of increased migration, and planning in an era of environmental uncertainty, threats and climate change. Claire Colomb and Mike Raco's Chapter 11 on planning for diversity raises some important questions about whether the policies planners implement have unintended consequences on ethnic groups, the distribution of housing and social infrastructure. Planners cannot simply embrace diversity, they are faced with dilemmas and difficult choices for which they are ultimately rather poorly equipped or trained to deal with. Catalina Turcu's Chapter 12 on sustainable development and planning elaborates on the broader global context within which planners work: an ageing population, rapid urbanisation, shrinking regions, climate change, resource scarcity and rapid technological advances. She highlights the difficulties in practice of delivering sustainable development, and the tensions with broader agendas such as deregulation and localism, which can work against it. One of the problems, she argues, is that planning for sustainable development in the UK is not governed by legally binding targets, but relies on moral commitments and political resolve. However, the 'presumption in favour of sustainable development' in national frameworks remains poorly defined (particularly in relation to the social dimension), leaving too much room for manoeuvre and mere lip service to be paid. In becoming aware of structural matters, and to plan more sensitively in the context of such structural constraints, planning practitioners face an increasing burden in terms of the knowledge, expertise and nuanced understanding of complex socio-economic and environmental-technical questions they are required to address to act fairly, justly and responsibly.

In Chapter 17, Claudio de Magalhães and Nikos Karadimitriou discuss the complexities facing planners in working to deliver large-scale urban regeneration schemes, and the range of skills and knowledges they require to do so. Planners are required to understand the dynamics of development, how to capture value without compromising viability, how to direct the benefits to the intended recipients, and how to manage risk and negotiate with all the parties involved – all of which, they point out, is not typically associated with their professional profile or planning education. Urban design and policy-making skills are insufficient to deal with the complexities faced by planners in delivering urban regeneration. Whereas private development companies will have multidisciplinary teams with the appropriate sets of skills, local authority planners can no longer rely on equivalent teams in their own authority (if they ever could). Often, the processes of negotiation and bargaining take place under the institutional umbrella of a public–private partnership, where decisions are taken outside the normal rules of accountability of local democracy.

Emphasising the structural and global context within which planners work, and how this affects professional practice, is a key contribution of this book. Throughout, the contributors have highlighted tensions that affect how planners can act – for example, tensions between decentralisation (giving more power to communities) and deregulation (taking away the ability of neighbourhoods and local planning authorities to control development), and between decentralisation and the privatisation of planning. Although previous accounts of practice (e.g. Thomas and Healey, 1991) have focused on recounting the day-to-day experiences and accounts from the perspective of practising planners, this book offers an analysis that links theoretical concepts of planning practice to everyday practice, importantly highlighting the changing political, social and economic context within which planners work. In doing so, it sheds light on why practitioners' day-to-day practice is so challenging, and how they might act within the structural constraints they face.

Shifting Character of the State

Planning is closely bound with debates on the changing nature of the state and evolving multi-level governance structures. The very nature of government and tasks and purposes constantly evolves. In the late 19th-century United States, Woodrow Wilson promoted the importance of 'administration' within government and the idea of the state as the guardian of society, with an aspiration to make the business of government 'less business-like' (Wilson, 1887). Large industries were perceived as having too close a relationship with government, and Wilson was concerned about resulting corruption. The end of the Second World War represented the height of enthusiasm for the state's role in society; planning as a discipline was born in this post-war excitement. More recently, however, we have seen an on-going rolling back of the state. In *Reinventing Government*, Osborne and Gaebler (1992: 34) documented the rise of the entrepreneurial government:

> Most entrepreneurial governments promote *competition* between service providers. They empower citizens by pushing control out of bureaucracy, into the community. They measure the performance of their agencies, focusing not on inputs but on *outcomes*. They are driven by their *goals* – their missions – not by their rules and regulations. They redefine their clients as *customers* and offer the choices. . . They prevent problems before they emerge, rather than simply offering services afterwards. They put their energies into earning money, not simply spending it. They *decentralise* authority, embracing participatory management. They prefer *market* mechanisms to bureaucratic mechanisms. And they focus not simply on providing public services but on catalysing all sectors – public, private and voluntary – into action to solve their community's problems.

But the move towards a more business-like, entrepreneurial state is fraught with problems. For a public governing body to be accountable, it has to demonstrate achievement of equality, impartiality, integrity, justice etc. (Haque, 2002). Yet for the state, demonstrating accountability is much harder than for private enterprise. It is harder to assess whether citizens are satisfied than whether shareholders are satisfied, since they have more complex needs and desires and it is often difficult to know what they want (Bogdanor, 2005). In the case of planning, there is an obvious tension between efficiency and accountability. The 'entrepreneurial' local authority is under pressure to speed up the decision-making process to make the system more efficient (and less costly) for developers, whereas councillors representing their constituents' interests may require more time to properly engage them in consultation on developments and affect accountability. A distinction between politicians who make the planning decisions (on larger schemes) and planners as administrators thus emerges – a tension that remains underexplored.

More fundamentally, there is now a sense – reinforced by several of the chapters in this book – that we are perhaps on the cusp of another transformation beyond the entrepreneurial state. After years of rolling back the state, particularly under Conservative-led administrations, there is now a sense that the 'entrepreneurial' state (as an entrepreneurial entity) is in crisis, with (even) the Conservative Party conceding the imperative for more state intervention, for instance in the direct delivery of social and affordable housing:

> We will invest an additional £2 billion in affordable housing – taking the Government's total affordable housing budget to almost £9 billion. We will encourage councils as well as housing associations to bid for this money and provide certainty over future rent levels. And in those parts of the country where the need is greatest, allow homes to be built for social rent, well below market level. Getting government back into the business of building houses. A new generation of council houses to help fix our broken housing market.
> (Conservative Party, 2017)

The decentralisation of authority has been part of the shift to the entrepreneurial state. As global flows have intensified under globalisation, so the role of the state in managing domestic economies (as it did under the Keynesian welfare state) has waned. Managing the economy and society became more complex as more actors became involved in decision-making, and power flowed away from nation states to other actors, signified in the formulation of a shift from government to governance. The state has not been replaced, but now acts in concert with other forces – markets, civil society, business, independent bodies and the courts (national, European and international). Changing governance structures have had a fundamental impact on planning practice – as John Tomaney and Claire Colomb show in Chapter 2. Planning occurs within a multi-level governance framework. The abolition of the regional tier and regional planning in England and the introduction of a new neighbourhood tier by the incoming Coalition government in 2010 has had profound implications for planning practice in England, with clear moves to recreate a strategic tier through Combined Authorities, City Deals and Local Economic Partnerships – although the emphasis is now on city-regions and 'functional economic areas' rather than administrative regions. Devolution to Scotland, Northern Ireland and Wales has provided the opportunity for a 'diversity of spatial plannings' to emerge, but the asymmetrical devolution we see (particularly the devolution of powers to city-regions) raises the prospect of inequality between dynamic metropolitan areas and their small town/rural hinterlands. The new political spaces offer the potential for different, potentially innovative planning practices to emerge, but this is by no means inevitable. Institutions matter, but so do the politics that govern them (see Chapter 2).

In the case of transport planning, in Chapter 16 Iqbal Hamiduddin and Robin Hickman reveal how the devolution of powers and budgetary responsibilities to new Local Transport Bodies (which co-exist with LEPs ostensibly over functional economic areas) has created fragmented institutional structures and problems of strategic coordination, which, alongside limited funding that is centralised and prioritised on a competitive basis, is resulting in patchy and unequal geographical coverage of public transport provision across the UK. However, drawing on good practice examples from other European cities, they claim it is not devolved governance arrangements that are the problem per se, but rather that such arrangements need to be matched with adequate levels of funding and authority if they are to maximise the potential for innovation and alignment with local objectives and needs (that devolved arrangements can more easily deliver).

The problems of strategic coordination between various parts of the splintering state, and between state actors and other actors in the process of planning, are increasingly evident. The failure of local authorities to coordinate strategically under the 'Duty to Cooperate' is a case in point. As Chapter 3 revealed in its assessment of the geographical coverage of Local Plans, part of the reason for the poor coverage of up-to-date Local Plans reflects the failure to cooperate under the duty. Incessant change, intended presumably to address identified problems, has now itself become part of the problem, with few signs of it slowing down. Devolution in the UK is on-going, and the role (and influence) of the private sector in governance continues to grow. The next section turns to the nature and implications of this latter turn.

Rising Power and Influence of the Private Sector

Traditionally, the distinction between the public and private sectors in planning and development was clear. Planners were effectively 'guardians of the public interest' in the face of private gain. We identify two significant changes, which blur the distinction rather radically.

Firstly, there is an increasing involvement of local government and community actors as partners in regeneration projects. Where development is entirely market-driven and private sector-led, the roles are clearer. However, where the public sector is engaged in a formal public–private partnership arrangement – either because it owns the land or because public sector involvement is required to de-risk development – the same organisation's role in the planning process either shaping the development or responding to planning applications as they come in is somewhat compromised, with the balance of power tilted towards the private sector. In Chapter 17, Claudio de Magalhães and Nikos Karadimitriou illustrate these tensions in relation to planning and regeneration. Such public–private partnerships, they point out, require compromises and adaptations to be made, both with regard to the development itself and the requirements of the local authority. The lack of accountability and representativeness in partnerships is an issue, given the many decisions they take about the shape, timing and outcomes of urban regeneration projects.

Secondly, we have yet to fully grapple with the implications of the growing consultancy sector and its influence in shaping planning policy and its outcomes. As Mike Raco shows in Chapter 8, the extraordinary growth of the consultancy sector has taken place in parallel with planning reform and a growth of regulations, which have – in the context of austerity – required more contracting out of work by local planning authorities to meet their obligations. Yet this growth is uneven. In plan-making, Chapter 3 documents local authority cut-backs to the use of planning consultants in spatial planning as part of the drive to find cost savings. Given the growth of the sector Raco documents, it might simply be that local authorities must look to areas where they can afford to reduce consultant input, given the regulatory requirements to produce technical assessments to, most notably, the production of viability assessments. Another aspect of private sector involvement revealed by Raco is the increasing concentration of work in the hands of a small number of large consultancies, with profound implications for the ability of the consultancy sector to lobby for planning reform that keeps them in work. Other private actors in the property industry are also involved in shaping planning reform to suit their interests: in Chapter 5, Patricia Canelas reveals how the Westminster Property Association – a developers' lobby – was influential in making the case for (what was to become) Planning Performance Agreements.

The lack of attention to the role of the private sector in planning to date – theoretically, politically and practically – is the starkest gap revealed in the book, and one which presents a clear opportunity and urgent need for further research and attention. Wolf-Powers (2005) and others (e.g. Fainstein, 2001; Harding, 1991; Logan and Molotch, 1987) limit their portrayal of planners to framing a dichotomy between the public sector (planners) and the private sector (developers), where planners are on one side of the divide, either reacting passively to development proposals and projects as they come in or preparing strategic plans to guide developers in their endeavours. This perspective overlooks the nuances of both public sector involvement in private development (de-risking) or private sector influence on planning policy, and the dominance of planning work by private planning consultants. Ultimately, planning is no longer merely a public sector activity, undertaken by public servants. The literature (mostly) still talks about it in these terms, and the education most UK planners receive does not reflect this new reality, but it has profound implications for planning practice, the skills and knowledges that planners require, the outcomes they are able to achieve, and the ethical and practical dilemmas they face. It offers a rich and fruitful area for future research.

Future Directions: the Changing Purpose of Planning?

As part of the Raynsford Review of Planning,[1] established by the Town and Country Planning Association (TCPA) in 2017, the very purpose of planning emerged as a fundamental question and area of disagreement. Hugh Ellis, Head of Policy at the TCPA, suggested (at a London event, as part of the evidence-gathering) that there were broadly two camps. In the first, people see planning primarily as a vehicle for the allocation of housing sites and permission for housing development. In the second camp, planning is seen as the means to secure wider community benefit and sustainable outcomes from development. This lack of agreement as to the very purpose of planning is, we would argue, an outcome of the restriction of planning's role – and its increasing dependence – on the promotion of 'growth'. In Chapter 8, Mike Raco focuses on the shift that has taken place in the wake of austerity cuts and the introduction of *viability planning regimes*, which has re-imagined and remade "the very ethos of what the planning system is for and what it should do". However, the seeds for this shift have a longer history, with increasing dependence on market-led development having taken place over the last three to four decades, during which time "planning as a purposeful state activity has become increasingly and more explicitly shaped by a dependence on growth" (Rydin, 2013: 15). Tensions arise when the role of the planner is reduced to facilitating a return to the market, and the space for the promotion of a just and sustainable society is lost.

Does this all amount to a shift in the purpose of planning? We would argue it signifies that planning's function has been transformed and increasingly co-opted by the development industry. Despite the anti-planning sentiment of government we described in Chapter 1, the planning system is functioning, despite austerity measures. Between April 2015 and March 2016, 1826 major planning applications were approved by 74 local planning authorities participating in the Annual Planning Survey – an average of 25 successful major applications per authority (GL Hearn and the British Property Federation, 2016). In examining the relationship between real estate and planning, in Chapter 10 Tommaso Gabrieli and Nicola Livingstone show how, in an increasingly internationalised and financialised real estate market, international actors rely on local professional planning services to accurately inform and support their decision-making process. The expertise and local knowledge of planners and their role in negotiating consultation with local communities are key. Hence, far from developers seeing planning as inefficient and a brake on development, international developers and investors – due to the capital under their command – have the luxury of being able to wait, and are willing to be patient to secure the best possible outcomes. As Patricia Canelas reveals in Chapter 5, it was a developer-led lobby – through the Westminster Property

Association – that prompted the introduction of Planning Performance Agreements, showing that developers are increasingly finding ways to shape and use the planning system to suit their purposes. For this group of actors, planning has a certain purpose. But, as Ben Clifford suggests (Chapter 4 in this volume; Clifford and Tewdwr-Jones, 2013), despite the structural pressures on planners and the subordination of the planning system to a narrow goal of housing delivery, public sector planners retain a strong determination to extract broader societal benefits and the notion of public service remains strong, albeit in a context where the scope for planners to actually 'make a difference' is limited.

The teaching of ethics is now established on the planning curriculum, but the spaces for considering our 'values' and their relationship to the 'good society' are limited. In a more devolved and divided UK, moreover, definitions of such values are more diverse than perhaps they were previously. However, the problem of socio-economic inequality is ascending the political agenda everywhere, providing opportunities for planners to be more intellectually assertive and self-confident in offering solutions to this crisis. The marginalisation of planning has played a part in producing these outcomes, but land use planning first emerged to deal with the excesses and inequalities arising from the manifest failures of the market at the end of the 19th century. Re-fashioning planning practice will be testing in an age where representative democracy appears fragile and faith in the capacity of governments to solve social problems is diminished. Nonetheless, this is the challenge that faces the profession today.

Note

1 The Raynsford Review of Planning (in England) was established in 2017, chaired by former Planning Minister the Rt Hon. Nick Raynsford. See https://www.tcpa.org.uk/raynsford-review.

References

All listed URLs were last accessed on 1 March 2018.

Allmendinger, P. and Haughton, G. (2012) Post-political spatial planning in England: a crisis of consensus? *Transactions of the Institute of British Geographers*, 37(1), pp.89–103.

Bogdanor, V. (2005) Introduction. In V. Bogdanor (ed.) *Joined-up government*. Oxford: Clarendon Press/British Academy.

Bowie, D. (2016) *The radical and socialist tradition in British planning: from Puritan colonies to garden cities*. London: Routledge.

Clifford, B. and Tewdwr-Jones, M. (2013) *The collaborating planner?* Bristol: Policy Press.

Conservative Party (2017) Theresa May's speech to Conservative Party Conference 2017, 4 October. Available at: https://www.conservatives.com/sharethefacts/2017/10/theresa-mays-conference-speech.

Davoudi, S. (2006) Evidence-based planning: rhetoric and reality, *disP*, 165(2), pp.14–24.

de Neufville, J. (1983) Planning theory and practice: bridging the gap, *Journal of Planning Education and Research*, 3, pp.35–45.

Ellis, H. and Henderson, K. (2014) *Rebuilding Britain: planning for a better future*. Bristol: Policy Press.

Fainstein, S. (2001) *The city builders: property development in New York and London 1980–2000*, 2nd edn. Lawrence, KS: University Press of Kansas.

Fischler, R. (2012) Reflective practice. In B. Sanyal et al. (eds) *Planning ideas that matter*. Cambridge, MA: MIT Press, pp.333–357.

Forester, J. (1989) *Planning in the face of power*. Berkeley, CA: University of California Press.

Forester, J. (1999) *The deliberative practitioner*. Cambridge, MA: MIT Press.

Forester, J. (2017) On the evolution of a critical pragmatism. In B. Haselsberger (ed.) *Encounters in planning thought: 16 autobiographical essays from key thinkers in spatial planning*. New York: Routledge, pp.280–297.

Friedmann, J. (1987) *Planning in the public domain: from knowledge to action*. Princeton, NJ: Princeton University Press.

GL Hearn and the British Property Federation (2016) *Annual Planning Survey 2016: a blueprint for the future of planning in England*. Available at: https://www.capitaproperty.co.uk/media/1834/2016_09_annual-planning-survey_england_final.pdf.

Grayston, R. (2017) *Slipping through the loophole: how viability assessments are reducing affordable housing supply in England*. London: Shelter. Available at: http://england.shelter.org.uk/__data/assets/pdf_file/0010/1434439/2017.11.01_Slipping_through_the_loophole.pdf.

Haque, S. (2002) Structures of new public management in Malaysia and Singapore: alternative views, *Journal of Comparative Asian Development*, 1(1), pp.71–86.

Harding, A. (1991) The rise of urban growth coalitions, UK-style? *Environment and Planning C: Politics and Space*, 9(3), pp.295–317.

Healey, P. (2012) Communicative planning: practices, concepts, rhetorics. In B. Sanyal et al. (eds) *Planning ideas that matter*. Cambridge MA: MIT Press, pp.333–357.

Logan, J. and Molotch, H. (1987) *Urban fortunes: the political economy of place*. Berkeley, CA: University of California Press.

Lord, A. and Hincks, S. (2010) Making plans: the role of evidence in England's reformed spatial planning system, *Planning Practice & Research*, 25(4), pp.477–496.

Mayor of London (2017) *Homes for Londoners: affordable housing and viability Supplementary Planning Guidance*, August. London: Greater London Authority.

Osborne, D. and Gaebler, T. (1992) *Reinventing government: how the entrepreneurial spirit is transforming government*. Reading, MA: Addison Wesley.

Özdemir, E. and Tasan-Kok, T. (2017) Planners' role in accommodating citizen disagreement: the case of Dutch urban planning, *Urban Studies*. Available at: https://doi.org/10.1177/0042098017726738.

Ryan-Collins, J., Lloyd, T. and Macfarlane, L. (2017) *Rethinking the economics of land and housing*. London: Zed Books.

Rydin, Y. (2007) Re-examining the role of knowledge within planning theory, *Planning Theory*, 6(1), pp.52–68.

Rydin, Y. (2013) *The future of planning: beyond growth dependence*. Bristol: Policy Press.

Schön, D. (1991) *The reflective practitioner: how professionals think in action*. Farnham: Ashgate.

Thomas, H. and Healey, P. (1991) *Dilemmas of planning practice: ethics, legitimacy, and the validation of knowledge*. Aldershot: Avebury Technical.

Tomaney, J. and Marques, P. (2013) Evidence, policy and the politics of regional development: the case of high-speed rail in the United Kingdom, *Environment and Planning C: Government and Policy*, 31, pp.414–427.

Wilson, W. (1887) The study of administration, *Political Science Quarterly*, 2(2), pp.197–222.

Wolf-Powers, L. (2005) Up-zoning New York City's mixed-use neighborhoods: property-led economic development and the anatomy of a planning dilemma, *Journal of Planning Education and Research*, 24(4), pp.379–393.

Young, K. et al. (2002) Social science and the evidence-based policy movement, *Social Policy and Society*, 1(3), pp.215–224.

Index

Locators in *italics* refer to figures and those in **bold** to tables.

accountability 2, 285–286, 292–293, 295–296
affordable housing 76–77, 294; *see also* housing
agglomeration 15–16, 237–238
allocations 214–216
Area Action Plan (AAP) 50
asset market bubbles 162
assistance tools, design 108
austerity: design 117–118; Development Management 58–61; economic progress 244; entrepreneurialisation of planning 124–128; infrastructure 61–62; local planning authorities 74, 124–128; plan-making 50; planning performance agreements 79–81; UK framework of planning practice 8–9

Bangladeshi populations 181
banking system, and housing 207–208
Barker Review of Housing Supply 212, 213
benefits of planning 10–12
Bicester planning delivery 195–199
Big Society 25–26
BME population: in Britain 174–176, *176*; engagement in planning 179–180; needs of 181–183; *see also* diversity in Britain
Brexit referendum: devolved administrations in UK 31; economic progress 246; sustainable development 195
budgets *see* austerity; costs of planning; marketisation of local government; public spending
build-to-rent market 76–77
built environment: London's real estate 160–163, 169–170; urban regeneration 266–267, 270–273

Camley Street, Camden, Neighbourhood Planning 151–153, 154
car use 250, 263
Caribbean migrants 174
case for planning 10–12
Central Activities Zone (CAZ) 78
Chicago School of Sociology 140–141, 142
city regeneration *see* urban regeneration
Coalition government (2010-2015): abolition of regional planning 8, 25, 87; austerity 124–125; Big Society 25–26; devolved administrations in UK 8, 21, 22, 25–27; localism 25–26, 87, 143; sustainable development 192
commercial real estate 14, 158–159, 171–172; globalisation and London 159–163; London professional reflections 164–170
Commission for Architecture and the Built Environment (CABE) 103, 106–107
common good *see* public interest
communicative planning: plan-making 40, 43; public engagement 2, 87, 90; theoretical context 16, 282, 284–286

community: diversity and planning 180; housing 214; sense of 141; sustainable development 190–191, 193–194, 198, 200; *see also* public engagement

Community Empowerment Act 2015 23

Community Infrastructure Levy 73–74, 78–79

Community Investment Programme (CIP), Camden 151–152

Community Land Trust (CLT), Camden 153

community participation *see* public engagement

community-led planning 146–147, 154–155

conflict, public engagement 95, 284

Conservative government (2015–present): austerity 124–125; devolved administrations in UK 24–25, 26–27; entrepreneurial nation state 294; localism 143; plan-making 41

consultancies 128–132, **130**, 296; *see also* private sector

consultation *see* public engagement

control in design 109–110

cost benefit analysis (CBA), transport networks 252

costs of planning: vs. benefits 10–12; privatisation 129–130, 132; UK framework of planning practice 7; *see also* planning as impediment

councils *see* local planning authorities (LPAs)

creativity, plan-making 47–48, 52

credit, global financial crisis 207–208

Croydon Urban Regeneration Vehicle 170

Cullingworth, Barry 88

decentralisation: and localism 28; Neighbourhood Planning 8; plan-making 50–51; process of 20–21, 30; *see also* devolved administrations in UK

deliberative practice 3, 16, 283–286

deliverability in planning 49–50, 245, 288

demographics *see* population

Department for Communities and Local Government (DCLG) 145

Department for Environment, Food and Rural Affairs (DEFRA) 191–192

deregulation: credit 207–208, 209; Development Management 289; devolution and localism 51, 56; economic progress 243; localism 289–290; permitted development 63, 77–78; plan-making 39, 51; UK context 8, 189–190

Deregulation Act 2015 8, 125

design 13; governance issues 103–110; historical challenges 101–103; implications for practice 116–118; propositional system 110–116; viability 288

design codes *115*, 115–117

design quality 104

development *see* economic development

development consent 226–227, 228

Development Control, as terminology 56–57, 58; *see also* Development Management

Development Management 13; ability to manage 62–64; austerity 58–61; challenges 66–68; executive arm of planning 55–56; market context 212; performance pressure and engagement 64–66; UK approach 56–58; viability and infrastructure 61–62

development plans: design 117–118; and plan-making 40; spatial planning 9; Town and Country Planning Act 1947 6

development value 13, 70–71, 81; capturing 71–75; challenges and novel approaches 76–81

devolution: England 25–30, 231–232; funding for transport 252–253, 263; and localism 138–139; Northern Ireland 23–24; process and impact 20–21, 30–31, 294, 295; Scotland 21–23; UK framework of planning practice 6; Wales 24–25

devolved administrations in UK 8, 12, 20–21, 30–31; Development Management 62–64; England's regional planning 25–30, **29**; infrastructure 231–232; Northern Ireland 23–24; plan-making 41–42,

50–51; Scotland 21–23; sustainable development 192; Wales 24–25
discretionary nature of planning 71–72, 192
discrimination legislation 177–178; *see also* diversity in Britain
diversity in Britain 14–15, 174, 185; application to planning 176–179; Bangladeshi populations 181; conceptions of 174–176; engagement of BME population in planning 179–180; needs of BME populations 181–183; Pakistani populations 181; planning for spaces of encounter 183–184; political context 176–177
diversity of the economy 236–241
DM *see* Development Management
due diligence 125–126

economic context *see* austerity; costs of planning; finance
economic crisis *see* global financial crisis (GFC)
economic development: benefits of planning 11; planning as impediment 4; pro-development approach 62–63
economic progress 15–16, 235–236, 245–246; from national guidance to local practice 242–245; specialisation vs. diversity 236–241
Economics Evidence Base 240, 243–244
eco-towns 195–199, 206
efficiency, production 236–237
Elephant Amenity Network (EAN) 150–151
Elephant and Walworth, Neighbourhood Planning 148–151, 154
Emissions Trading System (ETS) 195
employment designations 242–243
engagement *see* public engagement
England: employment designations 242–243; infrastructure governance 229–231; land use planning 215–217; Neighbourhood Planning 144–153; pro-development approach 62–63; public engagement 85, 91–92; regional planning 25–30, **29**; sustainable development 190, 193; *see also* United Kingdom
entrepreneurial nation states 293–294
entrepreneurial turn 72
entrepreneurialisation of planning 123–124, 124–128, 131–132
Environmental Impact Assessment (EIA) 194–195
equality legislation 176–178, 180; *see also* diversity in Britain
ethics in planning 298
ethnic minorities *see* diversity in Britain
European Union: Brexit referendum 31, 194–195, 246; migration to Britain 174–175; sustainable development 191, 194–195; transport case studies 253–261, 263–264; urban agenda 139
evaluation tools, design 108
evidence-based policy: design 107; plan-making 43–47, *46*, 286–288; theoretical context 286–288

fees *see* costs of planning
financial centre, London as 159–163, 167–169
financial context *see* austerity; costs of planning; development value; marketisation of local government; public spending
financial crisis *see* global financial crisis (GFC)
financialisation 167–169, 224
first-order design 106
flexibility in planning 49, 288
Forester, John 87, 283–284
forward planning *see* plan-making
Four Quadrant Model 161–162
frameworks of planning practice: international context 4–6; United Kingdom 6–10
Friedmann, John 284
funding *see* public spending
future of planning practice 133–134, 297–298

Glaeser, Edward 4, 239–240, 245
global cities: frameworks of planning practice 4–5; London as 159–163
global context: frameworks of planning practice 4–6; future of

planning practice 297–298; housing 205–209; London's real estate 159–163, 167–169; sustainable development 189; UK relations 9–10
global financial crisis (GFC): housing 207–208; London's real estate 158–159, 164
Good Friday Agreement 23
grassroots *see* community-led planning
Greater London Plan (1944) 142
Greater Manchester Agreement 28–30, 44
Green Belts 10, 206
Grenfell Tower disaster 85
Gross Domestic Product (GDP) 11, 238
guidance for design 109

Habermas, Jürgen 87, 284
Hammarby Sjöstad, Sweden 116–117, *118*
Healey, Patsy 2, 42, 87, 284–285
hierarchical nature of planning 71
higher-tier plans 50
housing 15; affordable housing provision 76–77, 294; demand for 205–209; development value 71, 72–73; diversity in Britain 181–182; global frameworks 205–209; local frameworks in a global context 209–216; North-South divide 30–31; place-making 216–217; plan-making 48–50; planning gain 73; regional differences 10; urban regeneration 268, 270–273
Housing and Planning Act 2016 8
Housing Land Availability Studies 211

imagination/creativity, plan-making 47–48, 52
impediment *see* planning as impediment
incentives, design 109
inequality: benefits of planning 10–11; diversity in Britain 176–177, 183, 185; equality legislation 176–178, 180
infrastructure 15–16, 220–226; definition of 221–222; Development Management 61–62; development value 72; multi-level governance 226–232; *see also* transport networks
Innes, Judith 87, 284
institutional entrepreneurs 60–61
Internal Energy Market (IEM) 195
international context *see* global context
International Financial Centres (IFCs) 159, 161, 164, 169, 171

Jacobs, Jane 239–240, 283–284
Jewish populations 181

Kassel, Germany, RegioTram System 257–261, *258–259*
Kitchen, Ted 2
knowledge in planning: design 107–108; evidence-based policy 43–47; London's real estate 168–169; plan-making 43, 45, 47

Lancashire, fracking public engagement case 92–93, 94, 96
Land Reform (Scotland) Act 2016 23
land use: housing 209–211; London's real estate 169–170; planning as impediment 4; UK regional inequalities 10; urban regeneration *275*
land values 10
Leeds Unitary Development Plan 91, 92
legal context: Brexit referendum 195; Development Management 55–56; diversity and planning 176–179, 180; England's regional planning 25–27; infrastructure 226–227, 228–229; Northern Ireland 23–24; plan-making 43–44; planning gain 61; privatisation 131; public engagement 89; Scotland 22–23; sustainable development 190–195; UK framework of planning practice 6–10; Wales 24–25; *see also individually named Acts*
legitimacy 87, 93, 147, 285; *see also* power relations
Local Agenda 21 88
local authorities *see* local planning authorities
Local Enterprise Partnerships (LEPs) 26
local planning authorities (LPAs): austerity 74, 125–126; BME

population 180; Camley Street, Camden 151–153; Development Management 58–61; development value 70, 76–81; economic progress 242–245; housing 214–216; land use planning 211; marketisation 123, 126–128
Local Plans: devolved administrations in UK 41–42; Economics Evidence Base 243–244; housing 215–216; London's real estate 165–166; Neighbourhood Planning 145–146; plan-making 44–45, 50; public engagement 91–92; urban regeneration 276
localism: economic progress 242–245; England's regional planning 25–28; housing 209–216; London's real estate 171–172; marketisation of local government 127–128; Neighbourhood Planning 138–140, 143; public engagement 87; sustainable development 193
Localism Act 2011: local planning authorities 126; Neighbourhood Planning 8, 138, 144, 145–146, 154; sustainable development 193
London: commercial real estate 159–170; development value 70–71; employment designations 243; housing 205; infrastructure governance 229–231; Neighbourhood Planning 146–153, *147–148*; permitted development 78; sewerage services 224; specialisation vs. diversity 238–239, 240–241; urban design frameworks 112–114; urban regeneration 267, *271*, 274, *275*
London Plan: economic progress 245; international context 163; Mayor's role 44; specialisation vs. diversity 240–241; strategic planning 27–28

Manchester Agreement *see* Greater Manchester Agreement
Maritime Spatial Planning Directive 195
market context: employment designations 243; framing the economy 236–241; housing demand 205–209; land use planning 210–214, 216–217; London's real estate 169–170; professional planners 72–73; urban regeneration 270–273
marketisation of local government 123, 126–128
megaprojects **225**, 225, 228–229
migration, diversity in Britain 174–176
minorities *see* diversity in Britain
multiculturalism 182–184; *see also* diversity in Britain

nation state, character of 292–295; *see also* public sector
national development taxes 73
National Infrastructure Plans 224–226, 230
National Planning Policy Framework (NPPF): development value 74–75; eco-towns 195–196; employment designations 242–243; housing 214; introduction of 8; local planning authorities 125; pro-development approach 62–63; public engagement with planning 285; sustainable development 192–194; viability 61; weight of 41
nationalisation, infrastructure 221; *see also* public sector
Nationally Significant Infrastructure Projects (NSIPs) 226–227
natural resources 5–6, 189, 191
Neighbourhood Development Plans (NDPs): in England 144–146; introduction of 138
Neighbourhood Forums 145, 147, 148–151, 152–153
neighbourhood participation 139
Neighbourhood Planning 8, 14; Camley Street, Camden 151–153; community-led planning 146–147, 154–155; design 112; Elephant and Walworth 148–151; England 26, 144–153; housing 215–216; ideologies and policy implementations 140–144; localism 138–140; London 146–153, *147–148*; public engagement 87, 91, 95–97, 284–285; sustainable development 193–194, 198
neo-liberal age 5; entrepreneurial nation states 293–294; Neighbourhood Planning 140; planning as impediment 235, 246

New Deal for Communities 90
New Labour: devolved administrations in UK 20; diversity in Britain 179, 182; evidence-based policy 43, 286; Neighbourhood Planning 142–143; plan-making 43–44; regional planning 25; spatial planning 9, 21, 47
New Towns Act (1946) 142
NIMBYism: housing 214; Neighbourhood Planning 154; public engagement 92, 93–94, 95–96, 285
North West Bicester (NWB) planning delivery 195–199
Northern Ireland 23–24, 41; *see also* United Kingdom
Northern Powerhouse 231–232, 237–238
North-South divide 30–31

One Planet Living (OPL) principles 196–197, **197**
outcomes of planning 15–16

Pakistani populations 181
participation *see* public engagement
performance pressure, Development Management 64–66
permission in principle 8
permitted development 63–64, 67, 77–78
permitting *see* Development Management
'Pink Book' *102*, 102, 110, 111–112, 117
place-based approaches 11
place-making 13; design 110–111; housing 216–217; London's real estate 163
plan-making 12–13, 39–40, 50–52; changing drivers of 48–50; England's regional planning 28; evidence-based 43–47, *45–46*, 286–288; process of 42–48; strategic vision 11; struggle to get a plan in place 41–42; Wales 25
planners *see* professional planners
Planning (Wales) Act 25
Planning Act 2008 226, 228
planning as impediment: economic development 4; neo-liberal age 235, 246; UK framework of planning practice 7–8; *see also* costs of planning
planning consultancies 128–132, **130**, 296
planning gain: development value 70; housing 73; legal context 61; privatisation 133
Planning Performance Agreements (PPAs) 74, 79–81
planning permissions *see* Development Management
planning policy *see* plan-making
Planning Policy Statement on Housing (PPS3) 212–213, 214–215
Planning Policy Statements (PPSs) 125, 192
policy *see* plan-making
political context: character of the state 292–295; diversity in Britain 176–177; inequality 298; infrastructure 226–227; London's real estate 166–167; practice of planning 1–4; UK framework of planning practice 6–10; urban regeneration 273
population: diversity in Britain 174–176; global context 189; housing demand 205–206; transport networks 251
power relations 1–2; accountability 285–286; Neighbourhood Planning 154–155; private sector 295–296; public engagement 90
practice of planning 14–15; global frameworks 4–6; historical context 1–2; purpose of 2–4, 62–64, 297–298; reflective and deliberative practice 16, 283–286; state's character 292–295; theoretical context 281–283; UK framework 6–10
practitioners *see* planning consultancies; professional planners
pre-application discussions 65–66
private sector: austerity 74, 124–128; consultancies 128–132, **130**, 296; creativity 47–48, 52; Development Management 57–58; future of planning practice 133–134; London's real estate 165–166; power 295–296; privatisation 123–124; urban regeneration 270–273, 274–277

privatisation 14, 123–124; austerity 124–128; future of planning practice 133–134; housing 207; infrastructure 221; planning consultancies 128–132
processes for planning 12–13
pro-development approach 62–63
production, efficiency 236–237
professional planners: consultancies 128–132, **130**, 296; creativity 47–48; historical context 3; London's real estate 164–170; as market actors 72–73; performance pressure and engagement 64–66; reflective and deliberative practice 283–286; skills required 2–3; theory and practice 281–283; urban regeneration 274–277
property *see* housing
propositional system, design 110–116
protests 95, 284
public engagement with planning 13, 85–86, 94–97; BME population 179–180; community participation 139; contradictions of participation 90; Development Management 55–56, 66; evidence-based policy 287; expanding public 86–89; housing 214–216; neighbourhood participation 139; Neighbourhood Planning 87, 91, 95–97, 284–285; plan-making 48–49; protests 284; success of engagement 91–94; *see also* community-led planning
public interest (common good) 1; Development Management 57; sustainable development 190–191; urban regeneration 274–277
public realm credits 79
public sector: creativity 47–48, 52; Development Management 57–58; equality legislation 178–179; future of planning practice 133–134; London's real estate 164–166; power of private sector 295–296; privatisation 123–124; state's character 292–295; urban regeneration 270–273, 274–277
public spending: economic progress 244–245; housing 207–208; infrastructure 61–62, 223–224, **227**; local authority Development Management 59–61, *60*; sustainable development 194–195; transport networks 252–253; *see also* austerity; costs of planning; marketisation of local government
public transport *see* transport networks
purpose of planning 2–4, 62–64, 297–298

quality vs. speed 65–66

race *see* diversity in Britain
Race Relations Act (RRA) 177–178
rail transport, UK 251–252; *see also* tramway systems
real estate *see* commercial real estate; housing
recognition, political context 177
reflective practice 16, 283–286
regeneration *see* urban regeneration
Regional Development Agencies (RDAs) 25
regional differences: devolved administrations in UK 8; land values 10; Local Plans 41; public engagement 86–87; *see also* England; Northern Ireland; Scotland; Wales
regulation *see* legal context
rental market 76–77
resources *see* natural resources
Ricardo, David 236
Royal Town Planning Institute (RTPI) 129, 177, 178
Rydin, Yvonne 88

Sanders, Lynn 95
scale: infrastructure governance 226–232; neighbourhoods 139; plan-making 40
Schön, Donald 283–284, 286
Scotland: 2014 referendum 21, 22–23; as devolved administration 21–23; infrastructure governance 229; local planning authorities 127; pro-development approach 63; public engagement 85–86; specialisation vs. diversity 241; *see also* United Kingdom
Scottish National Party 21–22
second-order design 106

Sheffield Unitary Development Plan 91
site masterplans 50
social justice 10–11
space, diversity in Britain 181–184
spatial planning: England's regional planning 25–26, 25–27; New Labour 9, 21, 47; Scotland 21–22
specialisation 15–16, 236–241
speed vs. quality 65–66
state, character of 292–295; *see also* public sector
Stormont Agreement 23
Strategic Housing Land Availability Assessments (SHLAAs) 211
Strategic Housing Market Assessments (SHMAs) 213
strategic planning *see* plan-making
strategy-making *see* plan-making
supplementary planning document (SPD) 50
sustainable development 15, 189–190, 199–200; fiscal context 194–195; legal context 190–195; in practice 195–199; pro-development approach 62–63; Wales 25
Sustainable Development Strategy: Securing the Future (DEFRA) 191–192

taxation, development value 73–74
technocratic approaches, rejection of 1, 2–3, 87, 111
territorial politics 20–21; *see also* devolved administrations in UK
testimony 95
Thame Town Council 215
theoretical context: diversity in Britain 177; evidence-based vs. viability-based planning 286–288; framing the economy 236–241; international framework of planning practice 4–6; Neighbourhood Planning 140–141; and practice 281–283; practice of planning 3–4; public engagement 86, 87, 95–96; reflective and deliberative practice 283–286; structural constraints 288–292; sustainable development 191; UK framework of planning practice 6–10
Third National Planning Framework (NPF3) 22, 192, 229
time context: first-order and second-order design 106; public engagement 89; speed vs. quality 65–66
tools for planning 12–13, 106–110, *107*, 111–116
Town and Country Planning Act 1947: Community Infrastructure Levy 78–79; development plans 6; local planning authorities 126; permitted development 77–78; planning gain 70; public engagement 88; public realm credits 79
town regeneration *see* urban regeneration
train network, UK 251–252; *see also* tramway systems
tramway system, Kassel, Germany 257–261, *258–259*
tramway system, Valenciennes, France 253–256, *254–255*
transport networks 16, 250–251; case studies 253–261, 263–264; infrastructure 220–226; London 230–231; Northern England 231–232; Northern Powerhouse 231–232; UK context 251–253, 262–264

United Kingdom: Development Management 56–58; frameworks of planning practice 6–10; framing the economy 236–241; infrastructure governance 226–229; privatisation 123–124, 133–134; transport networks 251–253, 262–264; *see also* devolved administrations in UK
urban design frameworks 112–114, *113*, *114*
urban regeneration 16, 266–268, 278; challenges 273–277; London's Neighbourhood Planning 146–153, *147–148*; meaning of 268–273
Urban Task Force report 235–236, 242
urbanism: BME population 175; real estate 158; transport networks 250

Valenciennes, France, single-track tramway system 253–256, *254–255*
value *see* costs of planning; development value
viability: Development Management 61–62; development value 74–75; economic progress 245; plan-making 49–50; theoretical context 286–288

Wales 24–25, 41, 238; *see also* United Kingdom
WebTAG (Web-based Transport Appraisal Guidance) 252
Welborne Plan *45–46*

York, Local Plan 42

zoning 105